Francis Hobler

Records of Roman History

From Cnæus Pompeius to Tiberius Constantinus...: Vol. I.

Francis Hobler

Records of Roman History

From Cnæus Pompeius to Tiberius Constantinus...: Vol. I.

ISBN/EAN: 9783337125615

Printed in Europe, USA, Canada, Australia, Japan

Cover: Foto ©ninafisch / pixelio.de

More available books at **www.hansebooks.com**

RECORDS

OF

ROMAN HISTORY,

FROM

CNÆUS POMPEIUS TO TIBERIUS CONSTANTINUS,

AS

EXHIBITED ON THE ROMAN COINS

COLLECTED BY

FRANCIS HOBLER,

FORMERLY SECRETARY OF THE NUMISMATIC SOCIETY OF LONDON.

IN TWO VOLUMES.

VOL. I.

WESTMINSTER:
JOHN BOWYER NICHOLS AND SONS,
25, PARLIAMENT STREET.

M.DCCC.LX.

TO

JOHN LEE, ESQ., LL.D.

F.R.S., F.R.A.S., &c. &c., FIRST PRESIDENT OF THE NUMISMATIC SOCIETY OF LONDON.

AND TO

VICE-ADMIRAL W. H. SMYTH,

F.R.S., F.R.A.S., &c. &c.

This Work is (by permission) dedicated, not only in admiration of the learning and ability which have won for them so high a reputation as Numismatists and Antiquaries, but also as a tribute of gratitude for the valuable assistance rendered by them during its Compilation and Arrangement

To their obliged Friend,

THE AUTHOR.

Canonbury Square, Islington, London,
January, 1860.

INTRODUCTION.

THE title I have placed on the first page of this work may to some appear rather pretentious, and of greater import than is warranted by the subject matter. I trust that I shall be able in a few words,—for the extent to which these volumes have run will not bear the addition of a lengthy Introduction,—to justify the choice I have made.

My experience in Roman Coins was very limited when I made the observation—that probably every one has made and will make under similar circumstances—namely, that, starting with the rude and heavy As, and following the series of Coins leading up to the fine types that commence with the reign of Augustus, thence tracing the series down again to the small and badly-executed Coins which make their appearance in the time of Gallienus, we have, from an artistic point of view, an epitome of the rise and fall of the Roman Empire. With but few wants, and those of the simplest character, and confined almost entirely to the necessities of eating, drinking, and fighting,—for the latter was a necessity to *him*, and the element of his greatness,—the early Roman was well content if the treasury coffers were filled with that primitive description of money the As. When luxury had increased the number of his wants, the polished Roman of the time of Augustus found in the money of his day a more ready and convenient means of satisfying his manifold exigencies than if the pristine system of barter had still prevailed. Advancing onward to the latter days of the Empire, the reckless and feverish haste in converting material into negotiable forms, or, as it may be expressed, the turning of principal into interest regardless of the future and of its claims, is clearly shown by the slovenly and careless execution of the Coinage; while the immense numbers still existing of the Small Brass, which then became the principal medium of circulation, points with equal distinctness to the loss of that simplicity of life which characterised the Roman under the Consuls.

My attention being thus, as it were, forcibly attracted to the consideration of the historic interest possessed by these stepping-stones across the flood of time, the artistic excellence of execution so worthy of admiration in the coins,—more particularly, of Claudius, Nero, Trajan, Hadrian, and Antoninus,—no longer entirely occupied my attention; and, although such magnificent specimens of die-engraving as the long and beautiful series of those respective Emperors discloses to us, still exacted their meed of commendation, I ceased to regard the selection of such specimens only, as the true end and aim of a collector in forming a Cabinet of Roman Coins. In pursuing the track thus opened to my view, subjects of infinite interest presented themselves before me and speeded me on. One of them has recently been treated by an esteemed friend, Professor Donaldson, with his wonted ability, in a work called "Architectura Numismatica," embellished with a great number of lithographs from drawings by his own hand, taken, some of them, from Coins in my Cabinet; this work so effectually exhausts the subject, that further allusion to it would be useless, and I can only refer the reader desirous of following it up to the book itself.

As would be anticipated from the character of the people under consideration in the following pages, the greatest historic interest is centred in the military types of the different Emperors. In this respect we have ample means of testing the value of these Records of Roman History, and most satisfactory is the result; for, on comparing the course of events in any one reign, as depicted on the coins, with that detailed by historians, we not only find each incident corroborated, but we are also frequently introduced to passages in the life of a man unnoticed by the historian, who, perhaps, was biassed in the view he took of contemporaneous and misinformed on past events. Nor must the quality of this corroborative and supplementary evidence be overlooked. No errors have crept into the text of these chronicles through the carelessness, or *nimium diligentiæ*, of transcribers: we have the fact itself, simple, and, however much perverted from the truth at the time it was indelibly recorded, at least free from false lights that might have been thrown upon it by historian or commentator, whose work would have been equally open to objection on the ground of want of veracity.

The points of history illustrated by coins are not confined to Architecture and War, although these two subjects prominently attract the notice of the Numismatist, for a well-arranged and selected series is valuable for many other branches of information. Indeed, I think that a Cabinet of Coins, though it be chosen with no other end in view than the compilation of a chronological table of events, is a necessary adjunct to every institution boasting the possession of historical works of reference. There are various subjects illustrated by coins which the reader will find treated of at some length in the body of this work; and I shall in this place content myself by alluding to some of them in a cursory manner only.

Foremost among these subsidiary details—and here I use the word subsidiary only in reference to the importance of the manner in which they are expressed on the medals, and not with reference to the intrinsic importance of the matter itself—stands the exposition of the religious ceremonials of this great nation. As might naturally be expected, the acts of devotion depicted are such as are chiefly personal to the Emperor in whose reign the pieces were struck, and there is little reference to the system of theology of the age. We find the attributes of various divinities ascribed to the different monarchs, or to members of their family, and we see them engaged in sacrificial duties pertinent to their office of Pontifex Maximus; or the same idea is thrown into an allegorical form. It would be useless to search for illustrations of the progress of religion; the subject is one that could not be treated of in this manner; and I may even venture so far as to say that no progress was made in Pantheism from the time of Ancus Martius up to the accession of Constantine, when the ice which had for so many centuries bound up the minds and consciences of the Romans dissolved before the sun of Christianity. But, in saying that no progress was made, I must be understood as confining myself strictly to the consideration of the question in connection with the State; for, undoubtedly, philosophers had, long before the days of Tiberius, entertained pure and clear views, far in advance of the gross and sensual creed of their time.

The enumeration of the points in the domestic economy of Rome, as portrayed on these coins, would, although of great value to the student of Roman history, be but tedious to the numismatist who is conversant with the subject; I will therefore mention two or three of them only, abstaining from further comment.

Among them shipping and the importation of corn justly claim a front rank, and in the next place I may notice the modes of transport adopted and the variety of conveyances used; various implements, as well domestic as agricultural, mechanical and sacerdotal, are accurately depicted, as are also armour and articles of dress, and the way in which they were worn.

One word on the artistic excellence of some of these "Records." Such is the skill displayed in many instances by the artist, not only in the execution of the design but in the design itself, and such is the elegance and refinement of the latter, that it is difficult to believe the artists were not brought to Rome from Greece, where alone the beauty of form was thoroughly understood and appreciated. Indeed, I would challenge a comparison of the medallions of Antoninus

Pius, page 448, Marcus Aurelius, page 494, and Lucilla, page 566, with any medallions of the present day, both for beauty of design, and, making a proper allowance for disparity of ages, as a specimen of die-engraving. Putting aside the restored coins, or such as were struck by various emperors in honour of predecessors, known by the word REST (*restituit*) in the reverse legend, and in which the engraver has diplomatically, and at the expense of him in whose honour they were designed, introduced a likeness to the Emperor by whom they were struck; —putting these aside, a Series of the Emperors forms a miniature Portrait Gallery of the greatest interest, giving in several instances the changes wrought by the finger of time on the countenance of a man during his whole life, if not from the cradle, at least from early youth, to the period of his death. Remarkable instances of this are given in the coins of the Emperor Marcus Aurelius and of his son Commodus. We are introduced to the former during the early part of the reign of Antoninus Pius, and find him represented as a beardless, curly-headed boy,—we leave him a venerable old man. His son Commodus first appears before us as a youth, and, if the last portrait we have of him does not leave on our minds the idea of a man as venerable as old Marcus Aurelius, it gives us at least an accurate notion of his age at the time of his death. The perfect resemblance of some of these portraits to the remaining busts of the same men, warrants the conclusion that in the majority of cases the likeness may be depended on.

The present work resembles, in its plan and arrangement, that of the Descriptive Catalogue of a Cabinet of Roman Large Brass Coins, by Rear-Admiral W. H. Smyth, F.R.S. After all that the Admiral has so cleverly written upon each coin in his Cabinet, it cannot be expected I can add much in the way of novelty, yet, as my series not only comprises nearly the whole or similar coins to those possessed by him, and is also continued to a much greater length, I am enabled to bring together a more extensive collection of historic matter, and, where I may differ from him in a point of chronology, or in the application of a type to any particular fact in history, I do so with great deference to his superiority as a numismatic antiquary.

My Cabinet was formed on the principle of embodying, as nearly as possible, the principal events in the life and reign of each of the Roman Emperors, commencing with Julius Cæsar, that are to be found on the Large Brass series of coins, but I found the Large Brass series at times too restrictive for historic purposes, and that it would be deficient in many interesting historic subjects which are only to be found on the Gold or Silver or the Second Brass, and latterly on the Third Brass, which was then the chief medium of circulation.

Consequently, coins not in the Large Brass series have been introduced which bear historic devices. I have thus enlarged upon Admiral Smyth's interesting series of types, which are strictly confined to historical Large Brass; and have also added a number of coins expressing the Moralities and Virtues ascribed to the different Emperors, which, although not customarily admitted into an Historic Cabinet by those antiquaries who seek only for the type of an event,—yet I contend that they are equally historical, by their evincing the feelings of the Roman people towards their Emperor, when a good prince, attending to their wants and safety, or their exultation expressed in a successful warrior being their ruler. These commendatory types may also be found on the coins of those Emperors who were of base, depraved, and tyrannic bearing towards the people; and, although the attributed virtues are direct falsehoods, yet the coins which bear their impress are historic evidences of the servile adulation of a weak and timid senate overawed by the insolence of the soldiery, who, by the large donations of an evil-disposed emperor, were always at his command to wreak destruction on those who were obnoxious to him.

This class of types possesses also a particular interest in an artistic point of view. On the earlier imperial coins the figures so introduced are for the most part very elegantly portrayed, and some fine specimens of die-engraving may be found among them, occasionally the copy of some ancient statue, which either no longer exists, or at best in a very imperfect condition. Again, the Roman artist differed very much from the modern in the representations of some of their Virtues and Moralities; for instance, the Hope of the Roman artist is a young female blithely tripping forward, holding up her robe with her left hand, while with her right hand she presents an opening flower; which it must be acknowledged is a far more elegant and expressive design than the modern representation of Hope as a female leaning on an anchor. The anchor with the ancients represented travelling by sea. On the Annona coins those female figures which rest their hands on the stem of an anchor usually have the prow of a galley in the back-ground, thus denoting that the corn for the supply of the city was brought by sea from some foreign port or province; for, when the corn came by land carriage or home produce, neither the anchor nor the prow appear, but Annona rests her hand on the staff of a rake or a plough-share.

In writing the following Records, and examining every coin therein mentioned, I have noticed several matters regarding the fabric and minting of Roman coins which are apt to escape the observation of the general collector.

The metal of which the genuine Roman brass coins are made is very peculiar.

INTRODUCTION.

The coins of the early Emperors are almost invariably made of what is termed AURICHALCUM. The true orthography of this word is ORICHALCUM—(ορειχαλκος), *i.e.* mountain brass, although the beautiful gold-like appearance which such coins often present gives great plausibility to the common but incorrect orthography. It is this peculiar metal which renders at times Roman brass coins so beautiful in the variety of colours which they present, and which variety is again assisted by the action of the salts or other chemical agents in the different earths or waters whence they may be exhumed, after an interment of many centuries. No forged brass coin has existed sufficiently long to have acquired naturally the tone and colour of the genuine orichalcum.

It will be frequently found on finely-preserved coins that the portrait of an Emperor is engraved with the utmost care and attention, whilst the letters of the legends are small and meagre, or thick and clumsy, sometimes uneven in size and straggling, or close and crowded. In these things may be seen the work of two artists: the Wyon of the day has executed his share of the work by producing a highly-finished portrait, whilst the lettering has been intrusted to an inferior workman. Such also may be the reason at times of different styles of work in the obverse and reverse of a coin. Again, it will be seen that an artist has massed the hair of the head and drapery of the bust of his portrait, throwing the features clearly into relief; thus giving the complete artistic effect without the minute detail of separate hairs in the head and beard.

I have added the weights and colours of most of the coins, which have not been given in the Brass Series in any numismatic work I have seen. The weights of the Gold and Silver coins we have had already given in some works, especially in Admiral Smyth's Descriptive Catalogue of the Consular Silver Coins in the Cabinet of His Grace the Duke of Northumberland. The weights I have introduced will be an additional source of information towards the identification of the specific coins, and of comparison with other coins of similar types.

The wood-cuts introduced of some of the more rare and unfrequent coins have been made from the coins themselves by Mr. Fairholt, well known as a numismatic artist.

The photographic frontispiece, by Messrs. Negretti and Zambra, is from a design of the celebrated artist G. B. Cipriani, and engraved by F. Bartolozzi, the subject being taken from the Orlando Furioso, canto XXXV. stanza XII.

I cannot close these few lines without acknowledging a debt of gratitude I have contracted to several estimable men, who have come forward on very many occasions, and have afforded me valuable assistance. Such of my readers as know

Dr. Lee will feel any allusion to his constant kindness and attention to those who enjoy that privilege, and indeed to archæologists generally, to be perfectly unnecessary; and the general reader would I fear deem it but flattery were I to express my appreciation of his worth. Rear-Admiral W. H. Smyth, whose valuable and interesting Catalogue of Roman Large Brass has formed the model of my own, has for so many years responded to my frequent inquiries, and that with such care and promptness, that I feel myself at a loss when I attempt to offer him adequate thanks. Nor can I place too high a value on the assistance rendered to me by my early friend Charles Roach Smith, esquire, the author of Collectanea Antiqua, of Roman London, and of other antiquarian works of sterling value. I deem myself to have been most fortunate in having been able to call the late Mr. Thomas Burgon, of the British Museum, my friend. No man with whom I have ever been acquainted possessed a more thorough knowledge of numismatics, although in the Museum his attention was directed to one branch of this study only, namely, to Greek Coins. My brother Secretary to the Numismatic Society, Mr. John Yonge Akerman, Sec. S.A.; Professor Donaldson (whose recent work, "Architectura Numismatica," I have before referred to); the Rev. Dr. Bruce, a gentleman deeply versed in the History of England under the Romans; and the Rev. E. Boden, may each and all justly claim the recognition of the services they have respectively rendered me. And now, with the hope that this work (not originally intended for the press), which has in thirty years grown up under my pen from a bare Index to its present size, may prove useful and instructive, and trusting that its imperfections may be viewed with a gentle eye, I introduce it to all who may feel interested in the history of the most mighty nation that has ever existed.

RECORDS

OF

ROMAN HISTORY.

CNÆUS POMPEIUS.

CNÆUS POMPEIUS, the son of Cnæus Pompeius Strabo and Lucilia, was born in the year of Rome 648. Having taken part with Sylla in the Civil War between that general and Marius, he acquired by his exploits the surname of MAGNUS, which was bestowed on him by Sylla in the year of Rome 673. Sylla, on his death about the year of Rome 678, left behind him Pompeius, then engaged in Spain at war with Sertorius, a former lieutenant of Cinna, and a friend of Marius; Lucullus, who was contending with Mithridates in the East; Julius Cæsar; Cato, Cicero, and Crassus, with several other men of rank, but opposite in their political opinions.

Mithridates, after suffering several defeats from Lucullus, not being completely subdued, Pompeius was sent against him, and overthrew him in a great battle, where the Eastern monarch was killed, leaving his kingdom a province of the Roman Republic. After this success, on his return to Rome, Pompeius joined with Julius Cæsar and Crassus, and with them formed that alliance which in the Roman History is called the First Triumvirate for the preservation of the Republic; this was accomplished in the year of Rome 694.

Soon after that time the Triumvirate was dissolved by the death of Crassus and his son in an expedition against the Parthians, by whom they were slain, and the legions which were with them were made prisoners. Pompeius, who remained, although supported by many of the most influential men in Rome, could not compete with Julius Cæsar. It is true Pompeius possessed talents of a very high order; he had met with very great success as a general; his address was eloquent and engaging; but he had been cruel upon several occasions, and had become envious of the success of Julius Cæsar.

In the latter part of his career Pompeius exhibits a great want of firmness and self-possession as a leader of armies, and this want of confidence in himself infused a corresponding damp into his troops; so that, when his struggle ensued with Julius Cæsar as to which should possess the supreme power, neither Pompeius or his legions could withstand the moral and physical courage and discipline of Cæsar and his warriors.

Cicero, who took part with Pompeius, had desired a peace with Cæsar, but Pompeius would not entertain the idea, and, being supported by the opinions of many men of rank and influence, war with Cæsar became inevitable. The result was that Pompeius lost the Battle of Pharsalia, and afterwards his life. This battle was fought in the year of Rome 706, about 48 years before the Christian æra. Pompeius fled to Egypt, where he was assassinated on his arrival by a slave, at the instigation it is said of Ptolemy the king, of whom he had sought protection.

As I do not profess to give long detailed biographies in the following pages, I must refer my reader to the most complete and scientific Roman History of the present day, entitled, "The History of the Romans under the Empire," by Charles Merivale, B.D., a most excellent and well-written work, in which he will find the biography and career of Pompeius and the several emperors carefully and elaborately set out from authentic sources.

1.

No legend. The heads of Cnæus Pompeius and his son Sextus back to back, in the style of Janus Bifrons, with ears of corn springing from the top. Dark-brown, very good.

℞. *No legend.* The prow of a galley to the right, with IMP underneath it.

The ears of corn are said to record the provision of corn made for the city by Pompeius when he was elected by the senate IMPERATOR, for the purpose of providing the annona or *rem frumentariam* of the city as usual.

By some writers the ears of corn are supposed to allude to the threat of famine made by Sextus Pompeius to the citizens of Rome if they did not oblige the Triumvirs to do him justice on his complaint of being deprived of his ancestral honours, Sextus Pompeius and his brother having at that time the command of a large fleet, and being in possession of the Island of Sicily, which was considered the granary of Rome.

2.

No legend. The heads of Pompeius and his son as Janus Bifrons, with ears of corn springing from them; over the heads are the letters MGN.

℞. PIVS over the prow of a galley to the right; in the exergum IMP.

The obverse of these coins of Pompeius is described by Argelati simply as "*Caput Jani spicatum.*"

There is only one other coin struck in brass to Pompeius, but it is rarely met with. It is noted in Occo.

The present, a fine dark-brown coin, is from the cabinet of Mr. Gwilt, in place of a very good one I had long previously possessed.

JULIUS CÆSAR.

CAIUS JULIUS CÆSAR was born in Rome in the year of Rome 654, of a most ancient Patrician family, assuming to be descended from the goddess Venus. He entered the army at an early age and achieved great honour. By birth he was the nephew of Marius the opponent of Sylla, who was then at the height of his power. At an early period Cæsar was married to Cornelia, the daughter of Cinna, the colleague of Marius. Cæsar was called upon to assert his courage and political principles at the very outset of his career; for Sylla, suspicious of the youthful nephew of his rival, and urged perhaps to destroy him by some of his own adherents, but restrained by some lurking feeling of mercy or sympathy with a kindred genius, required him to divorce his wife Cornelia, and thus loosen his connections with the Marians. That party at the moment was in its lowest state of despair. The proscriptions of Sylla had taken off all its leaders, and no one dared to raise his head above the ranks of the multitude who were protected by their insignificance. There was no one among them to whom Cæsar could appeal for protection; yet, although then only in his eighteenth year, he refused to comply. Sylla was staggered by his boldness, but refrained from striking. Pompeius and Piso had both by command of Sylla divorced their wives.

The firmness of Cæsar had caused Sylla to remark *that in Cæsar there was more than one Marius*, and to warn the magnates of the Senate *to beware of that young trifler*. Cæsar however did not entirely escape; he paid for his conjugal constancy by being obliged to fly from Rome and seek an asylum at a distance, and until his pardon was assured he wandered about in disguise among the Sabine mountains. There he was discovered, but saved his life by a bribe to his captor. He was displaced from the priesthood and deprived of his wife's fortune.

After the death of Sylla, Julius Cæsar became a prominent leader. With Pompeius and Crassus he formed the first Triumvirate for the preservation of the Republic; this was in the latter part of the year of Rome 694. In 695 he obtained the government of Gaul for five years, which was afterwards renewed to him for five years more.

During the time he was in Gaul, Cæsar, under the pretence that the Britons had assisted the Gauls in the war against him, passed over the sea to Britain. This was the first visit of the Romans to this island. They met with a vigorous opposition from the natives, but ultimately effected a landing. On his second expedition in the following year, by the valour of his troops and his skilful diplomacy with many of the British princes and chiefs, Cæsar laid the foundation of its future subjugation and conversion into a Roman province.

The exact place where Julius Cæsar landed in Britain has long been the subject of much discussion. I do not pretend in these pages to enter into a disputation on this topic, but I may refer to Professor Halley's paper, read to the Royal Society as far back as the year 1685, and printed in vol. xvii. of the Philosophical Transactions; likewise to an excellent antiquarian work of the present day, viz. Collectanea Antiqua, by my earliest numismatic friend C. Roach Smith, F.S.A., who in his first volume gives a paper on the subject by the Rev. Beale Poste, a skilful Roman antiquary. There is likewise the 4to work of C. R. Smith on Richborough, Lymne, and Reculver; likewise the work of Archdeacon Battely on Rutupiæ or Richborough; also the Rev. C. Merivale's History of the Romans under the Empire, vol. i. p. 464, &c.;[*] and the memoir of Professor Airy, Astronomer-Royal,

---

[*] From a close examination of Cæsar's description of the place on the sea-shore where he did land, my own opinion leads me to the open beach at Deal, a few miles beyond Dover, although subsequent explorations may have led the Roman commanders to prefer Rutupiæ as their best place of disembarcation and constant resort—using Dover nevertheless as an outpost or watch-tower, from its elevated position. In confirmation of my opinion I may add, there are no remains at Pevensey or St. Leonard's of Roman castra or other works to show that either of them had ever been used as a place of disembarcation by the Romans, whereas at Richborough such remains abound, and show the ruins of Roman fortifications on a very great scale, as may be fully seen in C. Roach Smith's book on Richborough, &c.; thus supporting by their existence the opinion of Professor Halley, the Rev. B. Poste, the Rev. Mr. Merivale, and Admiral Smyth.

communicated to the Society of Antiquaries in 1852 by Admiral Smyth, also an eminent Astronomer and Hydrographer. Professor Airy considers the spot to have been at Pevensey or St. Leonard's, to the west from Dover. Professor Halley, the Rev. B. Poste, Mr. Merivale, and a letter I have from Admiral Smyth, speak of the landing-place being to the east of Dover, at the Deal beach, just beyond which place is the entrance of the Stour river, on the banks whereof are the ruins of the Roman castrum of Rutupiæ. These remains are of such magnitude as to prove Richborough or Rutupiæ to have been a strongly-fortified place, and of great importance and resort in the time of the Romans.

Professor Airy, after giving a lengthened and learned discussion on the question of the locality, says, " It is impossible to admit Dover, Deal, or Walmer as Cæsar's landing-place; that, although there is not the same impossibility of admitting Folkstone and Romney Marsh, there are strong improbabilities; but that every possibility and probability are in favour of St. Leonard's and Pevensey."—After all, it is sufficient for our purpose to know that Julius Cæsar was the first Roman general who ventured to come over from Gaul into Britain.

Crassus and his son had been defeated and slain in their expedition against the Parthians, so that when Cæsar returned to Rome there was only Pompeius, with whom he soon after had a quarrel. Pompeius being supported by a great number of senators and other men of rank, a civil war ensued between them, which was terminated by the defeat of Pompeius on the plains of Pharsalia, in Thessaly, in the year of Rome 706.

After this battle and the subsequent death of Pompeius, Cæsar became the only surviving Triumvir,—he was afterwards nominated Dictator for one year. The title and office were renewed to him the following year, and in the year of Rome 710 he was created Perpetual Dictator; and he also held the office of Pontifex Maximus. Six months after receiving the honour and dignity of Perpetual Dictator, Julius Cæsar was assassinated in a full assembly of the senate on the 15th of March, and in the fifty-sixth year of his age, by Brutus, Cassius, and others, men of rank whose lives he had spared at Pharsalia, and Rome was thus in a few minutes deprived of her most accomplished statesman and most illustrious chieftain.

Amongst other matters which render the name of Julius Cæsar celebrated in history as a man of science, is the reform of the kalendar of the year, which had been first introduced by Romulus, who was more of a warrior then an astronomer: this was corrected by Numa, but the kalendar still continued faulty; and at last Julius Cæsar, with the aid of Sosigenes a celebrated astronomer, brought the year to the regular period of the earth's annual revolution of 365 days 6 hours. One other day was introduced every fourth year by increasing the month of February from 28 to 29 days. Thus was established the Julian Kalendar. This calculation was again reformed under Pope Gregory XIII. with the advice of Clavius and Ciaconius, celebrated men of that day; and this reformation, or New Style as it is called, commenced on the 4th of October 1582, and is the calculation used at the present time throughout all civilized countries.

Although Schlegel, the German writer, in his Lectures on the Philosophy of History, Lecture 9, cannot avoid noticing the ambition which formed a prominent part of Cæsar's character, yet on the whole he does fair justice to him, considering his character by the Roman standard of excellence. Schlegel says, he was by no means vindictive, nor in general subject to passion, nor cruel without a motive—but, whenever his interest required it, he was careless what blood he spilled. The war between Cæsar and Pompey extended over all the provinces and regions of the Roman world; but when conqueror he formed and followed up the plan of completing and consolidating his victory by a system of lenity and conciliation. With all his indefatigable activity and consummate wisdom, with all the equanimity, prudence, and energy of his character, he appears to have been still weak enough to imagine that the laurels he had acquired, in a way unequalled by any, were insufficient without the diadem; at least he gave occasion for such suspicion, and so the second Brutus perpetrated on his person the act for which the elder had been so highly commended by all Roman historians.

From Kuno Fischer, another German writer, we have another and harsher view of Cæsar's character. In his chapter "Of the want of Sense for Antiquity in Bacon" he speaks of Bacon's view in these terms:—

"In Julius Cæsar he saw combined all that the Roman genius had to bestow in the shape of greatness, nobility, culture, and fascination, and regarded his character as the most formidable that the Roman world could encounter, and giving what always seems as the proof of the calculation in the analysis of character.

"Bacon so explains the character of Cæsar as to explain his fate also; he saw, like Shakespeare, that Cæsar was naturally inclined to a despotic feeling, that governed his great qualities and also their aberrations, rendering him dangerous to the Republic and blind with respect to his enemies. He wished, says Bacon, not to be eminent amongst great and deserving men, but to be chief amongst inferiors and vassals; he was so much dazzled by his own greatness that he no longer knew what danger was. This is the same Cæsar into whose mouth Shakespeare puts the words—

> Danger knows full well
> That Cæsar is more dangerous than he.
> We were two lions littered in one day,
> And I the elder and more terrible.
> JULIUS CÆSAR, Act. 2, Sc. 4.

"When Bacon at last attributes the fate of Cæsar to his forgiveness of enemies, that by this magnanimity he might impose upon the multitude, he still shows the dazzled man who heightens the expression of his greatness at the expense of his security."—Pages 211, 212, Kuno Fischer.

But I consider the most complete and comprehensive and unprejudiced view of Julius Cæsar, his actions and policy, may be seen in Merivale's History of the Romans under the Empire, in which there is an equally good account of Pompeius his rival.

I have been thus diffuse over Julius Cæsar, for he was a man who stands alone from all the rest of the Roman worthies; and, being endowed by Divine Providence with those commanding and engaging qualities which give ascendancy in society, he must have swayed the destiny of his contemporaries in any age or nation in which he might have been born. Plutarch describes him as one who would rather be first in a village than second in Rome, and equally remarkable for bodily and mental vigour, courage, and vigilance. Britain, Gaul, Spain, Italy, and Ægypt bear witness to his military skill and prowess. As a writer he stands pre-eminent for purity of style and elegance and clearness of expression, and as an orator he has been described as only second to Cicero himself.

There is a singular village in Gaul that by tradition is connected with Julius Cæsar even at the present day—La Gaude, a village of Provence, containing 800 inhabitants. Tradition says it owes its name to its famous wine, still much prized, and known as far back as the days of Julius Cæsar; who, arriving there with his wearied troops, encamped and invited them to drink the wine, saying, "*Gaudete*." The whole country and the people in their habits of life are much the same as in the time of Julius Cæsar—their dialect borders as closely on the Latin as on French and Italian.

The Gold and Silver coins of Cæsar bearing his effigies were struck in his lifetime, he being the first of the Romans whose portrait was placed on coins when living—but the Large Brass coins, which are mostly cast coins, are considered to have been minted by order of Augustus after the death of Cæsar, and show his artifice to obtain supreme power in thus asserting his adoption by Cæsar. They may therefore be termed apotheosis coins of Cæsar; and are in no instance known to bear the S C, or mark of senatorial authority for being minted.

3.

DIVOS . IVLIVS. The laureate head of Cæsar to the right.

℞. CAESAR . DIVI . F. The youthful unlaureate head of Augustus to the right.

This inscription denotes the fact related in history of Julius Cæsar's adoption of his nephew Octavianus, who is here called his son, and was subsequently saluted with the name or title of Augustus.

These coins, although placed under the name of Julius Cæsar, may likewise by some persons be classed with the coins of Augustus; but, as they are intended to apply more particularly to Julius Cæsar, I have placed them under his name, which is the more usual practice with numismatic writers.

In DIVOS the o is used instead of the U, a practice not uncommon among the Romans.

The present coin, from the cabinet of Mr. Gwilt, displaced a very good one I had many years back from the Rev. E. C. Brice.

4.

DIVOS . IVLIVS. The laureate head of Cæsar to the right.

℞. CAESAR . DIVI . F. The youthful unlaureate head of Octavianus to the right —a star in the field in front of the face.

After the death of Cæsar, his nephew Augustus instituted games to his honour: at the first celebration of these games a blazing star or comet appeared, which has been recorded by Horace as the *Julium Sidus*, and by Virgil it is called *Cæsaris Astrum*.

It appeared at Rome for several days, and Augustus in commemorating Cæsar has also recorded the star by introducing it in the field of the brass coins, and by a denarius, as we shall see in the next coin—

———Micat inter omnes
Julium sidus, velut inter ignes
Luna minores.
HORACE, CARMINA, *Ode* xii. *de Laudibus Deorum et Hominum.*

Suetonius in Vita J. Cæsaris, ch. 88, says. " Siquidem ludis quos primos consecratos ei hæres Augustus edebat, stella crinita per septem dies continuos fulsit, exoriens circa undecimam horam, creditumque est animam esse Cæsaris in cœlum recepti, et hac de causa simulacro ejus in vertice additur stella; curiam in qua occisus est obstrui placuit idusque Martias parricidium nominari; ac ne unquam eo die senatus ageretur."

5.

DIVVS . IVLIVS across the field, on which appear eight points or lines as of a star, one of them having several waved lines on each side of it, corresponding with the words of Suetonius, *stella crinita*.

℞. CAESAR . AVGVSTVS. The head of Augustus to the left, decorated with a wreath of oak-leaves and acorns.

The legend is so placed as to read either way, Cæsar Augustus, or Augustus Cæsar. The wreath of oak-leaves and acorns is very singular in making its first appearance on the head of AVGVSTVS; the only other instance is to be found on the head of Galba.

The star which is here recorded, and is said to have been visible at Rome in broad daylight, is supposed by some antiquaries to be intended for the planet Venus, in allusion to the pretended genealogic descent of the Julii; others consider it was an appearance of the planet Venus occasioned by some peculiar state of the atmosphere for a few days; others again say that it refers to Cæsar's reform of the kalendar. The words *stella crinita* meaning also a comet, modern astronomers consider the Julium Sidus to have been a comet, but what comet cannot be determined for want of any data beyond the short account of Pliny, Suetonius, &c.

A scarce denarius from the cabinet of Mr. Gwilt.

6.

DIVOS . IVLIVS within a laurel wreath bearing large berries.

℞. DIVI . F. The head of Octavianus to the right; a star in the field in front of the neck.

The star here recorded is the star we have already noticed on the preceding coins.

A star in the most ancient times was a symbol of divinity. In the Gospel of St. Matthew it is related that when our Lord Jesus Christ was born the Magi from the East were guided to Bethlehem by a star, and they inquired for him by words expressive of His divinity : " Where is He that is born king of the Jews, for we have seen *His star* in the East and have come to worship him ? "

The laureated head does not appear on any coin until the time of Julius Cæsar. The Senate allowed, as a special honour to Cæsar, that he might at all times wear a laurel wreath, under the excuse that it was on account of his baldness. From this period the laurel wreath is invariably introduced on the heads of the emperors, excepting the instance of the preceding coin, and occasionally of the Emperor Galba: on some of his coins he is represented with a wreath of oak-leaves and acorns.

7.

CAESAR. The unlaureate head of Octavianus to the right.

℞. *No legend.* The prow of a galley to the right, having a forecastle and a pillar raised in front. The galley has a large scroll fiddle-head.

8.

..P.CAESAR.DIVI.F. The heads of Cæsar and Augustus back to back; a palm-branch is between them, and bending over the head of Augustus, which is to the right. The head of Cæsar is to the left, and laureate; that of Augustus is unlaureate.

℞. *No legend.* The prow of a galley to the right, having a bank of oars stretched from its side; close at the bow above them, and within the lines of the upper works, is an eye, by the side of which is a small square opening or porthole with a dot in it. Beyond this, the side of the galley is ornamented with diagonal lines. Standing above the front bar of the bulwark rail is a column, by the side of which in the field is a spiked ball.

The representation of an eye on the fore part of a galley is very ancient; it may be seen on the bow of a Greek galley represented in the paintings of Polygnotus in the Lesche at Delphi. The eye also appears on Charon's boat, which is introduced in the same paintings.

The eye is a type of the Divine Providence or the Deity, and is still retained on some of the Mediterranean craft. It is of the remotest antiquity: among the ancient Ægyptians the eye was a very frequent emblem, signifying the superintendence or watchfulness of Divine Providence. It is used by the Chinese at the present day on their war-junks as well as on the sampan. It also appears on some of the Hetruscan vases which were some years back discovered in the ancient tombs of the Hetruscans by Lucien Buonaparte.

There is in the Arschot Cabinet, as described by Gevartius, tab. vii. No. xvi. a coin which had been struck by Cnæus Domitius, who was præfectus classis in Mari Ionio temp. Marc. Antonii, similar to the present. Gevartius considers that the præfect placed the spiked globe above the galley as an emblem of the sun, meaning Antonius, as being under his auspices or command.

Vaillant, in his work Numismata Imperatorum in Coloniis cusa, p. 4, describes a coin of this type as belonging to the Colonia Valentia; and in his specimen he gives the word COPIA under the galley, from which word he conjectures that the coin may have been struck by another colony, and the letters C. O. P. I. A. as only initial, intended to signify Colonia Octavianum Pacensis Julia Augusta. The word *copia* appears indistinctly on the exergum of the reverse of this present coin.

9.

DIVI . IVLI . . . . . F . IMP. The unlaureate heads of Cæsar and Augustus back to back.

℞. C.I.V. Over the prow of a galley to the right, with a forecastle of four stories, in front of which is a straight column.

This is a colonial coin, the letters C.I.V. meaning Colonia Julia Valentia, a town in Spain, near Saguntum, founded originally by Junius Brutus. Mr. Burgon describes a coin of this type in General Ramsay's collection as having been struck at Vienne in Gallia Narbonensis; but I think he is wrong.

The pillar or upright column in front of the forecastle of the galley represented on this and the two preceding coins is an object the use of which I do not find noticed by any numismatic writer, and I am indebted to my worthy friend the Rev. E. Boden for reminding me of what is noted by Polybius. It appears to be described by him in the following manner, as translated by Hampton:—

"They erected on the prow of every vessel a round pillar of wood of about twelve feet in height and of three palms breadth in diameter, with a pulley at the top; to this pillar was fitted a kind of stage, eighteen feet in length and four feet broad, which was made ladder-wise of strong timbers, laid across and cramped together with iron, the pillar being received into an oblong square, which was opened for that purpose at a distance of six feet from the end of the stage: on either side of the stage, lengthwise, was a parapet which reached just above the knee; at the furthest end of the step or ladder was a bar of iron, whose shape was somewhat like a pestle, but it was sharpened at the bottom or lower part, and at the top of it was a ring. The whole appearance of this machine very much resembled those that are used for grinding corn. To the ring just mentioned was fixed a rope by which, with the help of the pulley which was at the top of the pillar, they hoisted up the machines, and as the vessels of the enemy came near let them fall upon them."

To this explanation of the pillar I may add the description of the *corvus*, which it appears was an apparatus to be used for much the same purpose. Pitiscus, Lexicon Antiquitatum Romanorum, *art.* Corvus, says :—

"*Corvus.* A manu ferrea sive harpagone diversus fuit, distinguunt enim. Curt. iv. 2, 12, Ferreæ quoque manus, harpagones vocant corvique præparabantur; et Diodor. xvii. 4!, Corvis autem manibusque ferreis in loricis consistentes abripiebant.—Videtur Corvus ferramentum fuisse triquetrum et acuminatum ad effigiem corvini rostri—inque summo capite habuisse annulum e ferro cui inserebatur catena, sicque postea vel balista vel alia machina conjectum navim hostilem aliquando retinuisse, sæpius perforasse, describit Polyb. i. 12. V. illum; Scheffer de Milit. Nav. ii. 7, Lips.; Poliorc. v. 8; Philand. in Vitruv. x. 19; Bald. lex Vitruv.; Stewech in Veget. iv. 44."

The corvus, or grappling-iron, was the invention of Duillius, the Roman consul who gained the first naval victory over the Carthaginians B. C. 260, for which he was honoured with a naval triumph, and a column was erected at Rome, in marble, decorated with the rostra of ships. This column still exists at Rome, in that part which was the Forum; it is called Columna Duillii.—Donati, p. 137.

10.

CAESAR . DIC . TER. The head of Victory to the right, a circular ring in the ear. Weight 236½ grains.

℞. C . CLOVI . PRAEF. Minerva armed, gradient to the left, the ægis on her breast, and bearing the shield with the Gorgon's head on her left arm; on her right shoulder she is carrying a trophy of arms; in front at her feet is a serpent in an erect undulatory posture.

The serpent or dragon was sacred to Minerva, and at Athens there was a statue of Minerva by Phidias, representing her with a serpent at her feet.

There are few facts better attested by historical evidence than that the serpent has by all the nations of antiquity been regarded and employed symbolically—it is conspicuous in their history, it stands out in their fables, and is visible in their religion; conjoined with Minerva on the present coin, it is evil or tendency to evil controlled by reason or wisdom—wisdom and prudence likewise, for among the most ancient people by a serpent was signified prudence or circumspection: the serpent is used in this sense by the Lord himself in St. Matthew, x. 16.—Rendell, Antediluv.

The Athenians had a tradition that the chief guardian of their Acropolis was a serpent. Herodotus (Euterpe, 74) informs us the serpent was sacred at Thebes. The hieroglyphics which have been brought to light in our own times abundantly show that it must have been used in an emblematic way among the ancients, and it was set apart as one of the objects associated with the religion of Egypt—not at first to be worshipped, nor for any good it could bestow—it was the symbol of something that might if not guarded against be disastrous to mankind. The figure of a serpent biting its own tail is very ancient, and is commonly regarded as an emblem of eternity. We would ask, is it not rather a representation of evil punishing itself?

The serpent surrounding an egg in Phœnician mythology plainly implies the danger of sensuality, with which life is beset from its very beginning.

Among the Greeks the hair of Medusa is represented as being turned into serpents, because she had violated the sanctity of the Temple of Minerva; the serpents representing the evil she had perpetrated.

The serpent Python, fabled to have sprung from the mud of the deluge of Deucalion, was an emblem of the evil occasioned to Greece by the inundations of Thessaly; the arrows of Apollo destroying Python representing the drying-up of the waters and marshes by the rays of the sun.

The serpents which the infant Hercules strangled were a representation of innocence overcoming the blandishments of sensuality; and the Hydra he afterwards slew was a representative of those evils which energy and fortitude may overcome.

Æsculapius is always represented with a serpent entwined around his staff, (see Caracalla,) to denote the power of the physician over the diseases of humanity. Apollo Medicus is also represented leaning on a staff with a serpent entwined around it. (See Galba.)

Of all the degrees of man's life the sensual and corporeal are the lowest, being actuated by merely earthly appetites, influences, and causes. As the serpent crawls upon the earth, so the sensual principle in man is the nearest akin to the earth, which if not elevated by the rational and spiritual principles of his nature, typified by Minerva, may be said to crawl upon the earth.

From the instances above mentioned it may be seen that the emblem of that whereby man fell from his first integrity was preserved among mankind for a long time after the reminiscence of its precise signification had passed away. They had retained the emblem with some general idea of its meaning, but had lost sight of its definite signification; for this we must go to analogy and the Scriptures; these will show us that by the serpent was meant the sensual principle of man; and his submitting himself to its influence, and no longer allowing himself to be led of God, was the fall or decline from a state of obedience to the Divine commandments, to the rule of self-love, the sensual principle.

Caius Clovius, or Cluvius, (for it is written both ways,) who struck this coin, lived in the time of Julius Cæsar, and is held by antiquaries to be the Clovius who was sent by Cæsar to take the command in Gallia Cisalpina. Before he departed for the province he was invited by Cicero to visit him, that they might have some conversation regarding his appointment. (Cicero's Letters, lib. xiii. ep. 7 and ep. 55.) Clovius was an intimate friend of Cicero, by whom he was held in much esteem. Cicero speaks of him in his oration for Roscius—" Petam a C. Cluvio equite Romano ornatissimo homine;" also " Venit ad Cluvium, quem hominem imo gravissimum nobilem imo constantissimum," &c.—Harrec. Thes. 90.

In Gruter, p. xiv. No. 2, we have an inscription quoted that was found at Puteoli—

C . CLVVIVS . M . F.
IIIVIR.
IVRIDIC . IIVIR . NOLAE .
IIIIVIR . QVINQVENNAL .
DE . SVO . FACIVND . COERAVIT.
IDEMQVE . RESTITVIT .
IOVI . D . M . SACR .

11.

CAESAR . DIC . TER. The head of Victory to the right, a circular ring in the ear.

℞. C . CLOVI . PRAEF . Minerva armed, and gradient to the left, preceded by the serpent.

The reverse of this coin is finely perfect.

12.

CAESAR . DIC . TER . The head of Victory to the right, having a circular ring in the ear, and a star in the field behind the head.

℞. C . CLOVI . PRAEF . Minerva armed, and gradient to the left, preceded by the serpent.

The star introduced in the field on the obverse is the star (*stella crinita*) we have already noticed.

These two coins, in good preservation, are from the cabinet of General Ramsay.

MARCUS JUNIUS BRUTUS.

MARCUS JUNIUS BRUTUS, the son of Junius Brutus and Servilia the sister of Cato, was born in the year of Rome 669. He joined the party of Pompeius against Cæsar, and held a command in the army of Pompeius at the battle of Pharsalia. After the death of Pompeius he was pardoned by Cæsar; and, being of ancient family and a learned man, he was treated by Cæsar with much consideration and favour. The desire of Julius Cæsar for curbing the ascendancy of the popular party, and his endeavours to make the three distinctions of the government, as *the supreme head, the deliberative*, and *the elective*, were not, or would not be, understood; and the radical opinions of Brutus, Cassius, and others (most of whose lives Cæsar had spared after the great battle) were called into action under the mistaken notion that they were patriots putting down tyranny, conceiving that Cæsar aspired to kingly power. These misguided hasty men put their benefactor to death in the year of Rome 710, four years after their lives and fortunes had been granted them, and before they had had the opportunity of seeing and forming a proper judgment on the plans which Julius Cæsar proposed to provide for the future security and good government of the Roman people.

Brutus was lineally descended from the Lucius Junius surnamed Brutus who expelled the Tarquins from Rome on the death of Lucretia, and he seems to have inherited all the intolerant republican spirit of his ancestor, and therefore did not scruple to plunge his dagger into the breast of his friend and benefactor Julius Cæsar when he imagined Cæsar intended to assume regal authority.

To persons who are at all acquainted with Roman history the name of Brutus is so conjoined with that of Cæsar, principally occasioned perhaps by the affectionate exclamation recorded of Cæsar, "*Et tu Brute*," when he saw Brutus with his hand raised to stab him, that the mention of either brings the other to the mind, with all the circumstances related of the death of Cæsar and the conduct of Brutus on the occasion, and the part he took in the murder.

The coin of Brutus is only found in gold and silver.

13.

BRVT . IMP . L . PLAET . CEST. The head of Brutus unlaureate to the right. A denarius, weight 53¼ grains.

℞. EID . MAR. Underneath a pileus or cap, on each side of which is a dagger.

Julius Cæsar was murdered on the Ides of March, which would be the 15th, or middle of the month, in the year of Rome 710. The actual day of the perpetration of the deed is marked on the coin in perpetual remembrance of the fact. After the murder of Cæsar in the senate-house the conspirators marched through the city accompanied by a numerous band of gladiators and many associates, proclaiming liberty to the people and peace to all, declaring they intended no further violence to any one. Upon this occasion they were preceded by one of their attendants, who carried a cap, the emblem of liberty, raised on the point of a spear. Thus the cap on the coin refers to the freedom of the citizens of Rome having (been supposed to have) been gained by the use of the dagger, implying that the Roman people had been held in slavery by Julius Cæsar, from which state of bondage they had been released and made freemen by the daggers of Brutus and his confederates.

The mode of manumitting a slave is described in Festus thus:—"Manumitti servus dicebatur cum dominus ejus aut caput ejusdem servi aut aliud membrum tenens dicebat, 'Hunc hominem liberum esse volo,' et emittebat eum è manu, servo autem prætori se sistente, quod prætor vindictâ, id est, virgâ ejusdem servi capiti impositâ ita dicebat, 'Dico eum liberum esse more Quiritum;' inde conversus ad lictorem addebat, 'secundum tuam causam, sicuti dixi, ecce tibi vindicta.' Tum lictor, acceptâ a prætore vindictâ, caput servi percutiebat, faciem palma tergumque verberabat. Quibus actis nomen manumissi in acta a scribâ referebatur."

Well-struck coins of Brutus are frequently termed false; but Mr. Cureton, a very skilful hand in detecting a forgery, and who bought this for me at the Pembroke sale, remarked to me he had never seen a coin of Brutus called genuine but what was equally as false as those commonly called false; and in fact it was only a fashion to say so, for one was quite as good and genuine as the other. This he said in consequence of my remarking to him that the similar coin in the sale preceding the present had brought 10*l*., and Mr. Cureton gave it me as his real and unqualified opinion that the present coin was quite as genuine.

MARCUS ÆMILIUS LEPIDUS.

MARCUS ÆMILIUS LEPIDUS was born of a patrician family, although it is not known in what year; he followed the fortunes of Julius Cæsar in opposing Pompeius, and took a part in the battle of Pharsalia. After the death of Julius Cæsar he joined with Octavianus and Antonius, and formed with them the second Triumvirate for the preservation of the Republic in the year of Rome 710-11.

He was afterwards deprived of the title of Triumvir, and banished by Octavianus, in the year of Rome 718, to Circei, a small town in Italy, where he passed his days in private life, and died in the year of Rome 741.

His coins are rare, and are only known in gold and silver.

14.

LEPIDUS . PONT . MAX . IIIV . R . P . C. The unlaureate head of Lepidus to the right.

℞. CÆSAR . IMP . IIIVIR . R . P . C. The unlaureate head of Octavianus to the right.

The present coin is a denarius, obtained from the cabinet St. Croix; it is in good condition, which is not usual with coins of Lepidus Weight 59½ grains.

MARCUS ANTONIUS.

MARCUS ANTONIUS was born about the year of Rome 671. He entered the army, and joined the party of Julius Cæsar, and contributed to the defeat of Pompeius at Pharsalia. Associating with Lepidus and Octavianus after the death of Cæsar, he formed with them the second Triumvirate for the preservation of the Republic, year of Rome 710. To strengthen this confederacy Octavianus married Clodia the daughter-in-law of Antonius; and Antonius, after the death of his wife Fulvia, married Octavia the sister of Octavianus. Antonius subsequently divorced Octavia, by whom he had three children, that he might marry Cleopatra the Queen of Ægypt.

Antonius being afterwards at variance with Octavianus, he engaged in war with him, and was completely defeated in a sea-fight off Actium, a promontory and sea-port town of Epirus in the year of Rome 723, B.C. 31, 2nd of September; and this date has been formally recorded by historians as signalising the termination of the Republic and the commencement of the Roman monarchy. Octavianus himself considered it as the inauguration of a new æra. As a perpetual memorial of this complete and final triumph, he founded a city upon the site of his camp, and gave it the name of Nicopolis, the city of victory.

After this defeat Antonius fled into Ægypt, whither he was pursued by Octavianus, and in the following year Antonius killed himself, his fleet and his army having surrendered to his opponent.

15.

M . ANTONIVS . IMP . COS . DES . ITER . ET . TER. The head of Antonius to the right, wreathed with ivy. The legend is also encircled with ivy leaves and berries alternately. Under the head is a small augural lituus, denoting the rank of Antonius as chief of the College of Augurs.

℞. IIIVIR . R . P . C. A small bust placed on a casket; to the right two snakes are entwined underneath, and raise their heads on either side.

Some authors have considered the bust on the casket as representing Octavia the wife of Antonius; others denote it as the bust of Cleopatra; while others again designate it as the bust of the goddess Libera, the female Bacchus, or more properly Ariadne, to whom the name of Libera was given by Bacchus, who was surnamed Liber. (Haverc. in Thes., also Oiselius *in Antonio*, p. 81., ed. 1677.)

I have little hesitation in considering the bust on the mystic cyst is intended for Octavia, for Antonius is termed in the legend IIIVIR . R . P . C., thus shewing the coin was struck whilst he was IIIVIR., and in amity with Octavianus; consequently it would have been an insult and out of character with the friendly feeling then existing between Antonius and Octavianus that the bust of any other lady than the sister of Augustus should be introduced on the coins of Rome.

Argelati *in Antonio* quotes two coins similar to this, both in brass, one ex Thes. Mauroc. J. C. Bon., the other in Musæo Fedriciano; and also one in silver which he describes, with similar legends to this, containing portraits of Antonius and Octavia on the obverse,—and which he quotes from Gorlæus, f. 5.

The present coin is a silver medallion from the cabinet of Sir John Twysden, and is of the class designated Cistophori. Weight 181½ grains.

16.

M . ANTONIVS . IMP . COS . DESIG . ITER . ET . TER.   The head of Antonius to the right, crowned with an ivy wreath. The legend is also encircled by a wreath of ivy leaves and bunches of ivy berries alternately.

℞. *No legend.* A quiver of arrows; two snakes entwining their tails raise their heads one on each side of the quiver, while a snake is seated on the top; on the left of the verge of the field is a star.

The ivy wreath around the head of Antonius on this and the preceding coin appears to record the fact mentioned in history that Antonius, when at Alexandria with Cleopatra the Queen of Ægypt, amongst other presumptions, allowed himself to be called Bacchus, also Osiris. He had before then, after the victory at Philippi, entered Ephesus with a procession of men, women, and children, clothed as Bacchantes and Satyrs, crowned with ivy and carrying thyrsi. See further Plutarch *in Antonio* p. 926; ii. Livy, c. 82. This unseemly conduct is also referred to by Eckhel, vi. 65, *in Antonio.*

The plant ivy was sacred to Bacchus; from this (the appropriation of the plant) the artist has encircled the head of Antonius with an ivy-wreath, emblem of Bacchus, whose godship Antonius had assumed.

A very good black coin from the cabinet of the Duke of Devonshire. Weight 487 grains.

17.

M . ANTONI . IMP . COS . DES . III. VIR . R . P . C.   The heads of Antonius and Octavianus side by side to the right; both are unlaureate. Facing them is the head of Octavia to the left, without diadem or any ornament to her hair. Bronze, fine.

℞. M . OPPIUS . CAPITO . P . R . PRAEF . CLASS . P . C.   A sailing galley with a bank of oars to the right, under it is the Greek letter Γ, and a triquetra.

This coin is classed by Morell as being of the *gens Oppia;* it was formerly in the Pembroke cabinet, and is well known from being cited by Eckhel *in M. Antonio,* vol. vi. p. 56, thus:—

"M . ANT . IMP . COS . DES . III . VIR . R . P . C .

"Capita tria ut supra (id est)—Duo capita virilia nuda, quorum anterius est Antonii, posterius juvenile, quibus adversum et tertium muliebre nudum.

" ℞. M . OPPIUS . CAPITO . PROPR . PRAEF . CLASS .

"Navis cum velo, infra Γ et triquetra.

"Æ. I. Pembrock. p. ii. tab. 58, et p. iii. tab. 46.

"Si hujus inscriptio numi talis est qualis perhibetur necesse est, notam III. bis accipiendam, sic ut primam efficiat cos . DES . III ., deinde III . VIR . R . P . C . etenim Antonius cos . DES . non fuit nisi anno V. C. 709, sed quo in tempore III . VIR . nondum fuit."

The present coin is also figured in Havercamp's Thesaurus; he describes the female portrait as being intended for a representation of Cleopatra. Vaillant, in his work Numismata Imperatorum, &c. in Coloniis percussa, p. 88, mentions a coin of Antonius with an inscription on the reverse similar to the present, giving no particulars of the coin from which he obtains his information; but I cannot help forming a different opinion to the numismatic authorities who quote this coin, and who all treat this portrait as being that of Cleopatra; first, I do not think the *triumviri monetales* would have ventured to place on a Roman coin, for circulation in Rome, the portrait of a foreigner male or female, more especially the portrait of a queen of another country, although she might be the paramour of a man high in office; next, Antonius must have lived with Octavia several years, for he had a family of three or four children by her, and there would not be the same objection with the master of the mint for the portrait of Octavia appearing on a coin jointly with her husband and her brother; and again, Octavia being afterwards divorced by Antonius to make room for Cleopatra, it is not at all probable the portrait of Cleopatra would be allowed to be placed on a Roman coin conjointly with the portrait of Octavia's brother.

The most complete authority in favour of my view is in Argelati *in Augusto* A.U.C. 714, a brass coin, thus, "Capita Aug. et Antonii jugata, cum capite Octaviæ illa respicientis. ℞. PRAE . ITER. . . . navis prætoria expansis velis, Seguin, f. 95, ubi illustrat nummum eruditissimo commentario." In A.U.C. 714, Fulvia, the wife of Antonius, died, and he married Octavia, the sister of Augustus.

The coin which gives in my opinion the greatest colour to the assertion of the female portrait being that of Cleopatra is one quoted in Argelati *in Antonio*, p. 19 :—

"M . OPPIVS . CAPITO . PRAEF . C . L . M .

"Antonius et Cleopatra in biga Hippopotamorum. *Schedæ Sponnianæ*."

The Hippopotami being natives of Ægypt suggests the doubt on the portrait, and then this coin must have been struck after the rupture with Octavianus, and the divorce of Octavia.

The battle of Actium took place in A.U.C. 723, and it was not many years before that Antonius, after repudiating Octavia, gave himself entirely to Cleopatra, and I think there is no doubt these coins were struck during the time there was a good understanding existing between Antonius and Octavianus. The divorce of Octavia and marriage with Cleopatra caused a complete rupture between Antonius and Octavianus, which had been long brooding in consequence of Antonius presuming on the youth of Octavianus. Civil war ensued, which in the end proved fatal to Antonius and Cleopatra.

The Greek letter Γ shews that the coin was minted in the third year of the triumvirate of Antonius, Lepidus, and Octavianus, A.U.C. 713, which therefore tends to confirm my view of the female portrait being that of Octavia. Havercamp, Thes. 305, says the Γ means the third year of OPP. CAPITO being *præfectus classis*, but I think he errs; the Greek Γ signifies the year of mintage, and the mintage of a coin applies to the person whose effigies is given on a coin, and who it was intended to commemorate, and not to a subordinate officer, as a prefect.

The Romans usually had a fleet stationed at Misenum in Sicily. Pitiscus in his Lexicon, under PRAEFECTVS, says, " Præfectus fuit custos potius quàm dux." The triquetra, or three human legs joined together, establishes it as a coin of Sicily, of which island the triquetra was the peculiar emblem, from the island being triangular and forming three promontories.

18.

M. ANT. IMP. TER. COS. DESIG. ITER. ET. TER. IIIVIR. R. P. C. The heads of Antonius and Octavia adverse, Antonius being to the right.

℞. L. ATRATINVS. AVGVR. PRAEF. CLASS. F. C.

A black coin, in good condition.

This coin is singular and very rare, or I should not have let it have a place in the cabinet. The legends above quoted are not on the coin, being worn off, except L. ATRATINVS. on the reverse. I have supplied them from Havercamp's Thesaurus, where this coin is described, p. 26, in the following words: After the legend on the obverse, he says—" Capita adversa Marci Antonii et Cleopatræ." The reverse he describes, " Duæ icunculæ in curru a quatuor equis marinis tracto, subtus litera Δ et arula, retro icunculas connexæ cernuntur in medio literæ H.S."

This is an accurate description of the present coin, less the legends, but I principally use it for the reason of the legend describing Antonius as IMP. TER. or *tertium*, or imperator for the third time, and consul designated for the third time; and I consider this legend as shewing Antonius at an early period of the Triumvirate, for which reasons I more safely conclude the female head to be that of the wife Octavia, although designated by Havercamp as Cleopatra; so, if this is an early struck coin of Antonius, as from the obverse may be concluded by the legend impressed, the female portrait cannot be that of Cleopatra.

Argelati speaks of a coin similar to the present coin being "ex Thes. Mediceo Reverendissimus Noris:" so it is apparently a very scarce coin.

I find in Argelati also several instances of coins which encourage the opinion of the female portrait being that of Cleopatra, but still I think it right to raise the doubt, especially as Argelati *in Antonio* describes a brass coin, "Capita M. Antonii, C. Cæsaris et Octaviæ jugata— ℟. Navis expansis velis; epigraphe non legitur. Ex Ind. Polatio;" and it must be conceded by antiquaries that a Roman mintmaster could not have dared to put the portrait of a Roman general's mistress on a coin for use in Rome in preference to the portrait of a wife, especially that wife being the sister of the reigning emperor.

In the time of the second triumvirate of Antonius, Lepidus, and Octavianus, the Roman legions played a very conspicuous part, and from some cause not now known Antonius had denarii struck recording all the legions. From their being almost the arbiters of the fate of Rome we have introduced these coins of the legions as historic coins of the period, although on their legends they record no more than their own names.

We have in English history books describing the origin and exploits of various regiments in the service of the Crown. The regiment is numerically equal to the Roman cohort; and it would be very interesting if a work could be written describing in like manner the origin and exploits of the different Roman legions, their campaigns, their victories, their retreats, their internal administration, anecdotes of the service of their officers, and acts of individual bravery, skill, and address. The only paper of the kind is one by the Rev. Beale Post on the Legio XX. contained in the volume of the Proceedings of the British Archæological Association at their meeting held at Gloucester in 1846; but it must have occasioned him immense labour to have collected sufficient materials to enable him to accomplish his task.

19.

ANT. AVG. A galley, rowing to the right, having a short mast, or bowsprit, at the head; under it IIIVIR. R. P. C.

MARCUS ANTONIUS.

℞. COHORTIVM . PRAETORIARVM. Three standards, the centre one being an eagle, standard of the legion.

20.

ANT . AVG . A galley, rowing to the right, as before, under it the words IIIVIR . R . P . C .

℞. COHORTIS . SPECVL. Three standards, each bearing a wreath, but no eagle.

21. ANT . AVG . A galley, as before.—℞. LEG . II . Three standards, the centre one being an eagle.
22. ANT . AVG . A galley, as before.—℞. LEG . III . Three standards, as before.
23. ANT . AVG . A galley, as before.—℞. LEG . IV . The three standards.
24. ANT . AVG . A galley, as before.—℞. LEG . V . The three standards.
25. ANT . AVG . A galley, as before.—R. LEG . VI . The three standards.
26. ANT . AVG . A galley, as before.—℞. LEG . VII . The three standards.
27. ANT . AVG . A galley, as before.—℞. LEG . VIII . The three standards.
28. ANT . AVG . A galley, as before.—℞. LEG . IX . The three standards.
29. ANT . AVG . A galley, as before.—℞. LEG . X . The three standards.
30. ANT . AVG . A galley, as before.—℞. LEG . XI . The three standards.
31. ANT . AVG . A galley, as before.—℞. LEG . XII . The three standards.
32. ANT . AVG . A galley, as before.—℞. LEG . XIII . The three standards.
33. ANT . AVG . A galley, as before.—℞. LEG . XIV . The three standards.
34. ANT . AVG . A galley, as before.—℞. LEG . XV . The three standards.
35. ANT . AVG . A galley, as before.—℞. LEG . XVI . The three standards.
36. ANT . AVG . A galley, as before.—℞. LEG . XVII . The three standards.

Obverse and reverse as before.

37. LEG . XVIII .
38. LEG . XVIII . LYBICÆ.
39. LEG . XIX .
40. LEG . XX .
41. LEG . XXI .
42. LEG . XXII .
43. LEG . XXIII .
44. LEG . XXIV .

In Argelati we have notice of thirty legions, and he describes them all on the reverse as—" Duo signa Castrensia, Aquila legionaria media."

All these legionary coins have an eagle as one of their standards. The bird called the eagle holds the highest rank, and has been emphatically called the King of Birds—in rapidity and power of flight, in strength and in keenness of vision, it far excels all others. An eagle with expanded wings formed the imperial standard of the Persians under Cyrus, very long before it became the principal standard of the Romans. As an emblem of sovereignty it was adopted by the Romans, and their conduct as warriors during the Republic and in the early period of the Empire was well symbolised by this emblem.

The eagle is also the attribute or attendant bird of Jupiter, the chief of the Roman deities. As the eagle was considered the chief of birds, it became a fitting associate with Jupiter.

AUGUSTUS.

CAIUS OCTAVIANUS CÆPIUS, the son of C. Octavius Rufus, and Atia or Actia, daughter of Julius Cæsar's sister, was born at Velitræ, an ancient town of Latium, on the Appian Road, about twenty miles east of Rome, year of Rome 691; his father died when he was about four years of age.

After receiving an excellent education, he was formally adopted by his great-uncle Julius Cæsar as his son, and by the will of Cæsar he was constituted his heir. At the time of Cæsar's murder he was about eighteen years of age, and was then studying at Apollonia, in Greece. On hearing of what had occurred he instantly quitted Apollonia for Rome, and declared himself Cæsar's heir and successor to the government. Antonius, who at first had received him with cordiality, grew cool and manifested designs for increasing his own power and diminishing the influence of Octavianus, who had received the support of Cæsar's soldiers.

After several disturbances and a little war, Antonius found it was more politic to keep friends with Octavianus, and accordingly about eighteen months after Cæsar's death Antonius, Octavianus, and Lepidus met at Mutina, and agreed to a firm friendship; and then constituted themselves Triumvirs for the preservation of the Republic.

Having taken measures to secure the government to themselves, the Triumvirs turned their attention to the murderers of Cæsar; and, after successive engagements, in which many of those who had conspired against Cæsar were slain, the armies of the two parties met at Philippi; where, after a very severe contest, the army of Brutus and Cassius was routed with great slaughter, upon which those commanders killed themselves. These events took place in the year of Rome 712. The authority of the new Triumvirate was now fully established, the few conspirators who survived the battle of Philippi surrendered, and were favourably received; but soon afterwards a number of men of rank, and among them Cicero, were set down in the list of proscriptions, and were searched out and put to death: by these means the Triumvirs got rid of all those who were, or were likely to be, opposed to their designs.

In the year of Rome 718, Octavianus having quarrelled with Lepidus, the latter was deprived of the honours of Triumvir, but allowed to retain the dignity of Pontifex Maximus; and was banished to Circei, where he died some years after. Subsequently the Roman people elected Octavianus Tribune for life.

Two or three years after this took place, disputes arose between Octavianus and Antonius. The former caused Antonius to be accused before the people. Antonius quitted Rome and withdrew to the legions that were quartered in Greece and Syria. In the end, both parties having taken up arms, various engagements ensued, and at last at the battle of Actium the forces of Antonius were defeated, and he fled to Egypt, where he soon after killed himself.

By this event Octavianus became sole master of the state. He consulted with his two most particular friends Mæcenas and Agrippa as to the course he should pursue—the latter recommended him to surrender his authority to the people, whilst the former advised he should maintain the power he had gained, but not to assume the title of King, it being detested by the Roman people. Octavianus preferred the advice of Mæcenas; he perceived on consideration that the Roman people had by such a long series of the wars of party factions in the city lost much of their ancient vigour and thirst for liberty; their foreign wars being no longer carried on by the citizens, but by hired legions of auxiliaries, the spirit and energy of the warriors of the olden time had disappeared, and the old Roman citizen was no longer to be found; while on the other hand the Senate, having lost a great part of its nobles and men of rank, influence, and patriotic principles, whose places were supplied by men of inferior grade and principle, they had not the firmness of character, independence, and resolution of former days. Added to these, so much corruption had crept in, especially amongst the military, that nothing but a vigorous hand to guide the chariot of the state could correct and remove the evils.

Octavianus clearly perceived this state of affairs, and he boldly resolved to abide by the advice of Mæcenas, and in the end his resolve was successful. Mæcenas was a nobleman of royal views and opinions, being himself, as noted by Horace, of royal descent (Hetruscan)—

Mæcenas atavis edite regibus.—Carm. i.

His aristocratic royal views coincided with the view of Octavianus, and he retained the position he had so gained.

The victory at Actium was gained in the year of Rome 723, and in commemoration of the event Octavianus built the town of Nicopolis and a temple to Apollo; and instituted games in honour of Apollo, who was then surnamed Actius. The games were called Actia, and were celebrated every five years with great pomp. The conduct of the games was placed under the care of the Lacedemonians.

Octavianus likewise shut up the Temple of Janus, and peace appeared to be general.

The Senate, perceiving it was to their interest to ingratiate themselves with Octavianus, after a time bestowed on him the title or surname of Augustus; by which he is now historically known.

The title of Imperator was also assumed, and he thus quietly obtained the whole power of government really in his own hands, although having the appearance of it being held at the will of the people.

The title of Imperator or Emperor, which had previously been a military distinction given usually on the field of battle to a successful general, became extended to signify the supreme governor, arbiter of all civil and military affairs, and thenceforward continued to be assumed as the hereditary title of the chief person in the state, and marked the change from a Republic to a Monarchy; the title of Rex, or King, being studiously avoided.

After a long life spent in reducing the government to consistency and order, curbing the vices of the people, and doing every thing in his power to raise the empire in the estimation of surrounding nations, and by his clemency and suavity of manner conciliating all parties, Augustus was suddenly taken ill of diarrhœa on his returning from a journey to Beneventum, which caused him to stop at Nola, near Capua, in Campania, where he shortly after died, being very nearly 76 years of age, in the year of Rome 767, and A.D. 14.

Augustus is one of the most remarkable of all the Romans of his period, and may properly be called the founder of the Roman empire, mostly on the plan his uncle Julius Cæsar had proposed to pursue. He won the affections of the Roman people to such an extent as to have obtained an absolute monarchy, a charge made against Julius Cæsar and causing his death. Cæsar appears rather to have coquetted with the title of King; had he, like Augustus, remained content with the title of Imperator, coupled with the Tribunicia Potestas as perpetual tribune, and the dignity of Pontifex Maximus, he might have reigned securely at Rome; but Cæsar was dazzled with the idea of being a King.

Augustus, on the contrary, took warning from the fate of his uncle. He accepted everything the Senate pleased to bestow on him in honours and power, but at the same time cautiously and craftily professing to hold his dignity at the will of the people, and being ready at all times to lay aside his honours if he were required. The people were however too indolent to resume their power, and, being charmed by his bounties and complaisant behaviour, the splendour and frequency of the shows he exhibited, and at which he made a point always to attend, they did not care to inquire too closely and distract themselves about his titles and government, and thus he remained in the undisturbed possession of the sovereignty and they became his slaves, and were never after able to throw off the yoke he had placed on their necks.

Although the coins of Augustus are generally speaking very common, yet it is difficult to fix the period of an event by any ty pewhich appears on them. The titles DIVVS and DIVO occur on many of the coins, but they are not all apotheosis coins, for it is related that Augustus was so vain as to allow himself to be saluted with the title in his lifetime, and even to have altars erected to him and incense burned as to a divine being, as the coins shew to us. See No. 46, *post*.

Among those coins which were struck during his life are some that record the assumption of the TRIBVNICIA · POTESTAS which was conferred on Augustus for life, and other coins which record the restoration of Roman citizens who were prisoners of war in other countries, especially those among the Parthians, the remains of the legions of Crassus, as well as the preservation of the lives of the Roman citizens by the cessation of civil wars. These were struck in conformity with decrees of the Senate by various masters of the mint whose names appear on some of the coins, and it is a singular fact that after the reign of Augustus all mention on coins of the name and title of the masters of the mint quite disappears, although the office of mint master or IIIVIR · MONETALIS was still continued.

The IIIVIR · MONETALIS is described—" Romæ magistratus iste Triumvirorum Monetalium dicebatur quorum providere numismata aurea, argentea, ærea probæ materiæ justique ponderis flatentur ac ferientur." Their origin is considered to be alluded to by Livy—" Et Romæ quoque propter penuriam argenti IIIVIRI mensarii, rogatione *Minutii Trib. Pl. facti L. Æmilius* qui Consul Censorque fuerat et *M. Attilius Regulus* qui bis Consul fuerat et *L. Scribonius Libo* qui Trib. Pl. erat, ex quo tempore IIIVIRI monetales originem traxisse." (Monumenta Patavina, p. 107, Patin. Imp. Romanorum Numismata, p. 20.)

The office of master of the mint was held by three individuals at one time; hence the title of Triumvir Monetalis. There is a sort of numismatic problem connected with the Triumviri Monetales, *i.e.* to ascertain who were in office at the same time at any one period. With the exception of the above names quoted from Livy, the nearest approach to this fact we shall notice presently on a set of coins of Augustus, in their proper place.

It is to be observed that the initial letters S. C., which now so constantly appear on Roman coins, denote that they were struck SENATVS . CONSVLTO, by a decree of the Senate. Although this is the invariable mark of the brass coins, yet there are instances of the S. C., sometimes E. X. S. C., appearing on the gold coins. Augustus reserved to himself the right of ordering the issue of gold and silver, leaving the brass coinage under the orders of the Senate; hence it is that no brass coins of the Roman mint of the Emperor Otho are as yet to be found, for the Senate, in silent disgust with his murder of the Emperor Galba, made no decree for a brass coinage. Otho, having power over the gold and silver, caused a coinage in those metals.

The absence of the S. C. is the distinctive signification of the medallion—a larger sized brass or silver coin, by some supposed to be proofs for the special use and approval of the Emperor and for presents to his friends. Augustus was a great coin collector, and had a cabinet of coins of foreign countries, from which he was accustomed at times to make presents.

45.

AVGVSTVS . TRIBVNIC . POTEST . inscribed in three lines within a palm-wreath.

℞. P . STOLO . IIIVIR . A . A . A . F . F .; in the centre of the field S. C. This is a Second Brass coin struck by Publius Stolo, a Triumvir Monetalis in the early part of the reign of Augustus, A . V. 730. We have on it the official title of the master of the mint in the figures and initial letters which follow after his name, which signify "Triumvir Auro Argento Ære Flando Feriundo," corresponding with the description given by Livy which we have already noticed.

Although the present is only a Second Brass coin and without portrait, yet I have placed it first, for I consider it one of the most important chronologically in the series of this emperor's coins, because it is the first in the order of time on which the Tribunicia Potestas appears.

Dr. Cardwell in his Numismatic Lectures, p. 189, believed he had discovered the earliest record of the Tribunicia Potestas of Augustus on a denarius of his eighth year struck by the Triumvir Monetalis L · VINICIVS . L . F . TR . POT . VIII . being, as Dr. Cardwell writes, "The first coin on which the TRIB · POT · appears, although assumed by Augustus eight years before."

On referring to Occo, small 4to edit. A.D. 1601, p. 60, he places the coin mentioned by Dr. Cardwell in anno urbis 737, and at p. 54 Occo quotes a silver coin of Augustus " AVGVSTVS . TR . POT . figura equestris ; Rev. P . STOLO . IIIVIR." This coin he places under date A.U. 730, being seven years earlier than the coin referred to by Dr. Cardwell. Eckhel, in vol. vi. p. 91., places the commencement of the Tribunicia Potestas in A.U. 731.—" Jam nunc Trib. Potestas monetæ inscribi incipit," quoting as his authority a denarius struck by P . STOLO . IIIVIR . in Mus. Caes. (Vienna Cabinet), and thus also reckoning Publius Stolo as the first mint master who recorded the TRIB · POT · of Augustus. Dr. Cooke also in his Medallic History of Rome, vol. i. p. 214., places a similar coin of P. Stolo as the first on which the TRIB . POT . is recorded. And in Argelati *in Augusto* I find the coins by P. Stolo with the TR . POT . placed in the year 731.

Assuming therefore that all these dates are correctly noted, and the right coins are quoted, it is evident P . STOLO was the first mint master who recorded the TRIB . POT . and would consequently cause this coin and the coins I have cited to take precedence of the coin quoted by Dr. Cardwell to the extent of seven years.*

Mr. Merivale also in his valuable work the History of the Romans under the Empire, vol. iv. p. 163, speaking of the time of Augustus, says, "The year 73 is memorable in the life of the first Princeps from his acceptance of the power of the Tribunate, the most important perhaps in a constitutional point of view of all his prerogatives."

The Publius Stolo we are speaking of was a descendant of that Licinius Stolo, the inveterate enemy of the patricians, who, after having introduced the law which restricted the possession of land to 500 acres, was himself convicted of having double the quantity. Havercamp speaks of him as a descendant of P. Licinius Calvus, Tribunus Plebis A. U. C. 377.

46.

CAES . PONT . MAX. The laureate head of Augustus to the right.

R̃. ROM . ET . AVG. Underneath a decorated altar between two short columns,

---

* When I wrote to Dr. Cardwell and called his attention to the error he kindly replied, saying he would correct it in his next edition.

on each of these a Victory is standing bearing a wreath and palm branch. There is no S. C.

This altar is usually called the altar of Lyons. The provinces in their servile adulation of Augustus erected temples and altars to him as to a deity, but Augustus refused these honours unless the city of Rome was to participate with him. Hence the inscription ROMAE . ET . AVGVSTO., and Rome was personified on the coins of the emperors subsequently.

Tacitus, iv. 56, says, the first temple to Urbs Roma was erected at Smyrna in the consulship of the elder Cato, A.U.C. 558. (Merivale, iv. 15.)

The earliest notice that I find of the type of ROM . ET . AVG on coins of Augustus is in Argelati A. U. C. 727, and again in 728 and in 741. Argelati quotes also a coin in brass entirely correspondent with the present coin, thus, " CAESAR . PONT . MAX . Caput Aug. laur.—ROM. ET. AVG . Porticus cum duabus Victoriis."

The origin of this altar of Lyons as it is termed is thus narrated by Merivale, iv. 223-4. At the time Drusus was in Germany A. U. C. 742, the German nations, in their discontent with the exactions made on them, were preparing again to cross the Rhine to contend with the Roman legions. Drusus was then at Lugdunum (Lyons), when he invited his subjects to display their loyalty to Augustus by erecting a stately altar at the confluence of the Rhine and Saone. Sixty of the Gaulish communities united in this work of flattery. It was dedicated to Augustus and Rome, the names of the sixty states were inscribed upon it, and the colossal statue of the Emperor before which it stood was surrounded by smaller representations of so many abstract nationalities. On the first day of the month of August, Drusus performed the act of consecrating this devotional tribute to the majesty of the empire; and instituted at the same time a festival, which continued to be annually solemnized on the spot with shows and musical performances for several centuries. The worship which was thus inaugurated in the province became extended throughout it, and in one place at least the Empress (Livia) herself was associated in the divine honours of her husband.

Virgil invokes Augustus as a deity—(Ecl. i.)

>Deus nobis hæc otia fecit;
>Namque erit ille mihi semper deus; illius aram
>Sæpe tener nostris ab ovilibus imbuet agnus.

And Horace says—(L. 3, Od. 5,)

>Præsens divus habebitur
>Augustus.

Argelati prefaces the year of Rome 741 with the remark that, Æmilius

Lepidus having died in March, Augustus was created Pontifex Maximus; yet Occo, p. 52 A. U. C. 727 quotes a silver coin of Augustus, the legend on the reverse being PONTIF. MAXIM., and in p. 62 A. U. C. 740, Occo states, " Hoc anno P. M. factus est Augustus:" and describes a gold coin bearing the title PONT. MAX., and also a silver coin with the same legends, obverse and reverse, as the present coin.

The portrait on this coin is youthful and Apollo-like; which Augustus affected, to correspond with the adulation of his courtiers. With respect to the dates above mentioned, it is possible, in order to account for their seeming discrepancy, that, after the banishment of Æmilius Lepidus in 718, inconveniences had arisen at certain ceremonials for want of the presence of the Chief Pontiff, and therefore Augustus took the office and dignity of Pontifex Maximus in order that such rites and ceremonies, in which the Pontifex Maximus must necessarily take a part, should not be interrupted or neglected. This would account for the office being held by Augustus before the death of Lepidus, who on his banishment, not having been deprived of his dignity of Pontifex Maximus, could not by reason of his exile perform the ceremonies of the office, although retaining the title.

It will be observed that the preceding coin records the TRIBVNICIA POTESTAS. or kingly power first held by Augustus; the present coin adds the first assumption of the chief ecclesiastical power, the Pontifex Maximus, thus making a union of the Church and State in the person of Augustus. This condition is correspondent with the most ancient times, for in the Book of Genesis, chap. xiv. ver. 8, we read that Melchisedek was " King and High Priest of Salem." The office of Pontifex Maximus therefore gave Augustus a large increase of power by the union of the imperial and ecclesiastical power and authority in himself; a course which caused his successors also to adopt and take upon themselves the office of chief pontiff.

Merivale, vol. iv. p. 210, says, " The year which followed (742) forms an important epoch in the life of Augustus; it beheld his elevation to the chief pontificate, the last of the great offices of the Republic which remained to complete the cycle of his functions as monarch of Rome. At the same time it left him alone in the possession of all their honours and burdens. The death of Lepidus, long grown grey in disgrace and retirement, removed the scruples he had long punctiliously maintained against wresting the sacred office from a living occupant, however unworthy; and early in 742 he became formally invested with the direction of the national rites, which he had long virtually exercised."

This is a scarce Second Brass coin, in fine condition.

47.

IMP . IX . TR . . . . . The unlaureate head of Augustus to the right.

℞. COM . . . . ASIAE . On either side of a temple of six columns, having on the frieze above the capitals of the columns the words, ROM . ET . AVGVST .

A coin in silver similar to the present is mentioned by Argelati *in Augusto*, A. U. C. 735, and the cause of the mintage of the device is thus described:—

"Regum Asiae Legati templum Jovis Olympici Athenis antiquitus a Deucalione inchoatum communi sumptu perficiendum locarunt absolutumque Genio Augusti dedicandum acreverunt."

The present is a silver medallion, in very good condition.

48.

CAESAR . AVGVSTVS . DIVI . F . PATER . PATRIAE . Reading from the left, the laureate head of Augustus to the right.

℞. ROM . ET . AVG . In the exergum, a decorated altar between two short columns, on each of which a Victory is standing, bearing a wreath and palm branch. No S. C.

49.

CAESAR . AVGVSTVS . DIVI . F . PATER . PATRIAE. The laureate head of Augustus to the left.

℞. ROM . ET . AVG. in the exergum, under a decorated altar, with Victories on either side, as on the preceding coin. No S. C.

The title of Pater Patriae, which appears on the obverse of this and the preceding coin, was first bestowed on Cicero for his discovery and punishment of the parties engaged in the conspiracy of Cataline, A. U. C. 691. The title of Parens Patriae was given by the Senate to Julius Cæsar. Pater Patriae came also to be given to Augustus.

Admiral Smyth, describing a coin of this type and legend, No. 6 in his cabinet, says, "From bearing PATER PATRIAE, this medal was probably struck in his thirteenth and last Consulate, as he only adopted that epithet in the year B. C. 2, or A. U. C. 751."

In Argelati, A. U. C. 729, a coin of Augustus in brass is quoted, with the legend CAESAR . AUGUSTUS . PATER .; and in A. U. C. 741, Argelati cites a gold coin, with the legend CAESAR . AVGVSTVS . DIVI . F . PATER . PATRIAE . The legend on the reverse being PONTIFEX . MAXIMVS . And again, in A. U. C. 746 Argelati quotes a brass coin with the legend on the obverse, AVGVSTO . DIVI . F . PONT . MAX . TR . POT . XVI . IMP . XIV.   On the reverse, COS . XI . PATRI . PATRIAE . S . P . Q . R.— S. C. in medio nummi. And the same title PATER PATRIAE is to be found in nearly all the subsequent years of Augustus.

I observe also in Occo, p. 52, a similar legend is quoted from a silver coin as on the obverse of the present coin; it is placed A. U. C. 742, and, again P . P . on a gold coin, A. U. C. 742, and another, in brass, A. U. C. 747, having COS . XI . as well as PATER . PATRIAE. So again P . P . in COS . XII ., and up to and after the year mentioned by Admiral Smyth, who also, in the coin of Agrippa, No. 16 in his cabinet, notices the legend of the crocodile coin of Nemausus or Nismes, being IMPERATOR . DIVI . FILIVS . PATER . PATRIAE. The coin of Nemausus with this legend was struck after the battle of Actium, about A. U. C. 724.

It is therefore evident from these coins that the P . P . or title of PATER PATRIAE was bestowed on Augustus many years before the time generally assigned. Eckhel, vol. vi. p. 112, states the title PATER PATRIAE to have been commenced B. C. 2, A. U. C. 751; which seems to be quite inconsistent with the before mentioned instances; and as to the coin of Nemausus, although it may be regarded as a colonial coin, yet it is highly improbable that a Roman colony would have dared to assign a title to an emperor or any other individual in high authority at Rome which had not previously received the sanction of the Senate, under whose charge the brass moneys were placed.

The present is a fine large spread coin from the cabinet of the Duke of Devonshire.

50.

CAESAR . AVGVST . PONT . MAX . TRIBVN . POT.   The laureate head of Augustus to the left; behind is a Victory volant, holding in her left hand a cornucopiæ, with her right hand she is placing a wreath on the head of Augustus.

℞. M . SALVIVS . OTHO . IIIVIR . A . A . A . F . F.   In the centre of the field S. C.

A coin of black bronze colour, from the Devonshire cabinet, weight 330½ grains.

Havercamp says, "Ab ipsa Victoria propter crebras et magnificas victorias coronari fingitur caput Augusti; cornucopiæ gerit Dea, quoniam abundè ut frumentum omnisque commeatus adesset Italiæ atque urbi sollicitè semper providet Augustus."

We have already remarked on the office of Triumvir Monetalis, or master of the mint, *ante*, and the type of this coin is singular, as being a means of showing who were the three mint masters who were in office at the time it was struck; for this particular type was only struck by the Triumvirs, Otho, Tullus, and Agrippa; and it is therefore not only probable, but it may also be reckoned a certainty, in the absence of any direct proof to the contrary, and it is a fair reason to conclude, that the three persons, M. S. OTHO, MAEC. TVLLVS, and L. AGRIPPA, being cotemporaries, and IIIVIRI MONETALES, were in office at the same time, and, in compliment to Augustus, each struck the type. This supposition and inference is the more credible from the fact that the type was not struck by any other Triumvir.

The Marcus Salvius Otho who struck this coin was the uncle of Marcus Salvius Otho who was emperor after Galba; he is considered to have been the son of the Tribune Salvius, friend of Cicero, whose tragic death is related by Appian, Bel. Civ. lib. iv. p. 598.

51.

CAESAR . AVGVST . PONT . MAX . TRIBVNIC . POT. The laureate head of Augustus to the left, with a Victory behind, as on the preceding coin, a globe at the point of the bust.

℞. M . MAECILIVS . TVLLVS . IIIVIR . A . A . A . F . F . In the centre of the field S. C. Yellow patina; from the cabinet of General Ramsay.

The globe at the point of the bust signifies that Augustus now has the empire of the world—the Victory placing the wreath on the head and holding a cornucopiæ implies the happy rule of Augustus, who from his constant victories had rendered everything abundant in the Roman empire. (Haverc. Thes. 256.)

52.

CAESAR . AVGVST . PONT . MAX . TRIBVNIC . POT. The laureate head of Augustus to the left, with a Victory behind as before.

℞. M . MAECILIVS . TVLLVS . IIIVIR . A . A . A . F . F . In the centre of the field S. C. A large Second Brass coin in red Cyprian copper, from the cabinet of Cavalier Campana.

I have not yet found any record of the length of time during which the mint-masters held office, whether they were appointed annually or *quamdiu se bene gesserint*, or *durante bene placito*, but in my opinion it was a triennial appointment, and this I infer from the number of Triumviri Monetales whose names appear on the coins of Augustus.

53.

CAESAR . AVGVST . PONT . MAX . TRIBVNIC . POT. The laureate head of Augustus to the left, with a Victory behind, as on the preceding coins.

℞. P . LVRIVS . AGRIPPA . IIIVIR . A . A . A . F . F . In the centre of the field S. C.

This coin completes the set of mint masters in office at the same time. To collect the three is a most difficult task; I believe they are only to be found in the Vienna Cabinet and my own. Having already the first two, I waited several years for the present coin; but hardly expected I should ever see the type of L. Agrippa, although I knew it existed. Fortunately the present coin made its appearance in a hoard found at Tunis. I obtained it against the British Museum bidding, and thus was enabled to complete the set and solve the problem. It is a fine dark green coin.

In the Imperial cabinet at Paris there are only the two coins by the Triumvirs Otho and Tullus. The British Museum has the same two; the Tullus bought against me from the Thomas Cabinet—so that in England the three coins are only to be met with in the present collection.

A fine coin of L . AGRIPPA of this type was sold at the sale of M. Herpin's cabinet, August 1857, but the British Museum did not bid for it or buy, and thus lost a chance which may not occur again for twenty years.

54.

OB . cIvIs . SERVATOS . inscribed in three lines within a double laurel wreath.

℞. P . LICINIVS STOLO . IIIVIR . A . A . A . F . F . In the centre of the field a large S. C.

A grass-green coin from the cabinet of M. Trattle; weight $374\frac{1}{4}$ grains.

The present coin and those which now follow seem from the inscriptions to have been struck after the battle of Actium, where Roman fought against Roman, but, by the defeat of Antonius and the surrender of his army and fleet to Augustus, the further effusion of the blood of Roman citizens was stayed.

This and the other coins with similar legends by different mint masters may well be considered as commemorating such events; for, although these coins of Augustus are reckoned of uncertain date, yet I see no sufficient reason why they should not be assigned to the services above mentioned, as well as the restoration of the Romans and their standards captured by the Parthians in the unfortunate expedition of Crassus. This last event was deemed one of the happiest of this reign, and is particularly recorded on the gold and silver coins of Augustus.

It was an annual custom at Rome to suspend laurel branches and oak wreaths at the doors of the palace of Augustus in remembrance of his victories and saving of the lives of citizens by the cessation of the civil wars. (Haver. Thes. 331.)

It will be observed that the I long is substituted for E in CIVES in all these coins.

55.

OB . CIVIS . SERVATOS . in three lines within a double laurel wreath.

℞. C . CASSIVS . C . F . CELER . IIIVIR . A . A . A . F . F . In the centre of the field a large S. C. Weight 404¼ grains.

This IIIVIR was of the Gens Cassia. The Celer was common to several families—of the present Cassius Celer nothing particular is known in history. (Morell.)

56.

OB . CIVIS . SERVATOS . within an outer wreath of laurel, the inner one of oak.

℞. T . QVINCTIVS . CRISPIN . SVLPIC . IIIVIR . A . A . A . F . F . A large S. C. in the centre of the field. Weight 386½ grains.

The *corona quercea* or oak wreath is rarely met with on these coins. This IIIVIR was Consul with Drusus senior, the brother of the Emperor Tiberius, B. C. 8.

57.

OB . CIVIS . SERVATOS . with a double wreath of palm and laurel.

℞. M . SANQVINIVS . Q . F . IIIVIR . A . A . A . F . F . In the centre of the field S. C. Weight 478¾ grains.

58.

OB . CIVIS . SERVATOS . with a double wreath, the outer one of palm, the inner being laurel.

℞. L . NAEVIVS . SVRDINVS . IIIVIR . A . A . A . F . F . In the field a large S. C. Weight 396½ grains.

Havercamp, (Thes. 292,) quoting this IIIVIR, says, "Surdini cognomen proprium genti Næviæ fuit, unde bona Naeviana agnoscit Valerius Maximus ubi de liberto Surdini agit qui vocabatur Nævius Surdinus, quique hæredem fecerat Gallum quendam Magnæ Matris sacerdotem Genucium, apud eundem Val. Max. lib. vii. c. vii. ex. 6."

59.

OB . CIVIS . SERVATOS . with a double wreath of palms.

℞. CN . PISO . CN . F . IIIVIR . A . A . A . F . F . In the field a large S. C. Weight 387¼ grains.

Cnæus Calpurnius Piso, who struck this coin, is the Piso who poisoned Germanicus in Syria, at the instigation of Tiberius; but, Tiberius in his dissimulation having condemned Piso for the act, the latter killed himself. (Haverc. Thes. 66.)

60.

ob . cIvIs . servatos . with a double wreath of laurel.

℞. Q . AELIVS . L . F . LAMIA IIIVIR . A . A . A . F . F.   In the field S. C.   Weight 302 grains.

61.

ob . cIvIs . servatos . with a double wreath, the outer one palm, the other oak.

℞. C . GALLIVS . C . F . LVPERCVS . IIIVIR . A . A . A . F . F.   In the field a large S. C.   Weight 388¼ grains.

Among the tribunes of the people A. U. C. 672 there is the name of C. GALLVS LVPERCVS. a provincial quæstor, and it appears that the present coin was struck by his nephew C . G . LVPERCVS. Suetonius, *in Augusto* cxxvii., speaks of Gallus; also Appian, Bell. Civ., lib. iii. p. 587. Lupercus was a family name derived from the Lupercal priests. (Havere. Thes. 191.)

62.

ob . cIvIs . servatos . with a double wreath of palm and laurel.

℞. C . PLOTIVS . RVFVS . IIIVIR . A . A . A . F . F.   In the field a large S. C.   Weight 389¼ grains.

Caius Plotius Rufus here mentioned is supposed to be the Rufus who was one of the conspirators against Augustus, spoken of in Suetonius, *in Augusto*, c. xix.

63.

ob . cIvIs . servatos . within a double wreath of palm and laurel.

℞. C . ASINIVS . C . F . GALLVS . IIIVIR . A . A . A . F . F.   In the field a large S. C.   Weight 403 grains.

64.

ob . cIvIs . servatos . with a double wreath of palm and laurel.

℞. TI . SEMPRONIVS . GRACCVS . IIIVIR . A . A . A . F . F.   In the field a large S. C.   Weight 341¼ grains.

65.

ob . cIvIs . servatos . within a double wreath of palm and laurel.

℞. C . MARCI . L . F . CENSORIN . AVG . IIIVIR . A . A . A . F . F.   In the field a large S. C.

This coin was struck by Caius Marcius Censorinus, who was Consul with Caius Asinius Gallus, A. U. C. 746. On the coins he is called Lucii filius, but on some marble inscriptions quoted in Gruter he is called N. (Nepos.) (Gruter, 196, num. i. and ii. 197, ii. 1078, num. x.; Havercamp, Thes. p. 268.)

The following coins are all of Second Brass, and on them the different mint masters have recorded the TRIBVNICIA POTESTAS. Amongst them are the names of the mint masters Otho, Tullus, and Agrippa, whom we have already mentioned, and whose present coins have different legends to the others.

66.

TRIBVNIC . POTEST . CAESAR . AVGVSTVS. The unlaureate head of Augustus to the right.

℞. C . ASINIVS . GALLVS . IIIVIR . A . A . A . F F. In the field S. C.

67.

TRIBVNIC . POTEST . CAES . . . . . . The unlaureate head of Augustus to the right.

℞. CN . PISO . CN . F . IIIVIR . A . A . A . F . F. In the centre of the field S. C.

68.

TRIBVNIC . POTEST . CAESAR . AVG. The unlaureate head of Augustus to the right.

℞. C . PLOTIVS . RVFVS . IIIVIR . A . A . A . F . F. In the field S. C. Weight 142½ grains.

69.

. . . . ST . CAESAR . AVGVSTVS. The unlaureate head of Augustus to the right.

℞. L . SVRDINVS . IIIVIR . A . A . A . F . F. In the field S. C. Weight 158½ grains.

70.

CAESAR . AVGVST . PONT . MAX . TRIBVNIC . POT. The unlaureate head of Augustus to the right.

℞. M . MAECILIVS . TVLLVS . IIIVIR . A . A . A . F . F. In the field S. C. Weight 170½ grains.

71.

. . . . . R . AVGVST . PONT . MAX . T . . . . The unlaureate head of Augustus to the right.

℞. M . SALVIVS . OTHO . IIIVIR . A . A . A . F . F. In the centre of the field S. C.

72.

CAESAR . AVGVST . PONT . MAX . TRIBVNIC . POT.   The unlaureate head of Augustus to the left.

℞. M . SALVIVS . OTHO . III VIR . A . A . A . F . F.   In the field S. C.

73.

CAESAR . AVGVST . PONT . MAX . TRIBVNIC . POT.   The unlaureate head of Augustus to the left.

℞. P . LVRIVS . AGRIPPA . IIIVIR . A . A . A . F . F.   In the field S. C. Weight 205½ grains.

On these last named coins we again have the coincidence of S . OTHO, M . TVLLVS, and L . AGRIPPA, being masters of the mint; and, from their using a legend on the obverse quite different to all the other masters of the mint, but in accordance with each other, there appears to be no doubt they were in office at the same time, although beyond these evidences we have no written record of the fact.

In all the following coins, which are also of Second Brass size, the T in Augustus is made long.

74.

AVGVSTVS TRIBVNIC . POTEST . in three lines within a laureate wreath.

℞. C . CASSIVS CELER—IIIVIR . A . A . A . F . F.   In the centre of the field S. C. Weight 186 grains.

75.

AVGVSTVS TRIBVNIC . POTEST . in the three lines within a laurel wreath.

℞. C . CENSORINVS . L . F . AVG . IIIVIR . A . A . A . F . F.   In the centre of the field S. C.   Weight 184¼ grains.

76.

AVGVSTVS TRIBVNIC . POTEST . in three lines within a laurel wreath.

℞. . C . ASINIVS . GALLVS . IIIVIR . A . A . A . F . F.   In the field S. C. Weight 269 grains.

77.

AVGVSTVS . TRIBVNIC . POTEST . in three lines within a laurel wreath.

℞. TI . SEMPRONIVS . GRACCVS . IIIVIR . A . A . A . F . F.   In the field S. C.   Weight 224⅜ grains.

78.

AVGVSTVS . TRIBVNIC . POTEST . in three lines within a laurel wreath.

℞. C . GALLVS . LVPERCVS . IIIVIR . A . A . A . F . F. In the field S. C. Weight 218½ grains.

79.

AVGVSTVS . TRIBVNIC . POTEST . in three lines within a laurel wreath.
℞. CN . PISO . CN . F . IIIVIR . A . A . A . F . F. In the middle of the field S. C. Weight 171½ grains.

80.

AVGVSTVS . TRIBVNIC . POTEST . in three lines within a laurel wreath.
℞. C . PLOTIVS . RVFVS . IIIVIR . A . A . A . F . F. In the field S. C. Weight 185 grains.

81.

AVGVSTVS . TRIBVNIC . POTEST . in three lines within a laurel wreath.
℞. M . SANQVINIVS . Q . F . IIIVIR . A . A . A . F . F. In the field S. C. Weight 172¼ grains.

82.

AVGVSTVS . TRIBVNIC . POTEST . in three lines within a wreath of oak leaves and acorns.
℞. T . CRISPINVS . SVLPICIAN . IIIVIR . A . A . A . F . F. In the field S. C. Weight 194 grains.

This mint master also struck a Large Brass coin OB . CIVES . SERVATOS . with a wreath of oak leaves and acorns.

83.

AVGVSTVS . TRIBVNIC . POTEST . in three lines within a laurel wreath.
℞. L . NAEVIVS . SVRDINVS . IIIVIR . A . A . A . F . F. In the field S. C. Weight 195¼ grains.

84.

DIVVS . AVGVSTVS . PATER. The head of Augustus to the right wearing a radiate crown. Weight 350½ grains.
℞. *No legend.* A Victory volant to the left, bearing a shield in her right hand. In the field S. C.

This and the following coins with DIVVS in the legend would seem to denote they were struck after the death of the Emperor, to the honour of the deified Augustus and by the decree of the Senate. Yet this and the next coin only record the military prowess of the emperor's generals in various parts of the empire, in Europe, Asia, Syria, which occurred at different times during the reign of Augustus.

AUGUSTUS.   41

The radiate crown was first applied to Augustus by the servile Senate, as a type of the sun's rays emanating from the head of the emperor, who was so weak-minded as to affect to resemble their idol Apollo. Hence it may be observed on many of the coins of Augustus that an endeavour is frequently made by the die engraver to give his portrait an Apollo-like cast of countenance.

A recent writer upon ancient coins, Mr. Noel Humphreys, speaking of the Roman coins, says, that the radiate crown which is found on the medallions of Trajanus Decius was first used by Jotapianus. This is a very great error, calculated to mislead those of his readers who might wish to learn a little of coins as connected with Roman history, and such as no person at all acquainted with the coins of the Roman imperial series could be guilty of. Jotapianus is not known as an emperor. Trajanus Decius did not assume the sovereignty until the death of the Philips in the year of Rome 1002, A.D. 249. Jotapianus was an usurper who assumed the purple in Syria in the latter part of the reign of Philip, and was defeated and put to death at the commencement of the reign of Trajanus Decius.

85.

DIVVS . AVGVSTVS . PATER. The head of Augustus to the right, wearing the radiate crown.

℞. *No legend.* A Victory volant to the left, bearing in her right hand a circular shield inscribed S . P . Q . R.

Black, very fine. Weight 216½ grains.

86.

DIVVS . AVGVSTVS . PATER. The head of Augustus to the right, with radiate crown.

℞. A wreath of oak leaves and acorns with S. C. in the middle of the field.

Brown, fine. Weight 226½ grains.

An eminent Ægyptian antiquary (Mr. Sharpe) treats these and the other coins with a similar legend as apotheosis coins, but, for the reasons I have already noted, I must differ with him, with all deference to his superior skill as an antiquary.

The present and preceding coin are of Second Brass size, as the weights denote.

G

87.

DIVVS . AVGVSTVS . PATER. The head of Augustus to the left, wearing the radiate crown. Weight 212¼ grains.

℞. *No legend.* A circular temple, having in front a square door; the friezes which encircle the temple are decorated. On the apex of the dome which forms the roof is a robed female figure standing, having in her right hand a wreath, in the left a *hasta pura*. The outer edge of the domed roof is supported by columns, which appear to be apart from the circular body of the building, and we may fairly conclude they encompass it. The door of the temple is approached by a flight of three steps; the top step seems to form part of a circular footpath around the building and within the columns supporting the roof. On either side of the temple, in relief, and apart from it, is a square base or pedestal; on the top of that to the right is the figure of an ox, on the opposite pedestal is a sheep. S. C. in the field on either side of the roof.

The present is a large spread Second Brass coin from the cabinet of the Duke of Devonshire. It is very rare and of much interest, but I cannot find it properly explained by any numismatic writer. The coin of this type in the cabinet of Queen Christina has not the figure standing on the top of the dome. Vaillant, (vol. i. p. 3,) describing a similar coin to the present, says it is "Templum Martis plurimis columnis suffultum, hinc et inde aries basi impositus." If we consider it a temple dedicated to Mars, the two animals represented on the present coin would be a bull and a ram, selected for their pugnacious qualities as appropriate emblems or attributes of the god of war; but, although in the worship of Mars the Romans paid him the most profound respect, considering him the father of the first of their kings and the patron of their city, yet neither the bull or the ram were objects of sacrifice to him. The horse, wolf, magpie, and vulture, were offered, as being of a warlike or ferocious nature. His most celebrated temple at Rome was built by Augustus after the battle of Philippi, and dedicated to MARS VLTOR. It is represented on the silver coins of Augustus, and, although with a domed roof, and surrounded by columns, yet it is without the adjunct of pedestals with animals, and it is differently decorated, as will be seen on the next coin.

Eckhel, vol. vi. p. 127, notes this coin—" s. c. Templum rotundum hinc et illinc basis quarum singulis quadrupes insistit, AE. II. Mus. Cæs.; Sacrarium Romæ D. Augusto ædificatum a Tiberio, domumque Nolæ in qua decessit in Templum mutatam refert Dio, proponitur illud in nummis Caligulæ, serius in nummis Antonini Pii inscriptis TEMPLVM . DIVI . AVG . REST."

In this conclusion I consider Eckhel errs; the temple represented on the coin of Caligula, and that on the coin of Antoninus, are as different in their structure as it is possible for two buildings to be, which any one on inspection of the several coins will at once perceive and acknowledge.

The Rev. W. Cooke, in his Medallic History of Rome, vol. i. p. 312, speaking of this type, says it represents the sacrarium or sanctuary raised in the Palatium until the temple to Augustus could be completed, and that the temple so completed appears on the coins of Tiberius. I consider Mr. Cooke has committed a great error—the temple on the coin of Tiberius is considered to be the Temple of Concord. The errors of these writers will quickly be seen by an inspection of this coin, and by comparing it with those they refer to of Tiberius, Caligula, and Antoninus Pius, which are all in this cabinet.

The present type is the representation of a temple in every way complete in itself, and not erected for a temporary purpose. The coin of Tiberius Mr. Cooke refers to for the representation of the complete building is a flat-fronted building, profusely ornamented with statuary, and is by many antiquaries supposed to represent the Temple of Concord, but in reality it more resembles the building usually called the Capitol.

Patin, Numismata Imperatorum, p. 52, noticing a coin of this type, says, " Eo spectant et agnus et vitulus juxta templum Augusti dicatum ; sive templum illud Romæ constructum fuerit, sive Nolanum intelligitur. Nolæ enim domus in qua decessit Augustus in templum mutata est inquit Dio."

88.

AVGVSTO CAESARI. Reading from the left. The youthful laureate head of Augustus to the right. Denarius.

℞. A circular temple.—MAR— V[LT] on either side. The roof is supported by columns, and the frieze above the capitals of the columns has a number of small ornaments projecting erect from it ; it is approached by a flight of three steps, which appear to be carried all round the building; the three columns in the front are wide apart, and between the two in immediate front there is a legionary eagle, and on either side of the eagle there are seen between the columns a standard, as of cohorts.

By the ascription of this temple to Mars Ultor it will at once be seen that the appropriation of the temple on the preceding coin to Mars Ultor must be quite erroneous; for there is not, except in being of circular form, the least similarity between them.

Before the time of Augustus there had been no temple erected at Rome to Mars Ultor; but he was now introduced into the city which he was supposed to have saved from overthrow and ruin; and the aid he had given in bringing the murderers of Cæsar to justice was signalized by the title of *Avenger*, by which he was now specially addressed. See also Merivale, iv. 145.

We read in Rosini, Antiquitatum Romanarum, p. 128—"Mars Ultor, ab ulciscendo dictus. Huic templum in foro suo maximum et sumptuosissimum cum opere tum artificio Augustus extruxit bello Philippico quod patris ulciscendi causa susceperat." (Suetonius.) Also, "Idem Augustus non multo post Templum Marti secundum Ultori, sive (ut ipse dici voluit) bis ultori in Capitolio erexit, in quo suspensa signa sunt a Parthis reddita." (Suetonius.)

From the description of the latter temple, as being the one in which the standards retaken from the Parthians were placed, one may fairly conclude that the present coin represents this latter temple, and the standards of Crassus intimated by the eagle and the two other standards there deposited. The standards taken by the Parthians were, when returned, taken by Tiberius (then general of the army in Armenia) to the Emperor Augustus, by whose order they were sent to the Temple of Mars Ultor.

89.

DIVVS . AVGVSTVS . PATER . The head of Augustus to the left, with radiate crown. In front of the face is a fulmen, and over the head is a star. These emblems of divinity mark strongly the adulation paid to Augustus.

℞. *No legend.* A large S. C. on either side of the field. Vesta seated to the right on a square seat: her left foot is supported by a low stool; her right hand, resting on her lap, holds a patera; in her left hand she has the *hasta pura* or wand of divinity.

This is a fine Second Brass coin (weight 170½ grains) from the Duke of Devonshire's cabinet, possessing much interest, for it is a type in the Augustan series which it appears could not have been known to Argelati, who mentions the coin of Caligula as bearing the earliest representation of the idol Vesta precisely as delineated on the present coin. There cannot be a doubt that the sedent figure on this coin is intended for the goddess Vesta. Moreover, comparison of the coin of Caligula and the present will prove it very exactly.

Sir Isaac Newton, in his Chronology, p. 175, ed. 1728, speaking of the Vestal temples amongst the Greeks, says, " From the word 'Εστια, fire, came the name *Vesta*, which at length the people turned into a goddess, and so became fire-worshippers, like the ancient Persians.

Clemens Alexandrinus and Blondus consider the worship to have been derived from the Egyptians, who they say used lamps, and kept a fire perpetually burning in their temples.

The worship of Vesta, or fire, had been early introduced into Italy. Virgil describes Æneas as carrying away from Troy the statue of Vesta as well as the sacred fire—

Vestamque potentem
Æternumque adytis effert penetralibus ignem.—Æn. ii. v. 296.

Numa Pompilius built the first temple at Rome to Vesta, and he appointed four priestesses, which number was afterwards increased to six by Tarquinius.

They were called Vestalia: their principal duties were to preserve the Palladium or statue of Minerva, which was said to have fallen from heaven, and the sacred fire, also asserted to have come from heaven, and keep it ever burning. Its being at any time extinguished was supposed to indicate some misfortune to the state, and the vestal who allowed the fire to be extinguished was subjected to whipping.

The vestals took a vow of chastity, and, if at any time a vestal violated her vow, she was punished by being buried alive in the Campus Sceleratus.

The nuns of the Romish church at the present day are, in their discipline and habits of life, very similar to the vestals, and are subject to the same sort of punishments. That of death was usually inflicted by being bricked up in a niche or recess in a wall of the convent; and, although we do not hear that the punishment of death is so inflicted at the present day, yet walls have no voices, and female skeletons have been found so bricked up in the walls of convents.

The Prytaneum in the ancient Greek towns and cities was a court with a place of worship, and a perpetual fire kept therein upon an altar for sacrificing. Dionysius says that the new kingdom of Rome, as Romulus left it, consisted of thirty courts or councils in thirty towns, each with the sacred fire kept in the Prytaneum of the court for the senators, who met there to perform sacred rites after the manner of the Greeks; but when Numa, the successor of Romulus, reigned, he, leaving the several fires in their own courts, instituted one common to them all at Rome, whence Rome was not a complete city before the time of Numa.

Besides the Temple of Vesta built by Numa, of which there are now no remains, another was erected on the banks of the Tiber, vestiges of which still remain, but by whom it was built is not known. It would seem that both these temples were standing in the time of Horace, who, describing (lib. i. ode 2) an inundation of the river, says:

> Vidimus flavum Tiberim, retortis
> Littore Hetrusco violenter undis,
> Ire dejectum monumenta regis
> Templaque Vestæ.

By the use of the plural word *templa* Horace may have intended both these temples of Vesta. Plutarch, *de Iside et Osiride*, speaking of the Temple of Vesta, says that it was of an orbicular form, intending thereby to express not so much the earth, or Vesta, as the whole universe, in the centre of which the Pythagoreans placed fire, which they called Vesta; thus it is quite probable that the worship of Vesta, or fire, had been borrowed, although not rightly understood, from Asia, and that it was in reality the worship of the Sun, which the astronomers of more ancient times had placed in the centre of the universe.

Some authors consider that no statue was erected to the goddess Vesta, but I think it probable that there was a representation of her, for we find her figure on coins both in a sedent and standing posture.

The idol statue of Pallas, or the Palladium as it was termed, was supposed to have fallen from heaven. It was about three cubits in height, and represented the goddess seated and holding a spear in her right hand; in the left she had a distaff and spindle. It was said to have been that on which the fate of Troy had depended, and had been saved from its ruins by Æneas, and by him it was brought into Italy, and ultimately came into the possession of Numa.

As universal dominion was supposed to be conferred on the people who possessed and preserved this Palladium. It was committed to the charge of the Vestals, by whom it was deposited in a secret place in the temple.

At Rome, festivals called Vestalia in honour of Vesta were celebrated on the 5th of the ides of June in every year. See further on the subject of Vesta and fire-worship in Vossius *de Idololatria Gentilium*, pp. 131-153. We likewise find in Higgins's Celtic Druids, p. 283, that the Druids had a sacred fire which was preserved with the greatest care at Kildare (Ireland). It was guarded from the most remote antiquity by an order of Druidesses, who were succeeded in later times by an order of Christian nuns.

About the year of our Lord 380 the Vestals were abolished and their fire extinguished by an order of Theodosius the Great, a Roman emperor and a Christian.

To the foregoing remarks on the idol-worship of Vesta, the fire-goddess, we may add that fire was an emblem of great import under the Jewish dispensation, for Moses, in Leviticus, ch. vi. ver. 13, says of the fire which was to be kept on the altar of burnt sacrifice, "The fire shall ever be burning, it shall never go out."

The sacrifices, whether of bird or beast, which were to be offered on the altar of the Tabernacle, were to represent the state of the affections of the person offering, and the fire, which was to be always burning to consume the sacrifices, represented the Lord's ardent and unceasing love towards his people; and thus by the sacrifice a conjunction between the Lord and his people was effected.

As the word *sacrifice* means *to make sacred*, therefore nothing impure could become an offering for sacrifice; thus it will be observed throughout the whole of the Mosaic injunctions no unclean animal or bird there designated could be offered in sacrifice, for, by clean animals, or such as were of gentle life, *e. g.*, lambs and oxen, were represented the good affections of mankind, and of the offerer in particular. By the unclean, as wolves, vultures, and the like, were signified the evil dispositions of mankind, and these, as such, were not allowed to be offered in sacrifice.

This will explain why several animals among some of the older nations became objects of such peculiar attention and respect. This circumstance was very remarkable among the ancient Egyptians. There can be no reasonable doubt that at some period of Egyptian History the animals had been understood as representatives of certain moral qualities; but by a succession of corruptions their proper signification was lost, and veneration was attached to them, so that the worship of certain animals was a perversion of the respect once paid to the human principles of which they were originally significant.

It would appear from Nibby (Foro Romano, 72) that the principal temple of Vesta at Rome was at the foot of the Palatine Hill on the Via Nova which led from the Forum to the Circus Maximus; it had annexed to it an Atrium once the Regia of Numa, and it had also a sacred grove.

90.

DIVVS . AVGVSTVS . PATER. The head of Augustus to the left, with a radiate crown.

℞. PROVIDENT. in the exergum; S. C. on either side of the field. Above the word is a square altar, the front of which is divided into different compartments.

A well-spread Second Brass coin, in fine condition. Weight 175½ grains.

This type is considered by some persons to be an altar dedicated to Divine Providence. By others it is supposed to be a representation of the doors of a granary or building in which Augustus stored corn for the city, thus signifying his care and providence for the wants of the citizens.

91.

DIVVS . AVGVSTVS. The head of Augustus to the left, with radiate crown. S. C. on either side of the field.

℞. CONSENSV . SENAT . ET . EQ . ORDIN . P . Q . R. A robed figure of Augustus sitting on a curule chair to the left, the right hand extended holding an olive branch, in the left hand a globe.

This figure has all the character and appearance of having been taken from a statue erected to Augustus, *quasi Orbis Pacator*, by a general vote of the Senate—the equites, and the people.

The present is a Second Brass coin in very fine condition. The First Brass coin of this type, although nothing like so fine in preservation, was bought away from me, at the sale of Mr. Thomas's coins, for the British Museum.

92.

DIVVS . AVGVSTVS. The head of Augustus to the left, with the radiate crown. S. C. on either side of the field.

℞. DIVA . AVGVSTA. Ceres seated to the left holding ears of corn in her right hand, in her left she has a long torch with fire burning on the top.

A Second Brass coin well spread and fine, from M. Rollin at Paris. Weight 263¾ grains.

The figure on this reverse is considered to be intended for Livia the wife of Augustus, under the character of Ceres, (Eckhel, vi. p. 158; Haverc. Christ. Cab. pl. xliv.) but I think this rather a forced interpretation occasioned by the reverse legend, amounting to a comparison of Livia with the goddess Ceres.

93.

DIVVS. AVGVSTVS. PATER. The head of Augustus to the right, with radiate crown.

℞. S. C. on either side of the field, between which is a massive winged fulmen, an emblem of divinity and power.

A Second Brass coin in fine condition, bronze colour. Weight 148¼ grains.

94.

DIVVS. AVGVSTVS. PATER. The radiate head of Augustus to the right.

℞. S. C. on either side of the field; between the letters, is an eagle with expanded wings, looking upwards, its feet resting on a globe.

The eagle, as the bird of Jove, was supposed to carry the souls of heroes to Heaven. Thus Dio, speaking of the ceremonies at the funeral of Augustus, says, "Post hæc centuriones, acceptis facibus, jussu senatus rogum succenderunt; eo absumpto, aquila ex eo emissa sursum volavit quasi animam Augusti in cœlum ferens."

A fine Second Brass coin, bronze colour. Weight 169 grains.

PROVINCIAL.

95.

DIVVS. AVGVSTVS. PATER. reading from the left. The head of Augustus to the left with radiate crown.

℞. *No legend.* A decorated square altar, the front compartment having on it a wreath suspended at each end from bullocks' heads; on the top of the altar is a small palm-tree with the letters c. v. on either side of it, and lower down in the field on either side of the altar are the letters T. T. The four letters c. v. T. T. are to be understood and read as Colonia Victrix Togata Tarraco.

Black bronze colour. Weight 388½ grains.

The city of Tarraco here mentioned is now known as Tarragona, in Spain. It is said to have been built by the Phœnicians, who called it Tarcon, which the Romans turned into Tarraco, and it gave the name to a considerable part of Spain called Hispania Tarraconensis. Tarraco was fortified by Scipio Africanus the elder and embellished by Scipio Africanus the younger.

Augustus, who visited all the provinces of the empire excepting Africa and Sardinia, stopped at Tarraco while he was in Spain, having been taken ill; on his recovery the inhabitants, in memory of his visit, and to ingratiate themselves with him, erected an altar to Augustus and burned incense before his statue as to a divinity.

At a subsequent period it was reported that a palm-tree had sprung up on the altar in a night; upon this a deputation was sent from Tarraco to Rome to congratulate Augustus on the event, as a presage of victory, peace, and eternal felicity. Augustus received the deputation, and in reply to their felicitations laconically remarked, "apparet quam sæpe accendatis."

After the death of Augustus the inhabitants of Tarraco used to regard the supposed miracle as a felicitous augury of good fortune, and a symbol of the immortal glory of Augustus, and placed it as a type on their coins.

The title т . т . Togata Tarraco, or the togated Tarraco, arises from the custom or privilege accorded to the Roman municipia of wearing the toga, the peculiar dress of the Roman citizen. Vaillant in his work on the coins of the Romans struck in the municipia and colonies, p. 45, speaking of Tarraco, says, "Tarraco cognomen *Togatæ* hoc in nummo assumit ut colonia ab aliis Hispanis per togæ usum distincta, cui adstipulari videtur Strabo, lib. iii. p. 151. At qui hanc formam sequuntur Hispani, stolati, seu togati, appellantur."

"Togati dicebantur etiam in præfecturis, coloniis, municipiis, qui Romanorum utebantur legibus, et victum cultumque Romanorum asciverant." Pitiscus, Lexicon Antiquitatum Romanarum, ii. 976.

It was termed *jus togæ*, or privilege of a Roman citizen, *i. e.* the right of wearing the dress of a Roman, and of taking, as they explained it, fire and water throughout the Roman empire.

"Roman" was a generical name given to every one who had a voice in electing magistrates or in enacting laws, although they did not reside in the city—whereas "Urbanus" or citizen was properly applied to those only who lived within the walls.

There is also a coin of Tarraco of Augustus mentioned by Vaillant representing Augustus on the obverse with the legend DEO . AVGVSTO ; on the reverse, C . V . T . T . AETERNITATIS . AVGVSTI.

There is also a coin of Tiberius with the same reverse as the present, but the legend of the palm-tree miracle is inappropriate to it.

96.

DIVVS . AVGVSTVS . PATER . reading from the left. The head of Augustus to the left with radiate crown.

℞. SCIPIONE . ET . MONTANO . IIVIR. A winged fulmen in the middle of the field with darts and four flames issuing from it; on the right side of the fulmen are the letters c . c, and A. on the left side. The names of the Duumviri in the legend read from the left. Brassy. Weight 403¼ grains.

This coin, like the preceding, bears symbols of divinity, and shows the adulation bestowed on Augustus in the different cities and provinces of the Roman empire. The colony here mentioned, and intended by the letters C. C. A, is now the city of Saragossa in Spain, situate on the river Ebro, and formerly called Salduba.

The fulmen on this reverse is a representative of divinity, or we should now more justly consider it as signifying Augustus being under the protection of the Divine Providence.

Vaillant in his Colonial Coins, p. 15, describes a coin of this type, and designates it "*rarissimus;*" it is also mentioned by Havercamp in Thesaurus 137.

97.

.... The unlaureate head of Augustus to the right.

℞. C. A. inscribed within a wreath of laurel-leaves and berries.

Havercamp, Pedrusi, and other antiquaries have ascribed this coin to Saragossa in Spain, and some give it to Cæsarea in Mauritania—Eckhel assigns it to Cæsarea in Palestine, in which city there was a temple and a colossal statue of Augustus.

Cities of the name of Cæsarea were founded in honour of Augustus in Bithynia, Armenia, Cilicia, Galatia, Palestine, Pisidia, and Mauritania. (Plin. Nat. Hist. v. vi.)

A large spread brass coin from the Thomas Collection. Weight 418 grains.

98.

AVGVSTVS. The unlaureate head of Augustus to the right.

℞. BILBILIS. placed underneath a warrior on horseback, galloping to the right, with lance in hand, brought to the charge.

Bilbilis was a city of Celtiberia in Spain; it is known as having been the birth-place of the epigrammist Martial.

Celtiberia is now the kingdom of Arragon. The town at present known by the name of Calatayud, and situated on the river Xalon, is supposed to be the ancient Bilbilis.

Strabo, lib. iii. p. 162, speaking of Celtiberia, says, "Segobriga et Bilbilis circa quas Metellus et Sertorius bellum gesserunt," and at p. 163, referring to the horses, says, "Multas alit Hispania capreas et equos feros;" he also adds, "Celtiberiorum equi sunt subvariegati et versicolores."

Martial in Epig. i. 49, alluding to the horses—

> Videbis altam, Liciniane, Bilbilim
> Equis et armis nobilem.

A well-spread black Second Brass coin.

99.

AVGVSTVS . DIVI . F . reading from the left. The laureate head of Augustus to the right.

℞. A bull gradient to the right; above it are the letters MVN . and in the exergum ERGAVICA .

Ergavica, now Alcaniz, was a Roman municipium or city of the Celtiberii in Hispania Tarraconiensis. The Roman legions under Gracchus took possession of this city, and it was constituted a municipium about the year of Rome 574.

An ox or a bull is the Roman symbol of an agricultural settlement. For the distinctions respecting the Colonia, Municipium, Civitas, and Præfectura, with their several rights and privileges, reference must be had to the work of Pitiscus, Lexicon Antiquitatum Romanarum, and the Dictionary of Greek and Roman Antiquities, by Dr. Smith.

A well-spread Second Brass coin—brassy. Weight $212\frac{3}{4}$ grains.

100.

AVGVSTVS . DIVI . F . reading from the left. The laureate head of Augustus to right.

℞. A bull gradient to the right; at the sides are the words B . ACCIO ... VICEL . and in the exergum M . FESTO ., and in front of the bull's neck IIVIR.

The size (Second Brass) and style of this coin in every respect resembling the preceding coin, designate it as belonging to a Spanish settlement, but its name is not marked on the coin.

A Second Brass coin—brassy. Weight $204\frac{1}{2}$ grains.

101.

DIVVS . AVGVSTVS . PATER . The head of Augustus to the left, with radiate crown.

℞. *No legend.* A broad arched gateway, having two porches or entrances, supported on each outer side by a round tower, in the middle of each tower is a square opening or window. An inscription, AVGVSTA . EMERITA ., in two lines is placed on the broad square front of the gate, over the porches.

The city of Emerita was situate in Portugal, then called Lusitania, near to the river Anas, now called Guadiana, and it is known at the present day as Merida. It was first colonised by the veteran soldiers who had been exempted by Augustus from further service after the Biscayan War, from which circumstance the city was called *Emerita*, or the deserved, and was surnamed *Augusta*, from Augustus, as its founder.

Havercamp (Christina Cabinet), speaking of this type, mentions three coins of Augusta Emerita, differing from each other in the description of the gate, towers, and fortifications, but all meaning the same city.

A well-spread brown coin.

102.

DIVVS . AVGVSTVS . PATER. The head of Augustus to the right, with radiate crown.

℞. An agricultural labourer, holding a plough, drawn by two oxen; to the left above in the field are the letters COL . A . A ., and in the exergum PATRENS.

Havercamp (Christina Cabinet) ascribes this coin to Patras, a city of Achaia, founded by Augustus, and he interprets the letters on it COLONIA . AVGVSTA . AROE . PATRENSIS .

The present is a Second Brass coin, from the cabinet of the Duke of Devonshire, encircled with a tortoiseshell ring, which was very frequent with coins in his cabinet.

103.

AVGVSTVS . DIVI . F . reading from the left. The laureate head of Augustus to the right.

℞. C . VAR . RVF . SE . IVL . POL . IIVIR . Q . The various pontifical apparatus; *i. e.* the axe in the centre; to the left the cap of Pontifex Maximus; to the right the aspergillum and simpulum.

A Second Brass coin, and evidently colonial, from its bearing the names of the duumviri, or chief magistrates of the colony, but the name of the colony is unfortunately omitted. The pontifical apparatus would seem to refer to Augustus, as chief pontiff. A well-spread Second Brass coin. Weight 225½ grains.

COINS STRUCK BY TIBERIUS.

104.

DIVVS . AVGVSTVS . PATER . The deified Augustus, robed and seated on a square stool to the left; the left foot rests on a footstool, and his head is encircled with a radius of twelve points, answering to the twelve signs of the Zodiac, to denote his divinity; before him is a square altar; in the right hand extended he holds an olive branch, in the left hand he has the *hasta pura*, or wand of divinity.

℞. TI . CAESAR . DIVI . AVG . F . AVGVST . P . M . TR . POT . XXIIII . In the field S. C.

After the death and deification of Augustus, Tiberius, who had been declared his successor, procured coins to be struck to his memory, bearing emblems of divinity; the present coin is one, and bears the mark of senatorial authority, by the S. C., and was struck A.D. 22.

It is related that the fact of Augustus having been seen to go into Heaven was publicly sworn to by one Numerius Atticus, whose sight no doubt was strengthened for the occasion by a handsome donation from the Empress Livia.

This is a remarkably fine coin, rich brown bronze colour. The portrait of Augustus is as well delineated as on any of the preceding Large Brass coins, although it is extremely small. Weight 419½ grains.

105.

DIVO . AVGVSTO . S . P . Q . R . in three lines on the upper part of the field, and over the heads of four elephants, that are drawing gently to the right, each having his driver. They are harnessed to a richly-decorated square car, adorned with wreaths and other emblems of Victory. On this car is placed a square seat, whereon is a robed figure of Augustus, wearing a radiate crown, holding an olive branch in his extended right hand; in the left hand he bears the *hasta pura*.

℞. TI . CAESAR . DIVI . AVG . F . AVGVST . P . M . TR . POT . XXXVII . In the centre of the field S. C.

This coin was struck A.D. 35, and by its type represents the car bearing the image of Augustus in his senatorial robes, as carried in the procession of the Circensian games, on which occasion the images of their gods and deified emperors and empresses were accustomed to be carried on cars with great pomp.

There is also another coin of this type, which has a slight variance from the present, inasmuch as the emperor is represented holding a globe in his right hand, instead of an olive or laurel branch.

A fine black bronze well-spread coin, from the cabinet of J. Knight. Weight 419½ grains.

106.

DIVO . AVGVSTO . S . P . Q . R . inscribed within the outer engrailment of the edge of the coin, and encircling a wreath of oak-leaves and acorns entwined around a small circular shield which is supported by two capricorns or sea-goats

AUGUSTUS. 55

placed back to back, their tails resting on a small globe. OB . CIVES . SER . inscribed in three lines on the shield.

℞. TI . CAESAR . DIVI . AVG . F . AVGVST . P . M . T . R . POT . XXXVII. In the centre of the field S. C.

This coin was struck by decree of the Senate A.D. 35. The capricorn is said to have been the nativity sign of Augustus.

In the minting of this coin, the Senate, with a view to please their master Tiberius, used the inscription OB . CIVES . SERVATOS . to remind the Roman people of the restoration of the soldiers and standards captured by the Parthians in the unfortunate expedition of Crassus, which we have already noticed.

RESTORED COINS.

107.

DIVVS . AVGVSTVS . PATER . The unlaureate head of Augustus to the right.

℞. IMP . T . CAES . AVG . REST . In the field S. C. A square altar, the front divided in compartments, PROVIDENT in the exergum.

A Second Brass coin struck by order of the Emperor Titus. Weight 194¾ grains.

108.

DIVVS . AVGVSTVS . PATER . The head of Augustus to the left, with radiate crown.

℞. IMP . D . AVG . REST . In the field S. C.; a square altar as on the preceding coin; PROVIDENT in the exergum.

A Second Brass coin struck by order of the Emperor Domitian.

These two coins are restorations of the coin 90 *ante*. Weight 168⅜ grains.

109.

DIVVS . AVGVSTVS. The head of Augustus to the right, with radiate crown.

℞. IMP . NERVA . CAES . AVG . REST . A globe banded by a zodiac; in front of it is the rudder of a galley; S. C. underneath it.

A type signifying the Roman power to be extended over sea and land, or I may say over the whole world. A Second Brass coin. Weight 188½ grains.

110.

DIVVS . AVGVSTVS . The laureate head of Augustus to the right.

℞. IMP . NERVA . CAESAR . AVG . REST. In the centre of the field S. C. Weight 436⅜ grains.

111.

No legend. A square temple approached by steps extending the whole length of the front. On either side of the temple is a square base, on which stands the figure of an animal, one apparently a sheep, the other an ox.

₿. IMP . NERVA . CAES . AVG . REST . In the middle of the field S.C.

The temple on this coin would not attract so much of our observation were it not for the two square bases on which animals are placed, similar to the representation on the coin No. 87 *ante*. There is, however, this difference, the temple we have already noticed is circular, the present is a square building.

The word REST. on this coin is equivocal, and may be read as applying to a restoration of the temple represented on the coin before noticed, which in the reign of Nerva may have fallen into a dilapidated state, and occasioned the emperor to have the necessary repairs made to it.

Or it is a representation of a restoration, or republication, of the coin of Augustus, on which the temple first mentioned is represented—so the word REST. may be understood either way.

This coin is not known in the British Museum, nor do I find it elsewhere in any foreign cabinet; it is of Second Brass size, like its predecessor; brassy, and but in middling condition.

Some collectors are very desirous of possessing restored coins, or I may say coins reproduced by other emperors, but they cannot be approved of in a strict and very select cabinet, for this reason: the restored coin being struck in the reign of a subsequent emperor, the mint masters, in compliment to the reigning emperor, represent the deceased emperor as resemblant in portrait to the reigning emperor. Thus such coins are not true in their portraiture, and therefore ought not to be considered other than as fanciful, and not as absolutely necessary to constitute a complete cabinet.

The few restored coins in this cabinet will show my view of the subject. They would not have been introduced, but they have come to me by accident and not design. I may also add that restored coins never bring out any new historic fact.

The only valid plea in favour of a restored coin is, that the original had by use disappeared, or nearly so, and the reigning emperor from respect to his predecessor, or to keep alive the record of some particular fact noticed on the coin, had caused a fresh coinage of the particular type; and, as it was long since past, he could not assume the type himself, and so of necessity the original imperial proprietor of the fact is also reproduced.

LIVIA.

LIVIA DRUSILLA, the daughter of Livius Drusus Calidianus, was born B.C. 57. She was of illustrious descent, her father having been adopted from the Claudian family into the Livii, and she herself being raised by the testament of Augustus into the family of the Julii. She was first married to Tiberius Claudianus Nero, by whom she had a son, Tiberius, who afterwards became emperor; having been adopted by Augustus in his testament and named as his successor in the empire. She was six months pregnant with Drusus when Augustus, divorcing his own wife Scribonia, wrested Livia from her husband and married her B.C. 38. After the birth of Drusus she bore no other issue, and died A.D. 29, aged 86 years. A.U.C. 782.

Livia was accounted the most witty, agreeable, and beautiful woman of her time; from her intellectual power and diplomatic skill she was termed by Caligula "Ulysses in female attire."

Notwithstanding she had waded through blood to procure the adoption and elevation of her son Tiberius to the empire, yet after her decease he expressly ordered that no honours public or private should be paid to her memory, especially the forms of religious worship and deification. We have therefore no Latin coins of Livia as funereal coins.

DIVA . AVGVSTA. The veiled head of Livia to the right, shoulders draped.

℞. DIVVS . AVGVSTVS. The radiate head of Augustus to the left. S . C . in the field.

This coin is I believe unique. It seems to be the only coin in brass on which an authentic portrait of Livia is to be found. The coins with heads of Pietas, Salus, and Justitia, which are usually claimed to be portraits of Livia, are really

I

not so; they are ideal heads created by the artist to represent the moralities or virtues the names denote.

The present coin is a black coin from the cabinet of General Ramsay; and Mr. Eastwood brought it to me as a coin which ought from its historic interest to be in this cabinet independently of its rarity, as until this came I had no authentic portrait of Livia. The portrait represents her to be about forty years of age, and, although time and stern passions have made their mark, yet the countenance bears the character of Livia being a woman of great intellectual capacity and power—usually termed a strong-minded woman.

113.

IVLIA . AVGVSTA . GENETRIX . ORBIS. The head of Livia, here called Julia, to the left, a globe under the neck which is undraped, and a crescent over the forehead; her head is encircled by a wreath, but whether it be of laurel or myrtle is uncertain.

℞. COL . ROM . PERM . DIVI . AVG . *i. e.* Colonia Romulea permissione divi Augusti. The head of Augustus to the right, with radiate crown, a star over the head and a fulmen in front of the face.

This coin is in fine condition; it was struck at Romulea, in Spain, a town to which the Romans granted the privileges of a Roman colony, and called it Julia Romulea, or little Rome; it was also called Hispalis, from the Phœnician word Spala or Spila, a plain or field of verdure: it is now known as the city of Seville.

The adulation of the citizens of this place is very strongly exemplified by the decorations and title given to Julia on the obverse, and likewise to Augustus on the reverse, each of them being complimented by the emblems of divinity.

Merivale, in vol. iv. p. 224, speaking of the altars and worship of Augustus, says, "The worship of the emperor (Augustus) which was thus inaugurated in the province (Gaul) became extended throughout it; and at one place at least the empress herself was associated in the divine honours of her husband."

In regard to the wreath which encircles the head of Livia, Havercamp, from the closeness of the leaves of the wreath on a specimen of this type in his own cabinet, considers it was a wreath of myrtle.

MARCUS AGRIPPA.

MARCUS VIPSANIUS AGRIPPA was born of an equestrian family about the year of Rome 691. Linked to Augustus by the bonds of friendship from an early period of their lives, and embracing his fortunes on the death of Julius Cæsar, he mainly contributed to the victories of Philippi and Actium, and by these secured to Augustus the possession of the sovereignty. It was the wish of Agrippa that Augustus should place Rome in its original condition as a Republic; but his views were overruled by the more aristocratic friend of Augustus, Mæcenas.

After the death of Marcellus, the son-in-law of Augustus, Agrippa by the desire of Augustus espoused the widow Julia; and he thus became most intimately allied to his friend.

In the year of Rome 736 he was invested by Augustus with the tribunician power, which he held during a period of five years, whilst Augustus made a tour of the Roman provinces.

Agrippa died in Campania about the year of Rome 742, on his return from an expedition to quell some hostilities in Pannonia. Augustus received the news of his illness while celebrating the festival of the Quinquatria; and on hearing of it he hastened from Rome to meet his son-in-law, but found him dead. The body of Agrippa was conveyed to Rome; Augustus pronounced his funeral oration, and caused his remains to be deposited in his own tomb, declaring that even in death he would not be separated from his friend.

After the battle of Actium a magnificent temple was erected by Agrippa at Rome, which he dedicated to Jupiter Ultor and all the gods; whence it derived its name of the Pantheon. It still exists, and is used as a place of worship at the present day, and is one of the most perfect and most splendid of the ancient temples of Rome: from its circular form it is frequently termed the Rotunda.

In the year of our Lord 607 the Pantheon was purified by Pope Boniface IV., who then dedicated it to the Virgin Mary and all the martyrs; he likewise placed the festival of the Virgin Mary and all the saints in the month of May, on the day when the festival of Cybele was anciently held in Rome. This was afterwards altered by Pope Gregory IV. to the 1st of November at the request of King Louis le Debonnaire of France, as a more proper time for the festival than the month of May on the day of a pagan festival.

114.

M . AGRIPPA . L . F . COS . III. A fine but stern portrait of Agrippa to the left, decorated with the rostral crown, which from the line of Ovid we may presume Agrippa was accustomed to wear in public on state occasions.

Navalique gener cinctus honore caput.

℞. S. C. in the field. Between the letters a figure of Neptune is standing, with a trident in his left hand; his right hand extended holds a dolphin; a mantle is suspended from his shoulders and pendent over each arm.

Of all the deities Neptune appears the least frequently upon coins. Augustus was offended with his godship, and from this period his effigies does not appear again on the brass coins until the reign of Nerva, and then only on one coin. It is again absent until Hadrian, after which time I do not find Neptune introduced on brass coins.

On the present coin it is a complimentary type to Agrippa, who commanded the fleet of Augustus at the battle of Actium, and by the victory there obtained, he had, like Neptune, acquired for Augustus the sovereignty of the sea; for which services the rostral crown was bestowed on him.

The great battle of Actium was fought on the 2nd of September, A.U.C. 723, B.C. 31. Mr. Merivale in vol. iii. p. 345 gives a very full and interesting account of this engagement, which was considered by Augustus as the crowning work in the dispersion of those who might interfere with his assumption of imperial or regal power.

This coin is encircled with the black ring of the Devonshire Cabinet; it is in Second Brass, in very fine condition, and black in colour.

Weight 191½ grains.

115.

M . AGRIPPA . L . F . COS . III. The head of Agrippa to the left, decorated with the rostral crown.

℞. *No legend.* Neptune standing rather to the left, with a mantle suspended from his shoulders and falling behind him. In his left hand he holds his trident upright. At his right side is a dolphin standing upright on its tail and supported by the rudder of a galley; Neptune's right foot is on the dolphin's tail, and he is putting some food into its mouth, which is wide open to receive it; above the large S on the right side of the field are a sun and a star, and below the large C on the left of the field is a star and a crescent in an oblique or falling position.

Virgil alludes to the battle of Actium and the part taken in it by Augustus and Agrippa respectively; also the Julium sidus, which he calls *Patrium sidus*, and likewise mentions the *corona navalis* or *rostrata* worn by Agrippa.

> Hinc Augustus agens Italos in prœlia Cæsar
> Cum patribus, populoque, Penatibus, et magnis Dîs,
> Stans celsâ in puppi; geminas cui tempora flammas
> Læta vomunt, *patriumque* aperitur vertice *sidus*.
> Parte aliâ ventis et Dîs Agrippa secundis
> Arduus agmen agens; cui, belli insigne superbum,
> Tempora *navali* fulgent *rostrata coronâ*.
>
> ÆNEID, viii. 678.

It is doubtful whether the *corona navalis* and the *corona rostrata* were one or different crowns; Virgil, in the above passage, combines both terms; but it is supposed that the former was given to any sailor who first boarded an enemy's ship, the latter only to the commander of a victorious fleet. M Agrippa is said, by various authors, to have been the first who received this honour, though others state that M. Varro obtained it from Pompeius Magnus. (Smith's Dictionary of Roman Antiquities.)

This is a unique Second Brass coin of brown colour, in excellent condition, quite unknown and unpublished; it was Lot 173 in the sale of some coins from Tunis on 21 December 1852. The type refers to the battle of Actium, and its interpretation may be taken thus,—

When Antonius was in Ægypt, being fascinated by the charms of Cleopatra, he forsook Octavia his wife, the sister of Augustus, and became so bewitched by the Ægyptian queen as to put on the garb of Osiris, whilst Cleopatra assumed that of Isis, allowing themselves to be worshipped as the personifications of those deities: they were also at times adored as Bacchus and Libera. The radiated globe was an emblem of the sun and a mark of divinity, and was applied to designate an emperor or royal personage. See the coins of Julius Cæsar *ante*.

The crescent or the moon was the emblem of divinity applicable to a queen or empress. See the coin of Livia. The junction of these two emblems, signifying the emperor and the empress, may be seen on the coins of Domitian, Hadrian, and of Antoninus Pius, *post*.

These emblems premised, we will pass to the battle of Actium, which was a sea-fight, where Antonius and Cleopatra, being opposed to Augustus, were defeated, and the complete sovereignty of the Roman empire became vested in Augustus.

The fall of Cleopatra and Antonius is therefore represented by the crescent and the star, which are placed low down on the left side of the field in an inclined or falling position; whilst a sun or star is placed high up on the right side of the field, to represent the fortune or star of Augustus having attained the ascendancy over his competitors.

With respect to Neptune and the dolphin, it may be stated that the dolphin is the peculiar emblem or attribute of Neptune; he cannot therefore be supposed to kill it; on the contrary, for he holds his trident in the left hand, upright, and not in an offensive attitude. With the right hand he is putting some food into the mouth of his dolphin, which is raised up on its tail, and supported in that attitude, with the mouth open to receive the food, by the rudder.

The whole interpretation I consider to be, that figuratively Neptune the god of the sea and his dolphin had contributed to the downfall of Antonius and Cleopatra, represented by the low and oblique position of the crescent and the star, by the engagement having taken place when there was a calm sea that favoured the manœuvres of the fleet of Augustus; and Neptune is rewarding his attendant dolphin for the success which has been obtained, and which placed in the ascendant Augustus, the friend of Agrippa, the commander of his fleet on that occasion.

This type is peculiarly applicable to Agrippa, and is complimentary to his conduct and success in the engagement at Actium.

Until a better interpretation of this device is given, the present may be received as the correct view of the meaning of the type, and in this view of its signification I am supported by my esteemed friends Admiral Smyth and Mr. Burgon.

116.

IMP. above in the field, DIVI. F. in the exergum. The heads of Augustus and Agrippa back to back; that of Augustus to the right is laureate, and that of Agrippa, looking to the left, has the rostral crown. P. P. on either side of the field.

℞. A palm-branch, to which a crocodile appears chained, looking to the right; above the crocodile and across the field are the letters COL. NEM. A wreath is suspended from the palm-branch over the word COL.

This coin in Second Brass was struck by the colony of Nemausus, now Nismes, in Gallia Narbonensis, in commemoration of the battle of Actium and the consequent subjugation of Ægypt, represented by the crocodile being chained to a palm-tree; the animal and the tree being indigenous to Ægypt.

The mintage and title P. P. PATER. PATRIAE we have already noticed on the coins of Augustus, *ante*.

117.

IMP. DIVI. F. arranged as on the preceding coin. The heads of Augustus and Agrippa back to back: the head of Augustus is laureate; that of Agrippa has a wreath composed half of laurel, and the front half the rostral crown. No P. P.

℞. COL. NEM. with the chained crocodile, palm-tree, and wreath, as on the preceding coin.

The city and colony of Nemausus were founded by Augustus after the battle of Actium, when he placed there a number of veterans selected from different legions who had been engaged in the wars in different cities and colonies, amongst others, Nismes; and, the veterans at Nismes having been engaged in the Ægyptian war, the present coin was struck by the colony. The wreath suspended from the palm-tree signifies the victorious result of the war, and also the share taken in it by the then veterans of the colony.

118.

IMP. DIVI. F. as before. The heads of Augustus and Agrippa exactly as on the preceding coin. No P. P.

℞. COL. NEM. with the chained crocodile, palm, and wreath, as before.

Both of these coins are in Second Brass and good preservation.

JULIA AUGUSTI FILIA.

JULIA was born in the year of Rome 715. She was the daughter of Augustus by his first wife Scribonia, and was married at the early age of fourteen to Marcellus, the son of Octavia, the sister of Augustus.

After the death of Marcellus she was married to Agrippa, and at his decease she became the wife of Tiberius. Her very dissolute and abandoned conduct was the cause of her being banished by Augustus to the island of Pandataria.

Ten years after this she was transferred to Rhegium, now Reggio, where she was left to die of hunger, as is said, A.D. 14, A.U.C. 767, and after her husband Tiberius had assumed the reins of government.

Julia is described as very beautiful and accomplished, and seems to have been one of the most elegant and fascinating women at her father's court. Her winning graceful ways often turned aside the rebuke of the old emperor, and it was long ere he could be induced to banish her to Pandataria, she then being in her 38th year, A.U C. 752. Merivale, vol. iv. c. xxxvii.

119.

S . P . Q . R . IVLIAE . AVGVST . inscribed in three lines over a *carpentum*, a sort of two-wheeled tilted cart decorated with carvings and drawn by two mules, moving at a slow pace across the field, to the right

℞. TI . CAESAR . DIVI . AVG . F . AVGVST . P . M . TR . POT . XXIIII. ; in the centre of the field S.C.

The coins of this type and legend are almost universally assigned to Livia, the wife of Augustus, called Julia after adoption into the Julian family under the will of Augustus.

I presume to dissent from this usual custom, for I deem it an error to assign this coin to Livia, for the following reasons :

The time of Julia's death was A.D. 14, and Livia did not die until A.D. 29, a period of fifteen years after Julia. The tribunician date on this coin shows its mintage to have been in A.D. 22, which will thus place it as an apotheosis coin eight years after the death of Julia, and consequently seven years before the decease of Livia ; and I think it more likely that Tiberius should permit the senate to commemorate his deceased wife, when her death, having occurred some years previously, may have weakened the impression formerly made on the citizens by her profligate conduct, but with whom she might still hold some favour from her being the only daughter of their favourite Augustus, than that the coin should have been struck for Livia, who was still living.

By this arrangement the difficulties which numismatic writers experience in making a correct attribution of this coin, arising from the difference between the tribunician date and the date of the death of Livia, are avoided.

It is acknowleged by all numismatists and numismatic writers, that the *carpentum* is a funereal type; if therefore the present coin is to be considered a funereal coin, it is far more reasonable to assign it to a person already deceased, or who had been deceased some few years, than to anticipate the death of a person still living, and who is proved to have lived for some years after the date when this coin was struck; and, although the hatred of Tiberius against Julia his wife was not at first to be pacified, yet it is more than probable that, when some years had elapsed after the death of Julia, Livia was enabled to persuade her son to permit the senate to strike an apotheosis coin to the memory of his wife, who was her own step-daughter, and the only daughter of her late husband and benefactor. More especially do I think so when we learn from Suetonius in Claudio, sec. ii. that Tiberius absolutely forbade all religious forms and deifications being bestowed on Livia when she died, and that such a memorial was not bestowed on her until Claudius became Emperor; but we find no coins of funereal or any other type struck by Claudius assigned to Livia. And thus while we find Tiberius forbade any honours to be paid to the deceased Livia, his mother, yet we do not find any such prohibitions by Tiberius of any such honours to be given to his wife Julia.

For these reasons therefore I have, with respectful deference to other numismatic authorities, assigned this coin to Julia, the daughter of Augustus, and wife of Tiberius. Rather confirmatory of this view of the appropriation of the coin, I find in Occo, under the title of Livia Augusti, mention made of three coins, thus,

One in brass—S . P . Q . R . DIVAE . IVLIAE . AVGVSTI . FIL.
℞. Carpentum drawn by mules.

One in silver—LIVIA . AVGVSTA.
℞. DIANA . LVCIFERA.

One in Brass—DIVA . LIVIA . DIVI . AVGVST.
℞. CONSECRATIO—a peacock.

The first of these three coins decidedly refers to Julia, the daughter of Augustus, the words AVGVSTI . FIL[IA] put the question beyond further dispute. The other two are as decidedly the coins of the wife Livia, for on these two coins Livia is styled Augusta or empress; but on the first coin it is Julia FILIA daughter of the emperor. The distinction is evident; and, the date of the present coin being seven years before the death of Livia, I hold that, the first of these three coins being confirmatory of my opinion, the appropriation that I have made of the present coin is correct.

The coin which is usually assigned to Julia, and is particularly noticed in Admiral Smyth's cabinet, No. 17, as a coin of Julia, is assigned to Iol, or Cæsarea, in Mauritania, and is without any date or mark to show its time of mintage. It is therefore clearly a colonial coin, and contains nothing in portrait or legend which will warrant it being called a coin struck to commemorate Julia, the daughter of Augustus. On the obverse there is an ear of corn behind the head, denoting it as intended for a Ceres. The portrait on the reverse is clearly a Minerva Galeata. Both the heads seem to be of fine Greek workmanship, and the coin is of Second Brass size, which circumstances render it still more unlikely that it was ever intended for a JuliaAugusti Filia.

TIBERIUS.

TIBERIUS CLAUDIUS NERO, the son of Tiberius Claudius Nero and Livia Drusilla, was born in the year of Rome 712. He was married to Vipsania, the daughter of Agrippa, whom he afterwards repudiated. Upon her death he married Julia, the widow of Agrippa and daughter of Augustus. In the year of Rome 748 he was invested by Augustus with the tribunician power for five years. After the deaths of Caius and Lucius Cæsar, the sons of Agrippa, who had been adopted by Augustus, Tiberius was adopted by Augustus at the same time with Agrippa Postumus. From that period he was named Cæsar, and invested anew with the tribunician power, which was at last renewed to him every year.

He succeeded to Augustus in the year of Rome 767, and died at Misenum in the year of Rome 790. He had been so bad a man that the joy at Rome was universal when his death was known. In the earlier part of his life he had been a very good soldier, and had the command of the troops in Pannonia and Germany, and passed through several campaigns during the latter part of the life of Augustus with much success and applause.

120.

TI . CAESAR . AVGVST . F . IMPERAT . V . The unlaureate head of Tiberius to the right.

℞. PONTIFEX . TRIBVN . POTESTATE . XII. In the middle of the field S.C.

A beautiful black Second Brass coin, from the cabinet of the Rev. E. C. Brice. Weight 173¾ grains.

121.

TI . CAESAR . DIVI . AVG . F . AVGVST. The unlaureate head of Tiberius to the left.

℞. PONTIF . MAXIM . TRIBVN . POTESTATE . XII. Vesta seated on a square seat to the right, with the *hasta pura* in her left hand; her right hand holds a *patera*; a large S.C. on either side of the field.

The earliest notice in Argelati of DIVI . AVG . on the brass coins of Tiberius is of the seventh year of empire, or Trib. Pot. xvii., five years later than this coin; nor is Vesta ever noticed by him on the coins of Tiberius.

The title of PONTIFEX . MAXIMVS, which appears constantly on the gold and silver coins of Julius Cæsar, was assumed and retained by Augustus, afterwards by Tiberius, and all subsequent emperors. It was an office that conferred great power on the individual who held it.

The consecration to the office was performed with extraordinary pomp and ceremony, and it exalted the individual to be the sovereign judge and director of the public and private obligations of worship. All priests and sacrifices were under his inspection. He approved of the Vestal Virgins, and appointed them their vestments and clothing; he chastised them when requisite, and condemned them to be buried alive if they violated their vows. To him also belonged the composing of the rituals, appointing religious ceremonies, feasts, and institutions, as well as digesting the public annals or history of the year, called "*Pontificum Libri.*" He was also astronomer to the state, and consequently regulator of the year; for it was his care and duty to see that the festivals appointed for certain days fell at their appointed seasons.

Julius Cæsar was the first who regularly assumed the office of Pontifex Maximus. He well knew the absolute dominion he thereby acquired over the minds and actions of men. Ovid says he preferred it to all other honours. In his office of Pontifex Maximus he reformed the calendar; the same thing was done in the year A.D. 1582 by the then Pontifex Maximus of Rome Pope Gregory XIII. Dionysius Halicarnassus gives a very long account of the functions of the Pontifex Maximus.

The Roman Catholic pope assumes the title of Pontifex Maximus, and is the temporal prince or ruler of those parts of Italy called the Papal States; but, not content with that, he assumes the right of possessing the bodies and souls and estates of all papists in whatever country they may dwell, things that Julius Cæsar neither dreamed of doing or possessing. The lust of dominion, temporal and spiritual, over mankind at the present day by the Pope of Rome, and his legions of monks and nuns and priests, is far greater than the ambition of Julius Cæsar ever led him to.

122.

.... AVGVSTI . F . IMPERAT . VII . reading from the left. The unlaureate head of Tiberius to the left.

℞. ROM . ET . AVG . No S. C. A representation of the altar of Lyons already noticed on the coins of Augustus, *ante*, No. 46. A countermark of the letter N intertwined with a D, is on the left side of the field by the altar.

A countermark on a coin may be considered a good proof of its being genuine, for I have not yet seen a false coin with a countermark.

This is a good brown coin from the cabinet of the Duke of Devonshire. Weight 366 grains.

123.

TI . CAESAR . AVGVST . F . IMPERAT . VII . reading from the left. The laureate head of Tiberius to the right.

℞. ROM . ET . AVG . in the exergum. No S. C. The altar of Lyons as on preceding coins.

A Second Brass brown coin in good condition. Weight 183¼ grains.

124.

TI . CAESAR . DIVI . AVGVSTI . F . AVGVSTVS. The laureate head of Tiberius to the right.

℞. PONT . MAXIM . COS . IIII . IMP . VII . TR . POT . XXI. No S. C. A winged caduceus upright between two cornucopiæ in saltier, filled with fruits. Weight 212¼ grains.

125.

TI . CAESAR . DIVI . AVG . F . AVGVST . IMP . VIII. The unlaureate head of Tiberius to the left.

℞. CIVITATIBVS . ASIAE . RESTITVTIS . In the field S. C. The emperor seated on a curule chair, to the left; his head laureate; his right hand extended holds a patera; in his left he has the hasta pura.

This coin was struck about the year A.D. 23; being struck in lead, it is extremely rare, and I consider it unique. It was found in the remains of some ancient Roman houses discovered at Bath many years since (from whence I had it), and which are, I believe, all now demolished. It is in very fine condition, the lead a little corroded, but not in any material part. Weight $421\frac{1}{2}$ grains.

126.

CIVITATIBVS . ASIAE . RESTITVTIS . Either side of the field S. C. The emperor laureate and in his robes, seated on a curule chair, to the left; in his left hand he has the hasta pura; his right hand extended holds a patera.

An incuse coin having only the impression of the obverse. There is one similar to the present in Admiral Smyth's cabinet, No. 22. I quite agree with his observation that they are so struck as original designs for coins, or proofs, for if it were otherwise the S. C. would not be on the obverse, the usual place for the S. C. being on some part of the reverse.

This coin incuse is extremely rare. I only know of Admiral Smyth's and the present, nor do I find such a coin noticed by any numismatic writer. It is of aurichalcum, and very fine; its weight $276\frac{5}{9}$ grains.

127.

CIVITATIBVS . ASIAE . RESTITVTIS. The emperor laureate seated to the left, as on the preceding coins.

℞. TI . CAESAR . DIVI . AVG . F . AVGVST . P . M . TR . POT . XXIIII. S. C. in the middle of the field.

This coin was struck at the same period as the preceding. By the legend on these three coins is recorded the restoration of various cities in Asia, which had been seriously injured or destroyed by an earthquake in A.D. 17. Twelve, as some writers say, and, according to Eusebius, thirteen, cities were destroyed. Tiberius not only remitted the taxes of the ruined cities for five years, but also presented them with large sums of money for rebuilding. Coins similar to these in type and legends were struck two years afterwards, and, it being subsequently decreed by the Senate that a colossal statue should be erected in honour of Tiberius for his munificence, Phlegon, who lived and wrote in the time of Hadrian, says the statue was erected in the Forum Cæsaris, with the personification of the twelve cities as an accompaniment.

In confirmation of this narrative, we find that in the year 1693 a piece of marble inscribed to the Emperor Tiberius was discovered at Puzzuoli. It had evidently been the base of a colossal statue, and around it, in accordance with the description of Phlegon, were figures representing the several cities, with their respective names.

In A.D. 30 Tiberius withdrew from Rome, and lived at Puteoli, now Puzzuoli, and from the basement so discovered we may conclude that the inhabitants of that place erected a statue to the honour of Tiberius, copied from that in the Forum at Rome, and then added the name of another city, Cibyra, which had been destroyed by earthquake after the twelve already mentioned, and had also partaken of the emperor's bounty.

The seated figure on these coins, representing Tiberius, is no doubt copied from the statue. It would seem from Dion Cassius that Tiberius was greatly respected in the provinces, and kept a check upon the severity and extortions of the præfects, which contrasted strongly with the tyranny he exercised at Rome, for proof of which, reference is generally made to the well-known anecdote of his reproof to Æmilius Rectus, governor of Ægypt, who, when he sent to Rome a larger amount of taxes than usual, was told by the emperor he wished his sheep to be sheared and not flayed.

Velleius Paterculus speaks of Tiberius as almost a demigod. It is well ascertained from history that he was very considerate towards the provinces and the enemies he had to encounter when he was general of the Roman armies in distant parts, and thus he made friends everywhere that he went, although he was feared, hated, and despised at Rome.

A brown coin in fine condition. Weight 395$\frac{5}{8}$ grains.

128.

IVSTITIA. A female head to the right, wearing an ornamented coronet; the bust draped; the word Justitia underneath.

℞. TI . CAESAR . DIVI . AVG . F . AVG . P . M . TR . POT . XXIIII . In the middle of the field S. C.

A very fine brown Second Brass coin, weight 221$\frac{5}{8}$ grains, usually assigned to Livia; but, being struck by decree of the Senate while Tiberius was emperor, it may therefore be termed an adulatory coin to Tiberius. It is certainly in my opinion in no way connected with Livia the wife of Augustus. I think the error of assigning the three Second Brass coins of SALVS, IVSTITIA, and PIETAS to Livia, as is so constantly done, arises from the circumstance of Livia having been reckoned in her time a very handsome woman. Antiquaries, finding the virtues or moralities of Justice, Health, and Piety represented by the portraits of a handsome female, have jumped, without due consideration, to the conclusion that these three ideal portraits represent Livia under those three different designations, a conclusion without sufficient evidence to warrant it, for, although they are representations of a handsome female, yet they are each of them different in the portraiture, so as in fact to be three handsome young women instead of one. Salus has a particularly sprightly cheerful look, and is different in features and dress of the hair from either of the others, as might be expected from the personification of Salus, or health.

129.

SALVS . AVGVSTA. A female head to the right, the hair handsomely dressed and formed into a knot at the back; the whole appearance being of a cheerful, lively, pretty woman—different in countenance to *Justitia*.

℞. TI . CAESAR . DIVI . AVG . F . AUG . P . M . TR . POT . XXIIII . In the middle of the field S. C.

This is a fine large spread Second Brass coin, usually assigned to Livia, but I consider it was struck by the Senate with the representation of the goddess Salus as guardian of the public health. It may likewise be a supplicatory coin for the restoration of the health of the empress Livia, who in A.D. 22, when the present coin was struck, was afflicted with a dangerous illness. Public supplications were made for her restoration to health, the great games were decreed, and Tiberius came from his residence in Campania to be present on the occasion

Salus was much worshipped by the ancients in Greece; she was called Hygeia, the daughter of Æsculapius, who was called the son of Phœbus Apollo, the god of medicine.

It is a curious circumstance that the Pythagorean problem of the pentagon, when formed in ancient archaic letters, becomes the Greek word ὑγεια, health; and amongst the most ancient oriental nations the women used to work a pentagon upon the swaddling-clothes of their infants to protect them against the influence of the evil eye; but in reality it was a prayer for the ὑγεια or health of the child, a more certain protection against the evil eye. It was subsequently called the mark of King Solomon's seal. It was also used on Greek coins, and may be seen on the coins of Antiochus Soter, a name significant as connected with ὑγεια, it meaning saviour. It is also found on the coins of the ancient Hetruscans. Lastly, the pentagon is a sign and emblem among Freemasons of the royal arch degree.

As health is undeniably the principal blessing of life, it is not very surprising that the ancients should personify the blessing as a female of sprightly, cheerful countenance, and designate her a goddess. The Romans consecrated many temples to Salus. Livy speaks of one dedicated to her by Junius Babulo, the censor, near to one of the gates of the city, whence it was called Porta Salutaris.

130.

SALVS . AVGVSTA . under the draped bust of a female to the right.

℞. TI . CAESAR . DIVI . AVG . F . AVG . P . M . TR . POT . XXIIII . In the middle of the field S. C.; in a small square above the S. C. is the countermark [N . C . A . P . R.] which letters have been considered by numismatic writers to signify *Nobis concessum a Populo Romano.*

131.

TI . CAESAR . DIVI . AVG . F . AVGVST . IMP . VIII. The laureate head of Tiberius to the left.

℞. MODERATIONI, on the outer verge of the field. A circular shield greatly ornamented, and encircled by a laurel wreath. A full-faced bust is in the centre of the shield. S. C. on either side of the field.

In the year of Rome 787, the 19th of the reign of the emperor Tiberius, Imperator VIII., tribunician date 35, 36, the Lord Jesus Christ was crucified at Jerusalem.

Eusebius, Eccl. Hist. lib. 3, c. 3, places the date of the crucifixion in the 18th year of Tiberius. Occo, p. 85, places it in the year of Rome 785, and of Tiberius 19. Argelati, in Tiberio, p. 61, says "U. C. 787, Christi 34, Tiberii 19, et mensibus tribus exactis ante diem viii. kal. April. pro humana salute cruci affixus est, et tertia die post, vivus apparuit; Olympiadis 202 anno quarto, aut Olymp. 203, anno secundo, ut alii."

The birth and death of the Lord are thus referred to :

>Imperante Augusto natus est Christus,
>Imperante Tiberio crucifixus.

The dates vary as to the year of the crucifixion from A.D. 27 to A.D. 33. Clinton gives many dissertations of ancient writers, but he seems inclined to fix it at A.D. 29, A.U.C. 782, the 16th of Tiberius. (Fasti Rom. vol. i. pp. 10—18.)

132.

No legend. A temple of large dimensions, decorated with statues on the slopes and apex of the pediment; in front, on the basement, a statue is placed on a large square block on each side of the steps leading up to the front of the temple, and between the columns in front a seated figure is placed. The tympanum is quite plain.

℞. TI . CAESAR . DIVI . AUG . F . AVGVST . P . M . TR . POT . XXXVII. In the field, S. C.

The splendid building portrayed on this and the next two coins is considered to be a representation of the Temple of Concord, which was originally erected in the capitol by Furius Camillus, the dictator in the time of the Republic, on the occasion of the suppression of a popular tumult among the citizens. This first temple was burnt down in the reign of Tiberius, who caused it to be rebuilt as here represented. There is scarcely any portion of it now remaining.

133.

No legend. A temple of large dimensions, similar in every way to the temple on the preceding coin; it is ornamented profusely with statues and sculptures, but differently arranged, and the tympanum is quite plain.

℞. TI . CAESAR . DIVI . AVG . F . AVGVST . P . M . TR . POT . XXXIIX. In the field, S. C.

The Temple of Concord, as the site is described by Nibby, was so near the forum, that it might almost be considered one of its buildings. It stood however between the capitol and the forum, its face turned towards the forum and to the comitium, and on its flank it was near to the Mamertine prison. It was erected by the Senate and people after Camillus had in his last dictatorship (when the two orders of the people, patrician and plebeian, came to an agreement) gained the privilege that one of the consuls should be elected from the plebeians. During the Republic it was a place where the Senate assembled to treat of important matters, and they met there on the occasion of the discovery of the conspiracy of Catiline.

134.

No legend. A temple of large dimensions, similar in every respect to the preceding, except that in the tympanum of the present there is a large hollow circle with some figures on each side of it; the circle appears to be pierced through to give light and air to the interior.

℞. TI . CAESAR . DIVI . AVG . F . AVGVST . P . M . TR . POT . XXXIIX. In the middle of the field, S. C.

L

135.

No legend. An empty triumphal chariot drawn by four horses slowly, to the right; it is richly decorated with figures of victories, trophies, and captives.

℞. TI . CAESAR . DIVI . AVG . F . AVGVST . P . M . TR . POT . XXXVII. In the field S. C.

A coin struck A.D. 36, and is supposed to allude to the triumph decreed to Tiberius many years before, but which was never celebrated owing to the grievous defeat of the Romans under Quintilius Varus in Germany, and the loss of three entire legions with their eagles and other standards. This event is said to have happened in A.D. 9, during the reign of Augustus, who was for a short time in a state of distraction from the misfortune, frequently raving and calling out, Varus, restore me my legions. The battle took place near to the river Visargis, now the Weser. The Romans were drawn into an ambuscade, and Varus, seeing all effort to save his army of no avail, threw himself upon his sword and died. His head, and afterwards his body, were sent to Rome in derision. The legions which were thus destroyed by the Germans were the seventeenth, eighteenth, and nineteenth, of which scarcely a man escaped; and most of the chief officers who were taken prisoners were offered in sacrifice to the idols of the country. See more of this under the coin of Germanicus, *post.*

136.

No legend. A triumphal car drawn by four horses slowly, to the right, with decorations as on the preceding coin, but no one in it.

℞. TI . CAESAR . DIVI . AVG . F . AVGVST . P . M . TR . POT . XXXIIX. S. C. in the field. Weight 413 grains.

These two coins are quoted by Argelati.

137.

TI . CAESAR . DIVI . AVG . F . AVGVST . IMP . VIII. The laureate head of Tiberius to the left.

℞. PONTIF . MAX . TR . POT . XXXIIX. S. C. on the sides of the field, between which is a globe. On the front of it is a rudder of a galley, with a small globe affixed to it on its lower end.

The type represents the sovereignty of the Roman people by sea and land.

There are no funereal or consecration coins of Tiberius. If the senate with its usual servility would have acquiesced in the apotheosis of a tyrant who had degraded and decimated it, the citizens interfered to forbid the honours, and Caius [Caligula] made no effort to enforce them. Vide Merivale, 375.

COLONIAL.

138.

TI . CAESAR . DIVI . AVG . P . AVGVSTVS . PON . MAX . TR . P . XXXIII. This legend is obliterated on the present coin, but I have supplied it from Vaillant. A seated figure to the left holding a patera in the right hand; the hasta pura in the left.

℟. C . C . A . [M] CATO . L . VETTIACVS . IIVIR. Then in three lines across the field the numbers of the legions with three military standards, the centre being a vexillum or cavalry banner.   LEG. IV. LEG. VI. LEG. X.

This coin was struck by Marcus Cato and Lucius Vettiacus, the duumviri of the municipium Cæsarea Augusta in Spain, now Saragossa, already noticed under the provincial coins of Augustus.

The Legions IV. VI. and X. named on this coin as colonists of Cæsarea Augusta, were transferred to that place by Augustus: these soldiers were of the class termed Veteran. Those of the Fourth legion were of the Legio IV. Scythica; the Sixth were taken, part from the Legio Sexta Victrix, and part from the Legio Sexta Ferrata; and the Tenth in like manner, part Legio X. Gemina, and part Legio X. Fretensis.

Some doubt has been expressed whether Legio IV. Scythica was not transferred to Syria instead of being located in Spain.

The standard in the middle is the vexillum, which was the standard of the cavalry, consisting of a square piece of cloth extended upon a cross. The standards on each side appear to have circular wreaths, and, being unaccompanied by an eagle, they indicate that the colonists were parts of the legions, or cohorts of the respective legions. The military colonists are usually distinguished on coins by the legionary eagle or other military standards, and the ordinary agricultural colonists were designated by bulls or oxen.

It was the custom at Rome, when a colony was to be sent forth, to put up a banner in the forum, with a tablet inscribed with the name of the chief under whose charge the colonists were to be placed, the number of persons who were to depart, and the name and situation of the place, thus inviting the citizens to join the emigrants who had already inscribed to go forth. When the intended number was completed, the colonists out of every 100 chose ten; from the whole of these tens, or decuriones as they were called, two were selected as the chief magistrates and were called duumviri, who were to exercise in the new colony similar powers and duties to those performed by the consuls at Rome; and when the colonists took their final leave of Rome they were preceded by the vexillarius or standard-bearer, who marched at their head, carrying the vexillum or ensign of the colony, or the aquila if it were a legionary colony.

Vaillant describing a coin of Tiberius similar to the present, says, " Hic nummus majoris moduli olim in cimelio Emin. Card. Maximi, rarissimus et præstantissimus est." It is also mentioned in Haver. Thes. 355-6, and an engraving of it in the Gens Porcia, tab. 2.

Of this coin I have never seen any example but the present at sale or elsewhere, it is so very rare. It is not in fine condition.

139.

TI. CAESAR. DIVI. AVG. F. AVGVST. IMP. VIII. The unlaureate head of Tiberius to the left.

℞. C. VIBIO. MARSO. PR. COS. D. R. CAE. Q. P. R. T. C. RVFVS. F. C. In the area of the field D. D. P. P. Caio Vibio Marso pro consule Druso Cæsare Quæstore Provinciæ Titus Cælius Rufus fieri curavit, Decuriones posuerunt.

A female seated to the right, the hasta pura in her left hand, a patera in the right. The figure very much resembles the representations of Vesta already noticed.

Vaillant, pp. 87, 88, speaking of similar provincial coins struck by the Proconsul Vibius Marso, says, " Ad Uticam pertinet nummus etsi nomen urbis desit." This type is also mentioned in Havercamp's Thesaurus, p. 56, as belonging to the Caelia Gens. A well-spread Second Brass black-green coin.

140.

TI. CAESAR. AVGVSTVS. The unlaureate head of Tiberius to the left; behind the head is an olive branch; in front of the neck, on the right, is an eagle with expanded wings, holding in its beak an ear of corn.

℞. IIOL. A laureate head, evidently female, to the right; her hair braided and in tresses falling on her neck, shoulders draped, and in front rather full on the bosom; in the field, in front of the face, is a cithara: the whole is encircled by a laurel-wreath.

From the word on the reverse, this coin seems to have been struck at the same place, Iol, in Cæsarea Mauritania, as that mentioned by Admiral Smyth, in IVLIA AVGVSTI, p. 14.

Black brown, fine.

RESTORED COIN.

141.

TI . CAESAR . DIVI . AVG . F . AVGVS . IMP . VIII. The unlaureate head of Tiberius to the left.

℞. IMP . T . CAES . DIVI . VESP . F . AVG . REST. A caduceus; in the field S. C.

A Second Brass coin, in fine condition (weight 194⅝ grains). It is a restored coin by Titus, whose resemblance in portrait may be seen disguised as Tiberius, a worthy for an unworthy personage.

DRUSUS JUNIOR.

NERO CLAUDIUS DRUSUS, the only son of Tiberius and Vipsania Agrippina, the daughter of Agrippa, was born at Rome, about the year of Rome 741, or B. C. 13. He was made quæstor A. D. 12, and elected consul A. D. 14. He was invested by his father with the tribunician power A. D. 22, and poisoned the following year by his wife Livilla, at the instigation of her paramour Sejanus. Drusus was a man of the most depraved and immoral character.

142.

DRVSVS . CAESAR . TI . AVG . F . DIVI . AVG . N. The unlaureate head of Drusus to the left.

℞. PONTIF . TRIBVN . POTEST . ITER. In the centre of the field S. C.

The coins of Drusus are common, although seldom so fine as the present; it was struck in A.D. 22, and records the title of Drusus as pontiff, and also his investiture with the tribunicia potestas, by which, for the time he held it, he became associated with his father in the sovereignty.

A black coin in Second Brass and of fine condition, from the cabinet of the Rev. E. C. Brice. Weight 175¼ grains.

143.

PIETAS. A beautiful female head to the right, with a plain coronet in front on the forehead; a veil is drawn over the back part of the head, descending on the shoulders, which are draped; the word PIETAS is under the bust.

℞. DRVSVS . CAESAR . TI . AVGVSTI . F . TR . POT . ITER. In the centre of the field S. C.

A large Second Brass coin from the Campana collection, unrivalled for beauty, of pale powdery white green. Weight 218¼ grains.

Numismatic writers usually assign this coin to Livia, although I do not see any reason why. It is possible—nay, more than probable—that it was struck by the Senate as a complimentary coin to Drusus as a pontiff, his father Tiberius being the chief pontiff, to both of whom *piety* could well be imputed *officially*. I therefore consider the head an ideal head to represent *Piety* as a devotional matter, and veiled according to the custom of the ancients when offering sacrifice; this custom was taken from the Jews, or the most ancient church.

144.

PIETAS. in the verge of the field, behind a veiled female head to the right, with a plain coronet; like the preceding coin.

℞. DRVSVS . CAESAR . TI . AVGVSTI . F . TR . POT . ITER . In the middle of the field S. C. A smaller Second Brass coin, black.

145.

No legend. A winged caduceus between two cornucopiæ in saltier, each having a child's head on the top, vis-a-vis.

℞. DRVSVS . CAESAR . TI . AVG . F . DIVI . AVG . N . PONT . TR . POT . I̅I̅. In the middle of the field S. C.

This coin was struck A. D. 23, and records the two young princes Drusus Gemellus and Tiberius Nero, the twin sons of Drusus. The first died in his infancy, and the other was put to death by Caligula.

The present coin, from the cabinet of Mr. Thomas (weight 418¼ grains), is in remarkably fine preservation, showing the portraits of the children with very great minuteness, which is owing to its being gilded; and there is no doubt this was done soon after it was struck, and thus is coeval with the coin, and renders it a unique specimen. It was one of the gems of the Thomas cabinet; and Mr. Cureton, who bought it for me, gave his decided opinion of it being Roman gilding.

The tribunician date being marked I̅I̅, having the line above, has created discussion with antiquaries. Some consider it to be the word *iterum* abbreviated, while others consider the line above the numerals always to indicate increase by one; thus in the present instance it would mean III; but there is no historic record of Drusus having on his coins a TR . POT . III. in full.

From this coin having been originally gilded when it was struck, it is not improbable it was for a birthday present to some young Roman lady or gentleman, and so all the sharpness of the dies has been admirably preserved. Romans of respectability were accustomed to make birthday presents of new coins. Augustus, who was a geologist, and had a collection of fossils, had also a large collection of coins of different countries, from which at times he was in the habit of making presents.

146.

No legend. A winged caduceus between two cornucopiæ in saltier, each having a child's head on the top, as on the preceding coin.

℞. DRVSVS . CAESAR . TI . AVG . F . AVG . N . PONT . TR . POT . I̅I̅. In the middle of the field S. C.

DRUSUS SENIOR.

NERO CLAUDIUS DRUSUS, the brother of the emperor Tiberius, was born in the year of Rome 716; he was made prætor in the year B.C. 13, and consul with T. Crispinus Sulpicianus, B.C. 8; soon after which, in the same year, he died from the effects of a fall from his horse when returning from a military expedition into Germany, A. U. C. 745. After his death he was styled Germanicus, from the successes he had gained in Germany. A very interesting account of the military achievements of Drusus will be found in the 4th volume of Merivale.

Argelati in reference to the coins of Drusus observes: "Drusi Germ. nummi quibus Ti. Cl. Imp. nomen aut effigies inest à Ti. Claudio filio in honorem patris Neronis Cl. Drusi Germanici cusa sunt, &c. ad renovandum actorum et victoriarum paternarum memoriam."

Claudius became emperor A.D. 41; his reign ended in A.D. 54; but, as the coins of Drusus are void of any distinctive mark of his time, the identification of any date of mintage is unimportant, the pieces having allusion only to the memorable victories of Drusus in Germany in B.C. 8, &c.

The coins of Drusus are very common, excepting in a good state of preservation.

147.

NERO . CLAUDIUS . DRUSUS . GERMANICUS . IMP. The unlaureate head of Drusus to the left.

℞. TI . CLAVDIVS . CAESAR . AVG . P . M . TR . P . IMP.. In the exergum S. C. Drusus seated robed and bareheaded on a curule chair placed over a mundus or globe, to the left; his right hand extended holds a branch of laurel; his feet rest on a cuirass, and around him are strewed broken arms and armour of various kinds, to signify his victories over the various tribes of German people.

Argelati describes this reverse rather differently: he says, "Figura sedens, dextrâ ramum lauri, sinistrâ sceptrum, ad pedes plura armorum genera." By the *figura* Argelati may possibly have intended to signify Drusus; there is no doubt the *figura* on this and the next coin is unmistakeably Drusus himself. Vaillant, in vol. i. p. 11, describes the reverse thus: "Nero Claudius togatus sedet in sellâ curuli, inter armorum spolia positâ; dextrâ ramum, sinistrâ chartam involutam."

Very fine black coin. Weight 473½.

148.

NERO . CLAVDIVS . DRVSVS . GERMANICVS . IMP. The unlaureate head of Drusus to the left.

℞. TI . CLAVDIVS . CAESAR . AVG . P . M . TR . P . IMP . P . P. S. C. in the exergum. Drusus seated to the left amongst arms, as above described.

149.

TI . CLAVDIVS . CAESAR . AVG . P . M . TR . P . IMP. The laureate head of the emperor Claudius to the right.

℞. NERO . CLAVDIVS . DRVSVS . GERMAN . IMP.; in the field S. C. An equestrian figure placed to the right on a triumphal arch, intended to represent Drusus on a prancing horse, with his right hand raised holding a spear, in the act of striking a foe.

ANTONIA.

ANTONIA was the daughter of Marcus Antonius and Octavia the sister of Augustus; she was born at Rome about the year of Rome B.C. 38. She was married to Drusus Senior, whom she survived until the year A.D. 38, when she died, as is supposed by poison, her grandson Caligula being privy to her death.

She was a lady of worthy and excellent character.

150.

ANTONIA . AVGVSTA. The head of Antonia to the right, her hair combed down the side of the face in plain wavy lines, and tied in a short loop-knot at the back of the neck, the shoulders draped.

℞. TI . CLAVDIVS . CAESAR . AVG . P . M . TR . P . IMP. In the field S. C. A veiled priestess standing to the left holding a simpulum in her right hand.

By Havercamp, Gevartius, and other writers, it has been supposed that this figure represents the Emperor Claudius; but it is evidently a female figure, and no doubt intended for Antonia habited as one of the priestesses of Augustus. The title of Augusta was bestowed on Antonia by Caligula when he became Emperor.

The present is a fine Second Brass coin from the cabinet of the Duke of Devonshire, mounted in a black ivory ring, according to the custom of the Devonshire cabinet. Weight 217¼ grains.

151.

ANTONIA . AVGVSTA. The head of Antonia to the right, her hair dressed as on the preceding coin.

℞. TI . CLAVDIVS . CAESAR . AVG . P . M . TR . P . IMP . P . P. In the field S. C. A veiled preistess standing to the left with a simpulum in her right hand.

A Second Brass coin. The legend on the reverse concludes with the title P . P .; not so the preceding coin either obverse or reverse. Weight 256¾ grains.

152.

ANTONIA . AVGVSTA. The head of Antonia to the right, as on the preceding coin.

℞. TI . CLAV . CA.
S. C.
AVG . P . M . TR . P.
} inscribed in three lines within a laurel wreath.

A coin similar to this is noticed by Vaillant in tom. i. p. 13; and by Havercamp in the Christina cabinet. It is a very rare coin, and not in the cabinets of the British Museum. It is a Second Brass, from Dr. Bird's sale.

GERMANICUS.

Germanicus was the son of Drusus senior and Antonia. He was born B.C. 15, and inherited the name of Germanicus from his father, to whom it had been decreed in perpetuity by the Senate, as we have noted *ante, in Druso*. He was adopted by Tiberius and invested with the title of Cæsar B.C. 4; he took the office of Quæstor A.D. 7, and in A.D. 11 he obtained triumphal honours for his successes over the Marsi, Catti, and other northern nations.

In A.D. 17 he had a still more brilliant triumph for his victories in Germany, on which occasion his children were with him in his triumphal chariot, to the great delight of the assembled multitudes who witnessed the procession. After a brilliant though short career, he died at Epidaphne, near Antioch, supposed to have been poisoned by Piso, the Governor of Syria, by the orders of Tiberius, who had become jealous of the fame and popularity Germanicus had obtained with the people of Rome.

Tiberius had also taken great offence with Germanicus for having visited Ægypt, where he made a tour and inspected all the antiquities and places of celebrity in that country. On this occasion, although he travelled as a private gentleman and was received every where in that character only, yet Tiberius reproved him for breaking the law made by Augustus by which every person of consular, senatorial, or equestrian rank, was strictly prohibited from entering Alexandria, the then capital city of Ægypt, without the permission of the emperor.

Germanicus was married to Agrippina, the daughter of Marcus Agrippa and Julia the daughter of Augustus; she was a woman of fine elevated character. They had nine children.

153.

GERMANICVS . CAESAR . in two lines, across the upper part of the field, above a triumphal chariot decorated with sculptures and drawn by four horses to the right, in which Germanicus is standing holding in his right hand a sceptre surmounted by an eagle.

℞. SIGNIS . RECEPT . DEVICTIS . GERM . across the field in four lines divided into two parts by a whole-length figure of Germanicus in full military costume excepting his helmet; he is standing looking to the left with his right hand raised in the attitude of command, in his left hand he holds a sceptre or short staff mounted with an eagle. S.C. under the legend on either side of Germanicus.

A Second Brass bronze-coloured coin in very fine condition; it was struck A.D. 17, the date of his triumph for the German victories, which Argelati, *in Germanico*, places to the kalends of July in that year. Merivale, v. 50, says, the triumph was celebrated on the 26th May, A.D. 17, A. U. C. 770.

This very interesting type records the victories obtained by Germanicus over the Germans, whom he defeated in several battles, and ultimately recovered the eagles and standards they had taken from the xvii., xviii., and xix. legions under Varus, in the year of Rome 762; they were thus recovered in the year 768, or according to Occo 769, and Argelati 770. This event gave the utmost delight and satisfaction to the people of Rome; and Argelati says the eagle held by Germanicus on this coin is one of those lost by Varus.

Tacitus in the first book of his annals, sect. 71, gives a very interesting account of the Roman army under Germanicus, when, in the expedition to Germany A.D. 15, they arrived at the places where Quintilius Varus and his legions were cut off, and the groves and forests where the officers and soldiers who were taken prisoners were offered up in sacrifice to the German idols. The Roman army collected the bones of their slaughtered friends and countrymen, and a memorial to the memory of the dead was raised with turf, Germanicus with his own hand laying the first sod, thus discharging the tribute of respect due to the legions, and sympathizing with the rest of the army in the loss of their fellow-soldiers and friends.

We have noticed this tragedy in the coins of Tiberius, *ante*.

154.

GERMANICVS . CAESAR. Across the upper part of the field in two lines, above Germanicus, who is in his chariot drawn by four horses to the right. The chariot displays more decoration than on the preceding coin.

℞. SIGNIS . RECEPT . DEVICTIS . GERM. S.C. under, on each side of the field. Germanicus standing with sceptre and eagle in his left hand, his right hand raised as already described.

This figure has been copied on a medal of the Buonaparte series, but that is not equal in its drawing to the Roman. On the French medal the body is made too elongated, which gives the figure a very awkward appearance.

155.

GERMANICVS . CAESAR . TI . AVG . F . DIVI . AVG . N. The unlaureate head of Germanicus to the left.

℞. C . CAESAR . AVG . GERMANICVS . PON . M . TR . POT. In the middle of the field S. C.

This Second Brass coin, which is in very fine condition, was struck by Caligula A.D. 19. Weight 181⅜ grains.

156.

GERMANICVS . CAESAR . TI . AVG . F . DIVI . AVG . N. The unlaureate head of Germanicus to the right.

℞. TI . CLAVDIVS . CAESAR . AVG . GERM . P . M . TR . P . IMP . P . P. In the middle of the field S. C.

A Second Brass coin in equally fine condition, struck by Claudius, the successor of Caligula.   Weight 170¾ grains.

AGRIPPINA SENIOR.

AGRIPPINA, daughter of Marcus Agrippa and Julia the daughter of Augustus, was born in the year B.C. 15. Afterwards she became the wife of Germanicus, and after his death she was banished by Tiberius to the island of Pandataria, A.D. 30, where she died three years after, being starved to death by order of Tiberius, A.D. 33, A . U . C . 786.

She was a woman of lofty mind and most excellent character, exemplary in every respect as a wife and a mother.

157.

AGRIPPINA . M . F . MAT . C . CAESARIS . AVGVSTI.   The head of Agrippina to the right, her hair in curls in front of the face, and a ringlet straying down the neck. The hair behind is drawn into a long knot braided with a string of pearls.

℞. MEMORIAE . AGRIPPINAE across the upper part of the right side of the field, and above them S . P . Q . R. A decorated carpentum drawn by two mules to the left, the reins held by a figure in front of the carpentum; under the tilt or roof is a seated figure, and another standing in front, as if in the act of presenting something to the one who is seated. The roof of the carpentum is divided in compartments as if tessellated.

The S . P . Q . R . denote the honours paid to Agrippina by the Senate and people of Rome by general assent in the reign of Caligula.

Gevartius, Havercamp, Pedrusi, and others, all pronounce coins of this type to have been struck by Caligula to the memory of his mother. Admiral Smyth, No. 32 of his Cabinet, attributes it to the emperor Claudius, but I suggest the former opinion to be the correct one. The legend on the obverse describes her as being MAT[ER] C[AII] CAESARIS; and Suetonius, in Caligula, sec. 15, says, "Et ea amplius matri circenses carpentumque quo in pompa traduceretur;" and, although Caligula affected to be ashamed of his really noble grandfather Marcus Agrippa, yet that is an insufficient argument in support of the assertion that he did not strike a coin to the memory of his illustrious yet unfortunate mother.

Weight, 398¼ grains.

158.

AGRIPPINA . M . F . MAT . C . CAESARIS . AVGVSTI. The head of Agrippina to the right, her hair braided as on the preceding coin.

℞. S . P . Q . R . over MEMORIAE . AGRIPPINAE . as already described; a carpentum drawn by two mules to the left; each corner of the roof of the carpentum is supported by a figure placed on a small plinth; the side of the carpentum is decorated.

Weight, 433¼ grains.

159.

AGRIPPINA . M . F . MAT . C . CAESARIS . AVGVSTI. The head of Agrippina to the right, as on the preceding coins.

℞. S . P . Q . R . over MEMORIAE AGRIPPINAE. A carpentum drawn by two mules to the left; the tilt or roof, which, with the sides, is much decorated, is supported by four small figures, but is differently adorned to either of the other specimens.

160.

AGRIPPINA . M . F . MAT . C . CAESARIS . AVGVSTI. The head of Agrippina to the right, as on the preceding coins.

℞ S . P . Q . R . over MEMORIAE . AGRIPPINAE. A richly-ornamented carpentum drawn gently by two mules to the left; the reins are fastened to a ball projecting from the front. The tilt or roof is supported by four figures, but the decorations are different to either of the other coins.

By reason of the varieties of the decorations on the carpentums I have retained all these coins; they are all in fine preservation; the colour of the first is an unpatinated drab colour, the others brown and brownish-green.

161.

AGRIPPINA . M . F . GERMANICI . CAESARIS. The head of Agrippina to the right, as on the preceding coins.

℞. TI . CLAVDIVS . CAESAR . AVG . GERM . P . M . TR . P . IMP . P . P . In the middle of the field S. C.

This coin was struck by the emperor Claudius to the memory of his unfortunate sister-in-law. On this coin it will be observed she is designated Marci Filia, wife of Germanicus Cæsar, the name of her son Caius Cæsar, *alias* Caligula, being omitted.

The difference between the coins struck by Caligula to the memory of his unfortunate mother, and of those struck to her memory by Claudius, is simply this: the coins of Caligula represent the funeral car or carpentum, while the coins of Claudius merely have an inscription and S. C. in the middle of the field on the reverse, as the coins we have just described fully show. The coins of Claudius designate her as the wife of Germanicus, while the coins of Caligula represent her as the mother of the emperor.

NERO ET DRUSUS CÆSARES.

NERO and DRUSUS were two of the sons of Germanicus and Agrippina. Nero was born about the year of Rome 760, or A.D. 7, and was starved to death in the island of Pontia, whither he had been exiled by his great-uncle Tiberius, about the year of Rome 784, or A.D. 31.

Drusus was born about the year of Rome 761, or A.D. 8. He was appointed præfect of Rome in A. D. 25, and in A.D. 32 he was starved to death in a dungeon under the palace of Tiberius by that emperor's orders.

162.

NERO . ET . DRVSVS . CAESARES . The two princes on horseback, galloping by the side of each, to the right.

℞. C . CAESAR . AVG . GERMANICVS . PON . M . TR . POT . In the middle of the field S. C.

A Second Brass coin struck by Caligula when emperor to the memory of his unfortunate brothers. Weight 205¾ grains.

Caligula went to the islands of Pontia and Pandataria for the purpose of bringing to Rome the remains of Nero and of his mother Agrippina.

The legend on the reverse sometimes concludes with the tribunician date and P . P . This coin, from not having a tribunician date, would appear to have been struck in the first year of Caligula.

163.

NERO . ET . DRVSVS . CAESARES . QVINQ . C . V . I . N . C . The heads of the two Cæsars adverse to each other.

℞. TI . CAESAR . DIVI . AVGVSTI . F . AVGVSTVS . P . M . The unlaureate head of Tiberius to the left.

From the legends on the obverse and reverse of this coin it is seen to have been struck in the reign of Tiberius, and whilst the two princes were in favour with that emperor.

The legend on the obverse shows it to have been struck by the colony of Carthagena in Spain, who, in compliment to the emperor Tiberius, had elected his grand-nephews to take the office of quinquennalian duumviri of their city.

This colony was said to have been originally founded by the Carthaginian general Asdrubal, in the year of Rome 527, whence its name Nova Carthago.

CAIUS CALIGULA.

CAIUS CÆSAR, one of the sons of Germanicus and Agrippina senior. He was surnamed Caligula from the *caligæ* or heavy military boots he used to wear when a youth, to inure himself to the fatigue of military duty.

He was born at Antium in the year of Rome 765, A.D. 12, and succeeded his great-uncle Tiberius in the year of Rome 790, A.D. 37. He was afterwards assassinated by Cassius Cherea, a tribune of the Prætorian Guard, in the year of Rome 794, A.D. 41.

The conduct of Caligula as emperor was of the most infamous description. At the commencement of his reign, being then quite a young man, his whole conduct and demeanour was so proper that the Roman people were in ecstasies at the exchange from the tyranny of Tiberius; but after the first year his conduct changed, and he became one of the worst men that ever was placed in sovereign power.

His coins are not particularly common, more especially in fine condition, for after his death his statues and coins were destroyed by order of the senate, so as to obliterate all record of such a man.

164.

C . CAESAR . AVG . GERMANICVS . PON . M . TR . POT . The laureate head of Caligula to the left.

℞. S . P . Q . R . P . P . OB . CIVES . SERVATOS . inscribed in four lines within an oak-wreath, the *corona quercea*.

The civic crown here represented was awarded to him who preserved the life of a citizen. On the present coin the allusion is to the recall of certain exiles and other acts of clemency which were performed by Caligula at the commencement of his reign, and gained him favour with the people.

Brown, remarkably fine.

165.

C . CAESAR . AVG . GERMANICVS . PON . M . TR . POT. The laureate head of Caligula to the left.

℞. ADLOCVT. in the upper part of the field, and COH. in the exergum—no S. C. The emperor robed, standing to the left on a low suggestum or tribunal; behind him is a curule seat; his right hand is raised in the attitude of addressing five soldiers, who stand before him armed, and bearing amongst them four eagles.

It was usual on the accession of an emperor for him to make an harangue to the Prætorian Guards and soldiers. Caligula is in the act of doing so, and, by the coin having no tribunician date, it may be considered as representing the oration made by him on his accession, the five soldiers with the eagles signifying the whole of the military forces.

Caligula was the first emperor whose allocution or address to the troops on his accession was introduced on his coins, a practice which was adopted by other emperors.

Tiberius died on the 17th of the kalends of April in A.D. 37, and Caligula was immediately declared emperor, so the present coin was struck in the first year of his reign, A.D. 37.

A very fine coin from the cabinet of the Rev. E. C. Brice. Weight 382½ grains.

166.

C . CAESAR . AVG . GERMANICVS . PON . M . PR . POT. The laureate head of Caligula to the left.

℞. AGRIPPINA, DRVSILLA, IVLIA. In the exergum S. C. The three sisters of Caligula in the characters of Piety, Constancy, and Fortune. Agrippina, as Constancy, leans her right arm on a short column at her right side, holding a cornucopiæ on her right arm; her left hand rests on the right shoulder of Drusilla, who as Piety holds a sacred patera in her right hand, on the left arm a cornucopiæ. Julia, as Fortune, holds a rudder in her right hand, on her left arm she bears a cornucopiæ.

Caligula bestowed on his sisters the rank of vestals, with similar privileges, although " cum omnibus sororibus suis stupri consuetudinem fecit." Drusilla, the favourite, was publicly espoused by him after her having had two husbands; and, upon her death, which occurred A.D. 38, he caused her to be deified, and one Livius Geminus swore that he saw her soul taken into Heaven and there conversing with the gods.

Agrippina and Julia were each twice married, but afterwards engaged in debaucheries with their brother, who subsequently banished them, and seized all their property. On the accession of Claudius they were recalled from their exile, but Julia, afterwards falling under the displeasure of Messalina, the first wife of Claudius, was again banished, and subsequently put to death by her order.

On the death of Messalina, Agrippina became the wife of Claudius, who was her uncle, and who she subsequently poisoned to make room for her son Nero.

167.

C . CAESAR . AVG . GERMANICVS . PON . M . TR . POT. The unlaureate head of Caligula to the left.

℞. VESTA . over a veiled female figure seated to the left on a square highbacked chair or throne much ornamented in every part; her right hand extended holds a patera, in her left hand she has the *hasta pura*. S. C. on either side of the field.

This coin of Caligula, with the type of Vesta sedent, is the first coin mentioned by Argelati as bearing this type, a type we have already noticed *in Augusto, ante*; which latter coin does not appear to have been then known to Argelati.

The present is a Second Brass black coin in most perfect condition.

168.

C . CAESAR . AVG . GERMANICVS . TR . POT. A sedent female figure to the left. The head veiled in the manner of PIETAS before noted, No. 143; her right hand extended holds the sacred patera, her left elbow rests on the head of a small figure of a robed female standing on a base at the side of the chair, with one hand on the bosom, the other at the side, intended as an ornamental support for the left arm, but seems to be quite distinct from the chair, which is perfect without the figure. The word PIETAS is in the exergum.

℞. DIVO――AVG . with S. C. under. Placed on either side of the front of a fine square temple of six columns decorated with garlands suspended among the columns; the pediment and tympanum are much ornamented with statues. In front of the temple is an altar, by which the emperor is standing habited in pontifical robes, holding in his right hand a patera to receive the blood of a steer which is held for sacrifice by a victimarius; behind the emperor is an attendant, who also holds in his left hand a patera.

This coin was struck in the first year of Caligula, the TR . POT . being without a number. By the inscription DIVO . AVG . on the reverse, it denotes the consecration of the temple erected to Augustus which was commenced by Tiberius, or, according to some writers, by Livia, who died before its completion, and the dedication here recorded was performed by Caligula in the first year of his reign.

On examining the coins of Antoninus Pius, it will be seen that the Temple of Augustus, having fallen into a dilapidated state, was repaired by Antoninus, which gave occasion to the coin with the legend on the reverse TEMPLVM . [sometimes AEDES] DIVI . AVG . REST.

Weight 489⅜ grains.

169.

C . CAESAR DIVI . AVG . PRON . AVG . P . M . TR . P . III . P . P. The laureate head of Caligula to the left.

℞. ADLOCVT . in the upper part of the field, and CON. in the exergum. The Emperor in his robes standing to the left in front of a curule seat placed on a low tribunal, his right hand raised as addressing five soldiers before him bearing four eagles. No S. C. From the TR . POT . III . on the obverse of this coin, it appears to have been struck A.D. 40, on occasion of Caligula's proposed expedition to Britain.

The first allocution already noticed was made on his accession, the present bearing the third year of tribunician date, being the year that he was in Gaul, and purposed making a descent on Britain. It therefore records his address to the troops, as related by Tacitus, "for gathering the spoils of the conquered ocean," as he vauntingly termed the ridiculous exhibition; for he did not venture his person or troops beyond the shores of Gaul, where by his orders the soldiers to the sound of trumpets collected in their helmets the shells lying on the beach in token of a victory, and he then made them a pompous harangue extolling their bravery. After which he had the folly to write letters to the Senate detailing his imaginary prowess, and binding his letters with laurel, as usual with generals who had gained a signal victory, he demanded a triumph, which of course he did not get.

Weight 416⅜ grains.

170.

C . CAESAR . DIVI . AVG . PRON . AVG . P . M . TR . P . IIII . P . P . A female figure seated to the left, her head veiled; her right hand extended holds a patera, her left arm rests on the head of a small female figure at her left side, but apparently distinct from the chair, and is also a different sort of figure to that on the preceding coin of this type. In the exergum PIETAS.

℞. DIVO . AVG . S. C . across the field, as on the former coin.

A temple of six columns, with garlands suspended in front, with a sacrifice going on in the presence of the emperor, as already described on the former coin.

This coin was struck in A.D. 41, in the last year of Caligula, who was killed in the month of February in that year. It is a repetition of the type of the dedication of the Temple of Augustus we have already noticed.

The sedent figure on the obverse of these coins is usually considered as representing the emperor in pontifical robes, but on the coins I have here described the bosom of the figure is decidedly that of a female, and I consider it to be a repretation of the goddess PIETAS, and emblematic of the piety of the emperor; for, being the Pontifex Maximus, he was pious *virtute officii*.

Eusebius, Hist. Eccles. l. ii. c. 7, says that in the last year of Caligula, A.D. 41, Pontius Pilate, the Governor of Judæa, temp. Tiberii, and who had been banished to Lyons [Merivale, vol. v. p. 349, says he was sent to Vienna], killed himself there, it then being eight years from the Crucifixion. Josephus, lib. iii. relates the same. Pilate was appointed governor of Judæa about the middle of the reign of Tiberius.

Weight 434 grains.

171.

C . CAESAR . DIVI . AVG . PRON . AVG . P . M . TR . P . IIII . P . P . The laureate head of Caligula to the left.

℞. ADLOCVT . in the upper part of the field, and COH. in the exergum. No S. C. The emperor in his robes standing to the left on a low suggestum ; behind him is a curule seat ; his right hand is raised, addressing five soldiers, who stand before him, bearing four eagles ; they wear their swords on their right side, and the first carries a shield on which there is the representation of a fulmen.

This allocutio is a repetition of the type of TR . P . III . on occasion of the soldiers gathering up the shells on the sea-shore of Gaul when Caligula had an idea of crossing over to Britain.

PROVINCIAL.

172.

C . CAES . AVG . GERMANICVS . IMP . reading from the left. The laureate head of Caligula to the left.

℞. LICINIANO . ET . GERMANO . II . In the exergum VIR .

Three military standards, the middle one being a legionary eagle; the outer ones are with hands or *manipuli*. cc. on one side of the eagle staff, A. on the other.

This is a coin of the colony Cæsarea Augusta, which we have noticed among the provincial coins of Augustus. The present coin is described by Vaillant in his book on the colonial coins, as "*inter rarissimos collocandus;*" it bears the names of Licinianus and Germanus, then being the Duumviri of the colony.

It would seem that the office of Duumvir was at times an object of competition among the colonists, for which there was much canvassing for votes by the competitors and their friends. An instance of this was lately discovered at Pompeii, as appears by a notice in the Illustrated News of the 10th March, 1855—

"In an establishment of ancient baths discovered some time since at Pompeii, in the street called the Odeon, there have been lately uncovered several grated windows looking into the street, and a door flanked by two pilasters, above which is painted this inscription—

P. FVR. IIV. V. B. O. V. F.

Publium Furium Duumvirum, virum bonum, oro vos faciatis. I beg of you to name as Duumvir Publius Furius, an honest man."

This is evidently a placard made for the time of an election for Duumvir of the town of Pompeii.

CLAUDIUS.

TIBERIUS CLAUDIUS DRUSUS GERMANICUS, the son of Drusus senior and Antonia, was born at Lyons in the year B.C. 10. Upon the death of C. Caligula in A.D. 41 he was raised to the empire by the soldiers, and afterwards confirmed as emperor by the Senate. He was subsequently poisoned by his wife Agrippina junior, the sister of Caligula and mother of Nero, A.D. 54. Claudius was the first emperor who on his accession made a donation to the soldiers, and this he did from fear and to save his life; but it was a pernicious example that in after-times was productive of the most serious evils to the welfare of the empire, and eventually caused the sovereignty to be entirely at the disposal of the military, who became always ready to sell to the highest bidder.

Claudius has generally been reckoned by historians as a man of very weak intellect and fond of table indulgences. Be that as it may, although he might not have possessed great physical power or courage, yet he possessed considerable thought and diligence. The port of Ostia bears testimony to this view of his character. Besides these works, although he might be so called a dull man, yet he was learned. He added three letters to the Roman alphabet. He also wrote annals of the empire, embracing a considerable period, and to which Tacitus and other Roman historians are said to have been indebted for many circumstances they have recorded, whereby their works are now the more valuable from the annals of Claudius having been lost.

173.

TI . CLAVDIVS . CAESAR . AVG . P . M . TR . P . The laureate head of Claudius to the right. In the field opposite to the face is a countermark | P. R. OB. | *i. e.* Populi Romani Oblatio.

℞. EX . S . C . OB . CIVES . SERVATOS . inscribed in four lines, within an oak wreath.

This coin was struck in A.D. 41, the first year of Claudius, when he suppressed the law of *lese-majesté*, which had been rigorously enforced by Tiberius and Caligula—recalled the exiles—relieved the people of many taxes—restored estates which had been unjustly seized by his predecessors—and did other benevolent acts at the commencement of his reign, and was therefore counted worthy of the civic wreath.

Weight 403½ grains.

174.

TI . CIAVDIVS . CAESAR . AVG . P . M . TR . P . PM . P . P . P . The laureate head of Claudius to the right.

℞. EX . S . C . PP . OB . CIVES . SERVATOS . in four lines, inscribed within an oak-wreath.

This coin and the next are peculiar in respect of having the P . P . or title of Pater Patriæ, both on the obverse and the reverse, and they are both struck from the same dies, which is the reason for my retaining both.

Coins struck from the same pair of dies are scarce and difficult to find, but yet are more frequent than is generally supposed.

Weight 467 grains.

175.

TI . CLAVDIVS . CAESAR . AVG . P . M . TR . P . IMP . P . P . The laureate head of Claudius to the right.

℞. EX . S . C . P . P . OB . CIVES . SERVATOS . in four lines, inscribed within an oak wreath.

This and the preceding coin were struck in A.D. 41, in commemoration of the events already noticed; on these two coins we have the title P. P. Pater Patriæ, mentioned twice, for the Senate and people of Rome were overjoyed with the bounties of Claudius, and would have bestowed on him all the honours which had been usually conferred on his predecessors, but which he declined, and forbade them erecting temples or altars to him. The significant and estimable title of Pater Patriæ seems however to have been retained on the coins by order of the Senate, as well as the honourable badge of the civic wreath.

Weight 406 grains.

176.

TI . CLAVDIVS . CAESAR . AVG . P . M . TR . P . IMP . P. P.   The laureate head of Claudius to the right.

℞. SPES . AVGVSTA . in the exergum S. C.   Hope gradient to the left; her right hand extended holds a flower; with her left hand she holds up her robes to enable her to walk more freely.

This coin was also struck at the commencement of the reign of Claudius, and expresses the satisfaction of the Roman people at his benevolent acts, and their hope for his continuance in the same path.

Claudius is the first emperor on whose coins Hope appears thus represented. Chocolate brown, very fine.   Weight $501\frac{1}{4}$ grains.

177.

TI . CLAVDIVS . CAESAR . AVG . P . M . TR. P . IMP . P . P.   The unlaureate head of Claudius to the right.

℞. LIBERTAS . AVGVSTA . in the field S. C.   Liberty, as a robed female, standing looking to the left, having a pileus in her right hand, the rudis in her left.

This and the next two coins are in Second Brass; they are very rarely, if at all, to be found in First Brass; they were struck A. D. 41. The type on the present coin denotes the change of circumstances with the Roman people under Claudius, as slaves who had received their manumission and liberty from him, as compared with what their condition had been under Tiberius and Caligula.

178.

TI . CLAVDIVS . CAESAR . AVG . P . M . TR . P . IMP . P . P.   The unlaureate head of Claudius to the right.

℞. *No legend.* S. C. in the field.   A figure of Minerva Jaculatrix armed, striding to the right, holding her spear and shield in a threatening attitude. Her helmet is Greek, and crested, and has the peculiar Greek vizor, which seems to be drawn down over the upper part of the face.

Weight $191\frac{3}{4}$ grains.

179.

TI . CLAVDIVS . CAESAR . AVG . P . M . TR . IMP . P . P. The unlaureate head of Claudius to the left.

℞. CONSTANTIAE . AVGVSTI . in the field S. C. The elegant figure of an armed female warrior standing full front looking to the left, holding a spear in her left hand; her helmet is open and finely crested; a short military cloak is pendant from her shoulders behind, and held by a clasp or fibula on the shoulder in front.

Weight 176¾ grains.

180.

TI . CLAVDIVS . CAESAR . AVG . P . M . TR . P . IMP . P . P. The unlaureate head of Claudius to the left.

℞. CERES . AVGVSTA . in the exergum S. C. Ceres robed and seated to the left on a throne; her right hand extended holds some ears of corn, a long torch lighted lies across her lap.

This also is a Second Brass coin, and from its want of a tribunician date appears to have been struck in A.D. 41, the first year of Claudius. It is rather a scarce coin, especially in good preservation.

181.

TI . CLAVDIVS . CAESAR . AVG . P . M . TR . P . IMP. The laureate head of Claudius to the right.

℞. NERO . CLAVDIVS . DRVSVS . AVG . GERMAN . IMP. In the field S. C. An equestrian figure placed to the right on a triumphal arch. A trophy of arms is at each corner of the building, and on either side of the equestrian figure, which is intended to represent Drusus senior, the father of the Emperor Claudius. The horse is in a prancing attitude, and Drusus appears with his right hand raised brandishing a spear, as against an enemy.

This coin records the triumphal arch which was erected by Claudius to commemorate the victories and martial achievements of his father, Drusus senior. The precise period of the coin's mintage cannot be well ascertained, for want of a consular or tribunician date. This circumstance would lead one to consider the arch to have been erected in the early part of the reign of Claudius, and the coin to have been struck soon after it was completed.

The arch of Drusus is mentioned by Suetonius, *in Claudio*, sect. i. It still exists at Rome near to the Porta San Sebastiano.

Weight 426¾ grains.

182.

TI . CLAVDIVS . CAESAR . AVG . P . M . TR . P . IMP . P . P. The laureate head of Claudius to the right.

℞. NERO . CLAVDIVS . DRVSVS . AVG . GERMAN . IMP.   In the field S. C.   An equestrian figure standing on an arch to the right, as on the preceding coin. The title P . P appears on the obverse, but it is not used on the preceding coin.

Weight 454½ grains.

TI . CLAVD . CAESAR . AVG . P . M . TR . P . VI . IMP . reading from the left. The laureate head of Claudius to the right.

℞. DE . BRITANN . on the frieze across the front of a triumphal arch, having trophies of arms at each corner of the platform above the arch, and between which is an equestrian figure gradient gently to the left.

The present coin is a denarius, in very good preservation (weight 56¼ grains), from the cabinet of the Cavalier Campana, and possesses very great interest for the historian of Britain, from the circumstance of it having been struck to record the victories gained in this island under Aulus Plautius, who was the commander of the Roman forces in Britain at the early part of the reign of Claudius.

In the year of Rome 796, A.D. 43, Claudius went himself to Britain, leaving Vitellius, his colleague in the consulship, in charge of the city; he proceeded by the route of Ostia and Massilia (Marseilles), attended by a retinue of officers and soldiers. His resolution was tried by adverse winds, which twice drove him back, not without peril, from the shores of Gaul. When he at last landed, his course was directed partly along the military roads and partly by the convenient channels of the navigable rivers, until he reached the coasts of the British sea. At Gessoriacum (Boulogne) he embarked for the opposite shores of Cantium, and speedily reached the Roman legions in their encampment beyond the Thames. The soldiers, long held in the leash in expectation of his arrival, were eager to spring on the foe. With the emperor himself at their head, a spectacle not beheld since the days of Julius Cæsar, they traversed the level plains of the Trinobantes, which afforded no defensible position until the natives were compelled to stand at bay before the stockades which encircled their capital Camulodunum. But the fate of the capital was decided by the issue of the encounter which took place before it. The Trinobantes were routed; they surrendered their city, and with it their national freedom and independence. The victory was complete, the subjection of the enemy assured; within sixteen days from his landing in Britain, Claudius had broken a powerful kingdom, and accomplished a substantial conquest. He left it to Aulus Plautius to secure by the usual methods the fruits of this signal success, and returned himself immediately to Rome, from which he had not been absent more than six months altogether.

Claudius had gained a victory—his soldiers had hailed him repeatedly in the short space of sixteen days with the title of IMPERATOR. The high estimation in which the exploits of Claudius were held appears from the inscription (the deficiencies in which are imperfectly and conjecturally supplied) upon his arch of triumph:

> * TI . CLAVDIO . Drusi F. Cæsari *
> AVGVSTO . Germanico Pio
> PONTIFICI . Max. Trib. Pot. IX.
> COS . V . IMperatori XVI. Pat. Patriæ
> SENATVS . POpulusque Rom. quod
> REGES . BRITanniæ perduelles sine
> VLLA . IACTVra celeriter ceperit
> GENTESQ. extremarum Orcadum
> PRIMVS . INDICIO . facto R. imperio adjeeerit
> (Merivale, vol. vi. p. 26.)

In the volume of the second annual Congress of the British Archæological Association, p. 185, there is a paper on this inscription, by the Rev. Beale Poste, and the inscription is given in the volume in the following manner:

> TI . CLAVDIO . CAES.
> AVGVSTO
> PONTIFICI . M . TR . P . XI.
> COS . V . IMP . XXII . P . P.
> SENATVS . POPVLVS . Q . R . QVOD
> REGES . BRITANNIAE . ABSQ.
> VLLA . IACTVRA . DOMVERIT.
> GENTESQVE . EXTIMAS . ORBIS
> PRIMVS . INDICIONEM . SVBEGERIT.

My early and much respected friend Charles Roach Smith, in his excellent work Collectanea Antiqua, vol. v. 1858, gives a very interesting letter from Mr. Fairholt, then being at Rome, with remarks on the remaining antiquities in the city; and in reference to the stone with this inscription he says:

---

* The letters in capitals are still legible upon the arch, and those in small type are introduced to show what time and the elements have destroyed.

"In the wall of the court-yard of the Barberini Palace is inserted a slab with an inscription commemorating the conquest of Britain by Claudius in the following words :*

```
TI·CLAVDIO·CÆS
AVGVSTO
PONTIFICI·MAX·TR·P·IX
COS·V·IMP·XVI · P · P ·
SENATVSPOPVLQ·R·QVOD
REGES·BRITANNIÆ·ABSQ
VLLA·IACTVRA·DOMVERIT
GENTESQVEBARBARAS
PRIMVS·INDICIO·SVBGERIT
```

"It was found in A.D. 1461 near the Sciarra Palace, in the Corso, where the arch is supposed to have stood; the inscription is deeply cut in the marble for the reception of bronze letters, and the holes by which they were fastened can be detected in the hollows of each letter. Only one half of the inscription is ancient (the first half of each line throughout) and that is again cut horizontally through the inscription, so that it is really two long slabs conjoined. The remainder is a conjectural restoration formed in stucco. The whole is surrounded with a foliated border. The Rev. Beale Poste, in his Britannic Researches, has devoted several pages to a disquisition on this important inscription, and a consideration of the various comments upon, and new readings of, the missing half offered by various scholars. It is evident that much confusion might have been spared had a *drawing* of the stone been accessible; for it does not appear to have been clear to them all whether the first or the second half of the stone is original, or whether the original portion is not lost, and the whole re-cut; and the conclusion is arrived at '*that it seems to be impossible,*'—that it is (as it really is) a closely-packed square inscription. In Mr. Hogg's essay in The Transactions of the Royal Society of Literature, vol. iii. he has correctly described it; but some of the conjectural readings of the latter half, given by him and other writers, it will be seen, cannot be admissible; they are too verbose, and could not be comprised in the space allowable; they are also constructed with an idea that the lines are irregular in a great degree, which is also not the

---

* The woodcut, engraved by Mr. Fairholt from the stone itself, has been kindly lent me by Mr. Fairholt and Mr. Roach Smith.

case. The mark over the V̄ in line four has been omitted by all writers. This is not of much consequence; but the very important letter which commences the word BARBARAS, in the eighth line, cannot be certainly pronounced a B, and allows the new reading which Mr. Poste suggests (*vide* Mr. Beale Poste's inscription, p. 97.) But then it must be taken into consideration that Mr. Poste's ingenious restoration requires *eleven* letters to follow the doubtful one in the eighth line, while the restoration at Rome has only *seven*, which the space seems to warrant."

The width of the slab bearing this inscription is eighteen feet; and, examining the words in the copy given by Mr. Fairholt from the inscription itself as it now is, and the inscription from Merivale, and from Mr. Beale Poste's paper, the preference must be given to the words of Mr. Fairholt's; for in its words and their meaning the copy by Mr. Fairholt certainly shows the object of the inscription, and for which the arch was erected, with greater certainty and correctness of appropriation than can be traced through the words of either of the others. For what connective signification have the words *extimas orbis* or *extremarum Orcadum* with the exploits of Claudius in Britain, who was only here sixteen days, and advanced no further into the country than to Camulodunum; but examine the words in the inscription given by Mr. Fairholt, and the whole subject and object of the arch falls into its place at once in connected signification and appropriation.

But the most important event to Britain which occurred in the time of Claudius was the defeat and capture of the British prince and chieftain Caractacus, one of the sons of the great Cunobelin, who held Camulodunum against Claudius when he was in Britain.

In the year of Rome 800, Aulus Plautius was recalled from Britain to Rome to enjoy the rewards of his great services. Claudius himself had been saluted by the Senate with the title of BRITANNICVS on his return to Rome, although we have no numismatic record; it is, however, the name by which his only son is known among historians.

On the return of Aulus Plautius, Ostorius Scapula went to Britain and took the command of the legions. For nine years Caractacus, at the head of the independent Britons, had kept the invaders in check: the genius of this patriot chief, the first of our national heroes, may be estimated not from victories, of which the Romans have left us no account, but from the length of his gallant resistance, and the magnitude of the operations it was necessary to direct against him. Mr. Merivale, in his History, vol. vi. 21, gives a very long and interesting account of the struggle between Caractacus and Ostorius; and, as he appears to have personally viewed at some time the scenes of the last encounter of the Briton with the Roman, we must refer to his excellent work for the full details. In the end Caractacus, being defeated, fled for refuge to Cartismandua, the Queen of the Brigantes, who betrayed him to the Romans.

Caractacus, whose fame had preceded him, was sent to Rome with his wife and family, who were also prisoners. When there, they were brought before the Emperor on an appointed day, when Claudius appeared on a tribunal in all the pomp of Roman majesty, his wife Agrippina in grand apparel seated by his side, the eagles and ensigns of Rome placed about them with the train of officers, military and civil, thus to strike terror, as it were, into the British hero.

On this occasion Caractacus made to Claudius that memorable speech recorded by Tacitus, the concluding words of which are truly noble and dignified, and must have produced a considerable sensation amongst the audience, accustomed on such occasions to hear only the exclamations of abject grief, and must have inspired the emperor and all who heard him with a profound respect for so manly a chieftain. "I am now in your power,—if you are bent on vengeance, execute your purpose, the bloody scene will soon be over, and the name of Caractacus will sink into oblivion;—preserve my life, and I shall be to late posterity a monument of Roman clemency!" Claudius, struck with the conduct and bearing of Caractacus, granted life and liberty to him, and also to his wife, his daughter, and his brother. They were enrolled among the clients of the Claudian house, and indulgence may be challenged for the pleasing conjecture that "Claudia, the foreigner, the offspring of the painted Britons," whose charms and genius are celebrated by Martial, was actually the child of the hero Caractacus, named Claudia after admission to the Claudia gens.—Martialis, ii. 54; iv. 13. Tacitus places this event in the year of Rome 803, A.D. 50.

	A.D.		
Feb.	41	.	1
1st Jan.	42	.	2
„	43	.	3
„	44	.	4
„	45	.	5
„	46	.	6
„	47	.	7
„	48	.	8
„	49	.	9
„	50	.	10
„	51	.	11
„	52	.	12
„	53	.	13
diedOct	54	.	14

It will be observed that the tribunician date on this coin is $\overline{\text{VI}}$. Considering the cross line above the figures to designate I, this coin would then have been struck in the seventh year of Claudius and A.D. 47; it therefore cannot have reference to any other victories than those of Claudius and Aulus Plautius, or of Ostorius Scapula before the defeat and capture of Caractacus, and the continued success which accrued to the Roman arms up to that year 47; for, as we have seen, Caligula was killed in February A.D. 41. The first tribunician date would then begin to his successor and end 31 December in A.D. 41. The second, commencing on the first of

January 42, would also end 31 December 42, and so on regularly. This would place the mintage of the present coin in A.D. 47, supposing the cross line to represent 1, and 46 if it does not, the defeat of Caractacus being in A.D. 50, and it is not probable this coin would be struck before the arch was erected or until it had been erected.

This much is said regarding the defeat of Caractacus because the arch on this coin is generally supposed to have been erected to record that event, from which opinion I decidedly differ.

Argelati, *in Claudio*, places the triumph decreed to Claudius in A.D. 44, but gives no coin with the triumphal arch DE . BRITANNIS . until A.D. 46, which makes two years interval between the time of celebrating the triumph and the erection of the arch, and he places the victory gained by Ostorius over Caractacus in A.D. 50, which also agrees with Tacitus, lib. xii., whose date, " anno urbis conditæ 803,"agrees with A.D. 50. By these calculations the tribunician dates I have described come perfectly in order; but whether the tribunician date on this coin is really VI. or VII. is immaterial to my purpose, for it is perfectly evident that, the defeat of Caractacus being in A.D. 50, neither the arch or this coin have any reference to that event.

Ex Suetonio à Pitisco in Claudio c. XVII. in notis, par. 18 : " Senatus rebus gestis cognitis Britannicum illum nominaverunt, illi triumphum concesserunt, ludos annuos et arcum tropæa ferentem in urbe aliumque in Gallia (unde in Britanniam trajecerat) decreverunt." Plin. xxxiii. 3. "Claudius, cùm de Britannia triumpharet, inter coronas aureas, unam vii. pondo habuit quam contulerat Hispania citerior, alteram ix. quam Gallia comata, sicut titulus indicavit." "Templum in Britannia illi constitutum fuit." Seneca, Apocol. p. 852. This temple is also mentioned in Tacitus, Ann. xiv. 31-5 : " Ad hoc templum D. Claudio constitutum quasi arx æternæ dominationis adspiciebatur, delectique sacerdotes specie religionis omnes fortunas effundebant." Pitiscus also in his Lexicon, *verbo* Templum, mentions a temple erected and dedicated to Claudius at Camulodunum.

The first coin of Claudius mentioned by Occo with the arch DE · BRITAN. is an aureus, which he places A.D. 47. TR . P . VI., and he refers to another aureus A.D. 50 TR . P . IX. It is therefore evident from the various dates of these coins representing the arch that the type, being one of conquest, was a favourite type, and struck in different years of Claudius, commencing A.D. 44 up to A.D. 50, but could by no means allude to the victory over Caractacus, and could only refer to one triumph for Britain, which we have seen took place in A.D. 44, according to Argelati.

In the Numismatic Journal for 1836, vol. i. p. 272, it is mentioned that the silver coins of Claudius DE . BRITAN . bear the legend on the reverse TRIB . POT . IX . COS . V . IMP . XVI . thus making it appear that the triumph decreed by the Senate to Claudius was while the emperor held the tribunician power for the ninth time. In fact the writer says, "thus showing that the triumph decreed by the Senate to Claudius was while that emperor held the tribunician power for the ninth, and not the eleventh, time, as Mr. Hogg supposes." This extract is from the letter of my friend Mr. J. Y. Akerman, in discussing the paper on the Barberini inscription read by Mr. Hogg before the Royal Society. I need hardly say I consider my preceding remarks and dates clearly show both these gentlemen to be wrong in their attribution of the date of the triumph.

Tacitus, Ann. xiii. 32. 2, says, "Pomponia Græcina, insignis fœmina, Plautio, qui ovans se de Britanniis retulit, nupta:" and Suetonius, *in Claudio*, xxiv. 8, says, "Aulo Plautio etiam ovationem decrevit." Thus Claudius on his return from Britain was decreed a triumphal procession, and Aulus Plautius on his return to Rome had an ovation, a minor sort of triumph.

Since writing these notes, I have read a paper in the "Gentleman's Magazine" for October 1858, by Dr. Bell, on the Barberini inscription. I see no reason whatever in all that Dr. Bell states to make any alteration in what I have written. There is no record whatever of Claudius having extended the walls of Rome so as to entitle him to an arch, as insinuated in the first paragraph. There is no historic record whatever of Claudius having had two triumphs, as Dr. Bell asserts in his second and third paragraphs; and there is no historic record of the arches of Drusus, Titus, Trajan, Severus, Constantine, or any other such arch having been erected for any other purpose than to celebrate victories gained; even the arch of Nero was for *supposed literary victories*. I may boldly assert, for there is no evidence to the contrary, that there is no record of Claudius having celebrated two triumphs. I am still of opinion, after examining several versions of the inscription, that Mr. Fairholt's copy, as presented by my friend Roach Smith in his Collectanea Antiqua, vol. v. is correct, and is of that character as should, in the absence of any further and better proof, be considered as final and conclusive on the question of the wording and attribution of this Barberini inscription.

184.

TI . CLAVD . CAESAR . AVG . GERM . P . M . TRIB . POT . P . P. The laureate head of Claudius to the right.

℞. AGRIPPINAE . AVGVSTAE. The head of Agrippina junior to the right—the wife of Claudius her uncle, and thus became saluted with the title of AVGVSTA;

her head is encircled with a wreath, but whether ears of corn or thin narrow laurel leaves I am uncertain.

The TRIB . POT . having no date shews this coin was struck in A.D. 41, the first year of Claudius. It is an aureus, in fine condition.

RESTORED COINS.

185.

TI . CLAVDIVS . CAESAR . AVG . P . M . TR . P . IMP . P . P.   The laureate head of Claudius to the right.

℞. IMP . T . VESP . . . REST.   In the field S. C.   Hope gradient to the left in the manner already described, *ante*, No. 176.

A restored coin, minted by the emperor Titus; it is a rare coin. Weight 354¼ grains.

Titus and his father Vespasianus, both of whom subsequently became emperors, were, in the reign of Claudius, generals in command in Britain under Aulus Plautius. The Isle of Wight, then called Vectis, was taken possession of by Vespasian, who held a command in Britain at the time of the visit of Claudius.

186.

TI . CLAVDIVS . CAESAR . AVG . P . M . TR . P . IMP . P . P.   The unlaureate head of Claudius to the right.

℞. IMP . T . VESP . AVG . REST.   In the exergum S. C.   Ceres seated to the left, holding ears of corn in her right hand, a long lighted torch placed across her lap, and supported by her left hand.

A very fine Second Brass coin, having the silver eagle at the back of the head on the obverse, showing it has once been in the cabinet of the Duke of Modena.

AGRIPPINA JUNIOR.

JULIA AGRIPPINA, daughter of Agrippina senior and Germanicus, was born in a town on the Rhine, afterwards called Colonia Agrippinensis, now the city of Cologne, A.D. 16. She was married at thirteen years of age to Cnæus Domitius Ahenobarbus, a man of cruel and debauched character, who died A.D. 30, leaving one son by her, who became the emperor Nero. Her incestuous intercourse with her brother Caligula, and her promiscuous adulteries, were notorious; but her intimacy with Lepidus, the son of Julia the grand-daughter of Augustus, brought upon her the vengeance of Caligula, who put Lepidus to death and banished Agrippina.

Upon the accession of her uncle, Claudius, in A.D. 41, she was recalled, and married Crispus Passienus, an orator, whom she soon made away with, and possessed herself of his wealth.

After the death of Messalina, she contrived to inveigle the emperor Claudius into a marriage in A.D. 49, and, although he was her uncle as well as her husband, yet she caused him to be poisoned to make room for her son Nero, who then became emperor.

Continuing her career of ambition, crime, and profligacy, she at last became so tyrannical and overbearing with Nero, that he caused her to be put to death at Baiæ, A.D. 59.

There are no Latin coins in brass of Agrippina, beyond one in Large Brass mentioned by Mionnet, but it is unique. There are gold and silver coins of the Roman mint, but they are generally scarce in good preservation.

187.

ΑΓΡΙΠΠΙΝΑ ΣΕΒΑΣΤΗ, in the field γ. The head of Agrippina to the right, the front of her hair entwined with ivy-leaves, and the back hair fastened in a long knot drooped on to the shoulders, the bosom draped.

NEP.KΛAY.KAI.ΣEBAΣ. The laureate head of Nero to the right.

An Alexandrian Greek coin, in fine condition (weight 196¼ grains), from the cabinet of Mr. Borrell of Smyrna; it is struck in billon as a substitute for silver. It was usual to mark on the Alexandrian coins the year of their mintage; from the mark on the obverse being the third letter of the Greek alphabet, Γ, is signified that the present coin was struck in the third year of the reign of Nero, but it is not easy to say what year of our Lord is intended by the Ægyptian year, although by the Roman computation it would be A.D. 56, calculating by tribunician dates from the death of Claudius in October, A.D. 54.

The Roman new year commenced on the first day of January. The Ægyptian year had three commencements,—the agricultural commencement, the hierophant commencement, and the vulgar period. I suspect, from seeing the Greek letters in the field, that the chronologic calculation may have been from one of the Ægyptian commencements, and not from the Roman tribunician date.

NERO.

LUCIUS DOMITIUS, son of Cnæus Domitius Ahenobarbus and Agrippina junior, was born at Antium. He was adopted by Claudius, at the instigation of his mother, and declared Cæsar A.D. 50, upon which occasion he took the names of Tiberius Claudius Nero Drusus. In the year A.D. 53, he married Octavia, the daughter of Claudius and Messalina, whom he soon after repudiated and caused to be put to death, A D. 62. She was then only twenty years of age, and beautiful, virtuous, and accomplished. She was only between ten and eleven years old when married to Nero. In A.D. 63 Nero married Poppæa Sabina, whom he killed three years after by a kick with his foot; and in the same year, A.D. 66, he married Statilia Messalina, the daughter of Statilius Taurus, a man of consular dignity.

In the year A.D. 54 he had succeeded to the empire on the death of Claudius. His conduct at the first was good, and gave satisfaction, but he afterwards became so bad, and was guilty of such infamous practices and wholesale murders, that at last, in A.D. 68, the armies in Spain, under Galba, revolted and declared that general emperor. The news spread to Rome, and, being joyfully received by the citizens, Nero fled from the city, and took refuge in a house in the vicinity, belonging to Phaon, one of his freedmen, where he killed himself on learning the Senate had condemned him to be put to death *more majorum*, and had sent soldiers in search of him, and bring him to Rome for execution, but who arrived too late to prevent his death. The punishment of death *more majorum* was by stripping the culprit, and fixing his head in a fork, and beating him with sticks until he died.

The coins of Nero, with some exceptions, are generally very common, but when in fine condition they show some of the die-engraving of the period to have been equal to any part of the Imperial series.

There is a peculiarity with regard to the coins of Nero, viz., that, excepting in the cases after mentioned, there is no record on them of consular or tribunician date. To form the present coins into chronologic series, as nearly as possible approaching the time when the event recorded on the coin took place, has occasioned me great research among the numismatic and other antiquarian authorities, and it is possible even now there may be some variations in the exact year occasioned by the variations in the chronologic reckonings of different authors.

There is one great event in the History of Britain which took place in the time of Nero, A.D. 60, and of which it is very remarkable, and much to be regretted, there is no record on any of his coins hitherto discovered,—I allude to the rising of the Britons under their queen Boadicea, but who was ultimately defeated by Suetonius Paulinus, at Battle Bridge, near London (not far from the present Pentonville). By some persons this defeat is said to have been near Camalodunum; but the localities of Battle Bridge, its name even, and all the lands adjoining rising on a gentle slope, yet flat lands, leading to the foot of the hills of Hampstead and Highgate, show it to be a place so admirably adapted for a general engagement of armies, such as is described by Tacitus to have taken place, that there cannot be much doubt that the fields leading down to Battle Bridge was the spot where this fierce encounter took place, the plain formerly known as the Forty-acre Field being admirably suited for it.

This opinion and tradition is much strengthened, one may almost be justified in saying confirmed, by two or three circumstances. Up to the year 1811, there was existing from the Roman times of the occupation of Londinium a large square plot of ground, having on each of the four sides a moat; it used to be called "The Roman Camp," and seemed as if intended for a small station for convalescent soldiers of the garrison of London, it being about $2\frac{1}{4}$ miles from the city: it might have been a sort of watching-station or outpost. This plot of ground was on an elevated part of the Pentonville fields, commanding a view of the rise of the hills of Hampstead and Highgate on the north and west, on the south stretching down to Battle Bridge, and on the east having a view all across the fields of Canonbury almost into Essex. The spot is well described in Nelson's History of Islington, and is also set out in Hone's Every-day Book. It is near to Barnsbury Park, in the manor of Bernersbury; and is now (1858) all built over, and scarcely can be recognised and defined even by those well used in former days to visit the spot. In the field adjoining this moated square there was formerly a large mound of earth, a sort of barrow, which seemed as if it had been a place of sepulture; and in building over those parts I am told several Roman remains and some coins were found. I am therefore inclined to believe the battle which decided the fate of Britain at that period took place at the part I have mentioned. There was for a long time, adjoining the road leading from Battle Bridge up to Hampstead and Barnet, a long range, apparently earthworks of defence, and which road intersects the old Roman road to the North known as Maiden Lane, Battle Bridge, which had some military tradition of former days attached to them; but what seems to me a very decisive point on the question is, that in July 1842 a part of an inscribed stone was dug up at Battle Bridge, a description whereof was published in the Times newspaper, 30 July, 1842, and also more fully in the Gentleman's Magazine for August, 1842. The following account is what appeared in the Times newspaper:—

ANTIQUITIES DISCOVERED.

A Roman inscription has within these few days past been discovered at Battle-bridge, otherwise, by an absurd change of denomination, known as King's Cross, New Road, St. Pancras. This discovery appears fully to justify the conjectures of Stukeley and other antiquaries, that the great battle between the Britons under Boadicea and the Romans under Suetonius Pauliuus took place at this spot. Faithful tradition, in the absence of all decisive evidence, still pointed to the place by the appellation of Battle-bridge; the inscription, which in parts is much obliterated, bears distinctly the letters LEG . XX. The writer of this notice has not yet had an opportunity personally to examine it, but speaks from the information of an antiquarian friend. The 20th legion, it is well known, was one of the four which came into Britain in the reign of Claudius, and contributed to its subjugation. The vexillation of this legion was in the army of Suetonius Paulinus when he made that victorious stand in a fortified pass, with a forest in his rear, against the insurgent Britons. The position is sketched by Tacitus, and antiquaries well know that on the high ground above Battle-bridge there are vestiges of Roman works, and that the tract of land to the north was formerly a forest. The veracity of the following passage of Tacitus is therefore fully confirmed: "Diligitque locum artis faucibus et a tergo silva clausum satis cognito nihil hostium nisi in fronte et apertam planitiem esse sine metu insidiarum." He further tells us that the force of Suetonius was composed of "quartadecima legio cum vexillariis vicesimariis et è proximis auxiliares, decem ferme millia armatorum erant;" and he describes the order of battle of the Roman troops, "Igitur legionarius frequens ordinibus levi circum armatura conglobatus, pro cornibus eques astitit."

The arrangement of the Britons is thus described: "At Britannorum copiæ passim per catervas et turmas exsultabant, quanta non alias multitudo et animo adeo fero, ut conjuges quoque testes victoriæ secum traherent, plaustrisque imponerent, quæ super extremum ambitum campi posuerant. Boadicea curru filias præ se vehens ut quamque nationem accesserat;" and then Tacitus gives her address to her troops just before the engagement commenced. Tac. Annal. lib. xiv. 34, 35.

This is a very important historic relic of Roman record. I think there can be no doubt this fragment was part of a sepulchral monument to the memory of some officer or soldier of the 20th legion. It was found placed as a stepping-stone in front of the garden of one of the cottages on the eastern side of Maiden-lane, Battle-bridge.*

The Roman legions which were in Britain in A.D. 43, under the command of Aulus Plautius, were the second, ninth, fourteenth, and twentieth. Claudius did not take them back with him when he returned to Rome. They continued under Ostorius Scapula, and part of them were engaged in the combats with Caractacus. When Suetonius Paulinus took the command in Britain, the twentieth legion, with others, was still remaining in Britain, being quartered at Deva, now Chester. For very full and very interesting particulars of the rising and discomfiture of the Britons under their queen Boadicea I must again refer to Mr. Merivale's work, A.D. 61, A.U.C. 814.

We shall have to notice presently several coins with the legend VICTORIA or VICTORIA AVGVSTI; but beyond these words there is no note of what events they apply to, so that they may have been struck either upon the suppression of the insurrection in Britain, or they may refer to the successes of the Roman armies in the East, under the command of Domitius Corbulo.

188.

NERO . CLAVD . CAESAR . AVG . GER . P . M . TR . P . IMP . P . P. The laureate head of Nero to the left.

℞. ADLOCVT . COH. in the exergum, and S. C. on either side of the field. The emperor in his robes, with an attendant standing to the left on a low tribunal in front of a building supported by three columns, with a cupola or round dome above, his right hand raised in the attitude of addressing three military persons who stand before him bare-headed; two of them bear standards, they wear their military cloaks, and their swords are girt on their right side.

This seems to be the earliest type of Nero's reign, and may therefore be well placed in A.D. 54, as recording the Allocutio or address made by Nero to the Pretorian soldiers then at the Pretorian camp immediately on his accession; for upon the death of Claudius, Nero, accompanied by his friend Burrhus, who was commander of the Pretorian guards, proceeded to the Pretorian camp, and, after making a speech to the soldiers, and promising them a donation, he was received with great acclamations by them and saluted emperor.

We therefore see on this coin Nero and his friend Burrhus, the former addressing the soldiers at their camp; the whole band of soldiers is represented

---

* By the kindness of Messrs. Nichols I am able to give an engraving of the stone so discovered.

by the centurion, who stands foremost, and is followed by the two signiferi or standard-bearers.

The present coin is in excellent condition, and was found many years since in the excavation of some Roman remains at Bath.

It is a light brown or drab unpatinated coin. Weight 392⅜ grains.

189.

NERO . CLAVD . CAESAR . AVG . GER . P . M . TR . P . IMP . P . P. The laureate head of Nero to the left, a small globe at the point of the bust.

℞. ANNONA . AVGVSTI . CERES. In the exergum S. C. Ceres seated to the left, having in her left hand a lighted torch; her right hand is extended towards a decorated altar placed in front at her feet; her left foot rests on a low stool; on the altar is placed a small modius or corn measure. A female is standing in front of Ceres bearing a full cornucopiæ on her left arm; in the background is the stern of a merchant galley, signifying the corn represented by Ceres having been brought to Rome by sea.

Nero commenced his reign by many acts of liberality to the citizens, and distributing a great deal of corn and money amongst them, which at the time made him very popular. He granted privileges or bounties to those who built large ships for the transport of corn from the provinces, and he continued to keep up a good supply for the use of the city—from which circumstance the annona is a frequent type on his coins; but there is not one in any cabinet that bears a number to denote it as a first, second, or third annona. The coins of Nero are the first of the imperial series on which the annona is depicted.

The word annona is derived from the word annus, the year; it being customary to distribute annually a supply of corn to the humble classes of the citizens.

This coin I consider was struck A.D. 54, in the first year of Nero; it is in fine condition, with beautiful emerald green patina. Weight 387 grains.

190.

NERO CLAVDIVS . CAESAR . AVG . GERM . TR . P . IMP . P . P. The laureate head of Nero to the right.

℞. ANNONA . AVGVSTI . CERES. In the exergum S. C. Ceres seated to the left with a lighted torch on her left arm; the altar and modius before her. A female with a cornucopiæ is standing in front, and the stern of a galley appears in the background, in the way the same objects are represented on the preceding coin.

The modius held about a peck of our corn measure, and was the usual quantity distributed. Argelati describes a similar coin in Nero thus: "Fortunæ stantis et Cereris sedentis typus cum tæda et rostro navis."

I have observed that there are four varieties of legends on the obverse of the annona coins of Nero, and also different positions of the portrait. The annona type as represented on the coins of Nero was first used by him; it was adopted by subsequent emperors, but not in the full display that is represented on these coins, excepting by Domitian, whose die-engravers appear to have copied the type on the coins of Nero which we are describing.

This coin we also place in A.D. 54. Weight 410¾ grains.

191.

NERO . CLAVD . CAESAR . AVG . GER . P . M . TR . P . IMP . P . P . The youthful head of Nero to the left.

℞. ANNONA . AVGVSTI . CERES . in the exergum S. C. Ceres as before described seated to the left, female with cornucopiæ in front, part of a galley in the background. All the design exactly as on the preceding coins.

A very fine large brown coin almost medallion size of the earliest mintage, the portrait being of a very youthful appearance.

192.

NERO . CLAVDIVS . CAESAR . AVG . GERM . P . M . TR . P . IMP . P . P. The laureate head of Nero to the right.

℞. ADLOCVT . COH . in the exergum. No S. C. Nero and his friend Burrhus standing to the left on a slightly raised base; Nero holds up his right hand towards three standard bearers who are in front of him, each of them carrying a standard, his sword at his right side, and wearing his military cloak. Nero's left hand is placed in his girdle.

This is a specimen of an early medallion, the size at a later period being much extended and increased in weight. The figure of Nero on the reverse is easily recognized, although the portrait is very minute. It is a first-rate coin—black in colour.

193.

NERO . CLAVD . CAESAR . AVG . GER . P . M . TR . P . IMP . P . P . The laureate head of Nero to the left, a small globe at the point of the bust.

℞. CONG ... DAT ... OP. In the exergum S. C. The emperor or his depute seated to the right on a curule chair placed on a high tribunal; beside him on the left hand is a statue of Minerva with an owl in her right hand, a spear in the left; a little in front of Nero another person is sitting in the act of writing at a small table placed at his left side, while a third person is ascending the steps of the tribunal to receive the donation, and behind him is another person. At the left side of the person who is sitting in front, a female figure is standing holding up a tablet in her right hand, her left hand extended as if inviting persons to approach.

The *congiarium* was a distribution to the citizens of wine and oil, which were measured out in a congius, a measure containing seven pints. The *annona* was a distribution of dry substances, as wheat, barley, beans, &c., distinguished from the *congiarium*, which was of liquids.

The type of congiarium ii. is very different in its arrangement, which makes me consider this as a representation of congiarium i.

Green. Weight 386¼ grains.

194.

IMP . NERO . CAESAR . AVG . PONT . MAX . TR . POT . P . P . The laureate head of Nero to the right, a small globe at the point of the bust in front.

℞. CONGI . . . DAT . POP. In the exergum S. C. The emperor or his depute and the attendant scribe with other persons sitting and standing in the same way as represented on the reverse of the preceding coin.

These two coins represent the distribution made to the citizens by Nero on his accession in the year A.D. 54, and they were coined after that congiary had been distributed. Argelati, *in Nerone*, also describes similar coins, and places them in A.D. 54. There is a variation between these two coins, but it is evident they are intended for the same congiary.

Brown. Weight 377¾ grains.

195.

NERO . CLAVD . CAESAR . AVG . GER . P . M . TR . P . IMP . P . P. The laureate of Nero to the right.

℞. ROMA . in the exergum. S. C. in the field. Roma as an armed female wearing her helmet seated to the left on a cuirass. Three shields are piled up behind her; a helmet on the ground supports her right foot; her right hand extended bears a small image of Victory, which presents a wreath to her. Her left hand grasps the hilt of her sword. She does not wear any military cloak, but the upper part of her dress is drawn over her shoulders to the left so as to expose her right shoulder and breast.

Roma is a very frequent type on the imperial coins, and when represented, as on the present coin, with a Victoriola or small figure of Victory in her hand, she is called Roma Victrix; sometimes she is standing, but never unarmed. Her clothes are generally full, but short to the knees, as on this and the two next coins; at other times the clothes extend to the ankles, but she never wears long clothes when standing up. Long *braccæ* or trousers were peculiar to the oriental or barbarian countries, as the Romans called all other nations and peoples. The personifications of countries on the subsequent coins of Trajan and Hadrian show the trousers or *braccæ* of the Dacians and other people.

Mr. Noel Humphreys has been guilty of a gross error regarding Roma, as we shall see in another place. The representation of Roma on these coins all differ, which accounts for my having so many.

A very fine black coin from the cabinet of Mr. Percival. Weight 417½ grains.

196.

NERO . CLAVD . CAESAR . AVG . GERM . PM . TR . P . IMP . P . P. The laureate head of Nero to the right.

℞. ROMA . in the exergum. S. C. in the field. Roma seated on a cuirass to the left, with shields behind, as described on the preceding coin. Her right hand extended holds a Victoriola, her left hand grasps the hilt of her sword. Weight 428½ grains.

197.

NERO . CLAVD . CAESAR . AVG . GER . PM . TR . P . IMP . P . P. The laureate head of Nero to the right.

℞. ROMA . in the exergum. S. C. in the field. Roma seated to the left on a cuirass with shields behind her; she wears a cuirass that has no lappets on the lower part, but instead of them she has a short petticoat extending to the knees. Her right hand supports a Victoriola presenting a wreath, her left hand holds a spear upright, and her shield is at her left side.

Weight 399 grains.

198.

IMP . NERO . CLAVD . CAESAR . AVG . GERM . P . M . TR . POT . P . P. The laureate head of Nero to the right.

℞. ROMA in the exergum. S. C. in the field. Roma seated to the left on a cuirass and other arms; at her left side is her shield, and she rests her left arm on the upper edge of it, the lower edge being placed on a helmet lying on the ground; her spear is held upright in her right hand, her right shoulder and breast are uncovered, and her clothes are folded over down to her ankles.

199.

IMP . NERO . CLAVD . CAESAR . AVG . GER . P . M . TR . P . P. P.   The head of Nero to the right with radiate crown.

℞. ROMA . in the exergum. S. C. in the field. Roma seated to the left on a cuirass and arms; her right hand extended presents a wreath, her left hand grasps the hilt of her sword; her right shoulder and breast are quite uncovered, and her clothes reach to the ankles.

A fine Second Brass brown coin formerly in the cabinet of the Rev. E. C. Brice. Weight 235½ grains.

200.

NERO . CLAVD . CAESAR . AVG . GER . P . M . TR . P . IMP . P . P.   The laureate head of Nero to the left, a small globe at the point of the bust.

℞. ROMA . in the exergum. S. C. in the field. Roma seated to the left on a cuirass, having some shields piled behind her, and a spear upright projects from amongst the shields; her right hand extended holds a Victoriola presenting a wreath, with her left hand she grasps the hilt of her sword, her right foot rests on a helmet lying on the ground; her clothes reach only to the knees.

A brown coin in very good condition from the cabinet of Sir George Musgrave.

201.

NERO . CLAVD . CAESAR . AVG . GER . P . M . TR . P . IMP . P . P.   The laureate head of Nero to the right.

℞. ROMA . in the exergum. S. C. in the field. Roma seated to the left on a cuirass with shields around her, as described on the preceding coin, and in addition to the spear amongst the arms are a bow and quiver of arrows.

This and the preceding type of Roma on the coins of Nero are the rarest of all the Roma types. The rarest of the coins of Nero are those with the tribunician date.

A bronze coin in very good condition from the cabinet of Mr. Gwilt.

202.

NERO . CLAVD . CAESAR . AVG . GER . P . M . TR . P . IMP . P . P.   The head of Nero to the right, unlaureate, a small globe at the point of the bust.

℞. GENIO . AVGVSTI. In the field S. C. A semi-nude virile figure standing, full front, looking to the left, having a cornucopiæ on the left arm, the right hand extended, holding a patera in the act of pouring on to a fire burning on an altar at the right side.

According to the religious opinions of the ancients, the genii were attendants upon the human race, and to every person a good genius was attached from his birth. They also considered a similar tutelage was extended to countries and cities. The belief that a spiritual and celestial guardianship is by divine mercy exercised over mortals is a truth of most ancient date, beyond either Judaism or Christianity. Archbishop Tillotson remarks, "This doctrine [the guardianship] of angels is not a peculiar doctrine of the Jewish or Christian religion, but the general doctrine of all religions that ever were, and therefore cannot be objected against by any but Atheists." In the book of the Acts of the Apostles, ch. xii. the Apostle Peter when in prison was roused from his sleep by an angel, who struck him on the side to awaken him, and said, "Arise up quickly, gird thyself, and bind on thy sandals, cast thy garment about thee and follow me." Peter was at the time bound by chains to two Roman soldiers, his chains fell from him, and the angel and Peter left the prison together. When the angel had conducted him into a street where he had friends he left him. Peter then went to his friends' house and knocked for admittance. The servant girl came to the gate, and seeing who knocked she ran back into the house overcome with joy, and told the folks inside, but they would not believe her, but they said, "It is his angel." Peter, however, continued knocking at the gate, and at last got into the house. There are several other accounts in the same book of angels appearing to and conversing with Christian men as well as others. In the book of the Revelation of St. John mention is made of the seven angels belonging to the seven churches of Asia, all of which are named, and an admonition is delivered to each of them in succession; thus shewing that each of the churches, that is to say, each of the community of Christians in those respective districts distinguished by the title of churches, was in charge of an angel. In the earliest literature of classical antiquity we find this belief. Hesiod speaks of angels—

> By great Jove design'd
> To be on earth the guardians of mankind.

And both Homer and Virgil in their works furnish instances of apparitions, warnings, and predictions of spirits to mortals. The Romans swore by their genius or good spirit. The Roman women also swore by their genii, called Junones. Both Greeks and Romans had their Lares and Lemures; the Lemures being their evil spirits—the Lares being good spirits, who were believed to exercise a special guardianship over families. At the feet of the image of the *Lar*, or guardian spirit, it was usual to place the figure of a dog barking, denoting vigilance. Plautus represents a Lar thus speaking—

> I am the family Lar
> Of this house whence you see me coming out.
> 'Tis many years now that I keep and guard
> This family; both father and grandsire
> Of him that has it now I have protected.

The statues of the Lares, resembling monkeys, and covered with the skin of a dog, were placed in a niche behind the door of the house or around the family hearth. Incense was burned on their altars, and a sow was offered in sacrifice on particular days. Their festival was observed at Rome in the month of May, when the statues were crowned with flowers and offerings of fruit were made.

The *Lares Publici* were the guardians of the city, and had a temple at the upper end of the *Via Sacra*. This temple, *Ædes Larum*, contained two images, probably those of Romulus and Remus, as the public guardians of the city.

The Koran assigns two angels to every man—one to record his good, the other his evil actions; they are so merciful, that if an evil action has been done it is not recorded until the man has slept, and if in that interval he repents they place on the record that God has pardoned him. Shakspere introduces a spirit, which is, I think, wrongly called the spiritual appearance of Julius Cæsar, to Brutus before the battle of Philippi, whilst he is in his tent—for why should Cæsar visit his murderer, and call himself his murderer's evil genius or spirit?

> How ill this taper burns——Ha! who comes here?
> I think it is the weakness of mine eyes
> That shapes this monstrous apparition——
> It comes upon me——Art thou anything?
> Art thou some God—some angel—or some devil—
> That mak'st my blood cold and my hair to stare?——
> Speak to me——What thou art.——
>   Thy evil spirit, Brutus.
> Why com'st thou?——
>   To tell thee thou shalt see me at Philippi.
> Then, I shall see thee again——
>   Ay, at Philippi.   JULIUS CÆSAR, Act iv.

A passage in Apuleius, with respect to the dæmon or angel of Socrates, explains this whole mythology; he says—"The Genius is the soul of man, disengaged and set at liberty from the bonds whereby it is united to the body. I find in the ancient Latin language it was named at that time *Lemur*. Of these Lemures, they whose province it is to take care of those who inhabit the houses where they themselves had dwelt, who are gentle and peaceful, are called Familiar Lares. Those, on the contrary, who for the punishment of their bad lives have no fixed residence, but are condemned to wander up and down, raising panic terrors in the good, whom they seek to disturb, and inflicting real evils upon the wicked, are named *Larvæ*, and both one and the other, whether *Lares* or *Larvæ*, go under the name of DII MANES, and the designation of gods is added to them by way of honour—Honoris gratia Dei vocabulum additum est."

In Antoninus we shall see a coin describing Antoninus as the Genius of the Senate—a compliment to him as the principal personage presiding over or giving life to their deliberations. Another coin, also of Antoninus, is the *Genius Populi Romani*. This last reverse was the common reverse in the latter period of the empire. Sometimes it was varied in legend by being *Genio* IMPERATORIS, as we shall see amongst the later emperors.

203.

NERO . CLAVD . CAESAR . AVG . GERM . P . M . TR . P . IMP . P . The head of Nero to the right, with radiate crown.

℞. SECVRITAS . AVGVSTI. In the field S. C. A female seated to the right, in an easy reclining attitude; her head, thrown back, rests on her right hand, her right arm being supported by the back of her throne; her left hand holds a *hasta pura* upright; in front at her left side is a decorated square altar, on which a fire is burning; at her feet is a lighted torch, placed obliquely, as if fixed to the side of the altar. In the exergum is the mark $\overline{\text{II}}$.

A coin obtained from the Thames. Water golden.

204.

IMP . NERO . CAESAR . AVG . P . MAX . TR . P . P . P . The laureate head of Nero to the left.

℞. SECVRITAS . AVGVSTI. In the field S. C. No mark in the exergum. A female seated on a throne to the right, in a reclining attitude, as on the preceding coin, with altar and torch in front.

These two coins are in Second Brass. I do not find that this type was struck in the time of Nero after the year A.D. 55. Nero commenced his reign with acts of clemency, moderation, and liberality which might well entitle the Senate to strike coins of this type, to signify the security likely to be enjoyed under a prince whose career commenced so auspiciously for the welfare of the Roman people, and in return the good feeling on the part of the people towards Nero would reciprocate a security to him, as the head of the government.

Green, in fine condition, from Mr. G. Gwilt's cabinet.

205.

IMP . NERO . CAESAR . AVGVSTVS. The laureate head of Nero to the right.

. IVPPITER . CVSTOS. Jupiter seated to the left, having the *hasta pura* in his left hand, the right holding a *fulmen* resting on his lap.

The present coin is an aureus, in good condition, from the Gwilt collection.

206.

NERO . CLAVD . CAESAR . AVG . GER . P . M . TR . P . IMP . P . P. The laureate head of Nero to the right.

℞. AVGVSTI . inscribed on the upper verge. S . POR . OST . C . on the lower verge of the coin. Pale brown. Weight 390½ grains.

The port of Ostia, represented on this coin, was situated at the mouth of the river Tiber. The entrance of the port is indicated by a statue raised on a square base under the word AVGVSTI; the right hand of the figure is extended, the left holds a long staff. This statue is said to have served as a mark by day and a pharos by night, a light being placed in the right hand to guide vessels entering the port after dark. The outer sides of the field, which at one time were supposed to represent granaries and warehouses for the storing of corn and merchandize, from more recent explorations are now ascertained to have been archways for the currents of water flowing to and fro from the Mediterranean Sea, and also temples.

The whole of the inner part of the field within the lines of the arches and other buildings represents the basin of the port occupied by shipping, consisting of four sailing galleys, and three rowing galleys. On the lower verge of the field is a recumbent figure of Neptune to the left; his right hand rests on the broad part of a rudder, a dolphin is on his left arm, and under him are the words s . POR . OST . C . as already mentioned.

The construction of the port of Ostia recorded on this coin was commenced by Ancus Marcius, the fourth King of Rome, in the year of Rome 127. He reigned 24 years, and during the last ten or twelve years of that period he was much engaged in public works for the benefit of the city; and Ostia was raised to a place of importance and became the port of Rome. When the Romans afterwards began to have ships of war, Ostia became a place of greater importance, and a fleet was constantly stationed there to guard the mouth of the Tiber. According to Plutarch, Julius Cæsar was the first who turned his attention to the construction of a port at Ostia by raising there a mole and other works; but it was to the emperor Claudius that this harbour was indebted for all the magnificence ascribed to it by the ancients: for Claudius repaired the dilapidations of the works erected by Ancus Marcius, and completed the port in the state it appears on the coins. A period of 669 years had elapsed from the death of Ancus Marcius, in the year of Rome 138, to the year A.D. 54, when this coin was struck.

There were no coins of Claudius (so far as is now known) recording this port in any way; it was therefore decreed by the Senate to record the completion of the port by striking this coin, and to compliment Nero on the politic measures he had taken to ensure regular supplies of corn to the city, and by his encouraging by bounties the building of large vessels for the conveyance of corn from foreign countries.

The town of Ostia itself was but a small place at the mouth of the Tiber, and built by Ancus Marcius coincident with the port. Being about 18 miles from Rome, it was much frequented by the citizens in the summer season as a watering place. Ostia is still remaining, and keeps its name, although no longer what it was when this coin was struck. The salt marshes formed by Ancus Marcius at the first foundation of Ostia also still subsist near the site now called Casone del Sale.

The importance of the town and port of Ostia, and which has been so imperfectly and unsatisfactorily explained upon an historical and proper basis by numismatic writers, must apologise for our making a lengthened notice of it, and also excuse a little seeming tautology in the following abstract of a very long and highly interesting memoir by Mons. Charles Texier, published in the Revue de l'Architecture et des Travaux Publics of 1857, vol. 15. Mons. Texier (as a skilful engineer) was commissioned by the French minister of the Interior to survey and examine (*inter alia*) this ancient port of Ostia; and from his memoir I derive the following account of this port and the additional works of the emperor Trajan, together with a plan of the remains as they now exist, and also a copy of a plan taken about 300 years ago, for both of which I am indebted to my kind friend Professor Donaldson.

"Rome had by the middle of the reign of Ancus Marcius, by an uninterrupted succession of victories, made herself mistress of the whole of the country extending along the banks of the Tiber from its source to its mouth; but, as the country did not produce an adequate supply of food for the greatly increased population, recourse was had to the products of foreign countries, and, the cultivated lands offering no reasonable proportion to the number of mouths requiring food, the people looked for assistance from the foresight of their kings. Ancus Marcius clearly saw the advantages of commerce, and his efforts in endeavouring to establish a communication by sea with other countries are thus described by Dionysius of Halicarnassus, book iii. c. 45.

"After speaking of the inclosure of Mount Aventine, he says, 'The other [public work] was of still greater consequence, as it increased the happiness of the city by supplying it with all the conveniences of life, and encouraged its inhabitants to undertake greater things. For the river Tiber, falling from the Apennine hills and running close by Rome, discharges itself into the Tyrrhene Sea, whose shore lies exposed to the weather without havens, and this river is of small or inconsiderable advantage to Rome by not having at its mouth any strong place to receive the commodities brought thither either by sea or by the river from the country and to exchange them with the merchants; but, as it is navigable quite up to its source for large boats, and even to Rome for trading ships of great burden, he resolved to build a sea-port at the entrance of it, and to make use of the mouth of the river itself for a haven; since the Tiber is very large where it falls into the sea and forms great bays equal to those of the best sea-ports. But the most wonderful thing is, that its mouth is not stopped up with sandbanks accumulated by the sea, which is an inconvenience that happens even to many great rivers, neither does it, by wandering through fens and marshes, spend itself in different places before its stream mixes with the sea, but is every where navigable, and discharges itself at one mouth; and, notwithstanding the violence of the west wind, to which that coast is much exposed, repels the surge that comes from the main. Ships therefore with oars, how great soever, and merchant ships of the burden of 3,000 bushels [75 tons], enter at the mouth of the river and are rowed and towed up to Rome. Those of a larger size ride at anchor at the mouth, where they are unladed and laded by lighters. Upon the elbow of land which lies between the river and the sea the king built a city, and encompassed it with a wall, which city, from its situation, he called Ostia; as we should call it θυρα, a door; and by this means he made Rome not only an inland town, but also a sea-port, and gave it a taste of those advantages that flow from a maritime commerce.' (Spelman's translation.)

"This description by Dionysius of Halicarnassus had evidently been made after a minute inspection of the places; the city of Ostia, although at the present time more than three miles distant from the sea, is to be found exactly in the situation indicated by the historian. The salt pans founded by Ancus Marcius (Tit. Liv. lib. i. c. 33) alone appear not to have changed their place; they were at first supplied from the sea, but, the sand accumulating around them, they have formed a lake (Lacus Ostiensis) which exists at this day.

"In the time of Julius Cæsar, the sea, by the accumulation of sand and otherwise, had very much withdrawn from the port. To remedy this state of things, he proposed to construct another port at the entrance of the river, but he afterwards abandoned the idea, being alarmed at the difficulties which presented themselves.

"The emperor Claudius took up the project which had been abandoned by Julius Cæsar, but, declining to restore the ancient port situate on the Tiber, he selected a place in firm ground for the purpose of excavating a basin; his work is thus described by Suetonius, *in Claudio*, xx.: 'Portum Ostiæ exstruxit circumducto dextrâ sinistrâque brachio, et ad introitum profundo jam solo mole objectâ. Quam quo stabilius fundaret navem ante demersit qua magnus obeliscus ex Ægypto fuerat advectus, congestisque pilis superposuit altissimam turrim in exemplum Alexandrini Phari, ut ad nocturnos ignes cursum navigia dirigerent.'

"Claudius took great pains to superintend the works himself; he often took up his abode at Ostia. Tacitus and Scutonius mention his frequent visits, and some fine ruins, as of a palace, have of late been discovered.

"Under the dictatorship of Julius Cæsar, the vessels which brought grain from Sicily were obliged to remain for a long time outside at the entrance of the Tiber until a dearth began to be felt at Rome. The import had sensibly diminished year by year throughout Italy, whence those frequent famines which desolated the city urged Claudius to undertake the immense works for the construction of the Port of Claudius.

"Strabo, who lived in the time of the emperor Tiberius, saw in the ancient port of Ostia the only emporium of Rome (Strabo, lib. v. 375). In his time it was choked up with the sand, mud, and rubbish brought down by the Tiber; the ships which brought provisions to Rome were obliged to lay outside at the mouth of the port, exposed to all dangers; this inconvenience in landing cargo was remedied by the employment of a multitude of barges or barques, which received the cargoes of vessels and returned to the Tiber, and thence on to Rome, a distance of about 16 miles.

"In reality, the name of the *port of Ostia* should only be applied to that which was founded on the banks of the river Tiber, near to the ancient city of Ostia; but the importance of the works established by Claudius, soon effaced the name of the original port, and transferred it to that of Claudius. The greater part of the commercial population installed themselves near to the new port, which at first was only a naval arsenal; but in the end, a city having sprung up in its vicinity, it absorbed the name of the ancient Ostia. At first is was known as the Portus Claudii, and the city was named Urbs Portuensis; some authors spoke of it under the name of Portus Ostiensis.

"The public acts transmitted to us by inscriptions give it the name of Portus Ostiæ; it seems that it received this last denomination rather from its situation at the mouth of the Tiber, than at the ancient city of Ostia.

"A little way above the ancient Ostia, the Tiber divides itself into two branches of unequal size; that on the right hand flows beneath the walls of the city, forming several sinuosities, and falls into the sea at four miles below the ancient Ostia. The other branch, which detaches itself from the principal course of the river, takes its course to the left almost in a straight line, and after a course of about five miles falls into the sea at about four miles to the north of the main entrance of the river; the branches thus form between them a triangular island usually called Insula Sacra.

"For a long time it was the opinion of antiquaries that the branches of the Tiber were of natural formation; but the Abbé Fea, in 1824, broached the theory that they were the work of Trajan. From a sentence in Pliny, it was conjectured that the direct communication between the Port of Claudius and the Tiber was the work of Trajan; but in the year 1836, an inscription was found at Ostia, an inscription on a marble tablet, pointing out the construction of the naval arsenal and the junction of the port and the river as the work of the emperor Claudius. The following is a copy of the inscription which was so discovered:

TI . CLAVDIVS . DRVSI . F . CAESAR.
AVG . GERMANICVS . PONTIF . MAX.
TRIB . POTEST . VI . COS . DESIG . IIII . IMP . XII . P . P.
FOSSIS . DVCTIS . A . TIBERI . OPERIS . PORTVS.
CAVSSA . EMISSISQVE . IN . MARE . VRBEM.
INVNDATIONIS . PERICVLO . LIBERAVIT.

"The hexagonal port of Trajan adjoins the port of Claudius, and was constructed so as to enjoy the benefits of this communication. This basin still exists in a perfect state; it is called Lago Trajano or Trajanello; it is surrounded by many ruins of warehouses and factories. In commemoration of the founding of the port by Trajan, a medal was struck, bearing on one side the portrait of Trajan, and on the reverse a representation of the hexagonal port.

"Juvenal, XII. Sat. v. 75, mentions the erection of the port of Trajan,—'Quia Trajanus portum Augusti restauravit in melius et interius tutiorem sui nominis fecit.' Pliny the younger mentions it in the same manner in his Panegyric."

Thus far I have taken from M. Texier's memoir.

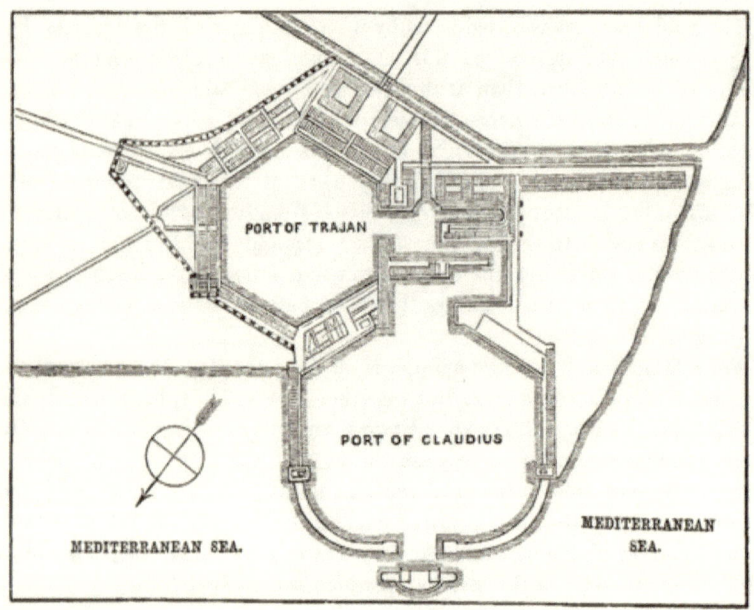

Sir John Rennie, President of the Institution of Civil Engineers, in his remarks on the port of Ostia, published in 1845, says:

"Taking into consideration all the various circumstances, the port of Ostia appears to have been one of the most complete of ancient times, and was considered by the Romans themselves as one of their greatest works. In these works may be discovered considerable novelty and ingenuity both in design and construction, the whole being artificial and attended with considerable natural difficulties; indeed, it should be observed that almost every principle adopted by the improved science and superior skill of modern times appears to have been carried into effect here with singular perseverance and ability."

The two coins of Nero and Trajan have hitherto been very unsatisfactorily explained; they have been regarded as referring to separate places, far distant from each other; whereas, now I think it is by this note clearly and satisfactorily shown that the two coins, PORT . OSTIA of Nero, and PORTUM . TRAJANI, or PORT . OST. of Trajan, should be read together. The two coins will show it quite plainly; and if they are put together, that is to say, the port of Ostia brought in front of the port of Trajan, a representation of the plan is produced, to which there is only one exception (but that does not alter my proposition)—the modern plan of Mons. Texier puts the port of Trajan a little on one side, although the water of the port of Claudius flows into it; whereas the old one makes the two ports conjoined, and the water flows in without any bend. I hope, therefore, in future, antiquaries who meet with this note will read the two coins as conjoined historically.

207.

NERO . CLAVD . CAESAR . AVG . GER . P . M . TR . P . IMP . P . P. The laureate head of Nero to the right.

℞. AVGVSTI . S . POR . OST . C. Placed in the same manner as on the preceding coin. The statue on its base at the entrance of the port—Neptune, with rudder and dolphin at the bottom; in the waters seven galleys appear, four of them being sailing galleys, the others row galleys; but of the large sailing galleys, three of them are at anchor with the sails furled, by which the varieties in their build are discernible; ranges of storehouses appear on one side, and on the other the arches to admit the flux and reflux of the waters; Neptune at the bottom is crowned with a wreath, possibly of sea-weed, and water is undulating beneath him.

Black brown, from Mr. Gwilt's collection.

208.

No legend visible. The heads of Ancus Marcius and Numa in profile, joined.

℞. CENS. In the exergum ROMA. Two arches: under the one on the right is a statue standing on a cippus; under the arch to the left is the prow of a galley, as if coming through the arch out into a river or dock basin.

This appears intended to represent two of the arches at the side of the Port of Claudius, which formed the *brachia* spoken of by Suetonius, and at times it is not impossible that the waters permitted small galleys to pass under the side arches instead of going out of port at the entrance, by the breakwater.

A black coin from the cabinet of General Ramsay.

209.

NERO . CLAVDIVS . CAESAR . AVG . GERM . P . M . TR . P . IMP . P. P. The laureate head of Nero to the right.

℞. CONG . II . DAT . POP. In the exergum S. C. The emperor or his depute seated to the left on a curule chair, placed on a suggestum. A person stands on his right hand, appearing to converse with him; beyond, on the right, is a statue of Minerva, with a spear in the left hand, a scroll in the right; behind the statue appears the entrance to some building. On the ground in front of the suggestum, a person stands holding up a tablet to another person, who is standing before him with his robe extended, as if to receive a donation.

The second congiary was given to the citizens of Rome A.D. 57, which may therefore be taken as the date when this coin was struck.

A very good brown coin. Weight 424¼ grains.

210.

NERO . CLAVD . CAESAR . AVG . GER . P . M . TR . P . . . . . . The laureate head of Nero to the right.

℞. PACE . P . R . TERRA . MARIQ . PARTA . IANVM . CLVSIT. In the field S. C. The temple of Janus right side, showing the front of the door, which is closed, and a garland is suspended across the upper part of the building, crossing the top of the door, which is arched; the side of the building shows the openings intended for the admission of light, above which are the scroll decorations.

This and the two following coins were struck on occasion of the victories gained by the Roman armies under Domitius Corbulo, an eminent general commanding the armies in Belgium, and afterwards in Armenia. For the former of these Nero was saluted Imperator, and upon the final overthrow of Tiridates, king of Armenia, and the destruction of Artaxata, Nero shut up the temple of Janus, in A.D. 58, after it had been open for a period of nearly 84 years.

This coin, on the reverse, is in very fine preservation, and in decorations and style of building is a complete copy of the beautiful coin No. 50, in Admiral Smyth's cabinet. The two reverses compared are scarcely to be distinguished for excellence. The obverse has been a little worn, but not injured; it was formerly in the cabinet of Mr. Neve.

211.

IMP . NERO . CAESAR . AVG . GERMANIC. The laureate head of Nero to the right.

℞. PACE . P . R . VBIQ . PARTA . IANVM . CLVSIT. S. C. in the field. The temple of Janus left side; a garland above the doors, and also on the side of the building.

A Second Brass black coin, very good, although rather small.

212.

NERO . CLAVDIVS . CAESAR . AVG . GER . P . M . TR . P . IMP . P . P. The laureate head of Nero to the left.

℞. PACE . P . R . TERRA . MARIQ . PARTA . IANVM . CLVSIT. On either side of the field S. C. The temple of Janus on the right side, showing the front and side of the building rather different to the preceding coin. A garland is suspended across the doors, which open in the middle in two halves, in which are fixed two large ring-handles or knockers; the upper part and side are quite plain, without any sort of ornament.

Black, very fine. Weight 434 grains.

213.

NERO . CLAVDIVS . CAESAR . AVG . GER . P . M . TR . P . IMP . P . P. The laureate head of Nero to the right.

℞. PACE . P . R . TERRA . MARIQ . PARTA . IANVM . CLVSIT. S. C. on either side of the field.

The temple of Janus on the left side, with all its parts, decorations, and wreath suspended across the door in front, are all perfectly set out.

Auricalchum. Weight $405\frac{1}{4}$ grains.

These coins, being in very perfect condition, give such correct representations of the front and both sides of the temple in all its detail and ornament, that complete architectural drawings might easily be made from them.

There were two sorts of temples at Rome erected to Janus—one to Janus Bifrons, and one to Janus Quadrifrons. The latter temples were built with four different sides, each having a door and three windows. The four doors represented the four seasons, and the twelve windows represented the twelve months of the year. The temple on these coins is the temple of Janus Quadrifrons.

Janus was said to have been the most ancient king who reigned in Italy. After his death he was deified; subsequently, he was worshipped at Rome under different names, as Quirinus, Martialis, Patuleius, and Clausius, because he was supposed to preside over peace and war; whence, in time of peace, his temple gates were shut, and he was Clausius—in time of war they were kept open, and he was called Patuleius.

From the reign of Numa Pompilius, the second king of Rome, to the time the present coins were struck, a period of 761 years, the temple of Janus had been shut only five times. The first in the time of Ancus Martius; the second in the year of Rome 523; the third in the year of Rome 725; the fourth in the year of Rome 729; and the fifth, as here recorded, in the year of Rome 811, and A.D. 58.

The temple of Janus represented on these coins is considered to be the one which stood in the Forum; it was originally built by Romulus and Tatius, and was distinguished by the above-mentioned title of Quirinus; and Suetonius, *in Augusto*, sec. 22, states it to be the temple which was closed after the battle of Actium, calling it Janum Quirinum.

214.

NERO . CAESAR . AVGVSTVS. The laureate head of Nero to the right.

℞. PACE . P . R . TERRA . MARIQ . PARTA . IANVM . CLVSIT. A representation of the gates or doors in front of the temple of Janus. There are no decorations whatever. There is an astragal from top to bottom, and three bars across the whole width of the doors.

An aureus.

215.

NERO . CLAVDIVS . CAESAR . AVG . GER . P . M . TR . P . IMP . P . P. The head of Nero to the right, with radiate crown.

℞. VICTORIA . AVGVSTI. In the field S. C. A Victory volant to the right, with a palm branch in her left hand, a wreath in the right.

Weight 254½ grains.

216.

IMP . NERO . CAESAR . AVG . P . MAX . TR. P . P . P. The laureate head of Nero to the right.

℞. VICTORIA . AVGVSTI. In the field S. C. A Victory gradient to the left, holding up a wreath in her right hand; in the left she carries a palm-branch. A Second Brass coin from the Thames, given me by Mr. C. Roach Smith.

Weight 152⅝ grains.

217.

IMP . NERO . CAESAR . AVG . P . MAX . TR . P . P . P. The unlaureate head of Nero to the right, a small globe at the point of the bust.

℞. *No legend.* A Victory volant to the left, bearing in her right hand a cirular shield inscribed S . P . Q . R. In the field S. C.

Weight 167½ grains.

These three Second Brass coins, one may consider, refer to the victories gained by Domitius Corbulo, already mentioned, which would make their date about A.D. 58.

218.

NERO . CLAVDIVS . CAESAR . AVG . GER . P . M . TR . P . IMP . P . P. The laureate head of Nero to the right.

℞. MAC . AVG. On either side of the field S. C. The macellum is represented as a circular building, surmounted by a dome and flanked by lateral porticoes, the whole having in the height two orders, apparently Doric. The lower columns with intercolumniations, the middle being considerably wider than the others, and an arch the whole height of the columns with each intercolumniation. A flight of steps of the width of the centre intercolumniation, flanked by two pedestals, leads up to the middle archway, in which is a lofty naked figure, colossal size, on a low pedestal, resting on a spear, or *hasta pura*, in his left hand. The upper order consists of three columns, one being in the centre, forming an open colonnade of two intercolumniations, filled in with an open parapet of one-third of the height of the opening, and two festoons hanging from capital to capital. There is a very lofty entablature equalling two-thirds the height of the column; and the dome is encircled with three rows of palm leaves, surmounted by a very remarkable apex, of large proportions, like two wings or horns, with a point in the middle. The lateral portion on the right side of the coin has two columniations next the centre, interrupted by a small arch, which, however, is omitted in some coins. The order above is only three-fourths as high as the lower order, and has a double festoon from capital to capital. The porticoes on the left side of the coin have three intercolumniations, and are not so high as those on the other side. The upper order has a podium under the columns, which does not exist on the other side, and only a single festoon hangs from capital to capital of the upper columns. There is the appearance of some ornament in the frieze over the columns of this upper order. The lateral porticoes have only two steps instead of the flight which leads up to the central building. With this description I have been favoured by Professor Donaldson, who has composed it, not from this coin only, but from comparison with other coins in the British Museum, the French cabinet, and other sources.

The building represented on this coin is usually called the macellum, or meat market, which Dio says was built by Nero, and consecrated; but he does not say to what deity it was dedicated. The year A.D. 60 is generally placed as the date of this coin, on which the building is commemorated.

The present coin is of the finest aurichalcum; weight 351¼ grains; and is so rare as a First Brass coin that I believe there is scarcely another known. There is not one in the British Museum, or in the French cabinet, or in any known cabinet, although Eckhel, vol. vi. p. 273, says there are such. The same author, describing a Second Brass coin of this type in the Vienna cabinet, says it is "ædificium perelegans pluribus columnis fultum." Argelati, *in Nerone*, describes the reverse, "ædificium pulcherrimum quod macellum Neronis vocant;" but he does not give the size of the coin he describes.

Some writers have supposed the MAC. to be MAG. reading it as MAGNVS . AVGVSTI . DOMVS . or MAGNVM . AVGVSTI . AEDIFICIVM . considering the building to be the celebrated DOMVS . AVREA . of Nero. The elegant appearance of the building renders it a more fit representation of the Domus Aurea than of a meat market; yet, notwithstanding such remarks, there is no doubt that the word *macellum*, as applied to a market for every description of viand, is correct; it is to be found used as such in Varro, Fulvius, Plutarch, &c., and in the Aulularia of Plautus, where in act ii. scene 5, the market is thus described:

> Venio ad macellum, rogito pisces, indicant
> Caros, aguinam caram, bubulam,
> Vitulinam, cetum, porcinam, cara omnia.

The macellum of Nero appears not to have been the only one at Rome.
This coin has been ignorantly stigmatised as a forgery. It is of pure Roman

aurichalcum not found in forgeries, and I unhesitatingly aver it to be a genuine coin of the Roman mint.

219.

NERO . CLAVD . CAESAR . AVG . GER . P . M . TR . P . IMP . P . P. The laureate head of Nero to the left.

℞. MAC . AVG. S. C. on either side the field. A representation of the building described on the preceding coin.

A fine brown Second Brass coin.

220.

NERO . CLAVDIVS . CAESAR . AVG . GER . P . M . TR . P . IMP . P . P. The radiate head of Nero to the right.

℞. MAC . AVG. S. C. in the field. Same type as on the preceding coin. In the exergum $\overline{\text{II}}$.

A fine Second Brass coin, green tint. Weight $247\frac{1}{4}$ grains.

221.

NERO . CLAVDIUS . CAESAR . AVG . GERM . P . M . TR . P . IMP . P . P. The laureate head of Nero to the right.

℞. DECVRSIO . in the exergum, but no S. C. there or in the field. A warrior on horseback to the right, bare-headed, his spear in his right hand couched for the charge; he is preceded by an armed foot soldier, bearing a shield on his left arm, and a standard over his right shoulder; in the back ground, rather behind the horse, is another foot soldier, running.

The word Decursio was applied by the Romans to signify, first, the training or discipline of their cavalry; secondly, it was also used to signify the Ludi Trojani; and, thirdly, the military procession round the funeral pile of a general or emperor.

On this and the following coins of Decursio type, it is a representation of the disciplina, or training exercises of the Roman cavalry. On the present coin, the horseman is accompanied by two foot soldiers, to represent their being in training to join the cavalry, and assist in their ranks during a battle.

The Decursio coins rank under date of A.D. 60, because in that year Nero instituted certain quinquenualian games, and some antiquaries have supposed the Decursio to relate to those games, but I am not of that opinion; others think it refers in the Ludi Trojani as performed by the young Romans in the Campus Martius, and in which Nero at one time took much pleasure, but

I do not think so; it is in my opinion the ordinary and regular exercise of the Roman cavalry.

This type is the rarest of the Decursios, and I have observed it never has the S. C. Weight 389½ grains.

222.

NERO . CLAVDIVS . CAESAR . AVG . GER . P . M . TR . P . IMP . P . P. The laureate head of Nero to the right.

℞. DECVRSIO . in the exergum. S. C. in the field. Two warriors bare-headed on horses galloping to the right. The coin is in such perfect preservation that it may be seen the one in front or foreground is a miniature portrait of Nero wearing his cuirass and military cloak, his spear in the right hand brought to the charge. The other horseman carries a vexillum erect on his right shoulder.

Pure auricalchum, very fine and perfect. Weight 350¼ grains.

Nero, in the early part of his reign, was very fond of athletic sports, and encouraged the horse and chariot races. He also at times led the Ludi Trojani, said to have been instituted by Æneas or Ascanius, to commemorate Anchises, the father of Æneas. These games were at times celebrated with great pomp and solemnity, and consisted of military exercises, both cavalry and infantry, performed by young men of the first families in Rome, their leader being either the emperor's heir apparent or the son of a senator of patrician family, and he was called PRINCEPS . IVVENTVTIS . Prince of the Roman Youth. It subsequently became a custom to elect the son of the emperor Princeps Juventutis, and the title was put on his coins.

I have seen this Decursio type also on an indifferently preserved medallion of Hadrian.

223.

NERO . CLAVDIVS . CAESAR . AVG . GER . P . M . TR . P . IMP . P . P. The laureate head of Nero to the right.

℞. DECVRSIO . in the exergum. S. C. in the field. Two warriors on horses, bareheaded, and galloping to the right, as described on the preceding coin, the one in front being a complete portrait of Nero.

A very fine red brown coin from the cabinet of the Duke of Devonshire. Weight 424½ grains.

224.

NERO . CLAVDIVS . CAESAR . AVG . GER . P . M . TR . P . IMP . P . P. The laureate head of Nero to the right.

♃. DECVRSIO. in the exergum. S. C. in the field. Two warriors on horses galloping to the right as before, the one in front intended for Nero.

A chocolate-coloured coin, very fine, a duplicate from the British Museum.

225.

NERO . CLAVDIVS . CAESAR . AVG . GER . P . M . TR . P . IMP . P . P. The laureate head of Nero to the right.

♃. DECVRSIO. in the exergum. S. C. in the field. Two warriors on horses as on the preceding coins, galloping to the left, one in the foreground with his spear brought to the charge, the other carrying a vexillum.

Weight 423 grains.

226.

NERO . CLAVDIVS . CAESAR . AVG . GER . P . M . TR . P . IMP . P . P. The laureate head of Nero to the left.

♃. DECVRSIO. in the exergum. S. C. in the field. Two warriors on horses galloping to the left as before.

The vexillum was the regular standard of the Roman cavalry. It is generally called the labarum. See in Pitiscus, Lexicon, art. *Vexillum*.

These two coins are from the Thames, a present from C. Roach Smith.

227.

NERO . CLAVD . CAESAR . AVG . GERMANICVS. The unlaureate head of Nero to the left, a small globe at the point of the bust.

♃. PONTIF . MAX . TR . POT . IMP . P . P. In the field S. C. Nero, as is usually supposed, in female attire, with a frontal coronet and the hair confined at the back of the head in a knot; gradient to the right, playing on a cithara or lyre of large size, held by the left hand and arm.

In the museum of the British Royal Academy, there is a colossal statue in plaster of Paris (the original marble being at Rome), which is known by the appellation of the Apollo Citharista or Citharædus, in the precise attitude represented on this coin, but on an inspection of this coin, and observing what is said by Suetonius and others in their biographies of Nero, of his fondness for playing the harp and singing on the public stage, the question may be fairly raised whether the colossal Apollo Citharista is not, after all, a complimentary statue to Nero on his attainments as a poet and musician, two arts in which he was very desirous of being esteemed a great proficient. For Suetonius, *in Vita Neronis*, sect. 25, says, "Item statuas suas citharœdico habitu, quâ notâ etiam nummum percussit." Here is a direct declaration of Nero being represented in sculpture, as well as on the coinage, in the costume of a harp player, and, Apollo being the patron deity of music and poetry, there could not be a more appropriate designation and compliment to the vanity of the emperor than to represent him as an Apollo Citharista.

The present coin is from the Thames; it is of Second size, in red Cyprian copper (weight 144½ grains), and most probably was struck in A.D. 65, being the year when Nero first ventured to play and sing in public. The coin is sometimes found without any legend on the reverse, simply the figure of the Apollo or Nero in the act of playing on the cithara.

I have never yet seen it in First Brass; it is not in First Brass in the British Museum, or in the French or Vienna Cabinets. See also Patin, 118.

228.

NERO . CAES . AVG . IMP. The laureate head of Nero to the right.

℞. CER . QVINQVE . ROM. In the exergum S. C. A square table, on which is placed a vase, the letter S. at the right side.

A small fine black coin. Weight 108¼ grains.

This coin records the institution by Nero of the quinquennalian games in A.D. 60. They were called Neroniana, and celebrated every fifth year as their name denotes, in imitation of the Olympic. They consisted of contests in music, gymnastics, and chariot racing. Being an imitation of the Greek games, they found no favour with the Romans, who always looked upon the Greeks as an effeminate people. After the death of Nero, they were not again celebrated until the time of Domitian, who revived them in honour of Jupiter Capitolinus, and they thenceforth continued to be repeated until the reign of Constantine.

The numismatic record of these games is only found on Third Brass of Nero. Consult Suetonius, *in Nerone*, sec. 12, and *in Domitiano*, sec. 4.

229.

IMP . NERO . CAESAR . AVG . PONT . MAX . TR . POT . P . P. The laureate head of Nero to the left, a small globe at the point of the bust.

℞. ADVENTVS . on the upper verge, and AVGVSTI . on the lower verge of the field. G. P. under the word ADVENTVS. No S. C. A large galley, or triremis prætoria, being rowed to the left by twelve rowers in sight, beside other figures.

This coin was struck A.D. 66, on the return of Nero from Greece, where he had been exhibiting at the Olympic games, in which the crafty and politic Greeks had awarded him the highest honours for the display of his talents and proficiency as a poet and musician, and concluded their adulation by crowning him victor. By the letters G. P. is signified Grecia Peragrata.

There is no coin of this type in the British Museum. Vaillant, Numismata Ærea, &c., p. 122, describes a coin somewhat similar; but he reads G. P. as C. P. and signifying Colonia Patrensis in Achaia, as if struck by that city to record Nero's visit there. From this I dissent, because in such case no galley was required; but, the galley having a more immediate application to voyaging by sea, it is a representation or record of the fact of his having been conveyed by sea to and from Greece.

This is a large flan, the obverse and reverse in fine condition, and engraved by the same die engravers who cut the dies for the annona coins before mentioned. From a continual and close observation of the coins of Nero in this cabinet, there do not appear to have been more than three artists employed in executing the dies, and they are fine specimens of art.

A fine coin, green patina, from the cabinet of the Duke of Devonshire. Weight 318½ grains.

230.

NERO . CLAVD . CAESAR . AVG . GER . P . M . TR . P . IMP . P . P . P. The laureate head of Nero to the right, a small globe at the point of the bust.

℞. *No legend.* S. C. in the field. A triumphal arch ornamented with sculptures and statues; the front is divided into several compartments in which are various sculptures. In a niche at the right side is the statue of an armed warrior standing on a square base; a garland is suspended from side to side under the crown of the arch. The arch is surmounted by a square base or plinth, whereon is placed a quadriga, in which is a figure to represent Nero in a triumphal car. A victory is standing to the left of the horses, holding up a wreath in her right hand, in her left hand a palm branch. Below her on the outer edge of the plinth is a small figure, as if about to jump off; on the other side of the horses another figure is standing with a cornucopiæ on the left arm; and another small figure below, as if flying off.

This is considered to be a representation of the Arcus Neronis, erected in the capitol on the return of Nero from Greece, A.D. 66. When he arrived in Italy, he entered Naples and other cities in great triumph, through breaches made in the city walls, until he reached Rome, where he was received with similar pomp and servility.

Tacitus, lib. xiii. section 41, states that an arch and statues were decreed to

Nero for the victories gained by Domitius Corbulo in Syria, Parthia, &c.; but Tacitus perhaps preferred giving the arch to the warlike achievements of a general of the empire, than that posterity should suppose they were literary victories which had caused the erection of the arch, whilst Nero preferred his own literary achievements to any military exploits of another person.

A fine coin from the cabinet of the Duke of Devonshire. Weight 387½ grains.

231.

NERO . CLAVDIVS . CAESAR . AVG . GER . P . M . TR . P . IMP . P . P. The laureate head of Nero to the right.

℞. *No legend.* S. C. on either side of the field. The arch of triumph represented on the preceding coin; the front is divided into compartments that are ornamented with sculptures; and on each side of the curve of the arch a figure is inserted in position, curving with the curve of the arch. The square base or plinth placed on the top of the arch is ornamented with sculptures; and above is a quadriga, with the four horses led on each outside by Victories; an armed figure in the niche at the side; but there is *no garland* suspended from side to side under the crown of the arch.

This coin is in a very perfect state of preservation, showing all the details differently and more accurately in the lower part, where there are evidently gladiators in combat. It is of brown colour, and was formerly in the respective cabinets of E. Edgar, R. Heber, and G. Gwilt.

232.

NERO . CLAVDIVS . CAESAR . AVG . GER . P . M . TR . P . IMP . P . P. The laureate head of Nero to the right.

℞. *No legend.* S. C. in the field. The triumphal arch, as on the preceding coins; a wreath suspended under the arch. The sculptured decorations are similar to those already noticed. The quadriga, and Victories, and other figures at the sides of the plinth surmounting the arch, are very perfect and fine.

233.

IMP . NERO . CAESAR . AVG . PONTIF . MAX . TRIB . POT . P . P. The laureate head of Nero to the right, a small globe at the point of the bust.

℞. ADLOCVT . COH. in the exergum. S. C. in the field. Nero robed, standing with an attendant on a low suggestum to the left, his right hand raised as addressing three soldiers, who stand before him with their swords on their right sides, and without their helmets. Two of them carry standards. In the background is the front of a building; it appears to be circular, and supported by columns.

This coin is supposed to have been struck A.D. 66, to record the circumstances related by Suetonius *in Vita Neronis*, section 19 : " In Achaia isthmum perfodere aggressus prætorianos pro concione ad inchoandum opus cohortatus est, tubáque signo dato, primus rastello humum effodit et corbulæ congestam humeris extulerit."

The year A.D. 66 is very remarkable in history, not of the Roman empire only, but to the world as being the year when the great war with the Jews, which was to decide the fate of their country, commenced. The cruelties of Gessius Florus in Judæa had excited an insurrection which Cestius Gallus advanced to Jerusalem from Antioch to suppress, but there he encountered the people in arms, and was suddenly overpowered and slain with the loss of an eagle and other standards. In the next year Vespasian was sent by Nero to take the command, which he assumed in February, A.D. 67, and Jerusalem was taken on the 8th day of the month Gorphæus Eliel, and second year of Vespasian, by the army under the command of his son Titus, whom Vespasian had left in charge when he went to Rome on his election as emperor after the death of Nero.

Weight 401¼ grains.

234.

IMP . NERO . CLAVD . CAESAR . AVG . GERM . P . M . TR . P . XIII . P . P. The laureate head of Nero to the right.

℞. ROMA . in the exergum. S. C. in the field. Roma armed, seated on arms, to the left; her left arm rests on the upper edge of a circular shield, the lower part of the shield resting on a square block, on one side whereof is a helmet, on the other side is the cuirass on which she is seated; her sword, suspended by the belt over the right shoulder, is at her left side; in her right hand she holds her spear erect, the point upwards. Her clothing reaches to her feet.

Black brown colour, very fine. Weight 385¾ grains.

The brass coins of Nero which bear any tribunician date are rare. There is not one Large Brass coin of Nero in the French or Vienna cabinets which bears a tribunician date, nor is there one noticed in the Christina, Arschot, or Vaillant cabinets, nor is it mentioned in Occo. There are three like the present in the British Museum, one of them having the wolf and twins on the shield of Roma; and there is one like the present in the collection of Mr. Bergne, which formerly belonged to Mr. Edgar. Excepting what are in this cabinet, these are all the Large Brass coins I have been able to trace out having the tribunician date XIII. Eckhel, vol. vi. p. 267, quotes a Second Brass coin with the TRIB. POT. XIII., rev. ROMA, as on the present, and says: "Singularis est hic nummus, cùm quod trib. pot. numerum addit, cujus exemplum in alio Neronis nummo æneo nondum observare contigit, tum quod in eodem nummi parte utrumque imperatoris titulum offert."

An aureus of TR. P. VII. COS. IIII. is among the coins found at Rutupiæ, now Richborough, in the cabinet of Mr. Rolfe of Sandwich, in Kent. The coin is mentioned in C. R. Smith's Richborough, p. 124. The collection of Rutupian antiquities of Mr. Rolfe is now with Mr. Mayer, at Liverpool. These coins with TR. POT. were struck in A.D. 66.

235.

IMP. NERO. CLAVD. CAESAR. AVG. GERM. P. M. TR. P. $\overline{\text{XIII}}$. P. P. The laureate head of Nero to the right.

℞. ROMA. in the exergum. S. C. in the field. Roma armed, seated on a cuirass to the left, holding her spear erect in her right hand. Her left arm rests on her shield, which is at her left side, the lower edge of the shield resting on a square plinth, and against which *ocrea*, or armour for the legs, are resting. This peculiarity (the *ocrea*) in the device is extremely rare.

236.

IMP. NERO. CLAVD. CAESAR. AVG. GERM. P. M. TR. P. XIII. P. P. The radiate head of Nero to the right.

℞. ROMA. in the exergum. S. C. in the field. Roma armed, seated to the left on a cuirass; her clothes only reach to her knees; three or four shields are piled at her side and at her back. Her left hand holds her spear, the point of it resting on the ground. Her helmet is well crested, and her sword is slung at her left side by its belt, which crosses her bosom from the right shoulder. In her right hand she holds out a wreath.

A Second Brass coin, black, in beautiful condition.

237A.

IMP. NERO. CLAVD. CAESAR. AVG. GERM. P. M. TR. P. XIII. P. P. The radiate head of Nero to the right.

℞. ROMA. in the exergum. S. C. in the field. Roma seated on a cuirass to the left; her left arm rests on her shield at her left side; the lower edge of it is placed on a helmet, and another helmet is by its side. Her right hand holds her spear upright; her sword at her left side, the belt passing over her right shoulder. Her clothes reach to her ankles.

A beautiful black Second Brass coin. From the description given by Eckhel of the Second Brass coin in the Vienna cabinet, with the TR. POT. XIII., it would seem the present completely answers to that.

237B.

IMP. NERO. CLAVD. CAESAR. AVG. GERM. P. M. TR. P. XIII. P. P. The laureate head of Nero to the right.

℞. PACE. P. R. TERRA. MARIQ. PARTA. IANVM. CLVSIT. S. C. in the field. The Temple of Janus: the left side with garlands.

A fine coin, in pure unpatinated aurichalcum.

238.

NERO. CAESAR. AVG. IMP. TR. POT. XIIII. The laureate head of Nero to the right, the bust full and in armour, a military cloak appearing to be buckled on the right shoulder and drawn over to the left, thus showing the cuirass and lappets on the right shoulder which fasten the front and back parts of the cuirass together.

℞. ROMA. in the exergum. S. C. in the field. Roma armed, seated on a cuirass to the left; behind her are shields. Her left hand grasps the hilt of her sword; her right hand extended holds a Victoriola presenting her a wreath. Her clothes reach only to her knees.

A very fine dark green coin, from the cabinet of the Duke of Devonshire.

This singular coin was struck in the last year of Nero's reign. He killed himself in the thirty-second year of his age, on the 9th of June, A.D. 68, being the same day of the same month on which he had some few years before put his young wife Octavia to death, she being then only twenty years of age.

The present coin may be considered from two causes unique. The only other such coin was said to have been in the cabinet d'Ennery, but on looking there I did not find it, nor any note of it, or any trace of it being in existence, so this is the only Large Brass coin known on which Nero is represented in armour; secondly, it bears the tribunician date XIIII, which has been supposed not to exist on any Large Brass coin of Nero.

This tribunician date on a Large Brass coin, or on any other coin of Nero, was apparently unknown to Eckhel. From the observation I have already quoted, in describing the coin No. 234 *ante*, he seems to have considered the Second Brass coin he mentions with the tribunician date XIII. *as most singular*, and in no way does he allude to any coin with the TRIB. POT. XIIII. being anywhere in existence, or known to him. The only approach to this tribunician date is a coin quoted by Argelati as being in the Museum Correrii, thus: "*Aes*, NERO . CAESAR . AVG . IMP.—XIIII. *in medio nummi.*" It is evident from the position of the XIIII. on that coin it formed no part of the legend, and is unconnected with anything that may be described on the coin; it cannot therefore be considered as referring to a tribunician date; and, no other numbers than the above being given by Argelati in describing the coin, it is quite clear it is not a tribunician date; but it is not improbable the numerals may have been added at some later period for some private or peculiar purpose. Argelati does not give the size of the coin, nor does he say what reverse is on it; but to say simply "XIIII. in medio nummi," would imply the numeral was in the middle of the field of the reverse of the flan and without any legend, which is a most unusual and improbable act of a Roman master of the mint, or of his die-engraver. Upon the whole, no satisfactory opinion can be formed from what he says respecting the quoted coin; but I feel perfectly satisfied it was not intended for a tribunician date.

The only reverses upon coins of Nero that I have found bearing a tribunician date have been ROMA . and the Temple of Janus. The coins we have described are all the varieties of the ROMA type on which the tribunician date is to be found; and, although they are all ROMA, yet they all vary, in the same manner as the coins of ROMA without the tribunician date which we have first noticed.

In the reign of Nero a great persecution was raised against the Christians; and it is said St. Peter was crucified at Rome, and St. Paul beheaded there.

With the death of Nero the line of emperors and chiefs professing to be descended from Æneas and Augustus was ended. We bid farewell to the Cæsars, and at the same time to the state of things which the Cæsars created and maintained in the empire. A new scene commences; the old system of hereditary descent commenced by Julius Cæsar is broken; and, the army having found the secret of creating an emperor, the republic is at once thrown into their power, and all the rights and authority of the consuls and senate, as the true legislators, are at once set aside, and they are treated as mere puppets, to be called into play at the caprice of the military.

239.

IMP . NERO . CAESAR . AVG . P . MAX. The head of Nero to the right.

℞. *No legend.* A person on horseback to the right, his right hand raised with a sword to strike at a person who has fallen on the ground in front of the horse, and raises his hand in supplication.

A contorniate.

POPPÆA.

POPPÆA SABINA, the daughter of Titus Ollius, was named after her uncle Poppæus Sabinus, a man of consular dignity, who appears to have been consul in A.D. 9, jointly with Q. Sulpicius Camerinus. She was married to Rufus Crispinus, a Roman knight, by whom she had a son; but afterwards seduced from him by Otho; and Nero, happening to see her, became so enamoured of her, that he repudiated his wife Octavia; and, sending Otho to be governor of the distant province of Lusitania, now Portugal, took possession of Poppæa, A. D. 63. Octavia was banished to the island of Pandataria, and put to death in the first glow of youth and beauty, at twenty years of age, and her head brought to Rome and presented to Poppæa.

In the year A.D. 66, Poppæa, being pregnant by Nero, was killed by him in a fit of passion, by a kick with his foot, and thus the death of Octavia was avenged.

There are no Latin coins of Poppæa.

240.

ΠΟΠΠΑΙΑ . . . . The head of Poppæa to the right. Her hair in curls over the forehead, and drawn down behind, then turned up and tied in a long braided knot. A love-lock strays down the neck. Her bosom draped.

℞. ΝΕΡΩ . ΚΛΑΥ . . . ΚΑΙΣ . . . . The radiate head of Nero to the right.

A Greek Imperial coin in billon, from the cabinet of Mr. Borrell of Smyrna.

GALBA.

SERGIUS SULPICIUS GALBA was born of an illustrious family in the year of Rome 751, or B.C. 3. He was raised to the consulate in A.D. 33, jointly with L. Cornelius Sulla Felix, and was afterwards sent into Germany to supersede Getulicus in the command of the Roman armies there. Upon the death of Caligula, he was urged to assume the empire, but he declined; which conduct, when Claudius was raised to the sovereignty, he rewarded by appointing Galba to be pro-consul of Africa.

In the year A.D. 68, Galba being then in Spain, the troops revolted against Nero and proclaimed Galba emperor, and the death of Nero happening soon after, he remained in possession of the empire. Very quickly after Galba had arrived in Rome, on his assumption of the sovereignty, he held a meeting of some friends, and, by their advice, he associated with him in the empire Piso Licinianus, a descendant of the Crassi and Pompeii, of high birth and noble character. He afterwards proceeded with Piso to the camp of the Prætorians, and announced to them the act he had done; after that he went to the Senate and made a similar announcement, which was received with much satisfaction. Not so with the Prætorians, who, although they did not openly express their dissatisfaction, yet, as they had received no largess or donative on the arrival of Galba in Rome, nor on his presenting Piso to them, they were ready, as the fact afterwards proved, to turn against him, at the instigation of Otho, whose friends took care to secure their swords on his behalf by presents of money.* Galba did not long enjoy his honours, being slain the following year in a tumult with the soldiers, occasioned by Otho, who instigated an insurrection and was proclaimed emperor. Galba had then only reigned seven months, and was seventy-two years of age when he was killed. Piso was slain at the same time as Galba, by the particular orders of Otho, who feared him greatly.

The brass coins of Galba, with a few exceptions, are not rare, although they were all struck between the month of June, A.D. 68, and the month of February, A.D. 69.

241.

IMP . SER . GALBA . AVG . TR . P . The laureate head of Galba to the right, shoulders draped.

℞. *No legend.* S. C. in the field. A Victory gradient to the left; her right

---

* Merivale, vi. 379.

hand, extended, holds a little figure of Minerva Jaculatrix, or probably a Bellona; in her left hand she bears a palm-branch.

Black brown, remarkably sharp and fine. Weight, 441¼ grains.

242.

SER . SVLP . GALBA . IMP . CAESAR . AVG . The laureate head of Galba to the right.

℞. ADLOCVTIO in the exergum; in the field, S. C. The emperor, bareheaded, and in military attire, standing to the right on a low basement. Behind the emperor is an armed figure, who holds him by the right arm; before them are assembled many armed soldiers, and a horse's head and forelegs are intermixed with the soldiers, some of whom carry standards, among which are some eagles and a vexillum.

Weight, 409½ grains.

This coin records the address made by Galba to his troops, infantry and cavalry, on their saluting him as Augustus; the cavalry are represented by the horse; an officer stands in front of the emperor with his back to him, and seems to be enforcing the address which is being made by the emperor to those assembled.

We have said that the revolt of the troops, under Galba, occurred before the actual death of Nero; on that event being notified to Galba, he did not hesitate any longer to assume the imperial dignity, and put himself in motion at the head of his troops to proceed to Rome. We may therefore fairly conclude that this and the next coin were struck to record the address made by Galba to his troops on his resolution being taken, when they saluted him Imperator.

243.

. . . . . . IMP . C . . . . . . The laureate head of Galba to the right.

℞. ADLOCVTIO in the exergum, with S. C. under. The emperor addressing a band of armed soldiers, both cavalry and infantry, as on the preceding coin, with this peculiarity, that one of the soldiers in the fore ground of the group seems to have a human head fixed on his shield, as if the head of an enemy for a trophy.

Weight, 429¼ grains.

244.

SER . GALBA . IMP . CAES . AVG. The head of Galba to the right, wearing an oak-wreath.

℞. S . P . Q . R . OB . CIV . SER . inscribed in three lines across the field, within an oak-wreath.

Weight, 376 grains.

This coin was struck by the senate to compliment Galba, and record his having saved the citizens of Rome from the tyranny of Nero and the horrors of civil war, by assuming the sovereignty with promptitude; it therefore stands in order as of the earliest part of his reign, in A.D. 68.

The coins of emperors with the head encircled with an oak-wreath are unknown; I do not believe, excepting the coin I have noticed of Augustus, there is any other emperor on whose coins it appears than those of Galba, and his are very scarce.

245.

SER . GALBA . IMP . CAES . AVG . TR . P. The head of Galba to the right, wearing an oak-wreath.

℞. S . P . Q . R . OB . CIV . SER . inscribed in three lines across the field, within a wreath of oak-leaves and acorns.

The civic crown, *corona quercea*, presented to a citizen who had saved the life of a fellow-citizen in battle, was considered more honourable than any other reward, although composed of no other materials than twigs of oak-leaves and acorns entwined together. It is called by Virgil, Æneid vi., *civilis quercus*—

"Atque umbrata gerunt civili tempora quercu."

It was a particular privilege conferred on the persons who gained this crown, that, when they came to any public shows, the whole company present, as well senators as people, should signify their respect by rising up on their entrance, and they should take their seat on these occasions among the senators. They were also excused from all troublesome offices, and procured the same exemption for their fathers and grandfathers, *ex parte paternâ*.

Being so highly esteemed, the civic crown was frequently awarded to an emperor at the commencement of his reign, more especially if his predecessor had been a man wanting in clemency, or had caused the death or exile of many of the citizens; it is in this latter view of the subject that Claudian compliments Stilicho, a celebrated general under Theodosius the Great:—

> Of old, when in the war's tumultuous strife
> A Roman saved a brother Roman's life,
> And foil'd the threatening foe, our sires decreed
> An oaken garland for the victor's meed.
> Thou who hast sav'd whole crowds, whole towns set free—
> What groves, what woods, shall furnish crowns to thee?

246.

SER . GALBA . IMP . CAESAR . AVG . TR . P. The laureate head of Galba to the right.

℞. EX . S . C . OB . CIVES . SERVATOS inscribed in four lines across the field, within an oak-wreath.

Weight 307¼ grains.

This device was struck on the same occasion as the preceding coin.

247.

IMP . SER . SVLP . GALBA . CAES . AVG . TR . P. The laureate head of Galba to the right. Shoulders draped.

℞. LIBERTAS . PVBLICA. In the field S. C. A robed female standing full front, looking to the left, with a pileus or cap of liberty in her right hand; in her left she holds the rudis.

248.

SER . GALBA . IMP . CAES . AVG . TR . P. The laureate head of Galba to the right.

℞. LIBERT . AVG. In the field S. C. A robed female standing with the pileus and rudis, as on the preceding coin.

Weight 423½ grains.

249.

IMP . SER . SVLP . GALBA . AVG . TR . P. The laureate head of Galba to the right. Shoulders draped.

Bright green, very fine.

℞. LIBERTAS . PVBLICA. In the field S. C. A robed female standing full front, looking to the left, holding a pileus in her right hand, in the left a rudis.

This type signifies that, by the death of Nero and the accession of Galba, the people of Rome had received their manumission, or had become free men instead of continuing to be the slaves they had been made under Nero.

It may also be considered to mean that the Julian and Claudian families had ended, and the sovereign power would no longer be permitted to descend from father to son, in family gradation; thus giving the citizens the freedom of electing the emperor, but which the military took good care they should not exercise.

250.

SER . SVLP . GALBA . IMP . CAESAR . AVG . TR . P. The laureate head of Galba to the right.

℞. LIBERTAS . RESTITVTA. In the exergum S. C. The emperor robed standing to the left, his right hand extended towards a female, who is kneeling before him on her right knee, her right hand raised towards him in supplication. At her left side, in the back-ground, Minerva is standing, her shield on her left arm to protect Roma while she is addressing the emperor.

Black brown. Weight 359¼ grains.

A coin struck upon the same occasion as the preceding coins, but it conveys a more extended signification of the restoration of liberty to the Roman people. The same idea is also represented on the next following coin, which, with the present, are both very rare.

This type has been copied on the coin of Vespasian *post*, ROMA . RESVRGES.

251.

SER . SVLP . GALBA . IMP . CAESAR . AVG . TR . P. The laureate head of Galba to the right.

℞. ROMA . RESTIT. In the field S. C. Roma wearing her helmet and military cloak, kneeling to the right on her right knee, and presenting her right hand to the emperor, who stands before her to the left, in military costume, with a spear in his left hand ; with his right hand he raises Roma by her right hand, she at the same time presenting the emperor with a little child she holds on her left arm and knee.

Black brown. Weight 426 grains.

This and the preceding coin, struck A.D. 68, by their types express the joy of the Roman people on their release from the despotic power of Nero, and the expectation of a happy reign, when Rome would be restored to its former youthful prosperity and good government, and the hope that such benefits would also be enjoyed by their families and descendants, typified by the little child Roma carries on her left arm. They are both of them very rare types, and are but in poor condition.

252.

SER . SVLPI . GALBA . IMP . CAESAR . AVG . P . M . TR . P. The laureate head of Galba to the right.

℞. SECVRITAS . P . ROMANI. In the field S. C. A female naked to the waist seated on a throne to the left; her left arm is resting on a rail crossing the upper part of the throne at the back, her right hand raised to her head; in front of her is a small circular altar, by the side of which is a torch with a light burning on the top.

Weight 226 grains.

This coin, struck A.D. 68, also denotes the security felt by the Roman people on the accession of Galba to the sovereignty. A somewhat similar type of similar import is in the series of Nero, Nos. 203 and 204 *ante*, and was struck in the early part of his reign, before his vicious character had displayed itself.

253.

IMP . SER . GALBA . AVG . TR . P. The head of Galba to the left, wearing a civic wreath of oak-leaves and acorns.

℞. *No legend.* In the field S. C. A Victory volant to the right, bearing in her right hand a wreath, in the left a palm-branch.

Weight 422 grains.

254.

IMP . SER . GALBA . CAE . AVG . TR . P. The laureate head of Galba to the right.

℞. PAX . AVGVST. In the field S.C. Pax standing to the left; her right hand, extended, holds an olive-branch; on her left arm she bears a full cornucopiæ, emblematic of riches and plenty, the offspring of peace.

A good Second Brass coin, weight $200\frac{3}{4}$ grains.

255.

SER . GALBA . IMP . CAESAR . AVG . TR . P. The laureate head of Galba to the right.

℞. *No legend.* In the field S. C. Three military standards, the centre one being an eagle with a fulmen in its claws, mounted on a plain staff. The other two have wreaths, and small circles under their signa, below which again are large crescents.

Weight $154\frac{1}{4}$ grains.

256.

SER . GALBA . IMP . CAES . AVG . TR . P. The laureate head of Galba to the right.

℞. *No legend.* S. C. in the sides of the field. Three military standards, each placed on the prow of a galley; the middle standard being an eagle; the staff being decorated with two wreaths, one above the galley and one under the eagle. In the centre of the staff, between the two wreaths, is a circular ornament. Each of the other standards bears a wreath, and underneath is a wreath, below which again is a circular ornament, that is placed within the concave bend of a crescent. Weight $183\frac{3}{4}$ grains.

These two coins, of second size, are in fine condition. By their types they denote the fidelity of the army, and by the prows of galleys of the navy also, to the cause of Galba.

257.

SER . SVLPI . GALBA . IMP . CAESAR . AVG . TR . P. The laureate head of Galba to the right.

℞. AEQV . . . . . S. C. in the field. A female standing in profile to the right, leaning on a *hasta pura* which she has in her left hand; in her right hand she holds a pair of scales or balance.

Weight 184½ grains.

258.

IMP . SER . GALBA . CAES . AVG . TR . P. The laureate head of Galba to the right.

℞. AVGVSTA in the exergum. In the field S. C. A robed female seated to the left on a square seat; her left hand holds a *hasta pura* erect, her right hand extended presents a patera.

Weight 409¼ grains.

259.

SER . GALBA . IMP . CAES . AVG. The laureate head of Galba to the right.

℞. CONCORD . AVG. In the exergum S. C. A robed female seated to the left on a square seat with low back on which her left arm is resting, and holding the *hasta pura* in her left hand transversely; her right hand extended holds an olive-branch.

Weight 407¼ grains.

260.

SER . GALBA . CAE . AVG . TR . P. The laureate head of Galba to the left.

℞. CONCORD . AVG. In the field S. C. Concordia seated to the left with olive branch and *hasta pura* as delineated on the preceding coin.

Weight 374 grains.

The coins of Galba with the head to the left are not very common.

261.

SER . GALBA . IMP . CAES . AVG . TR . P. The laureate head of Galba to the right.

℞. VESTA in the exergum. In the field S. C. The goddess seated to the left; her right hand extended holds a patera, on her left arm she supports a small palladium.

Weight 159¼ grains.

262.

IMP . SER . GALBA . CAESAR . AVG . TR . P. The unlaureate head of Galba to the right.

℞. VESTA in the exergum. In the field S. C. The goddess seated to the left; her right hand extended holds a palladium, in her left hand she holds a *hasta pura* transversely.

Weight 158¼ grains.

263.

SER . GALBA . IMP . CAES . AVG.   The laureate head of Galba to the right, shoulders draped.

℞. ADLOCVTIO in the exergum. S. C. in the field. This coin of the emperor making an address to the soldiers, such as we have before described, was the first coin ever bought by the late George Gwilt, and was purchased when he was in Florence in 1824; after then he became a collector, but not an historic collector. He shewed me this coin soon after his return to England.

Brown; no patina.

264.

SER . GALBA . IMP . CAES . AVG . TR . P.   The laureate head of Galba to the right.

℞. ROMA in the exergum. In the field S. C. Roma armed seated to the left on a cuirass; her left arm rests gracefully on the upper edge of her shield, the lower part whereof is resting on some shields, by the side of which are the *ocrea* or leg armour of some vanquished foe; her left foot rests on a helmet lying on the ground; in her right hand she holds her spear erect; her clothes, reaching to the feet, are displayed in rich folds at the left side.

Mottled greenish earthy colour. Weight 395¼ grains.

The figure of Roma just described has been arranged in a most elegant and graceful attitude, showing perfect ease and repose, coupled with firmness as the lady warrior. The die has been engraved by a first-rate artist; and, from the perfect condition of the coin, this reverse is a complete and artistic study. From the cabinet of Mr. Borrell.

Roma with *ocrea* among the armour of the vanquished is rare.

265.

SER . GALBA . IMP . CAES . AVG . TR . P.   The laureate head of Galba to the right, shoulders draped.

℞. ROMA in the exergum. S. C. in the field. Roma armed seated to the left on arms; her right hand holds her spear erect; her left arm placed on her shield, the lower edge of which rests on a small square base; her clothes come to her feet.

Weight 400¼ grains.

266.

SER . GALBA . IMP . CAESAR . AVG . TR . P. The laureate head of Galba to the right, shoulders draped.

℞. Roma standing full front, wearing a crested helmet, her spear in the left hand erect; her right hand extended holds a Victoriola presenting a wreath; the word RO—MA . across the field, divided by the female personification of the city. S. C. in the field, each letter being placed under the division of the word RO—MA.

Weight 362½ grains.

267.

IMP . SER . GALBA . CAES . AVG . PON . M . TR . P. The laureate head of Galba to the right.

℞. *No legend.* S. C. in the field. A victory gradient to the right; her right hand holds a wreath, in her left she bears a palm branch.

Weight 413¼ grains.

268.

SER . GALBA . IMP . CAES . AVG . TR . P. The laureate head of Galba to the right.

℞. *No legend.* S. C. in the field. A victory gradient to the left, holding out in her right hand a small figure of Minerva Jaculatrix, or Bellona; in her left hand she carries a palm-branch.

Weight 407¼ grains.

269.

SER . GALBA . IMP . CAESAR . AVG . P . M . TR . P . The laureate head of Galba to the right.

℞. XXXX . REMISSA. S. C. in the field. A plain double arch, the *arcus duplex* of Argelati. The front is approached by steps; a garland is suspended within the arch; on the top of the arch are four horses.

Weight 499¼ grains.

On this coin is recorded the remission of a tax or a collection of taxes to which the Roman people had been subjected by the predecessors of Galba, but of what the tax or taxes in particular designated by the Quadrigesima repealed by Galba consisted, I find no note anywhere. The coin only records the emperor's bounty to the citizens.

Spanheim has recorded this type, and has argued on its import, but is not able to come to a satisfactory decision on the question. (Spanheim, de Præstantia, &c. Elzevir small 4to, p. 797, second edition.) So with Eckhel, *in Galba*, vol. vi. p. 296. He notices the legend and coin of the *remissio quadrigesima*, but does not explain the particulars of what tax or taxes were remitted, and so gave rise to this coin; he notices, however, that Vespasian *revocasse*, revoked, or re-imposed the taxes Galba had so remitted.

270.

SER . SVLPI . GALBA . IMP . CAESAR . AVG . P . M . TR . P . The laureate head of Galba to the right, a small globe at the point of the bust.

℞. SENATVS . PIETATI . AVGVSTI . In the exergum S. C. The emperor in military costume standing full front to the left, holding a Victoriola in his extended right hand, in the left he has a small olive branch. At his left side a person stands in senatorial robes, who is with his right hand placing a wreath on the emperor's head, and holding a large olive branch in his left hand.

Weight 433¼ grains.

Galba was much respected for his exemplary conduct in private life; the present type is therefore quite appropriate, and records the sentiments of the Roman Senate on the excellent character of the emperor.

271.

SER . SVLPI . GALBA . IMP . CAESAR . AVG . P . M . TR . P . The laureate head of Galba to the right, the Modena eagle behind the head.

℞. *No legend*. S. C. in the field. Apollo as the god of medicine, without any drapery, standing full front with a staff in his left hand, around which a serpent is entwined.

From the Duke of Devonshire's cabinet. Black green, fine. Weight 414¼ grains.

This seems to be a supplicatory coin for the health and life of the emperor, who was an aged man; it is a type *very rarely* to be met with. The serpent we have already noticed *ante*, on coin of Julius Cæsar.

Amongst the Romans the serpent was a type of health, and on the coins is usually combined with Æsculapius or Hygeia, and almost invariably under the legend SALVS . AVG . or SALVS only, as indicating health. There is no doubt its origin is oriental, and most likely derived by tradition from the brazen serpent raised by Moses in the Wilderness in order to stay the pestilence which broke out among the Israelites, that all who looked on it might be restored to health.

Apollo Medicus is mentioned by Ovid, Met. 1, in the following terms :

> Inventum medicina meum est, opiferque per orbem
> Dicor, et herbarum subjecta potentia nobis.

Helios, or Sol, the Sun, was the same as Phœbus Apollo, the god of day and of light, and the father of Æsculapius, who is commonly termed the god of medicine; but he is more properly the god of medicine or healing in his own person, for, although in later times there were as many as four Apollos distinguished, yet this was probably but in keeping with the tendency of the Grecian mind to change the several attributes of a deity into as many distinct gods. The primitive idea was the sun (Helios or Sol), the fountain of light. To this, as a matter of course, followed life and health, and by another beautiful perception the same deity presided over music, one of the soul's chief comforters and healers, whence its medicinal fame from time immemorial. "The poets (says Lord Bacon) did well to conjoin music and medicine in Apollo, since the office of medicine is but to tune this curious harp of man's body and reduce it to harmony."

"Apollo was the pagan aspiration after Christ; one of his names was σωτηρ, saviour. His worship, his festivals, his oracles, all had more weight and influence with the Greeks than those of any other deity they worshipped. They would never have become what they were without the worship of Apollo; in him was the brightest side of the Grecian mind reflected. He who is the true light, the light which is the life of men, reveals himself also as healer of the nations in his lovely song of one that playeth well upon an instrument." (Grindon, 147.)

272.

SER . SVLPI . GALBA . IMP . CAESAR . AVG . TR . P. The laureate head of Galba to the right, shoulders draped.

℞. HONOS . ET . VIRTVS. S. C. in the exergum. Honos robed, and standing to the right with a *hasta pura* in her right hand; in her left she bears a cornucopiæ. Virtus stands opposite to Honos, in military costume; her cloak is drawn over the left shoulder, leaving the right breast bare, and falling in graceful folds behind and at her left side; her clothes reach to the knees, and are confined at the waist by a belt; her helmet is handsomely crested; a spear in her left hand, the point resting on the ground; her right foot placed on a cuirass lying on the ground, and in her right hand she holds her parazonium or dress-sword.

Temples were erected at Rome to many of the virtues or becoming acts of life. Marcellus erected two—one to Honos and the other to Virtus: they were so constructed, that to reach the Temple of Honos, it was necessary to pass through that of Virtus, a matter capable of being expanded into a beautiful allegory. The type is therefore highly interesting, and denotes the estimation in which Galba was held by the Senate and people of Rome.

Amongst the Romans, Virtus signified courage or valour. Courage was esteemed a great perfection, and was therefore represented by Virtus generally. Her appearance on coins is like that of Roma, excepting that she usually carries a sword in addition to her spear, but never a Victoriola.

The present coin is in the finest possible state of preservation (a drab colour), and is not easily found in such fine condition. It is from the cabinet of Captain Faber. Weight 414½ grains.

273.

SER . SULPI . GALBA . IMP . CAESAR . AVG . TR . P. The laureate head of Galba to the right, shoulders draped.

℞. MARS . VICTOR. In the field S. C. Mars unclothed, standing full front, with helmet on his head and spear in his right hand; on his left arm he bears a trophy of arms.

Brown-chocolate, reddish. Weight 460¼ grains.

OTHO.

MARCUS SALVIUS OTHO was of Hetruscan descent and illustrious parentage. He was born A.D. 32, at Ferentum, an Hetruscan city, now called Ferento, or Ferenti, five miles north of Viterbo. At the time of Galba's accession he was governor of Lusitania, now Portugal. He joined in the revolt against Nero, A.D. 68; and in the following year he conspired against Galba, who being slain, Otho was proclaimed emperor. Vitellius was at the same time proclaimed emperor in Gaul, and marched to Rome. Otho, who was at Rome, led out his troops to oppose Vitellius, and at the commencement of the war was successful in several skirmishes. A general engagement afterwards took place near to Bedriacum, now called Caneto, a village situate between Cremona and Verona. In this battle the troops of Otho were defeated; and, although he was entreated by his friends and followers to rally his troops and try again, and retrieve the fortune he had lost, he chose rather to kill himself, which he did on the 17th of April, A.D. 69, having reigned three months and seven days, being in the thirty-seventh year of his age.

Coins of Otho in First Brass are unknown. Some brass coins of Second size were struck at Antioch; but I avail myself of the denarii of the Roman mint, for both aurei and denarii were struck to him at Rome, and very probably coins in Large Brass, but they are all lost to us for the present.

274.

IMP . M . OTHO . CAESAR . AVG . TR . P. The head of Otho to the right, wearing a wig.

℞. SECVRITAS . P . R. A female standing looking to the left, having in her left hand a *hasta pura*; with her right hand she holds up an olive branch.

A denarius.

275.

IMP . M . OTHO . CAESAR . AVG . TR . P. The head of Otho to the right, wearing a wig.

℞. PAX . ORBIS . TERRARVM. Peace standing looking to the left, holding a long caduceus on her left arm; her right hand holds a branch.

A denarius.

The brass coins of Otho usually introduced in cabinets are from the Antioch mint. The type of the reverse is simply a laurel wreath with S. C. in the middle of the field. In the Numismatic Chronicle for January, 1841, there is mention made of a Large Brass Otho having been found at Autun, in France, the ancient Augustodunum; and an elaborate history of it is given by a gentleman who went to see it, and declares it is genuine; but at the same time he acknowledges his inexperience to detect a real coin from a forged one. I took the trouble to have some inquiry made at the Royal Library in Paris, for the opinion of the curators of the coins, as to the said Otho. The reply was that it was false. When I was in Paris, in September, 1847, I inquired of Mons. Le Normand, and the other gentlemen in the medal-room of the Royal Library, and they told me it was a Paduan. I had not the opportunity of going to Autun to see it, or I would have done so; and, taking some of the well-known forgeries of Large Brass Otho to compare with it, would have formed my own personal decision.

It is observed to me by my respected friend the Rev. E. Boden, that there may be a chance of a Large Brass coin of Otho being found in Portugal, for, as we have noticed (*ante*, POPPÆA), Nero, having taken a fancy to Poppæa, divorced her from Otho by sending him to Lusitania as governor, and took Poppæa to himself. On the revolt of the troops under Galba against Nero, and saluting Galba as emperor, Otho was still governor of Lusitania, and did not return to Rome until Galba was emperor. Poppæa, however, had been brutally killed by Nero long before the return of Otho. The governorship of Otho in Lusitania, calculating from the probable time when Nero took Poppæa, might be about three years, and during that time colonial Lusitanian coins may have been struck to Otho; but history says that Otho instigated the murder of Galba when they were both at Rome, and then Otho assumed the sovereignty, but no coins could before then be struck to him as emperor, and it was not allowable for the portraits of pro-consuls or provincial governors to be placed on the coinage, so that if any brass coins of Otho are to be discovered in Lusitania, they were struck there or at Rome, and sent there after Otho had assumed the imperial purple.

Eckhel, vol. vi. *in Othone*, p. 304, speaking of the absence of any brass coins of Otho, says: " Major corum pars adservere negatum hunc Othoni ab Senatu honorem (nam ad Senatum feriundæ monctæ æneæ jus pertinuit), quoniam ei infensus erat ob cæsum violentè Galbam, quodque à militibus, non ab se dictus fuerat Augustus, quod omnia ex militum voluntate gererentur; Senatus autem nihil haberetur, cujus varia exempla ipsis ex Tacito, Suetonio, Plutarcho, Dione præsto sunt."

Such was the jealousy of the election of Otho by the army, without reference to the Senate, who, feeling themselves offended at the usurpation of their rights by the soldiery, refused to exercise their right and power of striking a brass coinage; whereas Otho as the emperor had the power to coin in gold and silver. Hence gold and silver coins of Otho exist, but none in brass.

In Murphy's Tacitus, appendix to book xvi., speaking of Otho, it is noted that "Otho considered himself no better than a state prisoner (he was then governor of Lusitania) in a remote part of the empire. Resentment prompted him to revenge, and ambition like his was eager to come forth from obscurity and act a principal part on the great stage of public business. He melted down all his massive gold and silver [plate], and, having converted it into coin, went with his whole treasure and the forces of his province to support the enterprise of an old man (Galba) who he knew in the course of nature could not long enjoy the supreme authority. The other governors and propraetors followed his example."

In converting his gold and silver plate into coin, what dies were used? were they dies of Nero or Galba? and whence did he obtain them? Or, did he strike coin with his own effigies? If coin was struck with the head of Otho, some would be found in Portugal, or in the adjoining parts of Spain. Not much would be carried to Rome, except in the military chest. Therefore, Mr. Boden's conjecture may come right at last.

VITELLIUS.

AULUS VITELLIUS was born about the year A.D. 15. In A.D. 48, year of Rome 801, he was elected consul jointly with L. Vipsianus Poplicola. In A.D. 68 he was sent by the emperor Galba legate to Germany, where he revolted, and on news of the death of Galba he was proclaimed emperor by the troops under his command, and he then marched against Otho, who was defeated at Bebriacum, and after the battle slew himself, A.D. 69, by which event Vitellius was left in possession of the sovereignty, an honour he enjoyed but eight months and a few days, when he was killed in his turn on the 21st December, A.D. 69, by the soldiers of Vespasian, who had been proclaimed emperor in the East, and had marched to Rome to assume the reins of government.

The coins of Vitellius are rare, and are all of the mintage of A.D. 69.

276.

A . VITELLIVS . IMP . GERMAN. The laureate head of Vitellius to the left.

℞. FIDES . EXERCITVVM . in two lines across the field, between which are two right hands joined. S. C. in the exergum.

A Second Brass coin of red Cyprian copper, and by the legend being without the P . M . or TR . POT., or AVG., it may be considered one of the first struck to record the elevation of Vitellius to the sovereignty, as well as to conciliate the army, of whom Vitellius was doubtful and rather in fear. For these reasons I have placed it first in the series.

Weight 146¼ grains.

277.

A . VITELLIVS . GERMAN . IMP . AVG . P . M . TR . P. The laureate head of Vitellius to the right, shoulders draped.

℞. *No legend.* S. C. in the field. Mars gradient to the right, bearing a trophy of arms on his left shoulder; in the right hand he carries a spear, the point forward.

Weight 363¼ grains.

278.

A . VITELLIVS . GERMAN . IMP . AVG . P . M . TR . P. The laureate head of Vitellius to the right, shoulders draped.

℞. MARS . VICTOR. In the field S. C. Mars armed, striding to the left; his right hand extended holds a Victoriola. In his left hand he holds the staff of a trophy of arms, resting on his left shoulder; a short sword is girded on his left side.

A good red brown coin, presented by Mr. Cureton. Weight 387 grains.

279.

A . VITELLIVS . GERMANICVS . IMP . AVG . P . M . TR . P. The laureate head of Vitellius to the right, shoulders draped.

℞. MARS . VICTOR. In the field S. C. Mars in full military costume striding to the left hastily, with a Victoriola and trophy, as on the preceding coin.

280.

A . VITELLIVS . GERMANICVS . IMP . AVG . P . M . TR . P. The laureate head of Vitellius to the right, shoulders draped.

℞. VICTORIA . AVGVSTI. In the field S. C. A winged Victory naked to the waist, standing to the right, her left foot resting on a helmet lying on the ground; with her right hand she is inscribing on a shield affixed to the trunk of a tree, and held by her left hand, the words OB . CIVES . SER.

Black green, very fine. Weight 424½ grains.

The present and three preceding coins record the cessation of the war between Otho and Vitellius, and the stay of all further effusion of the blood of Roman citizens in contention with each other.

281.

A . VITELLIVS . GERMAN . IMP . AVG . P . M . TR . P. The laureate head of Vitellius to the right.

℞. *No legend.* S. C. in the field. A Victory gradient to the left, holding a Victoriola in her right hand, and in the left carrying a palm-branch.

Weight 359¼ grains.

282.

A . VITELLIVS . GERM . IMP . AVG . P . M . TR . P. The laureate head of Vitellius to the right.

℞. PAX . AVGVSTI. In the exergum S. C. Roma armed, standing to the right, her shield on her left arm and her sword on her right side; her right hand extended to the right hand of Vitellius, who is robed and stands before her to the left.

Weight 183½ grains.

283.

A . VITELLIVS . GERMANICVS . IMP . AVG . P . M . TR . P. The laureate head of Vitellius to the right, shoulders draped.

℞. PAX . AVGVSTI. In the field a large S. C. Pax standing full front, looking to the left; her right hand holds out an olive branch; on her left arm she bears a full cornucopiæ.

Black green, very fine.

284.

A . VITELLIVS . GERMAN . IMP . AVG . P . M . P . P. The laureate head of Vitellius to the right.

℞. ROMA . in the exergum. In the field S. C. Roma armed, seated on a cuirass to the left; two shields are behind her for support; her right hand extended, her left hand placed on the hilt of her sword.

It has been doubted whether the title P . P . Pater Patriæ, was given to Vitellius; but in Argelati, *tit.* Vitellius, there are three instances, one in silver SPQR . P . P . OB . C . S . in corona civica, musæo P. Cattanei; another in silver, A . VITELLIVS . GERM . IMP . P . P . ex thesauro Mauroceno J. C. Bon; and the third in brass, but he does not mention the size, A . VITELLIVS . GERMAN . IMP . AVG . P . M . P . P . musæi Moscardi.

Eckhel, *in Vitellio*, vol. vi. p. 309, gives examples of all the numismatic titles of Vitellius, but there is not one among them having the P . P .; but that is no reason why this coin and Argelati should be erroneous. It is in pure auricalchum, badly cleaned, from the cabinet of the Duke of Devonshire.

285.

A . VITELLIVS . GERMANICVS . IMP . AVG . P . M . TR . P. The laureate head of Vitellius to the right.

℞. CONCORDIA . AVGVSTI. In the exergum S. C. A robed female seated to the left on a square seat; in her right hand she holds a patera, at her feet is a decorated square altar on which a fire is burning; on her left arm she bears a cornucopiæ filled with fruits.

A Second Brass coin, black green, very fine.

286.

A . VITELLIUS . GERMAN . IMP . AVG . P . M . TR . P. The laureate head of Vitellius to the right, shoulders draped.

℞. L . VITELL . CENSOR . $\overline{\text{II}}$. In the exergum S. C. The elder Vitellius, father of the emperor, is seated in his robes on a curule chair placed on a suggestum to the left. Before him are three citizens, the foremost of whom he takes by the right hand; above them to the right, and facing the censor, another person is seated, apparently attending to what is going on.

This is a complimentary coin to the emperor, who was thus flattered by the cringing Senate recording the dignity to which his father had been advanced. The father of Vitellius was three times consul and once censor, as recorded in written history; but in numismatic history he appears to have held the latter office twice. By the Fasti Consulares, L. Vitellius was censor jointly with the emperor Claudius, A. D. 48, yet his name does not appear again in the Fasti as censor; but the coin cannot err, although written record may err or be uncertain, or omit a fact.

It is a dark brown coin from the cabinet of the Duke of Devonshire. Weight 524¼ grains.

287.

A . VITELLIVS . GERMAN . IMP . AVG . P . M . TR . P. The laureate head of Vitellius to the right, shoulders draped.

℞. L . VITELL . CENSOR . II. In the exergum S. C. L. Vitellius in his robes seated to the left on a curule chair placed on a suggestum; three citizens are in front, and a person is seated above them on the right, being a group similar to the preceding.

A brown coin from the cabinet of the Earl Pembroke. Weight 350¼ grains.

We have noticed the censorship of L. Vitellius on the preceding coin. The office of Censor was more honourable than that of consul; and its power was very great, without being amenable to any other. The censors were originally created in the year of Rome 310, and were of patrician family; the office was placed in the hands of two individuals for five years, and if either of them died while in office, there was no successor appointed, but the survivor continued for the remainder of the five years.

The first patricians who were appointed to the office were L. Papirius Mugillianus, and L. Sempronius Atratinus. Amongst other powers they had authority for correcting and reforming the manners of individuals of all ranks, not even excepting a dictator or consul; and if they thought necessary, could degrade senators, could take away a knight's horse and ring, and turn plebeians out of their tribes into lower rank. In every fifth year, the censors were to take a census of the Roman people in the Campus Martius, and this was called a Lustrum.

About the year of Rome 420, their time of office was reduced to eighteen months, and their powers were abridged; but, the republic subsequently becoming an empire, the censors were abolished, and the emperors took upon themselves the official duties. The robes of the censors were of scarlet cloth, with all the insignia of consular dignity, excepting the lictors.

The first enumeration or census of the Roman people was attributed to the founder of the state, and a law ascribed to Servius Tullus, the sixth king of Rome, B.C. 534, required that every birth should be registered by payment of a piece of money in the temple of Juno Lucina. At every death a piece of money was similarly offered at the shrine of Libitina. And the assumption of the robe of manhood (*toga virilis*) was verified in the same way by a fee to the goddess Juventas.

By these means Tullus was enabled to ascertain the number of the inhabitants of Rome, the living as children and men of full age, also the number of deaths. The census of Tullus shewed him 84,000 inhabitants of Rome.

The goddess Juno Lucina, supposed to preside over child-birth, had a temple erected to her in Rome, A.U.C. 396.

Libitina, supposed by some to be the same as Diana or Proserpina, presided over funerals; Servius Tullus first raised a temple to her at Rome, in which the registers of deaths were kept.

The goddess Juventas was the Hebe of the Greeks.

VESPASIANUS.

FLAVIUS VESPASIANUS was born A.D. 9, of a Sabine family, at Reate, now called Rieti, a place of very great antiquity, considered to have been the first seat of the Umbri in Italy. Vespasian became a senator, and, under the emperor Claudius, was appointed to the command of the Roman army in Britain, where he obtained many successes and made himself master of the Isle of Wight, called by the Romans Vectis. On the broad plains of Britain, Vespasian learned the art of war, which he was to practise among the steep defiles of Palestine, and against the walls of Jerusalem. He was afterwards appointed proconsul in Africa, and subsequently, on the defeat of Cestius Gallus, was appointed by Nero to the government of Palestine, and the command of the army destined for the conquest of Judæa.

In the disorders which ensued upon the death of Galba, the troops of Vespasian compelled him to assume the imperial title and dignity, and march towards Rome. The subsequent deaths of Vitellius and Otho left Vespasian sole master of the empire at the close of the year A.D. 69. Merivale says the date of the commencement of his reign was from the 1st of July, A.D. 69, being the day when the legions swore fidelity to him at Alexandria. It was from this city that he afterwards crossed the Mediterranean to Italy. His two sons, Titus and Domitianus, were named Cæsars; Titus being also appointed the colleague of his father in the censorship. And the census of the Roman people taken by them in A.D. 74 is the last recorded in history. Vespasian died at Reate in July A.D. 79, (Clinton says June,) and was succeeded by his son Titus. The coins of Vespasian, with the exception of some few particular types, are common.

288.

IMP . CAES . VESPASIAN . AVG . P . M . TR . P . P . P . COS . III. The laureate head of Vespasian to the right.

℞. S . P . Q . R . OB . CIVES . SERVATOS . inscribed in four lines within an oak-wreath.

The civic crown has already been very fully explained under preceding coins. This is a congratulatory coin upon the cessation of the strife between the armies of Otho and Vitellius, occasioned by the accession of Vespasian, by which the further effusion of the blood of Roman citizens was stayed. It was struck A.D. 71, in the third consulate of Vespasian.

A black coin, very fine. Weight 405 grains.

289.

IMP . CAES . VESPASIAN . AVG . P . M . TR . P . P . P . COS . III. The laureate head of Vespasian to the right.

℞. VICTORIA . AVGVSTI. In the field S. C. A winged Victory naked to the waist standing to the right; her left hand supports a shield against a palm-tree;

on the shield she has inscribed OB . CIVES . SER .; her left foot rests on a helmet placed on the ground at the foot of the palm-tree.

From the words inscribed on the shield, this coin was struck at the same period and to record the same circumstances as the preceding coin.

The inscription OB . CIVES . SERVATOS . within a wreath, or inscribed on a shield, seems to have been usually adopted at the commencement of a reign from the time of Augustus, when it first appears on the imperial coins.

This beautiful coin was in the cabinet of the Duke of Devonshire, at the sale whereof it was bought away from me by Dr. Rawlings, but I kept on watch, and afterwards got it at the sale of the doctor's coins.

From comparison of the reverse of this coin with the similar reverse type of Vitellius, I consider them as being struck from the same dies, which is not improbable. From the short reign of Vitellius, the dies of his coins were very little used, and with a fresh die for the head of Vespasian, the reverses of Vitellius were applicable, and would come in well; besides, the two coins are precisely alike in size and colour.

The weight of the Vitellian coin is $424\frac{1}{2}$ grains, that of this $413\frac{5}{8}$ grains. It is very fine, and of a black green colour.

290.

IMP . CAESAR . VESPASIANVS . AVG . P . M . TR . P . P . P . COS . III. The laureate head of Vespasian to the right.

℞. FIDES . EXERCITVVM. In the exergum S. C. Two right hands joined, holding between them a military ensign surmounted by an eagle; the foot of the ensign staff rests on the prow of a galley.

The present coin records the unanimity subsisting in the armies of the empire on the election of Vespasian, to which are added the naval forces, represented by the prow of the galley on which the staff of the eagle is set; thus signifying the conjunction of the army and navy in the selection of Vespasian for their emperor.

This coin (weight 425 grains) is one of the rare types of Vespasian. It was in the cabinet of Cavalier Campana, from whence I obtained it. I had never met with it before, nor have I seen it at sale since; and the same remark will apply to the next coin.

291.

IMP . CAES . VESPASIAN . AVG . COS . III. The laureate head of Vespasian to the right.

℞. *No legend.* In the field S. C. Three military standards, that in the centre being an eagle. Each standard is fixed on the prow of a galley. They are precisely the same in every respect as the type on the coin of Galba already described No. 256 *ante*.

It signifies the adhesion or fidelity of the army and navy to the cause of Vespasian.

This coin I obtained from the cabinet of Mr. Thomas, and its rarity is almost as great as that of the preceding coin. Weight $163\frac{1}{4}$ grains.

292.

IMP . CAES . VESPASIAN . AVG . COS . III. The radiated head of Vespasian to the right.

℞. LIBERTAS . PVBLICA. In the field S. C. Liberty standing looking to the left, holding a pileus in her right hand, a rudis in the left.

A fine Second Brass coin expressive of the fortunate change of the times and the benefits anticipated from the accession of Vespasian. Weight $235\frac{1}{4}$ grains.

293.

IMP . CAES . VESPASIAN . AVG . P . M . TR . P . P . P . C . . . . . The laureate head of Vespasian to the right.

℞. S . P . Q . R . ADSERTORI . LIBERTATIS . PVBLICAE . inscribed in four lines within an oak-wreath.

This coin is unique in its singular compliment, for the legend does not occur on any coin of any emperor before or after Vespasian, and strongly indicates, as well by the words used in the legend as by the civic wreath which surrounds them, the satisfaction that was felt by the citizens of Rome on the accession of Vespasian to the sovereignty.

The coin itself has been rather ill-used, and no doubt was formerly in the cabinet of the Duke of Modena; the small silver eagle at the back of the head has been cut out, but its place of insertion remains. Weight $361\frac{1}{2}$ grains.

294.

IMP . CAES . VESPASIAN . AVG . P . M . TR . P . P . P . COS . III. The laureate head of Vespasian to the left.

℞. S . P . Q . R . ADSERTORI . LIBERTATIS . PVBLICAE . inscribed in four lines within an oak-wreath.

This type we have described on the preceding coin.

A very good coin, of black-brown hue. Weight $401\frac{1}{2}$ grains.

295.

IMP . CAES . VESPASIAN . AVG . P . M . TR . P . P . P . COS . III. The laureate head of Vespasian to the right.

℞. SPES . AVGVSTA. In the exergum S. C. Hope standing to the left, holding up her robes with her left hand; her right hand is extended towards three military officers who stand before her. The first carries a standard, the second extends his right hand towards her, the third holds the hilt of his sword with his right hand, the sword being girded on his right side.

The present coin represents the salutation of Vespasian as emperor by the legions of Ægypt, Judæa, and Mœsia, who were the first to declare him emperor. It was only upon great persuasion, and almost threats of personal violence, that he was induced to consent to take the imperial dignity.

There is a similar type in the coins of Claudius. It is also the type of a coin that was sold in Dr. Mead's sale in 1755, but it is rather curiously described in the catalogue. "IMP . CAES . VESPASIAN . AVG . P . M . TR . P . P . P . COS . III. cap. lau. SPES . AVGVSTA. S. C. Dea Spes dextram porrigit Imperatori galeato, adstantibus Tito et Domitiano." It is a strange error to describe the soldiers as the emperor and his sons, for it may be observed on a careful inspection of such figures on a reverse, when it is intended to represent an emperor, that he is never depicted wearing a helmet; but soldiers, or Mars, or Minerva, or Roma always wear their helmet.

This is one of the very rare types of Vespasian. Weight $377\frac{1}{4}$ grains.

296.

IMP . CAES . VESPASIAN . AVG . P . M . TR . P . P . P . COS . III. The laureate head of Vespasian to the right.

℞. ROMA . RESVRGES. In the exergum S. C. The emperor in his robes standing to the left. With his right hand he is raising a female who is kneeling before him on her left knee. At her left side is Minerva with her spear and shield, who seems to be addressing the emperor. The legend is addressed by the emperor to the personification Roma, whom he is raising from the ground and promising to restore to her former state and dignity.

This coin was struck A.D. 71, and it would not only apply to the rebuilding of the capitol and other public and private buildings which had been burnt and destroyed in the civil commotions that followed upon the death of Galba, but also, morally, to the reform of abuses which had crept into almost every department of the state during the reign of Nero, and which the short reigns of Galba, Otho, and Vitellius had not given those emperors time to look into and reform had they been disposed to do so.

The grouping of the figures on this reverse resembles the group on the reverse of the coins of Galba, already noted.

This is also one of the very rare coins of this emperor.

297.

IMP . CAESAR . VESPASIANVS . AVG . P . M . TR . P . P . P . COS . $\overline{\text{III}}$. The laureate head of the emperor to the right.

℞. *No legend.* In the field S. C. A Victory flying to the right, bearing a palm-branch in her left hand, in her right hand she holds up a wreath.

This coin was struck A.D. 71, and refers to the conquest of Judæa and destruction of Jerusalem, an event which occasioned great rejoicings at Rome, and procured the honours of a triumph for Vespasian and his son Titus.

This type, although frequent with some emperors, Galba for instance, is very uncommon for Vespasian.

Weight 434¼ grains.

298.

IMP . CAES . VESPASIAN . AVG . P . M . TR . P . P . P . COS . III. The laureate head of Vespasian to the right.

℞. IVDAEA . CAPTA. In the exergum S. C. A palm-tree rising in the middle of the field, on the left side of which a female captive is seated upon armour, her head reclining upon her left hand in the attitude of grief. The emperor is standing on the right side, bare-headed and in military costume; in his right hand he holds a spear erect, and in the left hand a parazonium; his left foot rests on a helmet lying at the foot of the palm-tree.

Weight 395¼ grains.

This and most of the following coins relate to the conquest of Judæa and the victories of Titus; they were all struck about A.D. 71 and 72. They form a series of great interest, being the records of a heathen people, minted for the purpose of magnifying their own importance; but verifying to us that our Lord's prophecy of the destruction of the city of Jerusalem and the dispersion of the Jews, as related in the gospels, was fulfilled to the very letter, when, speaking of the magnificent temple which was in the city, he declared that not one stone should be left upon another.

At the death of Vitellius, Vespasian was in the East, and on his election by the armies as emperor, he quitted Judæa to proceed to Alexandria on his way to Rome, leaving his son Titus general of the Roman armies to complete the Jewish war and conquest of Judæa, which had been commenced by Vespasian when general under Nero, A.D. 67.

The siege of Jerusalem was prosecuted with great vigour by Titus, who ultimately made himself master of the place, notwithstanding the skilful and powerful resistance of the Jewish generals, more especially of Simon Gioras, who was eventually taken prisoner and sent to Rome. Titus, who had observed the beauty and grandeur of the temple, became desirous of saving it from destruction, and, when the final assault was made on the city, he gave strict orders for its preservation; but, in spite of his directions that this splendid structure should not be injured, a Roman soldier raised himself on the shoulders of a comrade and threw a lighted torch into one of the apartments, where some drapery taking fire it communicated to the rest of the building, and ultimately reduced the whole to ashes and ruin. Titus and some followers rushed into the Holy of Holies and other sacred apartments, and brought out the golden candlestick and several other superb ornaments and furniture of the temple, which were saved and afterwards carried in the triumphal procession at Rome.

The arch of Titus, yet extant at Rome, bears many sculptures, in which are represented various objects from the temple at Jerusalem being carried by Roman soldiers.

In this memorable siege, it is recorded that nearly two millions of Jews perished in various ways; but, notwithstanding so much slaughter, the end was not yet, for it was not until the time of Hadrian that the expulsion of the Jews from the city finally took place, as we shall see under the coins of Hadrian, *post*.

In the 79th Psalm we have four beautiful and affecting verses lamenting the devastation of Jerusalem, which it is supposed was to take place by the Chaldees under their king Nebuchadnezzar; but, although that king made great havoc amongst the Jews, yet the verses are continuous, and more strongly apply to the destruction committed by Titus and completed by Hadrian than to what was done by the Chaldees. From the periods of Titus and Hadrian to the present times, the Jews have ceased to be a nation.

"O God, the heathen are come into thine inheritance; thy holy temple have they defiled: they have laid Jerusalem on heaps.

"The dead bodies of thy servants have they given to be meat unto the fowls of the heaven, the flesh of thy saints unto the beasts of the earth.

"Their blood have they shed like water round about Jerusalem; and there was none to bury them."

"We are become a reproach to our neighbours, a scorn and derision to them that are round about us."

And in the book of Deuteronomy, chap. xxviii. 64, 65, 66, 68, we read,—

"And the Lord shall scatter thee among all people, from the one end of the earth even unto the other; and there thou shalt serve other gods, which neither thou nor thy fathers have known, even wood and stone.

"And among these nations shalt thou find no ease, neither shall the sole of thy foot have rest: but the Lord shall give thee there a trembling heart, and failing of eyes, and sorrow of mind.

"And thy life shall hang in doubt before thee; and thou shalt fear day and night, and shalt have none assurance of thy life.

"And the Lord shall bring thee into Ægypt again with ships, by the way whereof I spake unto thee, Thou shalt see it no more again: and there ye shall be sold unto your enemies for bondmen and bondwomen, *and no man shall buy you.*"

No man shall buy you was exhibited by the fact, that so many Jews were made slaves in Judæa, that three were sold for one piece of silver—taking the piece of silver to mean the denarius, it was at the rate of two pence each; if it were the drachma or tetradrachma, it would be about two shillings and six pence each.

299.

IMP . CAES . VESPASIAN . AVG . P . M . TR . P . P . P . COS . III. The laureate head of the emperor to the right.

℞. IVDAEA . CAPTA. In the exergum S. C. A type similar to the preceding coin, excepting that the figure of the emperor reaches nearly to the top of the palm-tree, on the left side of which a weeping female is seated on a cuirass.

Weight, 411¼ grains.

In addition to our Lord's prophecy of the destruction of Jerusalem, as related in the Gospels, there are, in the book of Deuteronomy, chapter xxviii., dreadful denunciations against the Jews for their disobedience, which were fulfilled in the siege of Samaria by Ben-hadad, king of Syria, as related in 2 Kings, chapter vi. verses 28, 29, as well as in the siege of Jerusalem by Titus, as related by Josephus.

In Patin, page 148, we read:—"*Effossum fuit superiori sæculo marmor in Circo in quo titulus hic erat sculptus—*

IMP . TITO . CAESARI . DIVI . VESPASIANI . F .
VESPASIANO . AVG . PONTIFICI . MAXIMO .
TRIB . POT . X . IMP . XVII . COS . VIII . P . P .
PRINCIPI . SVO . S . P . Q . R .
QVOD . PRAECEPTIS . PATRIS . CONSILIIS . QVE . ET .
AVSPICIS . GENTEM . IVDAEORVM . DOMVIT . ET .
VRBEM . HIEROSOLYMAM . OMNIBVS . ANTE . SE .
DVCIBVS . REGIBVS . GENTIBVSQVE . AVT . FRVSTRA .
PETITAM . AVT . OMNINO . INTENTATAM . DELEVIT .

Thus adding a further record to the fact of the destruction of the city of Jerusalem.

300.

IMP . CAES . VESPASIAN . AVG . P . M . TR . P . P . P . COS . $\overline{\text{III}}$. The laureate head of Vespasian to the right.

℞. IVDAEA . CAPTA. In the exergum S. C. A palm-tree, on the right side of which a man is standing with his hands bound behind him; he is looking at a female who is sitting on a cuirass on the other side of the tree weeping; behind the man are some shields and armour lying on the ground; a shield is also resting against the left side of the female.

Weight 399½ grains.

This coin was struck on the same occasion as the preceding; but, instead of the emperor, on this reverse we have a male captive, who, by the arms strewed on the ground behind him, is intended to represent a military personage. It is generally considered by antiquaries that the military captive represented on this coin is intended for Simon Gioras the Jewish general, who was taken prisoner and led in the triumphal procession at Rome, and on the same day put to death according to the barbarous custom of the Romans with such prisoners.

The female sitting weeping represents Jerusalem, or, we may say, the country of Judæa. A triumph being decreed for the conquest of Judæa, an arch was erected bearing an inscription, as follows:

SENATVS .
POPVLVSQVE . ROMANVS
DIVO . TITO . DIVI . VESPASIANI . F
VESPASIANO . AVGVSTO .

A good part of this arch is still remaining, but houses are built by the sides of it. On the sides under the arch are basso-relievos representing the Roman soldiers carrying the golden candlestick of seven branches, the tables of the law, the trumpet of jubilee, and other sacred instruments used in the Temple, as they were borne in the triumphal procession.

301.

IMP . CAES . VESPASIAN . AVG . P . M . TR . P . P . P . COS . $\overline{\text{III}}$. The laureate head of the emperor to the right.

℞. IVDAEA . CAPTA. In the exergum S. C. A palm-tree, on the left side whereof a man stands with his hands bound behind him, looking at a female seated on the other side of the palm-tree, with her head resting on her hands; in front of her are some shields, and some shields are on the ground behind the man.

Weight 407⅝ grains.

A coin struck on the same occasion as the preceding coins. The prisoner, with his hands bound, is to represent the Jewish general, as on the last coin.

Jerusalem was taken by the Romans on the seventeenth of the Jewish month Tamuz, coinciding with the nineteenth of the month of July. The temple was destroyed about the ninth of the month of August, or ninth of the Jewish month Ab; both of these days are kept by the Jews at the present time as days of fasting and humiliation.

302.

. . . . . . SPAS . AVG . P . M . TR . P . P . P . COS . III. The laureate head of the emperor to the right.

℞. IVDAEA . . . In the exergum S. C. A female in the attitude of grief, her head resting on her left hand, seated on armour on the left side of a palm-tree; on the other side of the tree, is a man who appears to be tied to the tree with his hands behind him; a helmet is on the ground before him.

Weight 393¾ grains.

303.

IMP . CAES . VESPASIAN . AVG . P . M . TR . P . P . P . COS . III. The laureate head of the emperor to the right.

℞. VICTORIA . AVGVSTI . In the exergum S. C. A palm-tree on the left side, to which a shield is affixed, and before it is a Victory, who, while supporting the shield with her left hand, is inscribing on it with her right hand; her left foot rests on a helmet lying on the ground; on the other side of the palm-tree a female is seated weeping.

Weight 378¼ grains.

304.

IMP . CAES . VESPASIAN . AVG . P . M . TR . P . P . P . COS . III.   The laureate head of the emperor to the right.

℞. VICTORIA . AVGVSTI.   In the field S. C.   A Victory inscribing a shield affixed to a palm-tree as described on the preceding coin, but there is no captive seated at the foot of the tree.

Weight 408 grains.

These two coins refer to the capture of Jerusalem as already noticed.

305.

IMP . CAES . VESPASIANVS . AVG . P . M . TR . P . P . P . COS . $\overline{\text{III}}$.   The laureate head of the emperor to the right.

℞. VICTORIA . AVGVSTI.   In the exergum S. C.   The emperor, bare-headed and in military costume, standing to the left with a spear in his left hand; his right hand is extended towards a Victory, who stands before him and presents him a small figure of Minerva Jaculatrix.

Weight 380¼ grains.

This coin also commemorates the conquest of Judæa. The little figure of Minerva, presented by Victory to the emperor, is a compliment to the wisdom and judgment he displayed in the arrangement of his plans for prosecuting the war to a successful termination.

306.

IMP . CAES . VESPAS . AVG . P . M . TR . P . P . P . COS . $\overline{\text{III}}$.   The laureate head of the emperor to the right.

℞. *No legend.*   In the field S. C.   Mars unclothed, gradient to the right, bearing a trophy of arms on his left shoulder, in his right hand he carries a spear with the point forward.

307.

IMP . CAES . VESPASIAN . AVG . PM . TR . P . P . P . COS . $\overline{\text{III}}$.   The laureate head of the emperor to the right.

℞. MARS . VICTOR.   In the field S. C.   Mars unclothed, standing full front, his head inclined to the right; in his right hand he holds a spear, and bears a trophy of arms in the left hand; at his right foot is an altar.

Reddish brown, very good.   Weight 411¼ grains.

308.

IMP . CAES . VESPASIAN . AVG . P . M . TR . P . P . P . COS . III. The laureate head of the emperor to the right.

℞. MARS . VICTOR. In the field S. C. Mars armed, striding hastily from left to right, holding out in his right hand a Victoriola, in his left hand he carries a small trophy of arms.

309.

IMP . CAESAR . VESPASIANVS . AVG . P . M . TR . P . . . . The laureate head of the emperor to the right.

℞. SIGNIS . RECEPTIS. In the exergum S. C. The emperor in military costume and bareheaded, standing on a low basement to the left, bearing a spear in his left hand, the point held downwards; his right hand extended to receive from a Victory who stands before him a legionary eagle, which she presents to him with her right hand, whilst in her left she holds a wreath and a palm branch.

Black brown, fine. Weight 428½ grains.

This is one of the rarest and most interesting coins in the Vespasian series. It records an event which occurred in the Jewish war, which is very imperfectly explained in history or by any antiquaries. Admiral Smyth follows Pellerin in describing a coin of similar type, No. 76, in his cabinet. He says, "It is very difficult to explain what event gave birth to this type. It may, in imitation of one by Augustus, allude to a recovered eagle, or perhaps to some standards taken from Fonteius Agrippa by the Sarmatic Jazygian."

This is the nearest explanation I have been able to obtain from any numismatic antiquary. Even Eckhel, vol. vi. p. 329, considers this type to refer to the recovery of the standards taken from the Romans in Belgium by Civilis in A.D. 78; but in that opinion Eckhel must also be in error, for the coin under consideration was struck in the third consulate, which was in A.D. 71, and therefore cannot by any possibility correspond with an event which took place in A.D. 78. But the solution of the question I venture to give as follows :—Tacitus, lib. xvi.

appendix, sect. viii. (Murphy), speaking of the Jewish war in its early part during the time of Nero, A.D. 67, states, "The Jews were in the field with a powerful army; they had defeated Cestius Gallus with great slaughter, and taken an eagle from one of the legions." Cestius Gallus, who was at that time governor of Syria, was himself slain upon this occasion, soon after which period Nero gave the command of the forces in Syria, including the country of Judæa, to Vespasian.

The legions which were usually quartered in Syria were the LEGIO . III . GALLICA.—LEGIO . IIII . SCYTHICA.—LEGIO . VI . FERRATA . and LEGIO . XII . FVLMINIFERA.—And in Judæa, the LEGIO . V . MACEDONIA.—LEGIO . X.—and LEGIO . XV . APOLLINARIS. It was therefore one of these seven legions which lost its eagle, but the particular legion is in no place mentioned, and Tacitus nowhere subsequently speaks of the eagle being recovered. Merivale, vi. 514, says, " Cestius Gallus put himself at the head of the twelfth legion with 6,000 men picked from other corps and several thousands of auxiliaries." This would make it appear that the captured eagle was that of the twelfth legion.

The present coin, with its peculiarly interesting type, steps in and supplies the omission of Tacitus, and we are thus enabled to complete the narrative of the loss of the eagle by the record of its recovery.

The coin in the cabinet of Admiral Smyth, from the corrosion of age, is imperfect in its detail on the reverse. The present coin, which was found at Pompeii, is very perfect in every respect, shewing what is not found on Admiral Smyth's coin, or on any other that I have been able to get access to, for the reverse represents Victory with a wreath as well as a palm-branch in her left hand, the one as an emblem of conquest, and the other the reward of success: with her right hand she presents an eagle to the emperor, and thus shows that the lost eagle had been recovered, and that she restored it to the emperor as the head of the army. The wreath that Victory holds in her left hand with the palm-branch is not mentioned by any writer; I apprehend because all previous specimens have been defective and corroded like Admiral Smyth's coin is.

The words on the reverse SIGNIS . RECEPTIS being in the plural number, signify that more than one standard was recovered, although Victory presents only the eagle; but that is selected as being the chief standard of a legion, and therefore more appropriately the standard to be presented to the emperor. No doubt the defeat of Cestius Gallus supplied the Jews, not only with an eagle, but several other standards, for Josephus, lib. vii. ch. 9, of the Jewish war, mentions that during the siege of the city the Jews killed a great number of standard-bearers, keeping such ensigns as they got possession of.

In the series of Titus, *post*, there is a Second Brass coin, the reverse being Victory placing a wreath on a vexillum fixed in the ground before her, the legend being VICTORIA . AVGVSTI. The two coins, I apprehend, may be considered conjointly, and will clearly make up and account for the loss and recovery of the eagle and standards, and supply the omission in Tacitus and other historians; for, as the capture of Jerusalem was the grand event of Vespasian's reign, including the entire reduction of Judæa, there is no reason why we should seek a solution of the types on this coin and the coin of Titus from any other events than those connected with the Jewish war, and in which both Vespasian and Titus were personally engaged, for Vespasian himself was wounded at the taking of Jotapata, which was defended by Josephus the governor, (the Jewish historian,) who was very soon after taken prisoner, and conveyed to Vespasian, who spared his life.

Another solution of the type has been suggested to me—that it does not refer to the recovery of any eagle, but is complimentary to the valour of the army, and, instead of erecting a trophy, an eagle is presented to the emperor as to the whole army, he, as the chief, being the impersonation of the army; but this is inconsistent with the words of the reverse legend and the facts we have noticed.

310.

IMP . CAESAR . VESPASIAN . AVG . P . M . TR . POT . P . P . COS . III. A smaller laureate head of the emperor to the right; the shoulder of the bust is notched.

℞. SIG . . . . S. C. in the exergum. The type of this reverse is similar to that of the preceding coin; but, from the corrosion of time and some ill usage, the wreath and palm-branch in the left hand of Victory are obliterated, and the remaining portions of the type are very defaced.

This coin, which is black and of poor condition, (weight 398½ grains,) is retained in the cabinet for the following reasons: the obverse appears struck from a bold Second Brass die. The coin in the cabinet of Admiral Smyth is from the same dies, both obverse and reverse, as the present coin, and it is equally injured by time. There is a coin also I have seen in the French cabinet, precisely similar in every respect, as well as in a like poor state of preservation, and by the plate of a coin of this type in Pellerin, the coin there delineated was precisely the same in every way—Pellerin calls it *unique* or *presque unique*, and I believe the three coins to have been struck from the same dies; but there is no coin of this type in the British Museum, nor in the Vienna cabinet, nor was it known to Occo, or Argelati, or Vaillant, nor in the Christina or Arschot cabinets.

311.

IMP . CAES . VESPASIAN . AVG . P . M . TR . P . P . P . COS . III. The laureate head of Vespasian to the right.

℞. ROMA . VICTRIX. In the field S. C. Roma armed, standing to the right, holding a spear in her right hand; in her left hand she has a parazonium, and her left foot rests upon a cuirass lying on the ground.

From the date on this coin it is likewise one recording the successful result of the Jewish war. It was struck A.D. 71, and is rather a scarce coin.

Weight 389 grains.

312.

IMP . CAES . VESPASIAN . AVG . P . M . TR . P . P . P . COS . III. The laureate head of Vespasian to the right.

℞. PAX . P . ROMANI. In the field S. C. Peace standing to the left, her right hand extended, holding an olive branch. On her left arm she bears a cornucopiæ, filled with fruits.

Weight 398¼ grains.

The type is emblematic of the benefits conferred on the people by the peace which followed the wars and deaths of Otho and Vitellius, as well as consequent upon the taking of Jerusalem, when the Jewish war ceased. In this year, A.D. 71, and the third consulate of Vespasian, he shut up the Temple of Janus, for the sixth time since the building of Rome.

In this year, likewise, a grand triumphal procession of the emperor and his son Titus was celebrated with great pomp, for the conquest of Jerusalem.

313.

IMP . CAES . VESPASIANVS . AVG . P . M . TR . P . P . P . COS . III. The laureate head of the emperor to the right.

℞. PAX . AVG. In the exergum S. C. Peace standing to the right; facing her on the left side of the field is a square altar; some arms are piled up before it, to which she is setting fire with a torch; in her left hand she holds erect what seems an olive-branch; behind her on the right is a column surmounted by a small figure; at the foot of the column in front are a helmet and shield, and a spear leans against it on the other side.

Weight 425¼ grains.

The present type shows an offering made to Mars of arms, the spoils of the vanquished, as was customary with the Romans. It has been suggested that this coin refers to the period when Vespasian, having by his son Titus finished the Jewish war, closed the Temple of Janus. That ceremony took place in A.D. 71, in the third consulate of Vespasian.

The small figure on the column behind Peace is by most writers termed a Bellona; and the column is itself supposed to be that from the side of which it was the custom of the Romans to throw a spear in the geographical direction of the country against which they declared war.

The custom of burning arms and military weapons gathered up from the field of battle, as an offering to Mars, is thus described by Silius Italicus, in his poem on the second Punic war :

> Ast tibi Bellipotens, sacrum constructus acervo
> Ingenti mons armorum consurgit ad astra :
> Ipse manu celsam pinum flammâque comantem
> Attollens, ductor Gradivum in vota ciebat;
> Primitias pugnæ et læti libamina belli,
> Hannibal Ausonio cremat hæc de nomine Victor.
> Et tibi, Mars genitor, votorum haud surde meorum
> Arma electa dicat spirantum turba virorum.
> Tum face conjectâ populatur fervidus ignis
> Flagrantem molem, et rupta caligine in auras
> Actus apex clarâ perfundit lumine campos.
>
> Lib. x.

314.

IMP . CAESAR . VESPASIANVS . AVG . P . M . TR . P . P . P . COS . III. The laureate head of the emperor to the right.

℞. PAX . ORBIS . TERRARV. In the field S. C. Peace standing to the right with a loaded cornucopiæ on her left arm, her right hand placed behind her back. Before her is a square altar, on which a fire is burning.

Weight 390¼ grains.

This coin was struck upon the conquest of Judæa ; and, when all the provinces had been reduced to tranquillity after the agitation created throughout the whole Roman empire upon the death of Galba, Vespasian then closed the temple of Janus, and peace prevailed over all the Roman world, whence the significant legend on this reverse.

315.

IMP . CAESAR . VESPASIAN . AVG . P . M . TR . P . P . P . COS . III. The laureate head of the emperor to the right.

℞. PAX . AVGVSTI. In the field S. C. Peace standing to the left. Her right hand extended holds an olive branch; on her left arm she bears a cornucopiæ filled with fruits.

Weight 411¼ grains.

316.

IMP . CAES . VESPASIAN . AVG . P . M . TR . P . P . P . COS . III. The laureate head of Vespasian to the right.

℞. PAX . AVGVSTI. In the field S. C. Peace seated to the left on a square seat with a low back. Her right hand extended holds an olive branch; her left arm rests on the back of the chair; in her hand she holds a *hasta pura* transversely.

Weight 376¾ grains.

All these varieties of Pax relate to the cessation of strife at Rome and abroad, as we have already noticed.

317.

IMP . CAES . VESPASIAN . AVG . COS . III. The laureate head of the emperor to the right.

R. *No legend.* In the field S. C. Victory gradient to the left, seemingly in great joy, with a trophy of arms over her right shoulder, her left hand raised to support it.

Weight 146¼ grains.

318.

IMP . CAES . VESPASIAN . AVG . COS . III. The head of Vespasian to the right, with radiate crown.

℞. *No legend.* S. C. in the field. Victory volant to the left, holding in her right hand a circular shield bearing the inscription S . P . Q . R.

Weight 212¾ grains.

These two coins are of Second Brass, and were struck A.D. 71, on the same occasion as the preceding.

319.

IMP . CAES . VESPASIAN . AVG . COS . III. The head of Vespasian to the right, with radiate crown.

℞. TVTELA . AVGVSTI. In the exergum S. C. A female seated on a square seat to the left. At her left side is a child, who she embraces with her left arm. Before her is another child, on whose shoulder the female places her right hand.

Mionnet, *Tit. Vespasien*, describes this type as " Femme assise entre Titus et Domitien," which seems to be its proper solution, considering these two individuals represented by the two children as the future support or guardians of the empire. It is a Second Brass coin of rare occurrence.

Weight 221½ grains.

320.

IMP . CAES . VESPASIAN . AVG . P . M . TR . P . P . P . COS . III. The laureate head of the emperor to the right.

℞. ROMA. In the field S. C. Roma armed, standing full front looking to the left; her right hand extended holds a Victoriola, which presents her a wreath; in her left hand she holds her spear upright; her dress reaches only to her knees.

Weight 426 grains.

321.

IMP . CAES . VESPASIAN . AVG . COS . III. The radiate head of the emperor to the right.

℞. ROMA. in the exergum; S. C. in the field. Roma armed, seated on arms to the left; her right hand extended presents a wreath; with the left hand she grasps the hilt of her sword; her clothes reach only to her knees.

The present is a Second sized coin, and with the preceding seems to be complimentary to the emperor on the successful termination of the Jewish war.

Weight 234 grains.

322.

IMP . CAES . VESPAS . AVG . P . M . TR . P . P . P . COS . III. The laureate head of Vespasian to the right.

℞. FORTVNAE . REDVCI. In the field S. C. Fortune, standing full front, looking to the left; her right hand extended holds an olive branch, and also the tiller of a rudder, the bottom of which rests on a globe; the left arm bears a cornucopiæ loaded with fruits.

As Vespasian did not come to Rome directly on his election to the empire, but remained in the Eastern provinces for a time, and ultimately came over to Italy from Alexandria, it is evident from the consulate marked on this coin that it was struck A.D. 71, to express the satisfaction of the people at Rome at the return of Vespasian from Syria, Judæa, and Ægypt, especially as his presence in Rome put down commotions and restored tranquillity to the city.

323.

IMP . CAES . VESPASIAN . AVG . P . M . TR . P . P . P . COS . $\overline{\text{III}}$.—The laureate head of the emperor to the right.

℞. CAESAR . AVG . F . DES . IMP . AVG . F . COS . DES . $\overline{\text{II}}$. In the exergum S.C. Titus and Domitian standing on either side, each bare-headed and in military costume; each holds a spear in the right hand; the one standing on the left has also a sceptrum on his left arm.

Rough mottled green; good condition. Weight 411½ grains.

According to the Fasti Consulares, it would seem this coin was struck in A.D. 71, when Domitian was nominated for consul the second time; for in A.D. 71 the consuls were the emperor Vespasian and M. Cocceius Nerva, afterwards emperor, and in A.D. 73 Domitian was full Consul II. with M. Valerius Messalinus.

In the year A.D. 71, being the year of triumph for the capture of Jerusalem, Titus was nominated Cæsar, and received the Tribunicia Potestas also; he became Imperator, and associated with his father in the government, and Domitian was nominated for Consul the second time.

324.

IMP . CAES . VESPASIAN . AVG . COS . III. The radiate head of Vespasian to the right.

℞. CONCORDIA . AVGVSTI. In the exergum S. C. A female seated to the left on a square seat, her right hand extended holds a patera; the left arm supports a cornucopiæ.

Weight 171½ grains.

325.

IMP . CAES . VESPASIAN . AVG . COS . III. The laureate head of the emperor to the right.

℞. AEQVITAS . AVGVSTI. In the exergum S. C. A female standing to the left; her right hand holds a pair of scales, in the left hand she has a palm-branch.

The two coins, of second module, were struck A.D. 71, to compliment the emperor on the peace, good order, and upright conduct with which the government of Rome was now managed.

326.

IMP . CAES . VESPAS . AVG . P . M . TR . P . P . P . COS . III. The laureate head of the emperor to the right.

A brown coin. Weight 389½ grains.

℞. *No legend.* S. C. in the field. The fountain, or, as it is usually termed, the *meta sudans*, which stood near to the amphitheatre. The present coin represents the fountain in the same manner, (excepting as to the flowing of the water, which is the artist's licence,) as it is figured by A. Donati in his excellent work, Roma Vetus ac Recens, ed. 1694, p. 188, and described by him, "Ante

Arcum Constantini et Amphitheatrum metam sudantem, fontem videlicet eorum qui ludos frequentabant extinguendæ siti percommodum, eminente Jovis simulacro, extante adhuc vestigio; constituunt, quam in nummis expressam habemus."

And he gives the portraiture of a coin of Titus exactly similar in its detail of the fountain to that the present coin exhibits.

The coin in Admiral Smyth's cabinet, and described as the *meta sudans*, is very different, being simply a column with very small base. I would suggest, may not Admiral Smyth's coin represent the *milliarium aureum* and not the *meta sudans?* Some slight remains of the *meta sudans* are still to be seen in the locality mentioned by Donati.

The coin of Titus with the *meta* was in the sale of Mr. Langdon's coins in fine condition; and very good in the sale of the Earl of Gainsborough's coins, 1858.

327.

IMP . CAES . VESPASIAN . AVG . P . M . TR . P . P . P . COS . III. The laureate head of the emperor to the right.

℞. SALVS . AVGVSTA. In the exergum S. C. A female seated to the left, her right hand extended holding a patera, in her left hand she holds a *hasta pura* erect. There is no altar or serpent.

This is one of the scarce coins of the Vespasian series.

328.

IMP . CAES . VESPAS . AVG . P . M . TR . P . P . P . COS . IIII. The laureate head of the emperor to the right.

℞. *No legend.* In the exergum S. C. The emperor on horseback, galloping to the right, casting a javelin at a warrior who has been thrown down under the horse, but is half raised from the ground, with a shield on his left arm and sword in his right hand, protecting himself from the assault of the emperor.

Weight 390¼ grains.

There does not appear to be mention in history of any act of single combat with an enemy having been performed by Vespasian in Britain or in the Jewish war. We must, therefore, consider this type, which was struck in A.D. 72, as allegoric, and referring generally to the military prowess of the emperor as a commander, and not to any specific act of valour.

Vaillant, Numismata, ed. 1692, p. 32, describing this type, says, "Hic nummus primæ magnitudinis rarior est quam in Tito et Domitiano."

329.

IMP · CAES . VESP . AVG . P . M . TR . P . P . P . COS . IIII . CENS .   The laureate head of Vespasian to the right.

℞. VICTORIA . NAVALIS .   In the field S. C.   A winged Victory standing to the right on the prow of a galley, holding a palm-branch in her left hand, in her right hand she holds up a wreath.

On referring to the Fasti Consulares it will be seen that Vespasian's fourth consulate was in A.D. 72, jointly with his son Titus, and by coins they were joint censors in the same year, and as the legend on the obverse of this coin concludes with the title of censor, the coin was struck in A.D. 72.

The event to which this coin and two coins of Titus and Domitian refer is related by Josephus in the Jewish War, lib. iii. ch. 17, and ch. 19, who says that Titus, having assaulted and taken Tarichæa on the lake of Genesareth, many of the besieged embarked and escaped. The day after Titus commenced the construction of some vessels, and in a few days Vespasian himself pursued the fugitives, whom he encountered and overthrew, and occasioned a loss of near ten thousand men, including those who were afterwards slain at Tiberias, and about eight to ten thousand more were sent into slavery. Josephus, speaking of the triumph of Vespasian and Titus for the capture of Jerusalem, must refer to this naval victory when he says, " Rostra navium à militibus portata esse."

This coin, and those of Titus and Domitian with similar type, are all of Second Brass. It is not known as a First Brass coin.

Black green, very good.   Weight 168½ grains.

330.

IMP . CAESAR . VESPASIAN . AVG . COS . IIII.   The radiate head of the emperor to the right.

℞. PAX . AVG.   In the field S. C.   A female standing to the left with a caduceus and olive branch in her left hand; her right hand holds a patera, from which she is in the act of pouring a libation on a fire that is burning on a decorated square altar placed on the ground at her right foot.

Weight 188½ grains.

331.

. . . . VESP . AVG . P . M . TR . P . P . P . COS . IIII . CENS.   The laureate head of the emperor to the right.

℞. *No legend.*   In the exergum S. C.   The emperor in a triumphal quadriga decorated with figures, passing slowly to the right; on the side a Victory is sculptured presenting a wreath.   Weight 390½ grains.

The triumph for the conquest of Judæa was celebrated in A.D. 71, and there are coins of that date with this type; the present coin was struck A.D. 72. The triumph was decreed to Vespasian and his son Titus.

Josephus gives a very full account of the procession. Amongst the trophies and spoils displayed were the golden candlestick, the golden table, and other articles of the costly furniture of the Temple; and amongst the captives walking in the procession was the Jewish general, Simon Gioras, who was put to death while Vespasian and Titus were ascending the steps of the capitol, and his body afterwards dragged to the Gemonia.

Occo places the triumph in the kalends of July, A.D. 72 (p. 148), and Argelati places it in A D. 71.

332.

IMP . CAES . VESP . AVG . P . M . TR . P . COS . IIII . CENS. The laureate head of the emperor to the right.

℞. *No legend.* S. C. in the field. A person in military costume on horseback to the left, his right hand raised as in the act of addressing spectators; on his left arm he bears a trophy of arms.

Weight 159½ grains.

Were it not that Vespasian had already been in Rome, and passed there the second and third consulates, this might be considered as representing his *adventus*. I should consider it most probably refers to the return of Titus from the Jewish war, when he was received into the city with demonstrations of great joy, and public festivals were held and the triumph decreed. We may thus fairly consider the person represented on this reverse to be Titus, on his arrival in Rome after his victorious campaign. Although the coin (Second Brass) was struck in the fourth consulate, it may still have reference to past events.

333.

IMP . CAES . VESPASIAN . AVG . COS . IIII. The laureate head of the emperor to the right.

℞. PROVIDENT under the base of a square altar. S. C. on either side of the field. Weight 165½ grains.

334.

IMP . CAES . VESP . AVG . P . M . TR . P . COS . V̄ . CENS. The radiate head of the emperor to the left.

℞. FELICITAS PVBLICA. In the field S. C. A female standing to the left; her right hand extended holds a caduceus, on her left arm she bears a cornucopiæ filled with fruits. Weight 195¼ grains.

335.

IMP . CAESAR . VESPASIANVS . AVG. The laureate head of the emperor to the left.

℞. PON . MAX . TR . POT . P . P . COS . V̄ . CENS. No S. C. Two cornucopiæ filled with fruits, in saltier, a caduceus between them.

Weight 201¼ grains.

These are three Second Brass coins, and, taken together, appear to represent the tranquillity, abundance, and consequent happiness the Roman people experienced from the discreet measures adopted by Vespasian for the preservation of the public peace and security.

336.

IMP . CAES . VESPAS . AVG . P . M . TR . P . P . P . COS . IIII. The laureate head of the emperor to the right.

℞. PAX . AVGVSTI. In the exergum S. C. Peace burning arms, as already described on the coin No. 313 *ante*.

Weight 413¼ grains.

The termination of the Jewish war, and capture of Jerusalem, to which this type refers, was a prolific subject for the Triumviri Monetales and their die-engravers, during the reigns of Vespasian and Titus.

337.

IMP . CAES . VESPASIAN . AVG . P . M . TR . P . P . P . COS . VII. The laureate head of the emperor to the right.

℞. FORTVNAE . REDVCI. In the field S. C. Fortune standing full front, looking to the left; her right hand extended holds an olive branch, and rests on the top of a rudder, the left arm bears a cornucopiæ filled with fruits.

Black, very fine, from cabinet of Rev. E. C. Brice. Weight 413½ grains.

When Augustus returned to Rome from his tour in Greece and Sicily in the early part of his reign, he built and dedicated a temple to Fortuna Redux, which is recorded on the gold and silver coins of Augustus, in the fourth tribunician date, the eleventh consulate and year of Rome 735; but the type does not appear on any brass coins of Augustus that are at present known. From this it became a custom with the emperors on their return to Rome from any expedition to a foreign country to make an offering at the temple of Fortuna Redux.

Although it does not appear from history that Vespasian ever went upon any foreign expedition after he came to Rome as emperor, yet Titus did. This coin I consider may therefore be appropriated in its type to commemorate the return of Titus from a tour of inspection in the provinces, for it is well known that after Vespasian had restored order in Rome he began the rebuilding of the capitol and other public buildings which had been injured or destroyed in the civil commotions of Otho and Vitellius. He also made reforms in the government and management of the provinces; and, as he did not travel himself, there is no reason to doubt but that Titus was deputed to carry out his father's plans and inspect the different provinces of the empire; and on the return of the prince he was received with great joy, and the present coin struck, with an appropriate type and legend, to record the event and the public satisfaction at his presence amongst them once more.

The date of the consulate, VII. would give this coin the date of its being struck A.D. 76, when Vespasian and his son Titus were joint consuls.

338.

IMP . CAES . VESPASIAN . AVG . P . M . TR . P . P . P . COS . $\overline{\text{VII}}$. The laureate head of the emperor to the right.

℞. *No legend.* S. C. in the exergum. A temple of six columns approached by steps ranging the whole front of the building; under the portico in front in the central compartment are the statues of three deities; two other statues are placed at the wings withoutside of the columns or portico. Of the three deities under the portico that in the centre is seated, and we may consider it to represent a Jupiter; the statue on the right hand is a figure of Minerva standing; and that on the left hand, also standing, would be a Juno. On the outside on the sloping lines of the roof are many sculptured figures, and in the tympanum there is an assemblage of figures; that in the centre is seated, and one standing on each side with other figures at the sides extending up to the corners of the base of the tympanum; two on the left side are like smiths forging iron on an anvil. The whole composition and arrangement of the building, architectural and sculptural, forms a very busy and brilliant group.

Although the temple portrayed on this and the following coin is by some writers supposed to refer to the Temple of Peace erected by Vespasian, yet, as the capitol had been burned in the civil commotions of former years, I believe from the deities in front being the Dii Majores, that it is a representation of the capitol which was rebuilt by Vespasian. The rebuilding commenced in A.D. 70, the first stone or ceremonial being laid on the 20th June of that year. The proceeding is described by Tacitus (Histor. iv. par. 52). It is noted by Mr. Merivale (vol. vi. p. 483) in the following terms:—

"With the return of abundance and tranquillity, the first care of the Senate was to commence the restoration of the capitol, for while the Temple of Jupiter lay in ruins the fortunes of the empire seemed to suffer an eclipse. This pious work was entrusted according to ancient precedent to one of the most respected citizens by name L. Vestinus, who, although only of knightly family, was equal in personal distinction to any of the senators. The Haruspices whom he consulted demanded that the ruins of the fallen building should be conveyed away and cast into the lowest places of the city, and the new temple erected precisely on the old foundations, for the gods, they declared, would have no change made in the form of their familiar dwelling.

"On the 20th of June [A.U.C. 823],* being a clear and cloudless day, the area of the temple precincts was surrounded with a cord of fillets and chaplets. Soldiers, chosen for their auspicious names, were marched into it, bearing boughs of the most auspicious trees, and the vestals, attended by a troop of boys and girls, both whose parents were living, sprinkled it with water drawn from bubbling founts or running streamlets.

"Then, preceded by the pontiffs, the prætor Helvidius Priscus stalking round sanctified the place with the mystical washing of sows', sheep's, and bulls' blood, and placed their entrails on a grassy altar. This done, he invoked Jupiter, Juno, and Minerva, and all the patrons of the empire, to prosper the undertaking, and raise, by Divine assistance, their temple founded by the piety of men. Then he touched with his hand the connected fillets, and the magistrates, the priests, the senators, the knights, with a number of the people, lent their strength to draw a great stone to the spot where the building was to commence. Beneath it they laid pieces of gold and silver minted for the occasion, as well as of unwrought metal, for the Haruspices forbade either stone or metal to be used which had been employed before for profane purposes.

"The temple rose from the deep substructions of Tarquinius exactly as was required on the plan of its predecessor. In the eyes of the citizens one thing only might seem wanting on this occasion to their prince's glory, that he should himself be present at the solemnity and conduct it in person. So natural was it,

* Tacitus says—" undecimo kal. Julias serena luce spatium omne quod templa dictabatur evinctum vittis coronisque. Ingressi milites quibus fausta nomina felicibus ramis, dein virgines vestales cum pueris, &c. Tum Helvidius Priscus prætor, præeunte Plauto Eliano pontifice, lustrata suovetaurilibus area," &c.

indeed, to suppose him there taking the part of an Augustus or Claudius in the expiation of his country's sins, that it came to be commonly believed that he was actually present, and such is the assertion of some writers of authority. Yet the circumstantial account of Tacitus proves clearly that this was not the case, and the discrepancy is worth noting from the hint it gives us of the causes which have helped to obscure the truth of facts at this period."

Admiral Smyth, p. 54, when he says that Vespasian himself was present and assisted at the ceremonial of laying the first stone for the rebuilding of the capitol, and carried the first basket of earth himself, is guided to that conclusion by what is said by Suetonius *in Vespasiano* 8.*

This is a dark brown coin from the collection of the Duke of Devonshire. Weight 371½ grains.

339.

IMP . CAES . VESPASIAN . AVG . P . M . TR . P . P . P . COS . VII. The laureate head of Vespasian to the right.

℞. *No legend.* S. C. in the exergum. A representation of the temple displayed on the preceding coin.

The present and preceding coins came from the same dies. There are two coins of this type in the French cabinet, and when I examined them I found they were marked in precisely similar manner to these two coins, having like them a line arching over the top of the temple, which satisfied me that all were from the same dies. The present coin had been in my possession several years before I obtained the preceding coin from the Duke of Devonshire's cabinet.

Havercamp, in the Christina Cabinet, p. 38, ascribes this coin to the capitol rebuilt by Vespasian. Weight 335¼ grains.

340.

IMP . CAES . VESPASIAN . AVG . COS . VIII . P . P. The laureate head of Vespasian to the right; a small globe at the point of the bust.

℞. *No legend.* S. C. on either side of the field. A small temple of six columns, having a flight of steps the whole breadth; the two centre columns are braced by an arch; in front under the portico are three figures, apparently intended for Jupiter, with Minerva on his right hand, Juno on the left; each figure is standing on a square base. Jupiter is standing up undraped, holding

---

* "Ipse restitutionem capitolii aggressus, ruderibus purgandis manus primus admovit, ac suo collo quædam extulit."

the *hasta pura* in his left hand. Minerva has her spear in her right hand, her shield held by the left hand, the lower edge of it resting on the base. Juno has nothing in her hands. In the tympanum above a figure is standing, with a *hasta pura* in the left hand, a recumbent figure on each side. On each angle of the pediment is a chariot with horses, and a quadriga is faintly appearing on the apex of the pediment.

This coin, which is of Second size, may be a representation in smaller form of the capitol; the Dii Majores are in front, and sculptured figures above, though much fewer in number than on the preceding coins. Weight 153½ grains.

341.

IMP . CAESAR . VESP . AVG . CENSOR. The laureate head of the emperor to the right.

℞. VES—TA . on either side of a dome, or baldaschino, supported by four columns, two in front and two of rather smaller circumference, as if retired; the top of the dome is divided in compartments, and the apex is decorated with a large ornament. Under the dome is a figure fully draped, holding a *hasta pura* in the left hand, the right hand extended. At each of the smaller columns is a figure holding a spear, or *hasta pura*; that to the right in the right hand; on the left the figure holds it in the left hand.

This is an aureus. A coin like it is noted in the Arschot Cabinet, plate xxx.

342.

IMP . CAES . VESPASIAN . AVG . P . M . TR . P . P . P . COS . $\overline{\text{VIII}}$. reading from the left. The laureate head of the emperor to the left.

℞. ANNONA . AVGVST. In the field S. C. A female seated to the left on a throne, her left foot resting on a footstool.

This type records a supply of corn provided by Vespasian for the support of poor citizens in his eight consulate, A.D. 77.

It is a coin of rare occurrence. Weight 412¼ grains.

343.

IMP . CAES . VESPASIAN . AVG . COS . VIII. The laureate head of the emperor to the right.

℞. FIDES . PVBLICA. In the field S. C. A female standing to the left; in her right hand she holds a patera, on her left arm she bears a cornucopiæ filled with fruits. Weight 160½ grains.

344.

IMP . CAES . VESPASIAN . AVG . COS . VIII . P . P. The laureate head of the emperor to the right.

℞. AEQVITAS . AVGVSTI. In the field S. C. A female standing to the left, holding a pair of scales in her right hand; in the left a *hasta pura*.

These two coins are by their types expressive of the confidence the Roman people still continued to have in the wisdom and good government of Vespasian.

Weight 130½ grains.

APOTHEOSIS COINS.

Vespasian died in July, A.D. 79, in the sixty-ninth year of his age, at his estate near Reate, his birth-place. The greatest stain on his character for unnecessary cruelty was the murder of Sabinus, told by Plutarch, Mor. pp. 770, 771.

345.

DIVVS . AVGVSTVS . VESPASIANVS. The laureate head of Vespasian to the right.
℞. *No legend.* Spes gradient to the left. S. C. on either side the field.

Weight 403⅔ grains.

The title DIVVS . implies the divinity assigned to the deceased emperor, reminding one of Vespasian's own impious boast, in allusion to the honours and titles awaiting his approaching decease, *ut puto Deus fio.*

346.

DIVO . AVG . VESPAS . in three lines in the upper part of the field. S . P . Q . R . in the exergum. A robed figure of the deceased emperor seated on a throne placed to the right, on a decorated car drawn by four elephants, each of them having a rider. The left hand extended holds a Victoriola, standing on a small globe, and has a wreath and palm-branch in its hands. A *hasta pura* is held in the right hand of the figure of Vespasian.

℞. IMP . T . CAES . DIVI . VESP . F . AVG . P . M . TR . P . P . P . COS . VIII. S. C. in the middle of the field.

A coin struck by Titus, and represents the effigies of the deceased emperor in the state in which it appeared at the annual procession of the deities to the Circensian games. Weight 328¼ grains.

347.

DIVVS . AVGVSTVS . VESP. A robed figure of the deceased emperor seated to the left, his head with a radiate crown; his right hand extended, holds an olive-

2 B

branch; in his left is the *hasta pura* held upright; his left foot rests on a footstool.

℞. IMP . T . CAES . DIVI . VESP . F . AVG . P . M . TR . P . P . P . COS . VIII. In the middle of the field S. C.

Weight 410⅜ grains.

The inscription denotes that this coin was struck by Titus to the memory of his deceased father. The effigies of the emperor, as exhibited on the obverse, is taken from a similar type on the coin of Augustus, *ante*, No. 104. The miniature portrait of Vespasian is very fine and perfect.

DOMITILLA.

FLAVIA DOMITILLA, the daughter of Flavius Liberalis, a Questorian scribe, was married to Vespasian in the year of Rome 793, A.D. 40. She died before Vespasian became emperor.

348.

MEMORIAE DOMITILLAE in three lines on the upper part of the field. A carpentum or funeral car, decorated with sculptures, placed on two wheels and drawn by two mules slowly, to the right.

℞. IMP . T . CAES . DIVI . VESP . F . AVG . P . M . TR . P . P . P . COS . VIII. In the middle of the field S. C.

A coin struck by Titus in A.D. 80. It has been much doubted by some antiquaries, whether the coins of this type are intended for the memory of his mother Domitilla, or of his sister, who was of the same name. Mionnet considers the coin to be applicable to the daughter only. It is however usual to rank Domitilla as the wife of the emperor Vespasian. I have therefore done so on the present occasion. Weight 382⅔ grains.

TITUS.

TITUS FLAVIUS VESPASIANUS, son of Vespasian and Domitilla, was born at Rome in January A.D. 41. After his father's elevation to the throne, he was named Prince of the Roman Youth, in A.D. 69. In A.D. 71, he was invested with the title of Imperator, and associated with his father in the sovereignty, and also in the censorship. On his father's election to the empire, and departure from

Judæa for Rome, Titus was left by him in command of the armies at the siege of Jerusalem. The capture of the city being accomplished, he returned to Rome, and, with his father, enjoyed the honours of a triumph for the conquest of Judæa. A magnificent triumphal arch was afterwards erected, decorated with sculptures recording many of the events of the Jewish war, and which remain nearly entire at the present day.

On the death of his father in A.D. 79, Titus succeeded to the empire, but died in two years, supposed to have been poisoned by his brother Domitianus, who then took upon himself the sovereignty.

With some few exceptions, the coins of Titus are not very rare, except for the condition of their preservation.

349.

T . CAES . VESPASIAN . IMP . PON . TR . POT . COS . II. The laureate head of Titus to the right.

℞. CAESAR . DOMITIAN . COS . DES . II. In the field S. C. A robed equestrian figure to the left bearing a long staff in the left hand, being the staff of the office of consul.

Weight 355½ grains.

Titus was consul for the second time, jointly with his father, in A.D. 72. This coin records Domitian being nominated (*designatus*) for consul the second time.

350.

T . CAES . VESPASIAN . IMP . PON . TR . POT . COS . II. The laureate head of the emperor to the right.

℞. *No legend.* S. C. in the upper part of the field. Titus, armed and on horseback, to the right, has struck down an armed warrior, who is under the horse and partly rising from the ground, and protecting himself with his shield from the impending blow, with sword in his right hand ready to repel the attack of Titus, whose right arm is raised holding a javelin in his right hand.

Weight 375¼ grains.

This coin has reference to the conquest of Judæa, represented by the prostrate warrior under the horse; it was struck in A.D. 72. We have noticed this device in Vespasian, *ante*, No. 328, and it is repeated in Domitian *post*. The three coins are rarely met with.

351.

T . CAES . IMP . PON . TR . P . COS . II . CENS. The laureate head of the emperor to the right.

℞. VICTORIA . NAVALIS. In the field S. C. Victory standing on the prow of a galley to the right; her left hand bears a palm branch; in her right hand she holds up a wreath.

Weight 155¼ grains.

The events recorded by this fine Second Brass coin have been already noticed under the coin of like device in Vespasian, *ante*, No. 329. It occurs again in Domitian, *post*.

352.

T . CAES . VESPASIAN . IMP . PON . TR . POT . COS . II. The laureate head of the emperor to the right.

℞. VICTORIA . AVGVSTI. In the field S. C. A winged Victory standing to the right; her left foot rests on a helmet lying on the ground at the foot of a palm tree, to which a shield is affixed, whereon she is writing.

This coin, struck in A.D. 72, records the capture of Jerusalem as already fully noticed on the coins of Vespasian, *ante*. It is a very rare coin.

Weight 400¼ grains.

353.

T . CAES . VESPASIAN . IMP . P. The laureate head of the emperor to the right.

℞. VICTORIA . AVGVSTI. In the field S. C. Victory standing to the right with a palm-branch in her left hand; before her is a cavalry standard, the vexillum, fixed in the ground; a wreath is fastened on the staff below the silk banner; the whole is surmounted by an ensign, but what it is, is too indistinct. Victory is placing a wreath on the top of the standard.

Weight 172¼ grains.

This coin is contemporaneous with the coin of Vespasian, SIGNIS . RECEPTIS . already noticed, *ante*, No. 309, and I consider it should be read together with that coin. It is, as to its legend, a coin apparently unknown to any numismatic writer; and, although Eckhel considers the coin of Vespasian to refer to the recovery of the Roman standards from Civilis the Belgian chieftain, which he had taken from the Romans, yet I am decidedly of opinion that Eckhel and those who take the same view of the types are quite wrong, as I have noticed in Vespasian, *ante*, No. 309, and that the present coin, coupled with that of Vespasian, make out a clear case that it is the recovery of the eagle and standards lost by Cestius Gallus at Jerusalem, which is recorded by these coins, and not the standards retaken from Civilis in A.D. 78, being a period of 7 years after the coins under consideration were struck.

There is no coin of SIGNIS . RECEPTIS . of Vespasian in the Arschot Cabinet, but there is a brass coin of Titus, pl. xxx., a Victory crowning a standard, as here represented, but without any legend on the reverse. It is described thus: "Victoria alata labaro Titi lauream imponens," but no reference to any event intended by the device. A similar coin of Titus is also mentioned by Oiselius, tab. xciv. 6, but he makes no reference whatever to the event it records, nor is there any legend, as on the present coin.

354.

T . CAES . VESPASIAN IMP . PON . TR . POT . COS . II. The laureate head of Titus to the right.

℞. CONG . PRIMVM . P . R . DATVM. In the exergum S. C. Titus or his legate seated to the left on a curule chair placed on a low suggestum, his right hand extended; Minerva is standing in front on his right hand. On the ground before him a person is standing holding up a tablet to a citizen who is before him, and extending his robe to receive a donation.

Weight $402\frac{1}{4}$ grains.

This coin was struck A.D. 72, and records the first donation made by Titus to the Roman people being citizens of Rome. Argelati, *in Tito*, quotes the present type on a coin of COS . II.; and in the same consulate, A.D. 72, he quotes a coin of CONGIARIVM . TERTIVM . *in Musæo Moscardi*, the grouping of the figures being similar to the present, and the coin in fine preservation. Eckhel, *in Tito*, vol. vi. p. 354, quoting the present type, and referring to the coin described as being in the Musæo Moscardi, designates it as a false coin. He says: "Nemo sanus erit cui non nummus spurius videbitur."

I do not find anywhere any mention made of the second congiary, and I should very much doubt the coin quoted from the Musæo Moscardi on account of its consular date being the same as the *congiarium primum*. It would be rather peculiar to make three congiaries in one year, of which I find no instance throughout the Imperial series; but there is a CONGIARIVM . TERTIVM . COS . VIII . in the Arschot Cabinet which seems to have been overlooked by Eckhel. Gevartius, in his description of that coin, tab. xxix., refers to Zonaras as his authority for Titus having made three congiaries, but he does not pretend or assume that they were all made in the same year.

355.

T . CAES . VESPASIAN . IMP . PON . TR . POT . COS . II. The laureate head of the emperor to the right.

℞. ROMA . on the verge at the right side of the field. S. C. in the field.

Roma armed, standing full front, looking to the left; her right hand extended holds a Victoriola having in its right hand a wreath, in the left a palm-branch; in her left hand she holds her spear upright, her cloak pendant from her shoulders in graceful folds at her left side; her clothes reach just to the knees.

Weight 418¼ grains.

356.

T . CAES . VESPASIAN . IMP . PON . TR . POT . COS . . . The laureate head of Titus to the right.

℞. *No legend*. S. C. in the field. Mars gradient to the right, bearing a trophy of arms on his left shoulder, and carrying a spear in his right hand, the point forwards.

Weight 351½ grains.

357.

T . CAES . IMP . PON . TR . P . COS . II . CENS. The laureate head of Titus to the right.

℞. VESTA. In the field S. C. A circular dome supported by four columns as if to protect from the weather a robed statue placed under it standing on a base, its left hand raised towards its head.

Weight 118½ grains.

Excepting the figures one on each side of the temple or dome not being here represented, one would consider this type to be a repetition of the type on the aureus of Vespasian already noticed, *ante*, No. 341.

358.

T . CAES . VESPASIAN . IMP . PON . TR . POT . COS . II. The laureate head of the emperor to the right.

℞. FORTVNAE . REDVCI. In the field S. C. A female standing full front looking to the left; on her left arm she bears a cornucopiæ filled with fruits, in her right hand she holds the tiller of a rudder.

Weight 394¼ grains.

This is one of the rare types of Titus, for in Large Brass it is not to be found in Occo, Vaillant, Argelati, Havercamp, Gevartius, Eckhel, or Mionnet. There are two in the Vienna cabinet, one COS . II . and one COS . V . DES . VI . although neither of them is noticed by Eckhel.

359.

T . CAESAR . IMP . COS . III . CENS. The laureate head of the emperor to the right.

℞. VICTORIA . AVGVST. In the field S. C. Victory standing to the right on the prow of a galley which has a large goose-neck; in her right hand she holds up a wreath, in her left hand she carries a palm-branch.

The Victory standing on the prow of a galley would seem to refer this coin to the same events that are recorded by the coin VICTORIA . NAVALIS . although the legend and consulate are different; like the other it is a Second Brass coin. Weight 158¼ grains.

360.

T . CAES . IMP . PONT. The laureate head of Titus to the right.

℞. TR . POT . COS . III . CENSOR. No S. C. Two cornucopiæ filled with fruits placed saltier-wise with a caduceus between them. Weight 119¼ grains.

361.

T . CAES . IMP . AVG . F . PON . TR . P . COS . V̄ . CENSOR. The laureate head of Titus to the right.

℞. IVDAEA . CAPTA. In the exergum S. C. A palm-tree in the centre of the field, on the right side of which is a man with his hands bound behind him; on the ground, behind him, is a shield; the man is looking at a female sitting on the left side of the palm-tree on a cuirass in an attitude of grief, resting her head on her left hand; some shields and spears are before her.

Weight 391¼ grains.

A coin recording the capture of Jerusalem, as we have already mentioned, under the coins of Vespasian. The dies for the portrait on the obverse of this and the next coin are engraved by the same artist.

362.

T . CAES . IMP . AVG . F . PON . TR . P . COS . VI . CENSOR. The laureate head of Titus to the right.

℞. ROMA . on the verge at the right side of the field. S. C. in the field. Roma armed standing to the left; her right hand, extended, holds a Victoriola; in her left hand she holds her spear, the point resting on the ground.

Weight 350¼ grains.

363.

T . CAES . IMP . AVG . F . TR . P . COS . VI . CENSOR. The laureate head of the emperor to the right.

℞. IVDAEA CAPTA. In the exergum S. C. A palm-tree, on the right side of which are some shields and spears; on the other side a female is seated on arms, with spear and shield before her, resting her head on her left hand in attitude of grief.

Weight 137¼ grains.

The type of this coin is an additional record of the conquest of Judæa and capture of Jerusalem.

364.

T . CAES . VESPASIAN . IMP . PON . TR POT . COS . VI. The laureate head of Titus to the right.

℞. *No legend.* In the exergum S. C. A temple of six columns in front, in every way resembling the temple already described on the coins of Vespasian *ante.* Were it not that the two centre columns are a little wider apart, it would seem the reverse of this coin and those of Vespasian were from the same dies. It may be therefore fairly considered that the temple on the present coin is intended for the temple represented on the coins of Vespasian, and which we have decided is intended for a representation of the capitol destroyed in the Otho and Vitellian disturbances, and rebuilt in the early part of Vespasian's reign.

365.

T CAES . IMP . AVG . F . TR . P . COS . VI . CENSOR. The laureate head of Titus to the right.

℞. PAX . AVG. In the field S. C. A female standing to the left; her right hand extended holds a patera, from which she is pouring a libation on fire that is burning on an altar standing in front. On her left arm she bears a caduceus and olive branch.

Weight 222½ grains.

366.

T . CAES . IMP . AVG . F . TR . P . COS . VI . CENSOR. The laureate head of the emperor to the right.

℞. PAX . AVG. In the field S. C. A female standing to the left; her right hand extended holds a caduceus; in her left hand she carries an olive branch.

Weight 182½ grains.

This and the preceding coin, both of Second size, allude to the peace procured by the conquest of Judæa and capture of Jerusalem.

367.

IMP . TITVS . CAES . VES . AVG . P . M . TR . P . P . P . COS . VII. The laureate head of the emperor to the right.

℞. *No legend.* S. C. in the field. Spes gradient to the left.
Weight 345¼ grains.

A fine coin of the seventh consulate of Titus, struck A.D. 79, and from its bearing the title IMP . precedent, and P . P added, there is no doubt it was struck soon after the death of Vespasian, which took place in July A D. 79. The spes is representative of the hopeful expectations of the Roman people from the accession of their favourite, Titus, as emperor; and that the advantages and blessings of peace they had enjoyed under Vespasian would still continue.

Coins of the seventh consulate (and I may say generally) bearing the name of Titus in full are rather scarce; they generally have the letter T only, distinguishing them from Tiberius, whose name is usually with the letters TI.

The year A.D. 79 is also memorable for the eruption of Mount Vesuvius, which overwhelmed the cities of Herculaneum and Pompeii. This event took place on the 23rd and 24th August. We are fortunately in possession of a very full and interesting account of the whole affair, in the letters of Pliny the younger, whose uncle lost his life on the occasion, in his desire to examine minutely into the progress of the eruption; for he was unfortunately suffocated by the sulphureous vapours, in spite of the precautions he had taken to prevent accidents.

368.

IMP . T . CAES . VESP . AVG . P.M . TR . P . P.P . COS . VIII. The laureate head of the emperor to the left.

℞. IVD.—CAP. across the field, under the branches of a palm-tree, by which the words are divided, and S. C. under the words in like manner. A female is seated in mournful attitude at the foot of the tree on the right side, her head resting on her right hand; on the left side of the tree a male captive is standing with his hands bound behind him to a tree; on the ground in front of him, and at the foot of the tree, are some arms and pieces of armour strewed about.

Weight 418⅛ grains.

369.

IMP . T . CAES . VESP . AVG . P.M . TR . P . P.P . COS . VIII. The laureate head of the emperor to the left.

℞. IVD.—CAP. across the field, with S. C. under, as delineated on the preceding coin. A captive and female on either side of the field, as before described.

Weight 418⅙ grains.

These coins were struck in A.D. 80, and, although obtained from different sources, I have found, on minute comparison in every particular, and also by their weights, that they were struck from the same dies.

They commemorate the capture of Jerusalem, as already set forth at length in Vespasian.

370.

IMP . T . CAES . VESP . AVG . P . M . TR . P . P . P . COS . VIII. The laureate head of the emperor to the right.

℞. *No legend.* In the exergum S. C. The emperor in a quadriga moving to the right; the body of the chariot decorated with sculptures of victory, wreaths, &c.; in his right hand he holds an olive-branch.

The present coin, although struck in A.D. 80, yet represents the emperor in a triumphal car as forming part of the triumphal procession which took place in A D. 71, for the conquest of Judæa and capture of Jerusalem, as already noticed in Vespasian. It is a very scarce coin.

Weight 491¼ grains.

371.

IMP . T . CAES . DIVI . VESP . F . AVG . P . M . TR . P . P . P . COS . VIII. The laureate head of the emperor to the right.

℞. *No legend.* In the field S. C. Mars gradient to the right, bearing a trophy of arms on his left shoulder.

This is also a scarce coin, but is in middling condition.

Weight 380⅛ grains.

372.

IMP . T . CAES . VESP . AVG . P . M . TR . P . P . P . COS . VIII. The laureate head of the emperor to the left.

℞. PIETAS . AVGVST. In the exergum S. C. Two robed figures representing Titus and Domitian standing opposite each other, the figure to the left being intended for Titus; between them in the background is a veiled female to represent the goddess Concordia, who joins their right hands; her head is turned towards Titus on her left hand, as if she were speaking to him; he bears a sceptre in his left hand. The person opposite seems likewise to bear a sceptre.

This coin was struck A.D. 80, and most probably records a reconciliation between the two brothers, they being joint consuls for the year A.D. 80.

Weight 368½ grains.

373.

IMP . T . CAES . VESP . AVG . P . M . TR . P . P . P . COS . VIII. The laureate head of the emperor to the left.

℞. *No legend.* S. C. in the field. Spes gradient to the right, in the usual manner.

Weight 425¼ grains.

A coin struck A.D. 80, signifying the continued hope and wishes of the Roman people for the tranquillity and good government of affairs under the rule of Titus, being a repetition of the expectations already noticed, *ante.*

374.

IMP . T . CAES . VESP . AVG . P . M . TR . P . P . P . COS . VIII. The laureate head of the emperor to the left.

℞. PROVIDENT . AVGVST. In the exergum S. C. Two robed figures representing Vespasian and Titus standing opposite to each other. Vespasian, who is to the right, is delivering to the other, Titus, a globe, which Titus receives with his right hand, which at the same time rests on the top of a rudder.

Weight 395½ grains.

Vespasian died in July A.D. 79, and, although this coin was struck in the following year, yet it seems to express the descent of the sovereign power to Titus by the demise of his father, signified by Vespasian delivering to him the *mundus* or globe, meaning the Roman world or empire.

A similar type is introduced on the coins of Hadrian in the first year of his reign, where he is represented receiving a globe or *mundus* from the emperor Trajan, who had adopted him as his successor in the sovereignty.

375.

IMP . T . CAES . VESP . AVG . P . M . TR . P . P . P . COS . VIII. The laureate head of the emperor to the right.

℞. FELICIT . PVBLIC. In the field S. C. A robed female standing to the left; her right hand holds a *hasta pura;* on her left arm she bears a cornucopiæ filled with fruits.

Weight 354¼ grains.

376.

IMP . T . CAES . VESP . AVG . P . M . TR . P . P . P . COS . VIII. The laureate head of the emperor to the left.

℞. FELICIT . PUBLIC. In the field S. C. A female standing to the left, with *hasta pura* and cornucopiæ, as on the preceding coin.

Weight 380¾ grains.

These coins were struck A. D. 80, and express the joy of the Roman people on the accession of Titus, which we have noticed being likewise indicated by the coin of Spes.

377.

T . CAES . DIVI . VESPASIAN . IMP . F . AVG . P . M . TR . P . P.P . COS . VIII.   The laureate head of the emperor to the right.

℞. *No legend.* A representation of the temple already noticed, *ante*, No. 338. On this reverse the graving tool has been used unsparingly to bring out the temple with its deities and sculptures in high relief; the work has been done with great skill and judgment, preserving the patina, and neither adding to or taking from any part of the device. From the Herpin collection.

378.

IMP . T . CAES . VESP . AVG . P . M . TR . P . P.P . COS . VIII.   The laureate head of the emperor to the right.

℞. PAX . AVGVST. In the field S. C. A female standing to the left; her right hand holds an olive branch, on her left arm she bears a cornucopiæ filled with fruits.

Weight 422¼ grains.

379.

IMP . T . CAES . VESP . AVG . P . M . TR . P . P.P . COS . VIII.   The laureate head of the emperor to the left.

℞. ANNONA . AVG. No S. C. A female standing to the left; her right hand extended holds a small figure of Equity with her balance and *hasta pura*; on her left arm she has a full cornucopiæ; at her right side is a basket, from which ears of corn project; in the background at her left side is the stern of a galley ornamented in wreath-work, and terminating in the neck and head of a goose with its mouth open.

By the galley is signified that the supply of corn for the city was brought in ships by sea.

This is rather a scarce coin, and not in very good condition.

Weight 371⅞ grains.

380.

IMP . T . CAES . VESP . P . M . TR . P . P . P . COS . VIII.   The laureate head of the emperor to the left.

℞. PAX . AVGVST. In the field S. C. A female standing to the left; her right hand holds an olive branch; on her left arm she bears a full cornucopiæ.

Weight 403¾ grains.

This and the preceding coin of Pax are of the mintage of A.D. 80, and commemorate the peace after the Jewish war, the cornucopiæ filled with fruits being an indication of the usual results of peace and tranquillity by agriculture and commerce bringing abundance for the use and enjoyment of the people.

381.

IMP . T . CAES . VESP . AVG . P . M . TR . P . P.P . COS . VIII. The laureate head of the emperor to the left.

℞. *No legend.* In the field S. C. Two cornucopiæ filled with corn and fruits in saltier; between them is a winged caduceus.

Weight 409$\frac{1}{r}$ grains.

This coin, also of the date A.D. 80, like the preceding coins, indicates the abundance and benefits enjoyed under the government of Titus.

382.

IMP . T . CAES . VESP . AVG . P . M . TR . P . COS . $\overline{\text{VIII}}$. The laureate head of the emperor to the left.

℞. GENI . P . R . In the field S. C. A male figure unclothed to the waist standing full front. On the left arm he bears a full cornucopiæ; at his right side is a decorated altar, on which a fire is burning; with the right hand he holds a patera, in the act of pouring on to the fire.

Weight 186$\frac{7}{r}$ grains.

383.

IMP . T . CAES . VESP . AVG . P . M . TR . P . COS . VIII. Head of the emperor to the left, with radiate crown.

℞. SECVRITAS . P . R. In the exergum S. C. A female seated to the left on a throne having arms to it, and from the square of the back a circular top rises, which at first view seems to be a veil floating round her head, but it is not so; her right hand holds a *hasta pura,* and her left arm rests on the elbow of the throne; in front is what appears to be a decorated altar, but it more strictly resembles a short pedestal terminating with the prow of a galley.

A Second Brass coin, in aurichalcum, in excellent condition, from the cabinet of Sir George Musgrave.

384.

IMP . T . CAES . VESP . AVG . P . M . TR . P . COS . VIII. The head of the emperor to the right, with radiate crown.

℞. CERES . AVGVST. In the field S. C. A female standing to the left; her right hand extended holds some ears of corn; in her left hand she has a long jointed torch.

Weight 225¼ grains.

385.

..T . CAES . VESP . AVG . P . M . TR . P . COS . VIII. The laureate head of the emperor to the right.

℞. VICTORIA . AVGVST. In the field S. C. A Victory standing to the right, on the prow of a galley, holding up a wreath in her right hand; in the left hand she carries a palm-branch.

Weight 165¼ grains.

Although the word NAVALIS may not occur in the legend of a type like the present, yet when a Victory is represented standing on the prow of a galley, as on the present coin, it cannot, I consider, be otherwise understood than as referring to some advantages gained over some adversary at sea. The only naval encounter by Titus with any enemies was the destruction of the vessels at Tarichæa and Gennesareth, which have been already noticed under the coin of Vespasian, with the legend VICTORIA . NAVALIS. I do not find any other naval affair during the times of Vespasian or Titus, or even Domitian.

386.

T . CAES . VESPASIAN . IMP . PON . M . TR . P . P . P . COS .... The laureate head of the emperor to the right.

℞. *No legend.* S. C. at the sides of the field. A temple of six columns; the two centre columns seem to project beyond the others, and the frieze and other columns are apparently retired, and the ascending steps at their bases project and retire at the sides to correspond. Between the centre columns is an arched recess, on which a statue is standing on a base; in the tympanum above are some figures, and figures are placed on each apex of the triangle of the pediment.

The appearance of this temple is different to that of any other temple usually depicted on coins. At first view it seems circular, but on examining closer the effect is produced by the positions of the columns being partly advanced and partly retired.

It is very doubtful what temple is intended. It is related that Vespasian erected a temple to Pallas that surpassed every building of the kind that had before been seen in Rome, not for its size, but for the beauty and elegance of its sculptures, paintings, carved work, and gilding. The temple delineated on this coin is very compact; and, having but one statue under the arch in front, the present may probably be intended as a record of the temple so erected to Pallas. We find on the coins of Domitian, *post*, a reverse with the emperor offering sacrifice to Minerva, whose statue is placed under an arch, or, as it may be termed by some, a shrine or *baldaschino*; but, although Minerva was the favourite deity of Domitian, we have no record of his having erected a temple to her.

Weight 327½ grains.

387.

IMP . T . CAES . VESP . AVG . P . M . TR . P . COS . VIII.   The laureate head of the emperor to the left.

℞. AETERNIT . AVGVST.   In the field S. C.   A female standing to the right, with a *hasta pura* erect in her right hand, in the left she holds a cornucopiæ filled with fruits, and her left foot rests on a globe placed on the ground.

Weight 187¼ grains.

There is a coin of Vespasian with this legend on the reverse, but I have not yet been able to obtain a specimen.

388.

IMP . T . CAES . VESP . AVG . P . M . TR . P . P . P . COS . VIII.   The laureate head of the emperor to the left.

℞. DIVO . AVG . T . DIVI . VESP . F . VESPASIAN.   In the exergum S. C.   A robed figure of Titus seated to the left, on a curule chair with a globe between the legs, holding in his right hand an olive branch; on the ground are various sorts of arms strewed about, and in front of him is an oblong shield standing upright, with a helmet on the top of it.

Weight 386¼ grains.

This device is similar to the one we have noticed on the coins of Drusus Senior, *ante*, No. 147. From the legends on these two coins, one using the word AETERNITAS and the other DIVO . AVGVSTO . TITO, it would seem as if they were intended for apotheosis or deification coins.

389.

DIVO . AVG . T . DIVI . VESP . F . VESPASIAN.   In the exergum S. C.   A robed figure of Titus, seated to the left amongst arms, as described on the preceding coin.

Weight 414¼ grains.

℞. *No legend.* The Flavian amphitheatre, having the *meta sudans* on the right side, and what is termed the *domus aurea* on the left. It represents the building full of spectators; in front there appears an arched box for the Præfectus Ludorum. There are two flights of steps in view leading from the bottom or area of the building to the upper row of seats, and for the use of all the intermediate rows. The outside of the building is decorated with many figures in small niches, and in one large space is the representation of a triumphal car with several horses.

There are three coins of this type in the French cabinet, but all of inferior preservation; the present is in very fine condition, and dark brown colour; it was found at Pompeii, and was obtained by Colonel Stewart, of whom I had it.

From the obverse and reverse legends of this and the preceding coin having the word DIVO, it gives them the character of apotheosis coins. I consider the present was struck soon after the death of Titus and inauguration of the Flavian amphitheatre.

This stupendous building was, from its vast size, originally called the Colosseum, now altered to Coliseum; it was also called the Flavian amphitheatre, from Flavius, the family name of Vespasian and Titus. It was commenced in A.D. 77, by Vespasian and Titus, but Vespasian did not live to see it completed; that was done by his son Titus, who kept about 30,000 Jewish captives employed in its erection; and in A.D. 81, it was finished and dedicated. Titus died shortly after on the 13th September in the same year, poisoned, as is supposed, by Domitian.

The amphitheatre is described by Publius Victor as containing seats for 87,000 spectators; but Admiral Smyth, when at Rome, took the pains to measure its *vestigia*, which still exist, and, allowing sixteen inches to each person, he could not find it would accommodate more than about 50,000 spectators.

A full description of the remains, as they were to be seen in A.D. 1694, is to be found in Donati, p. 192, and also in Pitiscus.

The festival of its dedication extended over a hundred days, during which the spectators were entertained with the slaughter of 5,000 wild beasts of various sorts, besides a large show of gladiators.

In the year A.D. 523 it ceased to be used for the games and contests of wild beasts, the gladiators having long before then been withdrawn from contests in the arena.

During the time of Macrinus, the Coliseum was struck by lightning, and greatly injured by the conflagration that ensued. Elagabalus and Severus Alexander made restorations, and a coin was struck by Severus on the occasion, and also one by Gordian III.

In the time of Trajanus Decius, it again suffered from fire, and was restored by him. Under Theodosius II. the Præfect Rufus Cecina Felix Lampadius restored the seats, and the podium and arena, which had become dilapidated.

There is little doubt that the theatres and amphitheatres at Rome originated from the theatres and amphitheatres of the Hetruscans; for at the ancient Hetruscan town of Sutrium the remains of an amphitheatre or coliseum in little are still (in 1847) to be seen perfect. The first permanent theatre erected in Rome was by Pompey, in the year of Rome 699, and it is still remaining.

390.

IMP . CAES . VESP . AVG . P . M . TR . P . P . P . COS . VIII.   S. C. in the field. Titus seated on a curule chair to the left, holding out an olive-branch in the right hand; armour and arms of various sorts are strewed around him on the ground.

℞. *No legend.* The Coliseum, with *meta sudans* and *domus aurea*, as on the preceding coin.

Pale white green, very good.

From the legend on the obverse, I consider this coin was struck at the time of the completion of the amphitheatre, and during the life of Titus.

JULIA SABINA, TITI FILIA.

JULIA SABINA was the daughter of Titus and Julia Furnilla. She was married to her first cousin, Flavius Sabinus, the son of Titus Flavius Sabinus, the brother of Vespasian the emperor. Domitian, her uncle, when emperor became enamoured with her; and, causing her husband to be put to death, he took her to himself, but she soon after died in a miscarriage. She was consecrated by Domitian, who struck coins in her commemoration. Nothing certain is known among historians as to the time of her birth or her death; the nearest approach to a knowledge of the day of her birth is an expression of Suetonius, *in Tito*, sect. 5; but in what year is not specified.

Her coins are not uncommon, but I have not yet seen a *consecratio* type of Julia with a *rogus* or a peacock, but only the *carpentum* type.

391.

IVLIA . IMP . T . AVG . F . AVGVSTA. The head of Julia to the right, her hair dressed in curls round the face, the rest drawn back and made into an ornamented knot behind. The shoulders and bust draped, with a beading on the edge of her dress over the neck and bosom.

℞. VESTA. in the exergum. S. C. in the field. Vesta seated to the left on a square seat, with a *hasta pura* in the left hand; her right hand extended holds a little figure of Minerva Jaculatrix.

This coin is encircled with the black ivory ring of the Devonshire cabinet, from whence I had it.

It is fine, and of a black bronze hue. Weight 210½ grains.

392.

IVLIA . IMP . T . AVG . F . AVGVSTA. The head of Julia to the right, her hair dressed much like the representation on the preceding coin; shoulders and bust draped.

℞. CERES . AVGVST. In the field S. C. A female standing to the left; her right hand extended holds some ears of corn; in her left hand she has a long jointed torch, the end resting on the ground.

Of a brassy green. Weight 190¾ grains.

Julia was styled Augusta by her father in his lifetime. These coins, which are of Second Brass, were struck in his lifetime; those which were struck to her after his death give the obverse legend, IVLIA . AVGVSTA . DIVI . TITI . F.

393.

IVLIA . IMP . T . AVG . F . AVGVSTA. The head of Julia to the right, her hair dressed to resemble the style on the other coins, but more prettily arranged and minute in its details; shoulders and bust draped.

℞. *No legend or device*, because it is incuse, and so perfect in all its detail of face and head-dress, I should not think it likely to be a flan, by accident placed on the obverse of a coin, accidentally left in the die. Its minute particularity seems to denote it as an entire or perfect and intended incuse coin. It is in Second Brass, and of a fine yellow tinge, very flat and a little split at an immaterial part of one side. It looks as if it came from an independent die, as a trial of the engraver at the mint. It was formerly in the cabinet of Sir George Musgrave.

394.

DIVAE . IVLIAE . AVG . DIVI . TITI . F. A decorated *carpentum* drawn by two mules to the right; in the exergum S . P . Q . R.

℞. IMP . CAES . DOMIT . AVG . GERM . COS . XV . CENSOR . P . P. In the middle of the field S. C.

Pale white green, very fine.

By the consular date of this coin, which is an apotheosis coin, it was struck A.D. 90, when Domitian, being emperor, was consul jointly with M. Cocceius Nerva, who afterwards became emperor.

395.

DIVAE . IVLIAE . AVG . DIVI . TI . F. A decorated *carpentum* drawn by two mules to the right; in the exergum S . P . Q . R.

℞. TI . CAESAR . DIVI . AVG . F . AVGVST . P . M . TR . POT . XXIIII. In the middle of the field S. C.

Fine, a brown bronze. Weight 322 grains.

The present is a very singular coin from the cabinet of the Duke of Devonshire; it has been examined by several most experienced numismatists, who have all pronounced it to be genuine in every respect, but the legend on the reverse is the legend of Tiberius, as may be seen by the coin of Tiberius, *ante*, No. 127. If it were not for the TI . F . at the close of the legend on the obverse, it would be quite apparent as a coin of Julia, the daughter of Augustus, and wife of Tiberius, and the reverse legend would fall in correctly.

In discussing the question of the reverse legend with my late esteemed friend Mr. Burgon, he was of opinion (in which I concur) that the only way in which the difficulty could be solved was, that one of the workmen, a tyro at the Mint, had accidentally used a reverse die of Tiberius, mistaking, for the moment, the commencement of the legend on the reverse, as applicable to Julia's father *Titus* CAESAR. There is no coin like it in any cabinet, neither in the French cabinet or in the British Museum. If it ever occurred before it has escaped notice.

DOMITIAN.

FLAVIUS DOMITIANUS, the second son of the emperor Vespasian and Domitilla, was born in the year of Rome 804, A.D. 51. On the accession of his father in A.D. 61, Domitian and his brother Titus were invested with the title of Cæsar, and also with that of Princeps Juventutis. On the death of his brother Titus, in A.D. 81, Domitian succeeded him in the sovereignty, and during the greater part of his reign his cruelty and immorality were quite equal to anything perpetrated by Caligula or Nero; his conduct became so bad at last, that a conspiracy was formed, and he was, in consequence, assassinated in October A.D. 96. With him ends the series of emperors usually termed "the Twelve Cæsars."

His coins are in gold, silver, and brass, and, with a few exceptions, are not particularly rare, except as to preservation. Coins with the head to the left are very rare; so also are coins representing him in armour, or the bust draped. A complete series of coins on which the celebration of the sæcular games is recorded is very difficult to obtain in good condition.

396.

CAESAR . AVG . F . DOMITIANVS . COS . DES . II.   The laureate head of Domitian to the right.

℞. *No legend*. A temple of six columns in front approached by a flight of four steps, extending the whole width of the building; there is a group of figures in the tympanum, and at each apex of the triangle of the pediment is a group with horses; in front of the temple, under the portico, are three arches, under each of which is a statue placed on a low base.

This is a Second Brass black coin of the first consulate, and of the time when Domitian was proposed for election to the consulate for the second time; it is therefore the first coin of the series of Domitian, and is in very beautiful condition.

397.

CAESAR . AVG . F . DOMITIAN . COS . II.   The laureate head of Domitian to the left.

℞. AEQVITAS . AVGVSTI.   In the field S. C.   A female standing to the left holding a balance in her right hand, in the left a *hasta pura*.

The types on the early coins of Domitian show the regard with which he was at first treated, but, as the early coins of Domitian were struck during the reigns of Vespasianus and Titus, the real character of Domitian was not then known.

398.

CAESAR . AVG . F . DOMITIAN . COS . II.   The laureate head of Domitian to the right.

℞. VICTORIA . NAVALIS.   In the field S. C.   A Victory standing to the right on the prow of a galley, holding up a wreath in her right hand; in her left she has a palm-branch.

This type we have already noticed in Vespasian No. 329, and in Titus No. 351. The present coin being struck upon the same occasion, and being the third, completes the series of coins with this legend applicable to Vespasian, Titus, and Domitian. They are all of Second Brass size, and are not known in any other. This is in a very good condition. Weight 146 grains.

399.

CAESAR . AVG . F . DOMITIAN . COS . ĪI. The laureate head of Domitian to the right.

℞. *No legend.* S. C. in the exergum. Domitian in a quadriga moving gradually to the right.

A Second Brass coin struck A.D. 73, Domitian being consul for the second time jointly with M. Valerius Messalinus. It is no doubt struck to commemorate the triumph in A.D. 71 for the conquest of Judæa, for it does not appear that any sole triumph was decreed to Domitian until his eleventh consulate, when he claimed a triumph for his imaginary victories over the Germans.

Eckhel, noticing this coin, says, "Indicat hic typus processum Domitiani consularum."

In First Brass this coin is very rare; it is far from common in Second Brass, like as the present, which is in Cyprian copper, but poor condition. Weight 145 grains.

400.

CAESAR . AVG . F . DOMITIAN . COS . ĪI. The laureate head of Domitian to the right.

℞. PAX . AVGVST. In the field S. C. A female standing to the left, holding out a caduceus in her right hand; in her left hand she has an olive-branch, and rests her arm on a short column standing at her left side.

A coin of the year 73. In this year his son by his wife Domitia Longina was born.

Weight 185¼ grains.

401.

CAESAR . AVG . F . DOMITIANVS . COS . IIII. The laureate head of Domitian to the right.

℞. PRINCEPS . IVVENTVTIS. Domitian bareheaded on horseback to the left, his right hand raised, in his left hand he bears a long staff having a ball at one end. S. C. under the forefeet of the horse, which is apparently in a gentle gallop.

Weight 184¾ grains.

402.

CAESAR . AVG . F . DOMITIANVS . COS . V. The laureate head of Domitian to the right.

℞. ANNONA . AVGVST. In the field S. C. A robed female seated to the left on a throne, her right hand holding a veil; her left elbow reclines on what seems a rest or short arm affixed to the left side of the throne, a fringed drapery is pendent from the seat of the throne on the left side, her left foot rests on a stool.

This type of Annona is very scarce; the more usual type will be noticed at a subsequent period.

Weight 376½ grains.

403.

CAES . DIVI . VESP . F . DOMITIANVS . COS . VII. The laureate head of Domitian to the left.

℞. *No legend.* Minerva Jaculatrix advancing to the right. A large S. C. on either side.

Were it not for the word Domitianus in the legend on the obverse, the portrait could well be spoken of as the portrait of Titus. The early coins of Domitian invariably bear portraits very much resembling his brother Titus, so that at first glance he might be mistaken for Titus, but the legend on the obverse will always correct the eye.

404.

CAES . DIVI . AVG . VESP . F . DOMITIAN . COS . VII. The laureate head of Domitian to the right.

℞. *No legend.* S. C. in the field. Minerva Jaculatrix advancing to the right, her right hand raised to throw a spear which she holds; on her left arm she bears a circular shield.

Of all the deities Minerva received the most adoration from Domitian, whence it is her effigies appears so often and variously on his coins, and he caused the Quinquatria to be exhibited every year with great magnificence.

The Quinquatria was a festival of five days' duration held at Rome in honour of Minerva, and answering to the Panathenæa of the Greeks. On the first day sacrifices and offerings were made without the shedding of blood, on the second, third, and fourth days there were shows of gladiators. On the fifth day a solemn procession throughout the city.

The scholars in the various institutions for learning offered prayers to Minerva as the goddess of wisdom, the patroness of literature, and they were accustomed to present their masters with a gift, which was called Minervalia.

405.

CAESAR DIVI . AVG . F . DOMITIANVS COS . VII. The laureate head of Domitian to the right.

℞ *No legend.* S. C. in the field. Spes gradient to the left, in the usual way. A fine Second Brass coin, one of my original purchases when about sixteen years of age. Weight 170¼ grains.

406.

CAES . DIVI . AVG . VESP . F . DOMITIANVS . COS . VII. The laureate head of Domitian to the right.

℞. PAX . AVGVST. In the field S. C. A female standing to the left; on her left arm she bears a full cornucopiæ; her right hand extended holds an olive-branch.

Weight 399½ grains.

The portrait now begins to be corrected, *i. e.* less Titus-like.

407.

. . . . AVG . VESP . F . DOMITIANVS . COS . VII. The laureate head of Domitian to the left.

℞. VESTA in the exergum. S. C. in the field. Vesta seated to the left, her left foot resting on a stool; her right hand extended holds a small statue of Minerva or Palladium; in her left she has the *hasta pura.*

Weight 346 grains.

This is one of the scarce coins of Domitian.

408.

IMP . CAES . DIVI . VESP . F . DOMITIAN . AVG . P . M. The laureate head of Domitian to the right.

℞. TR . P . COS . VII . DES . VIII . P . P. In the field S. C. Minerva Jaculatrix in her goat-skin dress, with tags at the side, standing to the right in an attitude of offence, having a spear in her right hand raised to strike and a circular shield on her left arm.

This coin was struck after the thirteenth of September, A.D. 81, the day of the death of Titus, and before the first day of January, A.D. 82. Domitian is described as the consul elect for the eighth time. The consuls entered on their duties on the 1st of January, and took the oaths of office within five days after.

The legends on this coin show Domitian to have assumed all the titles of sovereignty. It will be seen on subsequent coins, that he further assumed the title of CENSOR and CENSOR . PERPETVVS. The title of GERMANICVS is also to be found on coins of the seventh consulate; but they are very scarce, it being at that period assumed for the first time.

Beautiful dark green coin, from the cabinet of the Rev. E. C. Brice. Weight 384¼ grains.

409.

IMP . CAES . DIVI . VESP . F . DOMITIAN . AVG . P . M. The laureate head of Domitian to the right.

℞. TR . P . COS . VII . DES . VIII . P . P. In the field S. C. The emperor robed, standing to the left, holding a palladium in his right hand.

This is one of the rare coins of Domitian; the robes of the emperor have been refreshed very injudiciously with a graver, the rest of the coin is untouched.

Brown. Weight, 422½ grains.

410.

IMP . DOMITIAN . CAES . DIVI . VESP . F . AVG . P . M . TR . P . P . P . COS . VIII. The laureate head of Domitian to the right.

℞. *No legend.* S. C. in the field. Mars gradient to the right bearing a trophy of arms on his left shoulder, in his right hand a spear with the point forward. Weight 391 grains.

A coin of the date A.D. 82, in which year Domitian made another expedition to Germany, where he made an incursion into the territories of the Catti, but meeting with no enemies he returned to Rome and claimed the honours of a triumph for an imaginary victory, and the servile adulation or timid spirit of the senate granted his request for the triumph.

In this year likewise, the son of Domitian, born in A.D. 73, died, and was consecrated by his father; this event is recorded on a denarius of Domitia, on the reverse whereof the child is represented sitting on a globe on which stars are depicted, an emblem of the celestial sphere, and of his reception into Heaven.

411.

IMP . D . CAES . DIVI . VESP . F . AVG . P . M . TR . P . P . P . COS . VIII. The head of Domitian to the right, with radiate crown.

℞. ROMA . to the right of the field. S. C. in the exergum. Roma armed seated on arms to the left; her right hand extended presents a wreath, her right foot rests on a helmet placed on the ground, her left hand grasps the hilt of her sword at her left side, her clothes reach only to her knees.

A Second Brass coin struck A.D. 82, and is an adjunct to the preceding coin. The present type indicates Roma ready to present a wreath to the emperor for his supposed successes in Germany. Weight 188½ grains.

412.

IMP . CAES . DIVI . VESP . F . DOMITIAN . AVG . P . M. The laureate head of Domitian to the right.

℞. TR . P . COS . VIII . DES . VIIII . P . P. In the field S. C. Minerva standing full front looking to the left; her right hand holds her spear upright, her left placed at right angle on her left hip.

Weight 355¼ grains.

413.

IMP . CAES . DOMITIAN . AVG . GER . COS . X. The laureate head of Domitian to the right.

℞. *No legend.* S. C. in the field. Victory gradient, bearing apparently a standard or standards on her left arm, her right hand raised above her head to support what seems an eagle on the top of the standard.

Weight 192⅜ grains.

A coin struck in A.D. 84, and the first on which the title of GERMANICUS appears to have been assumed.

In A.D. 83, it appears the Romans first became certified of the fact of Britain being an island surrounded by water, for Agricola, then being in Britain, directed his galleys to sail to the north, keeping along the shore; some deserters seized three of the galleys and went entirely round by the west side, over the north, on to the east side, and were ultimately wrecked on, we should say, the coast of Holland. (Tacitus, Vit. Agricol. sec. 25 to 28; Eckhel, vol. vi. p. 378.)

414.

IMP . CAES . DOMIT . AVG . GERM . COS . XI . CENS . POT . P . P. The laureate head of Domitian to the right, an amulet on his breast.

℞. *No legend.* S. C. in the field. The emperor in military costume standing to the left, having a sceptrum or parazonium in his right hand; in his left a spear, one end resting on the ground; his right foot is placed on an old man prostrate at his feet, and whose right elbow rests on an urn from which water is flowing.

This coin was struck in A.D. 85, and, with the ten coins which now follow, represent the supposed subjugation of Germany. The present type represents the passage of the Rhine, that river being represented under the figure of the old man with his urn of water.

A black coin, in fine condition. Weight 454⅔ grains.

415.

IMP . CAES . DOMITIAN . AUG . GERM . COS . XI. The laureate head of Domitian to the right, amulet on the breast.

℞. *No legend.* S. C. in the exergum. The emperor on horseback galloping to the right, his right hand raised to throw a javelin at a warrior on the ground under the forelegs of the horse, and who is protecting himself from the attack with his sword and a long oblong shield; the emperor also has on his left arm a long shield like that of his antagonist.

An allegoric representation of the conquest of Germany. A similar type we have already seen on the coins of Vespasian and Titus, as applying with greater propriety to the conquest of Judæa.

Weight 337 grains.

416.

IMP . CAES . DOMITIAN . AVG . GERM . COS . XI. The laureate head of Domitian to the right, amulet on the breast.

℞. GERMANIA . CAPTA. In the exergum S. C. A trophy of armour and shields, on the right side whereof Germania, represented as a female naked to the waist seated on the ground, is bewailing her fallen condition, while her warriors are subdued and captive, which is represented by the man with his hands behind him, and apparently bound to the trophy on the left side. Various sorts of arms are strewed on the ground, indicating the violent resistance of the Germans.

A fine green coin. Weight 417½ grains.

417.

IMP . CAES . DOMIT . AVG . GERM . COS . XI . CENS . POT . P . P. The laureate head of the emperor to the right.

℞. GERMANIA . CAPTA. In the exergum S. C. A trophy of arms and captives, as on the preceding coin. On this coin, the helmet which surmounts the trophy is elegant and peculiar, having long horns at its sides, as seen sometimes in mediæval helmets.

The trophy and group on this and the preceding coin, when compared with the JUDÆA . CAPTA of Vespasian and Titus, will be found to have been copied from original designs.

A yellow-coloured coin from the cabinet of Mr. Thomas. Weight 349½ grains.

418.

IMP . CAES . DOMIT . AVG . GERM . COS . XI . CENS . POT . P . P. The laureate head of Domitian to the right, amulet on breast.

℞. *No legend.* In the field S. C. The emperor in military attire standing to the left, his right hand placed across his breast; in his left hand he bears a long pointless spear or *hasta pura*; at his left side is a short sword; a female is kneeling before him on her right knee; she is naked to the waist, and her hair streaming over her shoulders; she is presenting to him with both hands an oblong German shield, one end of it resting on the ground.

This type is an assumption of arrogance on the part of Domitian in supposing Germania, represented by the female, in so humble and abject a posture, making her submission to the emperor as to a conqueror.

The device is used on the coins of Marcus Aurelius, under the designation of CLEMENTIA. AVG., and with much greater justice and truthful assertion than on the present coin.

Black, very fine. Weight 428½ grains.

419.

IMP. CAES. DOMITIAN. AVG. GERM. COS. XI. The laureate head of the emperor to the right.

℞. *No legend.* In the field S. C. Victory standing to the right; her left hand supports a circular shield affixed to the trunk of a; tree with her right hand she is inscribing on the shield DE GER; her left foot is supported by a helmet lying on the ground at the foot of the tree; on the other side of the tree a female is seated on arms in an attitude of grief.

This is a very scarce coin, in good condition; it is copied from the coin of Vespasian, *ante*, No. 303.

A brown coin. Weight 321¼ grains.

420.

IMP. CAES. DOMITIAN. AVG. GERM. COS. XI. The head of the emperor to the right, with radiate crown.

℞. *No legend.* S. C. in the field. The trunk of a tree; on the upper part of it is affixed some body armour, completed by a helmet; on either side is a shield, each being different in form; on the ground, with their backs to the tree, are two figures seated; the one on the right of the field is a man with his hands tied behind him, on the other side is a female; they are both naked to the waist.

This coin, in Second Brass, of black brown colour, is rare; like the preceding coins, it is to signify and represent the pretended conquest of Germany.

421.

IMP. CAES. DOMITIAN. AVG. GERM. COS. XI. The radiate head of Domitian to the right.

℞. VICTORIAE . AVGVST. A winged Victory standing to the left, with a palm-branch in her left hand; before her is a trophy of arms affixed to the trunk of a tree, her right hand extended towards it as if placing some portion of the arms to complete the trophy. S. C. on either side the trunk.

422.

IMP . CAES . DOMIT . AVG . GERM . COS . XI . CENS . PER . P . P. The laureate head of Domitian to the right.

℞. VICTORIAE . AVGVST. Victory standing to the left arranging a trophy of arms, as on the preceding coin. S. C. as before. The arms are somewhat different to the others. The title CENSOR . PERPETVVS now first appears.

423.

IMP . CAES . DOMITIAN . AVG . GERM . COS . XI. The radiate head of Domitian to the right.

℞. *No legend.* S. C. in the field. Two oblong German shields; crossed above them in the middle is a fringed square banner resembling the Roman cavalry standard, the *vexillum*, which is surmounted by a crescent; on either side of the shield is a trumpet.

It seems from these insignia of war, which represent German arms, that the Germans used a standard like that of the Roman cavalry noticed *ante*, in Nero.

A water-gold Second Brass coin, from the Thames. Weight 156½ grains.

424.

IMP . CAES . DOMITIAN . AVG . GERM . COS . XI. The laureate head of Domitian to the right, with amulet on the breast.

℞. *No legend.* Peace standing to the left with a cornucopiæ on the left arm, and setting fire to a collection of arms piled in front of her with a torch she holds in her right hand. S. C. on either side of Peace.

The type represents an offering of arms to Mars for the successful termination of the pretended German war.

A coin with green patina. Weight 416⅜ grains.

425.

IMP . CAES . DOMIT . AVG . GERM . COS . XI . CENS . PER . P . P. The laureate head of the emperor to the right.

℞. IOVI . VICTORI. In the exergum S. C. Jupiter unclothed to the waist, seated on a low square seat to the left; his right hand extended holds a Victoriola, in his left hand he has the *hasta pura* erect.

Weight 364½ grains.

Domitian affected great gratitude to Jupiter as his preserver in his imaginary campaigns in Germany, and also against Decebalus, the King of the Dacians, and likewise against the Marcomanni. Whilst he was emperor he is said to have caused a magnificent temple to be erected to Jupiter.

426.

IMP . CAES . DOMITIAN . AVG . GERM . COS . XI. The radiate head of Domitian to the right.

℞. *No legend.* S. C. in the field. Mars in full armour advancing hastily to the left bearing a Victoriola in his extended right hand; on his left arm he carries a small trophy of arms; his sword at his left side, his military cloak pendent from his shoulders; his cuirass terminates with a double row of lappets.

This type of *Mars Victor* has reference to the pretended victories over the Catti, Daci, and other German nations. I have not yet seen the device in First Brass. The present is a pale green Second Brass coin in very good condition.

427.

IMP . CAES . DIVI . VESP . F . DOMIT . AVG . GERM . COS . XI. The laureate head of Domitian to the right, an amulet on the breast.

℞. *No legend.* No S. C. Roma armed sitting to the left on a square high-backed throne; her right hand extended holds a Victoriola, in the left she holds her spear transversely, the point resting on the ground; her left foot rests on a stool; her left arm resting on a circular shield, which, on its lower edge, rests on the side of the throne. The throne itself is supported by a low plinth, on which are two seated figures, whose heads support the seat of the throne in lieu of legs. On the shield is the representation of a building, and three persons are standing in front viewing the edifice.

The present coin, of the mintage A.D. 85, is unique, its type being unknown to any numismatic writer. The most peculiar feature is, that the shield of Roma should have on it the representation of a building. It is probable that the building is intended for the capitol, which was destroyed in the civil wars of Otho and Vitellius, and rebuilt by order of Vespasian, but accidentally was burnt in the last year of Vespasian, and again rebuilt and completed at great cost by Domitian, when the gilding alone is said to have cost twelve thousand talents.

In his twelfth consulate, A.D. 86, Domitian instituted a more famous sort of Capitoline Games, to be observed every five years, the first celebration whereof took place in A.D. 86.

A dark green coin from the cabinet of Mr. Thomas. Weight 332¼ grains.

428.

IMP . CAES . DOMIT . AVG . GERM . COS . X . C . . The laureate head of the emperor to the right.

℞. *No legend.* S. C. in the exergum. The emperor standing to the right; in front is an altar, on which a fire is burning; over this he joins right hands with a soldier who stands before him; by the side of the first soldier another is standing bearing a standard; two others are behind them, one bearing a standard, the other in armour, with his spear and shield.

Weight 405¼ grains

429.

IMP . CAES . DOMIT . AVG . GERM . COS . XI . CENS . PER . P . P. The laureate head of Domitian to the right, amulet on the breast.

℞. *No legend.* S. C. in the exergum. The emperor and a soldier join hands over an altar standing between them; behind the soldier is another in armour with spear and shield; a standard also on the right of the first soldier is held by another soldier.

Weight 388¼ grains.

430.

IMP . CAES . DOMIT . AVG . GERM .COS . XI . CENS . PER . P . P. The laureate head of Domitian to the right, with amulet on the breast.

℞. *No legend.* S. C. in the exergum. The emperor standing to the right, an altar in front with fire burning, joining hands with a soldier before him; another soldier in armour with spear and shield is standing behind his comrade; a standard is by the right side of the first soldier.

Argelati, *in Domitiano*, quotes a coin with this type in COS . X., the legend being FIDES . EXERCITVVM, which shows that this and the two preceding coins exhibit the army, represented by the soldiers and standards, taking the oath of fidelity or allegiance to Domitian. I am therefore surprised it should bear a consulate equal to A.D. 85, four years after he had possessed the sovereignty.

A dark green coin, in fine condition, from the cabinet of Rev. E. C. Brice. Weight 405⅝ grains.

431.

IMP . CAES . DOMITIAN AVG . GERM . COS . XI. The laureate head of Domitian to the right, with amulet on the breast.

℞. *No legend.* S. C. in the field. The emperor with his head veiled standing to the left, offering sacrifice at an altar on which a fire is burning, placed in front of a shrine or *baldaschino*, under which is a statue of Minerva.

Question has been made what deity is intended to be represented on this reverse. The statue is that of a female with helmet and spear; and, as Minerva was adopted by Domitian as his patron, there cannot be much doubt that she is the deity represented. The specimens which have given rise to the doubt must have been imperfect in her figure.

A fine dark brown coin, a present from my respected friend Dr. Lee.

432.

IMP . CAES . DOMITIAN . AVG . GERM . COS . XI. The laureate head of the emperor to the right.

℞. SALVTI. above a square altar, the front being divided in compartments. AVGVSTI. underneath the altar. S. C. on either side of the field.

Weight 170½ grains.

433.

IMP . CAES . DOMITIAN . AVG . GERM . COS . XI . CENS . POT . P . P. The laureate head of the emperor to the right.

℞. AETERNITATI . AVGVSTI. In the field S. C. A female standing to the left; both her hands extended, the right hand being more elevated than the left; in each hand she holds a bust, the one in the right hand is with a radiate crown, that in the left hand has a crescent.

By these busts are represented the emperor and empress under the symbols of the sun and moon; and they not only express the adulation, but also by the legend the hypocritical prayer of the Senate and people of Rome for the perpetuity of the imperial breed of Domitian.

This type is used with greater propriety on the coins of Antoninus Pius, *post*; also in the Hadrian series.

Weight 184½ grains.

434.

IMP . CAES . DOMIT . AVG . GERM . COS . XI . CENS . PER . P . P. The laureate head of Domitian to the right, amulet on the breast.

℞. ANNONA . AVGVST. In the exergum S. C. Ceres and Annona with attributes exactly as represented on the coins of Nero already noticed *ante*, No. 189.

Weight 415¼ grains.

435.

IMP . CAES . DOMIT . AVG . GERM . COS . XII . CENS . PER . P . P. The laureate head of Domitian to the right, amulet on the breast.

℞. ANNONA . AVGVST. In the exergum S. C. Ceres and Annona with attributes as on the preceeding coin and the coins of Nero; both Ceres and Annona wear wreaths of wheat-ears on their heads.

A very fine brown coin. Weight 513 grains.

436.

IMP . CAES . DOMIT . AVG . GERM . COS . XII . CENS . PER . P . P. The laureate head of the emperor to the right.

℞. ANNONA . AVG. In the exergum S. C. A robed female seated to the right, her right arm resting on the back of her chair; her left hand is extended towards a person who stands before her with hands held out to receive some gift she appears to hold in her left hand; the stern of a galley appears in the background.

Weight 171⅞ grains.

437.

IMP . CAES . DOMIT . AVG . GERM . COS . XII . CENS . PER . P . P. The laureate head of Domitian to the right, with amulet on the breast.

℞. PACIS . on the upper part of the field. S. C. in the exergum. The reverse of this coin represents an altar rather in the form of a temple, with a tetrastyle portico of the Ionic order, raised on a base which is extended on each side beyond the outer column at the front corners of the altar; the entablature is highly enriched, and terminated by large acroterial ornaments at the angles forming the horns of the altar; the doorway of the temple in the centre intercolumniation is divided by a central mullion, and approached by four steps formed in the base of the temple; the two other intercolumniations are ornamented with groups of figures in bas-relief, in two heights—the figures in the lower squares or compartments being standing figures, and those in the upper squares being sedent figures; on each part of the lower base, which extends on each side outward beyond the square of the building, a robed figure is standing, having a patera in the right hand; there is also a small altar by the side of the figure on the right.

I do not find this singular reverse noticed in any writer. It is intended, no doubt, as an ARA. PACIS, from the word PACIS. being above the altar; thus leaving the altar itself to supply the word ARA. The *ara pacis* of Nero is a square altar, like to that usually on coins with the word PROVIDENT., as seen in the series of Augustus *ante*, No. 90.

A dark green Second Brass coin, in very good condition.

438.

IMP. CAES. DOMIT. AVG. GERM. COS. XII. CENS. PER. P.P. The laureate head of Domitian to the right, amulet on the breast.

℞. FIDEI. PVBLICAE. In the field S. C. A female standing with her head turned to the right; her left hand raised is holding a small basket of fruits; in her right hand she has two ears of corn and a poppy.

A pale green Second Brass coin. Weight 142¼ grains.

This type in Domitian is not in Large Brass, but it is to be found on the Large Brass coin of Antoninus Pius, *post*.

439.

IMP. CAES. DOMIT. AVG. GERM. COS. XII. CENS. PER. P.P. The laureate head of Domitian to the right, amulet on the breast.

℞. MONETA. AVGVST. In the field S. C. A female standing to the left with a pair of scales in her right hand; on her left arm she bears a full cornucopiæ.

Weight 166¼ grains.

This type also is not found in Domitian in Large Brass, but it occurs in the Large Brass of Hadrian, and also of Antoninus Pius.

440.

IMP. CAES. DOMIT. AVG. GERM. COS. XII. CENS. PER. P.P. The laureate head of Domitian to the right, with amulet on the breast.

℞. *No legend.* A large S. C. in the field. The emperor in military costume standing to the left, his right foot on an old river-god prostrate before him.

Weight 317½ grains.

This type has been fully noticed *ante*, No. 414.

441.

IMP . CAES . DOMIT . AVG . GERM . COS . XII . CENS . PER . P.P.   The laureate head of the emperor to the right, with amulet on the breast.

℞. IOVI . CONSERVAT.   In the field S. C.   Jupiter standing full front looking to the left; a robe pendant behind the left side from the left shoulder, and passed round the loins; the rest of the figure is undraped.   In the right hand he holds a *fulmen*, in the left a *hasta pura*.

In this consulate, A.D. 86, the first celebration of the new games, instituted by Domitian to the honour of Jupiter Capitolinus, was made with much ceremony.

A fine black Second Brass coin.   Weight 190½ grains.

442.

IMP . CAES . DOMIT . AVG . GERM . COS . XIII . CENS . PER . P.P.   The laureate head of Domitian to the right.

℞. FORTVNAE . AVGVSTI.   In the field S. C.   Fortune standing to the left, her right hand resting on a rudder; on her left arm she bears a cornucopiæ filled with fruits.

A Second Brass coin of the mintage of A.D. 87.   Weight 154½ grains.

443.

IMP . CAES . DOMIT . AVG . GERM . COS . XIIII . CENS . PER . P.P.   The laureate head of the emperor to the right.

℞. VIRTVTI . AVGVSTI.   S. C. in the field.   An armed female standing to the right; in her right hand she holds a spear; in the left she has a sceptrum, and rests her left elbow on her left knee, her left foot being placed on a helmet lying on the ground.

A Second Brass coin in Cyprian copper, but middling.   Weight 164 grains.

444.

IMP . CAES . DOMIT . AVG . GERM . COS . XIIII . CENS . PER . P.P.   The laureate head of Domitian to the right, amulet on the breast.

℞. *No legend.*   S. C. in the exergum.   The emperor in full military costume, except his helmet, standing to the left, holding a fulmen in his right hand, a spear in his left hand; at his left side Victory is standing with a palm-branch in her left hand, with her right hand she is placing a wreath on the head of the emperor.

This large and splendid coin was struck A.D. 88, and it refers to a victory gained this year over the Dacians, not by Domitian in person, but by one of his generals.

A very fine black coin from the cabinet of the Duke of Devonshire. Weight 420 grains.

The next following thirteen coins relate to the sæcular games which were celebrated at Rome in the time of Domitian; they form a more complete series in brass than are to be found in any other cabinet, either public or private, and are all in excellent preservation, nothing being wanting in any one of them to elucidate the subject of its type. There is only one other coin of this series known (in First Brass, I believe), and that I have never yet seen, although for many years I have watched for it.

445.

IMP . CAES . DOMIT . AVG . GERM . P. M . TR . P. VIII . CENS . PER . P. P. The laureate head of the emperor to the right.

℞. COS . XIIII . LVD . SAEC. On the exergum S. C. A robed figure seated to the left on a curule chair placed on a low tribunal supported by four balls; on the side of the tribunal is inscribed SVF . P. D. Two large vases stand in front on either side of the tribunal; a citizen stands in front with his right hand extended, as receiving something from the person who is seated; by the side of the citizen is a boy holding up his hands also to receive a donation; in the background is a building, having four columns in front.

Weight 372¼ grains.

This coin was struck in A.D. 88, and is the first of a very interesting series on which are recorded the sæcular games which were celebrated in the fourteenth consulate of Domitian, L . MINVCIVS . RVFVS. being consul jointly with the emperor, and in the year of Rome 841.

The donation represented on this reverse is of the purifying stuffs and perfumes, which were distributed to the people before the commencement of the festival by the Quindecemviri in the capitol, and also at the Palatine Hill, whence the inscription in front of the tribunal SVF . P. D.—*suffimenta populo data*. The person seated on the tribunal is supposed by most writers to represent the emperor, but to me it seems more likely to mean the tribunal of one of the Quindecemviri in the exercise of his official duties on the occasion.

These games, the most celebrated in Roman history, were instituted in compliance with the Sybilline Oracles, to the honour of Pluto, Proserpine, Juno,

Apollo, Diana, Ceres, and the Parcæ, and according to the oracle they were (as recorded by Horace) to be celebrated every 110 years:

<blockquote>Certus undenos decies per annos.</blockquote>

Some account of the ceremonials, as illustrated by these coins, may not be uninteresting here.

In the Sybilline Oracles was one famous prophecy to this effect,—"That if the Romans, at the beginning of every age, should hold solemn games in the Campus Martius to the honour of Pluto, Proserpine, Juno, Apollo, Diana, Ceres, and the Parcæ, their city should ever flourish, and all nations be subjected to their dominion."

The whole manner of their celebration was as follows:—Previously to the commencement of the festival, the fcciales or heralds traversed the city, and made a pompous proclamation inviting "all the world to come to a feast they never had yet seen, and should never see again."

Some few days before the beginning of the games, the Quindecemviri, taking their seats in the capitol and in the palatine temple, distributed among the people parcels of torches, brimstone, and other stuffs, for purification. From thence the people went to the temple of Diana, on the Aventine Hill, carrying wheat, barley, and beans as an offering at her shrine. This done, they passed several nights in prayer and devotion to the Parcæ. At length, when the time of the festival was actually arrived, and which lasted three days and three nights in succession, the people assembled in the Campus Martius, and offered sacrifices to Jupiter, Juno, Apollo, Latona, Diana, the Parcæ, Ceres, Pluto, and Proserpine.

On the first night of the festival, the emperor, accompanied by the Quindecemviri, caused three altars to be erected on the banks of the Tiber, which altars they sprinkled with the blood of three lambs, and then proceeded to burn the offerings and victims.

After this a space was marked out which served for a theatre, and was illuminated with a large number of torches and fires; here certain hymns composed for the occasion were sung, and various sports performed.

On the second day, sacrifices and victims were offered at the capitol; the people then returned to the Campus Martius, and celebrated sports in honour of Apollo and Diana. These lasted until the following day, when noble matrons, at an appointed hour, went to the capitol to sing hymns to Jupiter.

On the third and last day of the festival, twenty-seven young boys, and as many girls, both of whose parents were living, went in procession with palm-branches in their hands to the temple of the Palatine Apollo, where hymns and verses in Latin and Greek were sung in praise of the deities to whom the city was recommended for their protection. The *Carmen Sæculare* of Horace was composed by him for the last day of the sæcular games held by Augustus, and it was always afterwards used at their celebration.

It has been a subject of much controversy whether the Ludi Sæculares were celebrated every 100 years or every 110 years. For the former opinion, Censorinus, De die natali, c. 17, cites Antias, Varro, and Livy, the derivation of *sæculares* being from *sæculum*, an age, a computation among the Romans amounting to 100 years. For the contrary view of the question, Censorinus quotes the book of the Quindecemviri and the edicts of Augustus, besides the evidence of Horace in his poem already named:—

Certus undenos decies per annos.

The last period of 110 years is the time expressly enjoined by the Sybilline oracle, the verses of which are transcribed by Zosimus in the second book of his history; but as the emperors felt the uncertainty of their living to celebrate them if they let the full period of time elapse, we find that they were generally anticipated. The dates of their celebration seem to be as follows:—

The first was held in the year of Rome 245 or 248.

The second in the year of Rome 305 or 408.

The third in the year of Rome 518.

The fourth either Y. R. 605—608, or 628.

The fifth by Augustus, Y. R. 736; sive ut alii numerant 737.

The sixth by Claudius, Y. R. 800.

The seventh by Domitian, Y. R. 841; he took his computation from the celebration by Augustus.

The eighth by Septimius Severus, Y. R. 957.

The ninth by Philip, Y. R. 1000, when he struck a coin with the legend SAECVLVM . NOVVM.

The feciales or heralds, when they proclaimed the games in the life of Claudius, were scoffed at by the people, for many persons were then still living at Rome who had witnessed the festival celebrated by Augustus.

See Pitiscus, Lexicon, &c. art. *Ludi Sæculares;* also Hooke's Roman History. In Merivale, vol. iv. p. 179, we have the following note:—" Much has been written upon the mode of computing the time to which the sæcular games should be referred; I will try to compress within the limits of a note the most important points for consideration. We learn from Censorinus (c. 17), that Valerius, Antias,

Varro, and Livy make 100 years the period of the sæculum, while Augustus himself, and Horace, specified 110. The notices we have of the celebration of these games anterior to the time of Augustus are so inconsistent, that we must conclude there was no such regular celebration of them at all. The discrepancy, however, in the number of years as stated to us (100 and 110), may, perhaps, be accounted for by comparing the ordinary year of Numa, 355 days, with the intercalary years of 377-8 days; multiplying the first of these numbers by 110, and the second by 100, the results will come sufficiently near to one another to satisfy the condition of a round number. I take the hint of this solution from Walckenaer (Hist. d'Horace, ii. 269) though I cannot subscribe to the method by which he arrives at still closer results; but, however this may be, succeeding ages soon lost the clue to this synchronism. The emperor Claudius repeated the games A.U.C. 800, disregarding those of Augustus as irregular. Claudius was disregarded again in his turn by Domitian, who renewed the celebration in 841, anticipating in his impatience by six years the period prescribed by Augustus. To the Augustan computation Severus conformed precisely, and repeated the solemnity in 957, after two intervals of 110 years each. Philippus, however, returned once more to the precedent of Claudius in the year of the city 1000; this was the last celebration, although Zosimus, in the year 1067, suggests that the time has arrived for another sæcular festival according to the computation of Severus."

446.

IMP. CAES. DOMIT. AVG. GERM. P. M. TR. P. VIII. The laureate head of the emperor to the right.

℞. A cippus, or square upright tablet, on the right side whereof in the field cos. on the left side XIIII. on the tablet is an inscription:

LVD.

COS. SAEC. XIIII.

FEC.

the whole surrounded by a laurel wreath.

A denarius that has been originally gilded; from G. Gwilt's cabinet, very perfect.

447.

IMP. CAES. DOMIT. AVG. GERM. P. M. TR. P. VIII. CENS. PER. P. P. The laureate head of the emperor to the right.

℞. COS. XIIII. LVD. SAEC. In the exergum S. C. A coin similar in every respect to the preceding, save that there are no vases placed at the sides of the tribunal on which the quindecemvir is seated.

Weight 372½ grains.

448.

IMP . CAES . DOMIT . AVG . GERM . P . M . TR . P . VIII . CENS . PER . P . P.   The laureate head of the emperor to the right.

℞. COS . XIIII . LVD . SAEC . A . POP.   In the exergum S. C.   A person robed and seated to the right on a low square seat placed on a tribunal supported by four balls; on the side and front of the tribunal are the abbreviated words FRVG . AC : before him are three persons standing, the foremost of whom empties out a quantity of fruits from a sort of sack on to the ground; in the background is a building with four columns in front.

Weight 427⅔ grains.

Some writers consider this reverse represents an offering of first-fruits made to the emperor on the occasion of the game; but, as after the people had received their purifying stuffs and perfumes they proceeded to the temple of Diana, on the Aventine hill, where they made offerings of wheat, barley, and beans, the present type may represent the receiving of the fruits for the purpose of offerings, and which may be the offerings here recorded, for I do not find the word PRIMITIAE, or first-fruits, used on any coin, or any mention made of first-fruits being offered to the emperor, nor was it usual at this festival to make any offering whatever to him.

Eckhel, in vol. vi. p. 387, mentioning a coin similar to the present in the Vienna cabinet, quotes an opinion that the words on the reverse should be read— A . POPULO . FRUGES . ACCEPTAE.   Thus it was not the emperor, but the people of Rome "a quo fruges acceptæ sunt."

It may be so read, but that reading does not bear out the view I take of this type, viz.—that it represents the quindecemvir on his tribunal, receiving *from* the people (*a populo*) the offerings at the temple of Diana, or the offering made (*a populo*) *by* the people.

449.

IMP . CAES . DOMIT . AVG . GERM . P . M . TR . P . VIII . CENS . PER . P . P.   The laureate head of the emperor to the right.

℞. COS . XIII . LVD . SAEC . A . POP.   In the exergum S. C.   A coin similar in every respect to the preceding; no vases, however, on the *suggestum*, but the words FRVG . AC. are on the side and front.

Weight 407⅞ grains.

450.

IMP . CAES . DOMIT . AVG . GERM . P.M . TR . P . VIII . CENS . PER . P.P.   The laureate head of the emperor to the right.

℞. COS . XIIII . LVD . A . POP.   In the exergum S. C.   A person robed and seated to the right on a curule chair placed on a low tribunal resting on four balls, having on its side and front FRVG . AC.; at each corner of the tribunal are vases, and the person seated on the curule chair extends his right hand, in which he holds a patera, towards two other persons who stand before him, the foremost of whom also extends his right hand with a patera as if to receive something; in the background is a building having four columns in front.

Weight 383⅜ grains.

The acts of the persons represented on this reverse are more in accordance with the reading of the words on the present and preceding coins as quoted by Eckhel; but the letter A I consider duplex: in one reading it may be A populo, *by* the people; in another it may be A populo, *from* the people: thus on the first two coins it would be the *suffimenta* received A *by* the people; and the second series would read, the offerings received A *from* the people. I consider by these various readings the acts represented on these reverses are to be reconciled; thus, considering the first two coins to represent the first part of the ceremonial, the presentation and acceptance of purifying stuffs,—the next two coins as the offerings made by and received from the people at the temple of Diana, on the Aventine Hill,—and the present coin descriptive of the offering as made by the people; all the types would represent the ceremonies of distributing the perfumes and receiving and giving the fruits; then follow the coins of the sacrifices made by the emperor. Thus as nearly as possible the coins would bear record of all the proceedings on so interesting an occasion, closing with the procession which took place on the third day.

It is to be observed also that the word FEC only appears on the coins representing the sacrifices, which coins, with one exception, are only known in Second Brass. The coins already cited represent acts done by the people,—their share of the ceremonials; the others represent the acts of the emperor, closing with the procession.

451.

IMP . CAES . DOMIT . AVG . GERM . P . M . TR . P . VIII . CENS . PER . P . P. The laureate head of the emperor to the right.

℞. COS . XIIII . LVD . SAEC . FEC. On the exergum S. C. The emperor standing to the right; before him is an altar, with fire burning, on which he is making an offering; two musicians are standing near him, the one on his left hand at the back of the altar is playing on a cithara, the one opposite to him is playing on the double flute; on the opposite side of the altar is a hog; by its side is a *victimarius*, in a stooping attitude, as if preparing to slay the animal; in the foreground in front to the right is a female naked to the waist, and reclining on the ground, having on her left arm a cornucopiæ.

This coin is very rare; it is the type I missed at the Pembroke sale, but the present coin is finer and untooled. It was bought at the sale of the coins of M. Herpin, of Paris, by the Rev. E. Boden, who very kindly exchanged with me for other coins, and thus he let me complete a Large Brass series of the coins of the sæcular games. It is in very nice condition, and is one of the rarest. It is figured very accurately in Morell *in Domitiano*. There is only one Large Brass coin more rare than this, which I have not yet seen anywhere, although I know it exists, but I cannot tell where.

452.

IMP . CAES . DOMIT . AVG . GERM . P . M . TR . P . VIII . CENS . PER . P.P.

℞. COS . XIIII . LVD . SAEC . FEC. On the exergum S. C. The emperor robed standing to the left; in front of him is an altar with fire burning, on which he is pouring a libation; two musicians are standing before him, one of whom is playing on a cithara; on the ground to the right is a bearded male figure recumbent, with his back and face in profile; in the background is a temple having a triangular pediment on each side, and a cupola in the centre between the two pediments; the whole front is supported by six columns, evidently being a portico, from the intercolumniations which appear within the first row of columns, giving to the whole the appearance of a large building.

Second Brass. Weight 177½ grains.

The temples or buildings represented on this and the five following coins are nearly all different, and the types I consider represent the emperor offering sacrifice at the temples of different deities during the three days of the festival. The temples were on the banks of the Tiber, which river is here represented by the recumbent figure of the bearded old man or river-god.

These sacrificial coins are all in Second Brass. With the exception of the preceding coin, they do not appear in First Brass.

453.

IMP . CAES . DOMIT . AVG . GERM . P . M . TR . P . VIII . CENS . PER . P.P. The radiate head of the emperor to the right.

℞. COS . XIIII . . . . . On the exergum S. C. A temple of six columns, in front of which is an altar with fire burning on it; the emperor robed is standing to the left in the act of sacrificing by pouring a libation on the altar; opposite to the emperor are two musicians, one of them is playing the double flute, the other a cithara; by the side of the second musician is a person holding a goat and a lamb, as if intended to be offered in sacrifice.

454.

IMP . CAES . DOMIT . AVG . GERM . P . M . TR . P . VIII . CENS . PER . P.P. The laureate head of the emperor to the right.

℞. COS . XIIII . LVD . SAEC . FEC . On the exergum S. C. The emperor robed is standing to the left in the act of performing sacrifice by pouring a libation from a patera in his right hand on to a fire burning upon an altar before him; in front are two musicians, one playing on a cithara, the other a double flute; at the right side is a *victimarius* in the act of striking a mallet on to the head of an ox, which is held with its head bent down by another person who is kneeling in front of the animal.

455.

IMP . CAES . DOMIT . AVG . GERM . P . M . TR . P . VIII . CENS . PER . P.P. The laureate head of the emperor to the right.

℞. COS . XIIII . LVD . SAEC . FEC . On the exergum S. C. A type similar to the preceding coin; the animal on this coin is evidently an ox, by the horns which appear; on the preceding coin it is possible the animal may be a sheep which is being slain by the *victimarius*, for the sheep was an object of sacrifice at these ceremonials.

456.

IMP . CAES . DOMIT . AVG . GERM . P . M . TR . P . VIII . CENS . PER . P.P. The laureate head of the emperor to the right.

℞. COS . XIIII . LVD . SAEC . FEC . In the exergum S. C. The emperor standing to the left before a temple of six columns; a wreath is in the tympanum of the pediment; in front is an altar, whereon a fire is burning, and the emperor is pouring on to it a libation from a patera he holds in his right hand; before the emperor is a person playing on the double flute, behind whom is another person playing on a cithera.

457.

IMP . CAES . DOMIT . AVG . GERM . P . M . TR . P . VIII . CENS . PER . P . P .   The laureate head of the emperor to the right.

℞. COS . XIIII . LVD . SAEC . FEC .   In the exergum S. C. A coin of precisely similar type to the last, except that in the tympanum of the temple there is the figure of a bird, which I should consider is intended for an eagle, not only as the (attribute) bird of Jove, but also as the distinctive ensign of Rome and the Roman people.

458.

IMP . . . . GERM . P . M . TR . P . VIII . CENS . PER . P . P.   The laureate head of the emperor to the right.

℞. COS . XIIII . LVD . SAEC . FEC .   In the exergum S. C. The emperor with a scroll in his left hand, an official personage at his left side, both of them in robes, are following a procession of young people walking to the right and carrying branches in their right hands, which branches should be either of laurel or palm.

This is a representation of the procession of youths and virgins which took place on the third day of the games, and concluded their celebration. Twenty-seven youths, and as many young girls, all of the best families in Rome, and of each of whom both parents were still living, chaunted in procession throughout the city the well-known *Carmen Sæculare* of Horace, as well as other hymns of praise both in Greek and Latin, as mentioned by Zosimus.

This is a very rare type; the present coin came out of the cabinet of General Ramsay, displacing a very good one I had from the cabinet of Mr. Thomas. It is a very fine green coin, but the finest coin of this type I have yet seen is in the cabinet of Admiral Smyth.

Vaillant, Numism. Imperat. Rom. Selectiora, says of a coin of this type, "Hic nummus primi moduli inter rarissimos Sæcularium Ludorum collocatur."

Further particulars of the nature of the ceremonies of the sæcular games may be collected from Horace, Carm Sæc.; Tacit., Ann. xi. 11; Zosimus, ii. *init.* The origin of the festival is narrated by Zosimus and Valerius Max. ii. 4-6. For a lively description of them see also Walckenaer, Dezobry, Rome, &c. ii. 412 fol. and Merivale, iv. 181.

459.

IMP. CAES. DOMIT. AVG. GERM. COS. XV. CENS. PER. P. P.   The laureate head of Domitian to the right.

℞. *No legend.* In the exergum S. C. The emperor in military costume, except the helmet, standing to the left, holding in his right hand a fulmen, in his left hand a spear; at his left side Victory is standing with a palm-branch in her left hand, with her right hand she is placing a wreath on the head of the emperor.

Weight 400¾ grains.

A coin struck in A.D. 89, and occasioned by the continued success of the Roman armies in Germany.

In this year also the Vota Decennalia were performed; but I have not yet met with a First or Second Brass coin recording them.

460.

IMP. CAES. DOMIT. AVG. GERM. COS. XV. CENS. PER. P. P.   The laureate head of Domitian to the right.

℞. IOVI. VICTORI. In the exergum S. C. Jupiter, unclothed to the waist, seated on a square seat to the left; his right hand extended holds a Victoriola, in the left he has the *hasta pura*.

Weight 332⅛ grains.

461.

IMP. CAES. DOMIT. AVG. GERM. COS. XVI. CENS. PER. P. P.   The laureate head of Domitian to the right.

℞. IOVI. VICTORI. In the exergum S. C. Jupiter seated to the left as before with a Victoriola and *hasta pura*.

Weight 355¼ grains.

462.

IMP. CAES. DOMIT. AVG. GERM. COS. XVII. CENS. PER. P. P.   The laureate head of the emperor to the right.

℞. *No legend.* S. C. on either side of a winged Victory who is standing on a globe to the left; in her right hand she holds up a wreath, on her left arm she bears a small trophy of arms.

Weight 214¼ grains.

This coin in its type is taken from the gold and silver coins of Augustus. The type is repeated on the coins of Antoninus Pius relating to Britain, minus the trophy.

463.

IMP . CAES . DOMIT . AVG . GERM . COS . XVII . CENS . PER . P.P. The laureate head of the emperor to the right.

℞. IOVI . VICTORI. In the exergum S. C. Jupiter seated to the left as on the preceding coins with Victoriola and *hasta pura*.

Weight 351½ grains.

All these last-mentioned coins have reference to successful actions of the Romans with the Quadi, Dacii, and other German nations, although of no particular note in history.

464.

IMP . CAES . DOMIT . AVG . GERM . COS . XVII . CENS . PER . P.P. The laureate head of Domitian to the right, shoulders draped.

℞. *No legend.* S. C. on either side the field. A square building having an open archway on each side. On the top are two quadrigæ of elephants placed back to back, each car having a charioteer.

This coin is of the mintage A.D. 96. The arch is considered as referring to the emperor's supposed German victories. Vaillant describing this type says of the arch, " Ille erectus est in Germanico triumpho." The coin in First Brass he terms "rarissimus." Eusebius speaks of Domitian having a triumph for victories over Dacians and Germans in his sixteenth consulate.

The coins of Domitian that represent him in armour, or with the shoulders draped, are extremely rare.

465.

IMP . CAES . DOMIT . AVG . GERM . COS . XVII . CENS . PER . P . P. The laureate head of the emperor to the right.

℞. *No legend.* A fine eagle, with his wings partly expanded, standing on the stem of an ear of corn; in its beak it holds a wreath. S. C. on either side of the bird.

This type signifies the victories supposed to have been gained in Germany, the wreath held by the eagle being a complimentary adulation of the emperor as having triumphed over his enemies; its standing on the ear of corn signifies the benefits of agricultural abundance being obtained by a return of the armies to a peaceful occupation of the country.

This coin is of the date A.D. 96, and last of the reign of Domitian. It is, I believe, an unknown type.

A beautiful dark green and very perfect coin.

466.

IMP . CAES . DOMIT . AVG . GERM . COS . XVII . CENS . PER . P.P. The laureate head of the emperor to the right, the bust apparently in armour with military cloak over.

℞. *No legend.* S. C. in the exergum. The emperor on horseback to the right; his right hand raised as if he were addressing spectators.

This coin was struck A.D. 96, being the last year of the life of Domitian, who was slain in October A.D. 96, in the forty-fifth year of his age.

This type I have never yet seen in any cabinet. The equestrian statue of Domitian in bronze gilded, "Equum æneum auro superfusum," stood near the centre of the Forum, near to the Milliarium Aureum. It is supposed to be alluded to by Statius in the lines—

> Ipse loci custos cujus sacrata vorago
> Famosusque locus nomen memorabile servat.
> SILV. lib. 66.

The present coin represents that statue as it was originally placed in the Forum, on that part of it which was in former days the lake into which Quintus Curtius was said to have cast himself, and it was near this spot that the emperor Galba was slain.

This type is copied on the coin of Antoninus Pius, *post*, on which an equestrian statue of that emperor is represented. Types on coins of equestrian figures representing such statues as were erected to various emperors are very rare, and very difficult to be procured.

The present type of Domitian is extremely rare. The coin is rather injured by time and not by wear in any purse or scrip. Weight 335½ grains.

DOMITIANI FILIUS.

467.

No legend. The veiled head of a child to the right, with a wreath of sedge or sea-weed.

℞. S. C. within an olive garland or wreath.

This coin is of Third Brass size, and in fine preservation, of a pale green colour, and from the cabinet of General Ramsay. It is of the workmanship of the Domitian period, but hitherto has not been appropriated to any one person. After a thorough consideration of the subject, I coincide with Mr. Sparkes:

" *Where certainty is not attainable, probability is desirable,* and with this view I would suggest the appropriation of this coin to the infant son of Domitian—

" 1st. Because the fabric resembles that of the other Third Brass coins of Domitian. 2nd. Because the infant is commemorated in other metals and sizes, and is therefore probably commemorated in Third Brass, a coinage which under Domitian was struck in such unusual quantities and with such variety of type. 3rd. The infant is anonymous on all coins, and the omission on this coin of any inscription, as DIVVS. CAESAR. may possibly have arisen from his being the first deceased infant thus honoured.

" For testimonies as to the importance attached at the time both to his birth and death, see Eckhel, vi. p. 400; with respect to the crown of sea-weed, if sea-weed it be, I have neither explanation or conjecture to offer."

The crown is one of sea-weed or sedge, and is quite similar to one of the same material encircling the head of the river-god Tiberis on the reverse of the coins of Antoninus Pius, *post*. I find no other Small Brass coin of the time of Domitian, or of any other emperor, like this coin, or with any similar or apparently similar device or portraiture upon it. I feel therefore the less hesitation in following the opinion of Mr. Sparkes. The child not only being mentioned, but actually represented on the coin of his mother, the empress Domitia, still adds to the probability of the appropriation of this coin to the young son of Domitian being correct. The boy died, it must be observed, when he was about eight to nine years of age.

DOMITIA.

Domitia Longina, daughter of the celebrated general Cnæus Domitius Corbulo, was married to Lucius Lamia, who was murdered by order of Domitian, that he might obtain possession of his widow. After the death of her husband, Domitia lived with Domitian, and was subsequently married to him.

From an inscription found among the ruins of Gabii, a city formerly of the Volsci, and taken by the Romans and afterwards inhabited by them, but now in a state of ruin, which inscription was published by Visconti, in the Musæo Pio Clementino, it would appear that she lived to attain extreme old age, and died about the year A.D. 140.

The coins of Domitia are of the greatest rarity in brass. The denarii are occasionally seen at sales. Her portrait is also found occasionally on Greek colonial coins.

468.

DOMITIAE . AVG . IMP . CAES . DIVI . F . DOMITIAN . AVG. The head of Domitia to the right. Her hair in front is dressed like Julia Titi; the back hair is wound round in large bands, and the ends turned in; the shoulders and bosom draped.

℞. DIVI . CAESARIS . MATRI. In the exergum S. C. The empress robed and seated on a throne to the left; her right hand is placed on the shoulders of a little boy, who stands with his back to her, holding up his right hand; in her left hand she holds a *hasta pura* transversely.

From this reverse it is seen that the persons here represented are the empress and her little son, who was born in the second consulate of Domitian, A.D. 73, and created Cæsar by his father, but died A.D. 82. The present coin was, from the legend on the reverse, apparently struck after the death of the child.

This very interesting coin is of dark green patina, a streak of brown red oxide being mixed with the green in the hair at the back of the head. It was obtained from the cabinet of the Cavalier Campana. Weight 332½ grains.

DOMITIA.   233

Eckhel, vol. vi. *in Domitia*, describing a similar coin *in Musæo Cæsareo*, says, "Nummus hic rarissimus est, si modo certæ fidei." It is a coin rarely to be seen in any cabinet. That which is in the British Museum was formerly in the cabinet of M. D'Ennery, of which coin Eckhel says, "Etiam is qui fuit in Musæo D'Ennery nonnullius suspectus est visus." The Museum coin is exactly like the present in legends and head-dress, but is without patina, and brassy.

There is also another in the British Museum, which is certainly genuine. It is of the same type and legends as the D'Ennery coin, and as the present; but this second coin is in a very poor condition, and the reverse is cut out almost entirely anew from the metal, and thoroughly blacked afterwards. The figures on the reverse also are made very stiff and erect, and the obverse has been very much tooled. It was in the Duke of Devonshire's sale, Lot 279, and was purchased by Dr. Rawlings; and at the sale of his coins was bought for the British Museum at a small price. It is by no means a coin to be desired, or I would have bought it at the duke's sale.

In the French cabinet there are two with similar legends and types, and with the hair dressed similar to the present; and there are two other coins like the next mentioned coin; but they are none of them very good or fine.

The D'Ennery coin, now in the British Museum, is thus described in the printed catalogue of the Cabinet D'Ennery, a thick volume quarto:

"Grand Bronze. No. 2,617. DOMITIAE . AVG . IMP . CAES . DIVI . F . DOMITIAN . AVG . Tete de Domitia.

" ℞. DIVI . CAESAR . MATRI. Domitia assise, tenant un sceptre de la main gauche, etend sa droite sur l'epaule du jeune Domitien son fils (qui ne vecut que neuf ans); il est debout à ses pieds.

"On a eu quelques doutes sur cette medaille, qui est d'un grand prix si elle est vraie comme elle le paroit. Elle vient du cabinet du Prince de Rubempré, qui M. D'Ennery n'acheta que pour avoir cette Domitia."

469.

DOM . . . A . . . . . . S . DIVI . F . DOMITIAN . AVG. The head of Domitia to the right, her hair dressed in front as on the preceding coin; but the back hair is drawn and tied in a long looped knot, similar to the coins of Agrippina Senior and Antonia. Shoulders and bust draped.

℞. . . . . . AES . . . MATER. In the exergum S. C. The empress seated to

2 H

the left; her right hand placed on the shoulders of a child standing before her; in her left hand she has the *hasta pura*.

From the words DIVI CAESARIS in the legend of the preceding coin, some persons have considered these coins as apotheosis coins of the child of Domitian.

There are two coins of this style of obverse in the French cabinet, one of them having the Modena eagle in the field on the obverse. They are but in middling condition. The head on one of them has a sprig of laurel drawn through the hair, and the other has been tooled. The present coin is of brown colour, from the cabinet of Baron Koller, and is perfectly genuine, although in but middling preservation; but it is untooled, and is almost unique, even in its present condition.

The Domitia in Admiral Smyth's cabinet I need only mention, for the purpose of saying, without any the least disrespect to him, that it certainly is not genuine.

A really genuine and well preserved coin of Domitia has never made its appearance at a sale but in the Campana cabinet, and it may well be classed as one of the rarest of the rare Roman coins in Large Brass.

With these coins of Domitia, the series of the coins of the Twelve Cæsars, as they are termed, is ended.

NERVA.

MARCUS COCCEIUS NERVA was born in A.D. 32, at Narnia, in Umbria. His parents were M. C. Nerva, a man of consular dignity, and Plautilla, a lady of respectable family. He was early distinguished by civil dignities, and rendered himself exceedingly popular by his mildness, his generosity, and the active part he took in the management of public affairs. After having served as prætor and twice as consul, he was elected emperor on the death of Domitian, in October, A.D. 96.

Finding, after a time, the soldiery becoming turbulent and troublesome, he chose for his successor Ulpius Trajanus, a measure which gave great satisfaction to the people of Rome.

After a reign of sixteen months and a few days, he died of fever in January, A.D. 98.

His coins are not particularly common.

470.

IMP . NERVA . CAES . AVG . P . M . TR . P . COS . II . P . P. The laureate head of Nerva to the right.

℞. CONCORDIA . EXERCITVVM. In the field S. C. Two right hands joined; between them is a military standard surmounted by an eagle, signifying the fidelity plighted to the emperor by the army. The foot of the staff rests on the prow of a galley, indicating the good feeling of the naval forces, as well as of the army, towards the newly elected emperor.

From there being no number to the Tribunicia Potestas, this coin was doubtless minted early in the first year of Nerva's reign, probably very soon after his accession to the sovereign power.

A good water-gold coloured coin. Weight 387½ grains.

471.

IMP . NERVA . CAES . AVG . P . M . TR . P . COS . II . P . P. The laureate head of the emperor to the right.

℞. CONGIAR . P . R. In the exergum S. C. The emperor or his deputy seated to the right on a curule chair, the legs being crooked like an S. and placed on a high tribunal. Rather before him another person is seated on a low square seat; at their left side is a figure standing, and below another person stands holding up the *tessera frumentaria*. On the ground is a person about to ascend the steps in the front of the tribunal, and behind him is another citizen.

A good coin, green colour. Weight 346¼ grains.

472.

IMP . NERVA . CAES . AVG . P . M . . . . The laureate head of the emperor to the right.

℞. CON . . . . . . The emperor or his deputy, and another person in front seated to the right, with the other persons standing as on the preceding coin, but there is only one citizen who is ascending the steps of the tribunal.

These coins were struck in A.D. 96, and record the first donation made to the people on the emperor's accession to power.

A mottled green coin. Weight 393½ grains.

473.

IMP . NERVA . CAES . AVG . P . M . TR . P . COS . II P . P. The laureate head of the emperor to the right.

℞. ROMA . RENASCENS. In the exergum S. C. Roma seated to the left on a throne; her left foot rests on a stool, her right hand extended holds a Victoriola presenting a wreath to her; in her left hand she holds her spear erect.

A coin of the year A.D. 96, recording the hopes of the Roman people for the restoration of good order in the city, and empire generally, after the arbitrary power and cruelties which had been so wantonly exercised by Domitian, that the city should, as it were, be born again, or restored to its former healthy, moral state.

A dark brown coin. Weight 418½ grains.

474.

IMP . NERVA . CAES . AVG . P . M . TR . P . COS . II . P . P. The laureate head of the emperor to the right.

℞. FISCI . IVDAICI . CALVMNIA . SVBLATA. In the exergum S. C. A palm-tree with fruit.

The palm-tree, indigenous to Judæa, is introduced as the type, which, with the legend, records the remission of a tax laid on the Jews as tributaries before the conquest of Judæa, and which had been oppressively increased by Domitian. Nerva, in his liberality and love for liberty of conscience, abolished this tax: and the senate, to applaud and commemorate the kind feelings and benevolence of the emperor, caused this coin to be struck in A.D. 96.

Mr. Sharp says, "The word CALVMNIA marks that the tax was an insult to the sacred tribute granted to the Temple (at Jerusalem), but diverted by the conquerors."

A good black coin from the Devonshire cabinet. Weight 402¼ grains.

475.

IMP . NERVA . CAES . AVG . P . M . TR . P . COS . II . P . P. The laureate head of the emperor to the right.

℞. CONCORDIA . EXERCITVVM. In the exergum S. C. Two right hands joined; no military standard.

This type has the similar signification as the coin first mentioned, with a like legend.

A Second Brass coin. Weight 165¾ grains.

476.

IMP . NERVA . CAES . AVG . P . M . TR . P . COS . II . P . P. The radiate head of the emperor to the right.

℞. IVSTITIA . AVGVST . In the exergum S. C. A female seated to the right, unclothed to the waist; her feet resting on a stool; her left hand, extended, holds a branch, seemingly olive, her right hand has the *hasta pura*.

A very good dark Second Brass coin. Weight 191½ grains.

477.

IMP . NERVA . CAES . AVG . P . M . TR . P . COS . II . P . P . The laureate head of the emperor to the right.

℞. PROVIDENTIA . SENATVS . In the exergum S. C. The emperor, standing to the left, is receiving a *mundus* from a senator who is on the right, and holds in his left hand a *sceptrum*, or a wand of ceremony.

A very rare coin, unknown to Occo. It is a record of the confidence the senate felt and reposed in Nerva when entrusting him with the sovereignty, represented by a senator delivering a *mundus*, signifying the Roman world or empire, to the care of the emperor.

A very good brown coin from the cabinet of General Ramsay.

478.

IMP . NERVA . CAES . AVG . P . M . TR . P . COS . II . DESIGN . III . P . P . The laureate head of the emperor to the right.

℞. FORTVNA . AVGVST . In the field S. C. Fortuna standing to the left, holding a full cornucopiæ on the left arm; her right hand rests on the tiller of a rudder.

The present coin, struck A.D. 97, records the circumstance of Nerva being nominated consul for the third time; his first two consulates having occurred before he was elected emperor.

A beautiful pale green colour, fine condition. Weight 350¼ grains.

479.

IMP . NERVA . CAES . AVG . P . M . TR . P . II . COS . III . P . P . The laureate head of the emperor to the right.

℞. FORTVNA . AVGVST . In the field S. C. Fortuna standing to the left with rudder and cornucopiæ, as on the preceding coin.

Whilst on the preceding coin we have the nomination of Nerva for the consulate for the third time, on the present we have the second tribunician date acknowledged, and the third nomination for the consulate confirmed, which shews the mintage of this coin to have been after the election of consuls had taken place.

A fine bright green coin. Weight 378¼ grains.

480.

IMP . NERVA . CAES . AVG . P . M . TR . P . II . COS . III . P . P. The laureate head of the emperor to the right.

℞. FORTVNA . P . R. In the exergum S. C. Fortuna seated to the left, her right hand extended, holding some wheat ears; in her left hand she has the *hasta pura*.

This reverse is the Fortuna of the people of Rome: the other coins are the Fortuna of the Augustus or emperor.

A very good dark brown coin, from the Devonshire cabinet. Weight 462¼ grains.

481.

IMP . NERVA . CAES . AVG . P . M . TR . P . II . COS . III . P . P. The laureate head of the emperor to the right.

℞. PAX . AVG. In the exergum S. C. Peace seated to the left; her right hand extended holds an olive-branch, in her left she bears the *hasta pura*.

In A.D. 97, and the third consulate of Nerva, Trajan, who commanded in part of Germany, gained a successful victory in Pannonia, on which occasion Nerva was saluted *imperator* for the second time, and received the title of GERMANICVS, but which honours I have not yet met with on a Large Brass coin until the fourth consulate, as may also be observed in Argelati, whose work contains the most extensive numismatic series.

On this occasion also, and in this consulate, Nerva adopted Trajan as his successor, and in the month of October cos . III. nominated him CAESAR.

A good brown coin from the cabinet of Count Bruna. Weight 403¼ grains.

482.

IMP . NERVA . CAES . AVG . P . M . TR . P. COS . III . P . P. The laureate head of the emperor to the right.

℞. CONCORDIA . EXERCITVVM. In the field S. C. Two right hands joined; between them is a military ensign with a legionary eagle at the top; the foot of the standard is placed on the prow of a galley.

In the third consulate of Nerva disturbances were made by the Prætorian Guards, under pretence of avenging the death of Domitian. Nerva endeavoured to pacify them, but they would not be appeased until they had killed Petronius Secundus and Parthenius, who had been the principal actors in the death of Domitian. This conduct awakened Nerva to a sense of his precarious position as head of the state, and he at once very prudently made choice of Marcus Ulpius Trajanus, then being one of his generals, as his successor, and adopted him, and associated him in the sovereignty shortly before his death.

The date of this coin being of a later consulate than the first coin of this reign, it may therefore be considered as expressing the satisfaction of the armies, both of land and sea service, in the choice which had been made, as well as the return to their duty by the military and naval commanders after they had gratified their revenge upon Parthenius and others.

A fine brown coin, from the Devonshire cabinet. Weight 419¾ grains.

483.

IMP . NERVA . CAES . AUG . P . M . TR . P . COS . III . P . P.   The laureate head of the emperor to the right.

℞. LIBERTAS . PVBLICA .   In the field S. C.   Liberty standing to the left, having the *rudis* in her left hand, a *pileus* in the right.

A type emblematic of the peace and tranquillity, as well as the freedom, which the Roman people now enjoyed under the rule of Nerva, contrasted with the tyranny they had before endured under his predecessor Domitian.

A fine brown coin from the cabinet of the Rev. E. C. Brice. Weight 418¼ grains.

484.

IMP . NERVA . CAES . AVG . P . M . TR . P . COS . III . P . P.   The laureate head of the emperor to the right.

℞. VEHICVLATIONE . ITALIAE . REMISSA.   In the exergum S. C.   Two mules grazing, their heads being respectively outward to the legend; behind them are two carriage-yokes.

This coin was struck to record the munificence of the emperor in relieving the Italian states from the obligation of providing horses, mules, and carriages for persons professing to be travelling on the business of the state—a privilege which was a constant source of imposition. These things had become so burthensome as to cause several of the towns to petition the emperor for relief, who at once abolished the obligation, and regulations were adopted for preventing a repetition of the grievances

This interesting subject is most aptly represented by the mules relieved from their yokes and quietly grazing; the date of its mintage is A.D. 97.

See this subject very fully discussed in Spanheim, De Præstantiâ et Usu Nummorum Antiquorum, Elzevir 4to. ed. 1570, p. 800 *et seq.*

A fine dark green coin from the Devonshire cabinet. Weight 491¼ grains.

485.

IMP . NERVA . CAES . AVG . P . M . TR . P . COS . III . P . P .   The laureate head of the emperor to the right.

℞. PLEBEI . VRBANAE . FRVMENTO . CONSTITVTO . In the field S. C. A corn modius with ears of corn and a poppy sticking out of it at the top.

The present coin records another proof of the benevolence of Nerva's character in his directing that the towns of Italy should supply their poor with corn and other necessaries, or, in other words, making a decree for the institution of parochial relief in the several towns of Italy. There is another coin of similar import bearing the legend of TVTELA . ITALIAE . but it is extremely rare. I have not yet seen it at any sale.

There is a continuance of these benefactions to the poor in the towns of Italy by Trajan, as we shall have to notice under the coins of Trajan.

A good coin, without patina. Weight 406⅜ grains.

486.

IMP . NERVA . CAES . AVG . . . .   The laureate head of the emperor to the right.

℞. NEPTVNO . CIR . . . . VT . . . In the field S. C. Neptune unclothed standing to the right, in his left hand holding a trident, in his right hand a branch; at his feet is a prostrate figure.

The legend on this reverse evidently refers to the Circensian Games, which were originally instituted in honour of Neptune. Eckhel considers it to be one of the rarest coins of this emperor. He seems only to have known of three specimens. A fourth is in the cabinet of my friend C. R. Smith; it was dug up opposite to his house in Lothbury; and the present is the fifth, but where it was found I never could learn. Yet, strange to say, not one of the five possesses the reverse legend legibly perfect, so that whether the words are NEPTVNO . CIRCENSES . CON-

STITVIT. or RESTITVIT. or RESTITVTI. or CONSTITVTI. or RESTITVTORI. is a disputable point, until some truly perfect specimen is discovered.

Some reverses at sea occasioned the exclusion of Neptune from among the Dii Majores by Augustus; possibly Nerva restored the honours which were formerly accustomed to be paid to Neptune, and RESTITVTI would then be the as yet undiscovered word. The figure at the feet of Neptune represents the river Tiber, near to which the Circensian Games were exhibited.

There is no coin of Nerva of this type in the British Museum; for, except the instances I have given, I believe it to be as yet inedited and unknown, and it is a curious circumstance that all the specimens I have referred to are Second Brass coins like the present.

In addition to the preceding note, I may add the following extract from Eckhel, vi. 406, respecting a coin of Nerva of this type, which he had never seen, but found it in an English publication :—

"IMP . NERVA . CAES . AVG . P. M . TR . P . COS . III . P . P. Caput laureatum. ℞. NEPTVNO . CIRCENS . CONSTITVT . S . C . Neptunus nudus stans d . demissa . s . tridentem, pro pedibus ancora. Æ. II.

"Nummum hunc a Rev.^{do} Ashby, Anglo, editum, reperio in opere quod *Archæologia, published by the Society of Antiquaries of London*, inscribitur, ubi exstat volumine iii. p. 165. Auctor cum integerrimum, tectum viridi patina, repertumque ante annos non multos in horto prope Colcestriam adserit. Explicandæ epigraphes tres modos proponit, legendo, vel NEPTVNO . CIRCENS*es* . CONSTITVT*i* . vel NEPTVNO . CIRCENS*i* . CONSTITVT*a* . scilicet statua, vel NEPTVNO . CIRCENS*ium* . CONSTITVT*ori* . omnesque varios hos modos exemplis ex vetere moneta petitis stabilere satagit. Præterea jure unicum vocat, neque ex quocunque alio musæo, vel catalogo cognitum. Obtulit is dissertationem suam cruditæ Societati mense Maio anni 1772. Verum en tibi similis argumenti nummum alium et hunc quoque unicum, quem singulari dissertatione academiæ Cortonensi dedicata illustravit Philippus Becchettus, Ord. Præd. Eccum!

"IMP. NERVA . CAES . AVG . P . M . TR . P . COS . IIII. Caput laureatum. ℞. NEPTVNO . CIRCENSES . RESTITVT . S . C . Neptunus nudus stans d. flagellum s. hastæ innixus, humi genius Tiberis jacens. Æ. II."

See a further notice of coins of Nerva with this reverse, published long after these notes were written, in the Numismatic Chronicle, vol. vii.; Proceedings of the Numismatic Society, p. 22.

A Second Brass coin of pale green, in good condition. Weight 156¾ grains.

487.

IMP . NERVA . CAES . AVG . GERM . P . M . TR . P . II. The laureate head of the emperor to the right.

℞. IMP . II . COS . IIII . P. P. In the field S. C. Fortuna standing to the left, with a rudder in her right hand, a full cornucopiæ on her left arm.

This coin was struck in A.D. 98, and commemorates the fortune of the emperor in having, by means of his general, Ulpius Trajanus, gained considerable successes in Pannonia, which occurred A.D. 97, and for which Nerva was saluted Imperator the second time, and was also decreed the title of Germanicus; both of which circumstances we see recorded on this coin. It was struck in the last year of the reign of Nerva, and Large Brass coins with these inscriptions and of this year's mintage are rare. Such coins, however, as have the TRIB . POT . III . are much more rare.

It has been a question whether it is correct to count the years of an emperor's reign by the tribunician dates; but on comparison of times I have generally found it correct. In the case of the present emperor it is doubted by some whether the TR . POT . III . is a correct date, but the proof would, I think, be as follows:—

Domitian was killed, according to some authors, in September, others say October, year of Rome 849; and Nerva, immediately after that event, succeeded Domitian. Now, to reckon as the Romans did, from September or October 849 to 31 December 849, would be TRIB . POT . I. January 1st 850, to 31 December 850 would be TRIB . POT . II . and, having commenced January 851, he would commence TRIB . POT . III . and, although dying in January 851, or as some say February 851, would bring three annual dates in little more than sixteen months, and TRIB . POT . III . would be quite correct.

An instance of dating coins somewhat analogous to the present notice may be seen in the coinage of our own sovereigns, William the Fourth and Queen Victoria. William died in June, 1837, and coins were struck with his effigies in 1837; and coins were struck also to Queen Victoria in 1837, yet neither of them reigned the whole of the year 1837.

There are coins of Nerva quoted, in gold, and brass also, TR . POT . III . in Occo, though not in Eckhel.

A very good brown coin from the Devonshire cabinet. Weight 346¼ grains.

TRAJAN.

The tribunician dates of the reign of Trajan are as follow :—

Anno Domini—

98.	February to 31st December		Trib. Pot.	1
99.	1st January to 31st December	.	ditto	2
100.	Ditto	ditto		ditto	3
101.	Ditto	ditto		ditto	4
102.	Ditto	ditto		ditto	5
103.	Ditto	ditto		ditto	6
104.	Ditto	ditto		ditto	7
105.	Ditto	ditto		ditto	8
106.	Ditto	ditto		ditto	9
107.	Ditto	ditto		ditto	10
108.	Ditto	ditto		ditto	11
109.	Ditto	ditto		ditto	12
110.	Ditto	ditto		ditto	13
111.	Ditto	ditto		ditto	14
112.	Ditto	ditto		ditto	15
113.	Ditto	ditto	.	ditto	16
114.	Ditto	ditto	. .	ditto	17
115.	Ditto	ditto	. .	ditto	18
116.	Ditto	ditto	. .	ditto	19
117.	Ditto	to August, tunc obiit. .		. .	20

MARCUS ULPIUS TRAJANUS CRINITUS, a Spaniard by birth and extraction, was born at Italica (Italica Hispaniæ), in Bætica, in the year of Rome 806, A.D. 51. His father had the command of troops in the East at the same time as Vespasian, who became emperor. Trajan was the governor of Lower Germany under Domitian, and afterwards under Nerva, by whom he was subsequently adopted, A.D. 97, and associated with him in the empire. On the death of Nerva, which took place in January (or February "ut alii numerant") of the following year, A.D. 98, he assumed the government with the title of *Augustus*, and continued to reign until A.D. 117, when he died of paralysis at Selinus, in Cilicia.

There is a fine anecdote related of Trajan on his accession to the empire. He said to the commander of the prætorian guard on delivering to him his sword, which was the usual mode of conferring the rank and appointment, " Hoc pro me si juste imperavero, si perperam contra me utere."

Shakespere would seem to have used this anecdote in the delivery of the sword of justice by Henry the Fifth on his accession, to the Lord Chief Justice Gascoigne, who is said to have committed him to prison on one occasion for his youthful misconduct during his father's life:

> —— That you use the same
> With the like bold, just, and impartial spirit
> As you have done 'gainst me.

With some few exceptions the coins of Trajan are not rare or of great value. A very interesting series may be collected together; but it is their state of preservation that forms their real value. They are found in gold, silver, and brass.

488.

IMP . NERVA . CAES . TRAIANI . AVG . GERM . P. M. The laureate head of Trajan to the right.

℞. TR . POT . COS . II. In the field S. C. A female standing to the left, veiled and in full robes; at her feet is an altar with fire burning; her right hand is raised as if in supplication, her left hand supports her robes.

This is a type of *Pietas*, and is appropriate to the first mintage of Trajan's coins, imploring a blessing on the newly created emperor. The first consulate of Trajan was in A.D. 91, *temp. Domitiani;* the present coin is of the date A.D. 98, immediately on the death of Nerva, for there is no number to the *tribunicia potestas;* it therefore takes place as first in the series, although only in Second Brass.

A good light green coin. Weight 172½ grains.

489.

IMP . CAES . NERVA . TRAIAN . AVG . GERM . P . M . TR . P. The laureate head of the emperor to the right.

℞. COS . II . P . P . CONG . PR. In the exergum S. C. The emperor, or his deputy, seated to the left on a curule chair placed on a high tribunal; another person is seated in front on a lower tribunal, making a donation to a third person who is standing before him, whilst a fourth is ascending the steps.

The coins of Trajan hitherto known only record three congiaries bestowed on the people of Rome. The present coin is PR, which is ambiguous, and may be read PR*imum* or *Populo Romano;* but I incline to the opinion that the PR. refers to the word PR*imum*, because the coins recording the second and third donations are marked SECVNDVM and TERTIVM respectively at length; and Eckhel,

vi. 413, says the letters mean PRimum, because there is no dot between the P and R as in Populo Romano.

At the time of Nerva's death Trajan was in Germany, but he only continued there part of the year following his accession, and Pliny in his Panegyric, cap. 25, sec. 6, speaking of Trajan's liberality, says that "a congiary was given to the people and a donative to the soldiers when Trajan first arrived in Rome;" which circumstance, in the absence of a tribunician date, would clearly indicate this PR to be the first congiary, and in the year 98. Although he was in Germany during his first year, yet the donation might have been made in his absence by his legate or deputy for the occasion.

A good dark green coin. Weight 369½ grains.

490.

The legend obliterated. The laureate head of the emperor to the right.

℞. PROFECTIO . AVG . in the exergum, and S. C. under.

The emperor on horseback, bareheaded, trotting to the right with a spear in his right hand, the point forwards. He is preceded by an armed warrior marching with his spear in his right hand, and his shield on his left arm. Three other armed soldiers follow the emperor.

The present coin is much corroded on the obverse. I have never seen but this one at sale, for it is a coin of great rarity. In Argelati *in Trajano*, A.D. 100, it is noted in the Gold and the Brass series, but with this difference, the Brass has the legend PROFECTIO . AVG . GERMANIAE. Vaillant speaks of this type, "Hic nummus primæ formæ inter elegantiores reponendus;" and in the Gold series he describes the expedition recorded as referring to the Parthian war, because the word OPTIMUS on the obverse legend of the coin he quotes was not used until after the reduction of Armenia, and he designates the coin "ex rarissimis habendus;" but Argelati quotes two coins with OPTIMO in the reverse legend in A.D. 101. Thus Vaillant is wrong in ascribing this coin to the expedition to Parthia, for that did not take place until several years after the Dacian war; but from legends on coins described by Argelati, which are more perfect than on the present, there is no doubt that this coin was struck on the expedition against Dacia, and the date, A.D. 100, given to it by Argelati is correct.

A coin of this type is in the British Musuem, but in very poor condition.

491.

IMP . CAES . NERVA . TRAIAN . AVG . GERM . P . M . TR . P.   The laureate head of the emperor to the right.

℞. TR . POT . COS . III . P . P.   In the exergum S. C.   A robed female wearing a coronet or frontal crown, seated to the left on a throne, her feet crossed resting on a foot-stool; her right hand extended holds an olive-branch; her left hand bears a *hasta pura*.

A coin of the mintage of A.D. 100.

Yellow green in colour, and very fine condition.   Weight 379¾ grains.

492.

IMP . CAES . NERVA . TRAIAN . AVG . GERM . P . M.   The laureate head of the emperor to the right.

℞. TR . P . COS . III . P . P.   In the field S. C.   A soldier fully armed standing to the right; his left hand rests on his shield; in the right hand he holds his spear.

A coin of the year A.D. 100. In this year Trajan undertook an expedition against Decebalus, to abolish the infamy which attached to the Roman name occasioned by the tribute which Domitian had been accustomed to pay to Decebalus, under the disguise and pretence of his being a stipendiary ally of the Roman empire.

A very good dark green coin.

493.

IMP . CAES . NERVA . TRAIAN . AVG . GERM . P . M.   The laureate head of the emperor to the right.

℞. TR . POT . COS . IIII . P . P.   In the exergum S. C.   A robed female seated to the left, on a square seat; at her right side is a decorated altar on which a fire is burning; in her right hand she holds a patera, from which she is pouring a libation on the fire; on her left arm she bears a full cornucopiæ.

A fine brown coin from Mr. Cureton.   Weight 385¼ grains.

494.

IMP . CAES . NERVA . TRAIAN . AVG . GERM . P . M.   The laureate head of the emperor to the right.

℞. TR . POT . COS . IIII . P . P.   In the exergum S. C.   A female seated on a throne to the left, having an olive-branch in her right hand; her left arm rests on the arm of her chair or throne.

A very fine earthy green coin, from the Ramsay cabinet. Weight 431¼ grains.

495.

IMP . CAES . NERVA . TRAIAN . AVG . GERM . P. M. The laureate head of the emperor to the right.

℞. TR . POT . COS . IIII . P. P. In the field S. C. A winged Victory standing full front naked to the waist, her head turned to the left; her right hand raised holds a wreath; in the left she bears a palm-branch.

A good black Second Brass coin.

496.

IMP . CAES . NERVA . TRAIAN . AVG . GERM . P . M. The head of the emperor to the right, with radiate crown.

℞. TR . POT . COS . IIII . P. P. On the exergum S. C. A female seated to the left on a seat, formed of two cornucopiæ; her right hand holds a *hasta pura*, her left elbow rests on the top of one of the cornucopiæ.

A good brown Second Brass coin.

497.

IMP . CAES . NERVA . TRAIAN . AVG . GERM . TR . P . VI. The laureate head of the emperor to the right.

℞. IMP . IIII . COS . IIII . DES . V . P . P. In the exergum S. C. A female seated on a throne to the left; her right hand extended holds an olive-branch; the left bears a *hasta pura*, her left foot resting on a stool.

This coin was struck A.D. 103. The Dacian war was ended in the course of this year by the taking of the capital of Dacia, called by Eckhel, vi. 414, *Sarmizegethusa*, whereupon Decebalus became a suppliant to Trajan and obtained a peace. For these exploits the emperor was saluted with the title of Dacicus, and decreed a triumph, which was duly celebrated with much ceremony. The olive-branch held by the female is therefore an emblem of the peace.

Dacia comprised the countries which are known in modern times as Transylvania, Wallachia, and Moldavia. The former of these is at present under the dominion of Austria. Wallachia and Moldavia are termed principalities, and are under the control of Turkey.

Some of the fortifications raised by Trajan are still to be found in the part called the Dobrudscha, and are called Trajan's Wall, and were of some use during the recent war with Russia; and within the last three years an ancient Roman canal has been discovered leading from the lower part of the River Danube, which flows by Trajan's Wall into the Euxine Sea, and a company is now forming to cleanse and re-establish this canal, so as to allow merchant vessels to pass into the Danube by a shorter cut than by Sulina, and what are called the mouths of the Danube. Trajan's Wall, and the track of the canal, I have also seen delineated on a very old Dutch map of Turkey, &c., and of which a small map is published by a railway company intending to run a line parallel with the canal. The opening of these works on the Black Sea or Euxine is at a place called Kostendjie.

A good dark green coin from the Devonshire cabinet. Weight $358\frac{1}{2}$ grains.

498.

IMP . CAES . NERVAE . TRAIANO . AVG . GER . DAC . P . M . TR . P . COS . V . P. P. The laureate head of Trajan to the right.

℟. S . P . Q . R . OPTIMO . PRINCIPI. In the field S. C. Spes gradient to the left, holding up her dress with her left hand; in her right hand she has the lotus flower.

This type seems to express the joy of the Roman people at the prosperity likely to ensue under the reign of Trajan, and the device is aptly joined with the title of OPTIMVS bestowed on the emperor.

The coins of Trajan up to the fifth consulate are without this title of OPTIMVS, which would prove that, although Trajan was greatly applauded by the Senate and citizens when he returned to Rome, and was then called OPTIMVS, yet it was not until some time afterwards that the word was used on the coins.

The present coin is of the mintage A.D. 104; and it is to be observed that all the following coins referring to the final overthrow of Decebalus and the conquest of Dacia are of the fifth consulate of A.D. 104; but there is not much doubt that the pride of the Romans was so elevated by these events that the types were continually renewed for several years in succession, still bearing the date COS . V. as they had been originally struck, and to record the time when the overthrow of Decebalus took place. The title DACICVS now appears on the coins in further record of the Dacian victory.

A good brown coin. Weight $422\frac{1}{4}$ grains.

499.

IMP . CAES . NERVAE . TRAIANO . AVG . GER . DAC . P . M . TR . P . COS . V . P. P. The laureate head of the emperor to the right.

℞. S.P.Q.R. OPTIMO. PRINCIPI. In the exergum S. C. A river-god to the left, pressing with his right knee and right hand against a female who wears a Dacian cap and long trousers to the ancle, and is falling backward on the ground; in his left hand he holds a sedge or reed, and a robe floats around him at the back.

This type is considered to represent the passing of the river Danube by Trajan and his armies on his route for another campaign in Dacia.

Trajan built a stupendous bridge of hewn stone over the river Danube in the course of the summer, to enable him to pass into the country of Decebalus, who we have seen had shortly before been obliged to acknowledge himself vanquished, and sue for peace; but on Trajan and his armies retiring from the country he had rebelled, and refused to fulfil the conditions of the peace, and ill-used Longinus, the ambassador deputed to him by the Senate. For this conduct Decebalus was declared by the Senate to be an enemy of the state, and Trajan again marched his army into the country to take revenge upon him.

A very fine light brown coin, from the Devonshire cabinet. Weight 380 grains.

500.

IMP. TRAIANO. AVG. GER. DAC. P.M. TR. P. The laureate head of the emperor to the right.

℞. COS. V. P. P. S.P.Q.R. OPTIMO. PRINCIPI. In the exergum DANVVIVS. The river-god reclining to the left; his right hand resting on a boat; the left appears supported by an urn, from which water is flowing; his robe is floating around his head, forming an arch.

This type has reference to the preceding coin, as representing the river Danube yielding to the pressure of the emperor.

A fine denarius, from the cabinet of Mr. George Gwilt.

501.

IMP. CAES. NERVAE. TRAIANO. AVG. GER. DAC. P.M. TR. P. COS. V. P.P. The laureate head of the emperor to the right.

℞. S.P.Q.R. OPTIMO. PRINCIPI. In the exergum S. C. A bridge or an arch of a bridge, generally appropriated to the bridge said to have been constructed by the order of Trajan for the purpose of crossing the river Danube; but, on examining various coins of this type in various cabinets as well as my own, and on conferring with my friend Professor Donaldson, the architect, I have decided on adopting his view of the question in his own words, viz.: "This and the arched bridge on the coin of Sept. Severus are two most valuable illustrations of the wooden bridges of the ancient Romans. There is a conventional indication of running water, upon which there appears to be a small boat attached to the bridge by a rope [the boat I consider was for the use of the soldiers on guard at the guard-room of the bridge]. To the left is a species of arched entrance to the bridge, surmounted by an entablature; and above there is a figure of a warrior, with a spear between two trophies; on the opposite side of the bridge are indications of a like group at top. Steps seem to lead up to the archway; and probably there was a guard-room at either end to defend the approaches, as indicated by the blank space next the entrance on the left. The bridge itself consists of a one-spanned arch, with apparently three tiers of curved ribs and upright storey posts, securely framed together, the storey posts of both sides of the bridge being seemingly intended to be indicated. The ends of the transverse beams of the roof (for it is evidently a vaulted covered bridge) are distinctly shown. To the right the under part of the bridge is in perspective, and exposes to view the transverse ribs, to form the floor or gangway, and diagonal wind-braces to tie in securely the whole framing.

"It is obvious that wooden bridges were of frequent occurrence with the Romans, and doubtless there were many in the campagna of Rome thrown across the Tiber, which above the city narrows to a moderate width, and might be spanned easily by a single arch. From a passage in Plutarch's life of Numa we are led to conclude there was only one wooden bridge in Rome, probably that which Horatius Cocles defended against the Hetruscans, while the Romans were cutting it away behind him in order to prevent the enemy entering the city by it."

After mentioning the tradition, which he condemns as ridiculous—that the term *pontifex* for the high priest was derived from *pons*, from their offering sacrifices on the bridge—Professor Donaldson adds, "their priests too are said to have been commissioned to keep the bridges in repair, as one of the most indispensable parts of their holy office, for the Romans considered it as an execrable impiety to demolish the wooden bridge which we are told was built without iron, and put together with pins of wood only, by the direction of some oracle. The stone bridge was built many years after when Æmilius was quæstor. Some, however, inform us that the wooden bridge was not constructed in the time of Numa, having the last hand put to it by Ancus Marcius, who was grandson of Numa by his daughter. Pliny, lib. xxxvi. cap. xv. describing the altar of Proserpine at Cyzicum, notices a building at Cyzicum built of wood, the timbers of which were put together without iron fastenings, so that the beams appear without joinings (*sine suturis*); which, he adds, is also scrupulously observed in the Pons Sublicius, when it was restored after being defended by Horatius Cocles.

It is not impossible that the present reverse may be intended to represent the Pons Sublicius, so called because it rested on posts and beams, and which united the Janiculum to the Mons Aventinus at Rome.

The earliest complete description we have of a wooden bridge is that in the commentaries of Cæsar, lib. vi. c. 17, who threw one over the Rhine; in that case it consisted of piles driven into the river, and beams to form the roadway, over which the army had to pass. An able illustration of this was made by Palladio, and is also given by Rondolet, Art de Bâtir, and by Canino in his Architettura Romana.

The next example is that of Trajan's bridge over the Danube, the piers of which were in stone, and the superstructure of wood with arches, and which was considered by Dion. Cassius the finest of all the works of that emperor. The architect was Apollodorus of Damascus, who was subsequently put to death by Hadrian for some expression he used which gave offence to that emperor; there were twenty solid stone piers, each one 120 feet high above the foundations, and 60 feet wide, they were 170 feet apart. His successor, Hadrian, fearing that the bridge might equally serve the purpose of the enemy, and afford the barbarians the facility of invading the Roman territory, had the upper parts destroyed, so that the piers alone remained in the time of Dion.

A valuable illustration of this stupendous work exists on the Trajan column, and may therefore be considered as an authentic record of its construction. This is shewn in the seventy-ninth plate of Bartoli's work, descriptive of the Trajan column; the piers are marked with their courses of stone that serve as abutments to the wooden arches; above is a framework; on these piers is a horizontal plate which supports the transverse beams of the gangway; the open parapets on both sides are shewn, framed with cross braces. As there were nineteen arches, it must have been above a mile in length."

502.

IMP . CAES . NERVAE . TRAIANO . AVG . GER . DAC . P . M . TR . P . COS . V . P . P. The laureate head of the emperor to the right.

R̂. S . P . Q . R . OPTIMO . PRINCIPI. In the exergum S. C.

Another specimen of the bridge, showing in perspective the transverse ribs and under part intended for the support of the flooring or roadway of the bridge. Both of these bridge coins are in fine condition.

503.

IMP . CAES . NERVAE . TRAIANO . AVG . GER . DAC . P . M . TR . P . COS . V . P.P.   The laureate head of the emperor to the right, bust in armour, with military cloak over.

℞. S . P . Q . R . OPTIMO . PRINCIPI.   In the exergum S. C.   The emperor, bareheaded, on horseback at full speed to the right, darting a javelin at a person who has fallen on one knee in front of the horse, with his hands raised in attitude of supplication.

A fine dark green coin from the cabinet of Mr. Thomas.   Weight 393½ grains.

This type represents the Victory gained over Decebalus by Trajan on his second visit to Dacia, after building the bridge over the Danube to facilitate the operations and advance of his armies.

In this campaign Decebalus was completely overthrown, his kingdom and his life being taken, and his head sent to Rome as a trophy of conquest. His treasures had been buried in the bed of the river Sargetia, now called Jotrigu, the stream of which had been for a time diverted to admit of the necessary excavations for concealment being made; but that work was subsequently disclosed to Trajan, who again turned the course of the river and recovered the hidden treasures.

504.

IMP . CAES . NERVAE . TRAIANO . AVG . GER . DAC . P . M . TR . P . COS . V . P.P.   The laureate head of Trajan to the left, the whole bust full front and in armour.

℞. S . P . Q . R . OPTIMO . PRINCIPI.   In the exergum S. C.   The emperor armed on horseback at full speed to the right, throwing a javelin at a person bending in front of the horse with hands uplifted, as on the preceding coin.

Coins of Trajan with the head to the left, and especially with the bust full front and in armour, are very rarely to be met with.

A fine dark green coin from the Devonshire cabinet.   Weight 395⅔ grains.

505.

IMP . CAES . NERVAE . TRAIANO . AVG . GER . DAC . P . M . TR . P . COS . V . P.P.   The laureate head of the emperor to the right.

℞. S . P . Q . R . OPTIMO . PRINCIPI. In the exergum S. C. The emperor bareheaded in full armour on horseback at full speed to the right; his horse is richly caparisoned, and he is casting a javelin at a person who is under the horse supporting himself on his left hand and left knee.

The condition of this coin is so extremely perfect as to show every minute article of dress as well on the emperor and his horse as on the person who is prostrate under the horse, and is attired in a close-fitting tunic with a band round the waist and a cloak pendent from the shoulders, long trousers on the legs, and a round pointed cap or mitre on his head.

As the type records the victories gained over Decebalus, it is no great stretch of the imagination to presume that the prostrate figure under the horse is intended to represent that monarch cast down by the powers of Trajan.

This is a remarkably fine black brown coin from the Brice cabinet. Weight $408\frac{1}{2}$ grains.

506.

IMP . CAES . NERVAE . TRAIANO . AVG . GER . DAC . P. M . TR . P . COS . V . P.P. The laureate head of the emperor to the right.

℞. S . P . Q . R . OPTIMO . PRINCIPI. In the exergum S. C. A winged Victory in full flowing robes standing to the left, with a palm-branch in her left hand decorating a trophy before her consisting of coat armour, helmet, and shields, fixed on the trunk of a tree, at the foot of which are two shields of different shapes, and a spear with two falchions or curved swords.

A very fine black coin from the Gwilt cabinet.

507.

IMP . CAES . NERVAE . TRAIANO . AVG . GER . DAC . P. M . TR . P . COS . V . P.P. The laureate head of the emperor to the right.

℞. S . P . Q . R . OPTIMO . PRINCIPI. In the exergum S. C. A winged Victory decorating a trophy as on the preceding coin, but the arms suspended are rather different, and there are no swords or spear at the foot of the tree, only two ornamented shields, each of different form.

A very fine black coin from the Percival cabinet. Weight $402\frac{3}{4}$ grains.

508.

IMP . CAES . NERVAE . TRAIANO . AVG . GER . DAC . P. M . TR . P . COS . V . P.P. The laureate head of the emperor to the right.

℞. S . P . Q . R . OPTIMO . PRINCIPI. In the field S. C. A winged Victory naked to below the waist, standing to the right; her left foot rests on a helmet placed at the foot of the trunk of a tree, on which a shield is resting supported by her left hand, whilst with her right hand she has inscribed on the shield VIC . DAC.

A very good brown coin. Weight 394¾ grains.

509.

IMP . CAES . NERVAE . TRAIANO . AVG . GER . DAC . P . M . TR . P . COS . V . P.P. The laureate head of the emperor to the right.

℞. S.P.Q.R . OPTIMO . PRINCIPI. In the exergum S. C. A trophy of arms on the right consisting of body armour, helmet, and shields, fixed on a trunk of a tree, and at the foot on the ground are decorated shields of various forms, with spears and swords; in front of the trophy, and looking to the left, is a female wearing a peaked-round cap and seated on a pile of arms of different sorts, with her head resting on her right hand in the attitude of grief.

A very fine dark green coin from the Devonshire cabinet. Weight 390¼ grains.

510.

IMP . CAES . NERVAE . TRAIANO . AVG . GER . DAC . P . M . TR . P . COS . V . P.P. The laureate head of the emperor to the right.

℞. S.P.Q.R . OPTIMO . PRINCIPI. In the exergum S. C. A trophy of arms on the right, with a female seated in front as on the preceding coin, only there are arms and decorated shields different to the other.

A fine yellow brown coin.

511.

IMP . CAES . NERVAE . TRAIANO . AVG . GER . DAC . P . M . TR . P . COS . V . P.P. The radiate head of the emperor to the right.

℞. S.P.Q.R . OPTIMO . PRINCIPI. In the field S. C. A fine trophy of Dacian arms, consisting of coat armour with helmet above, a circular shield and spear on the left hand, an oblong shield and spear on the right; two smaller shields on the ground.

A fine black Second Brass coin.

512.

IMP . CAES . NERVAE . TRAIANO . AVG . GER . DAC . P . M . TR . P . COS . V . P.P. The radiate head of the emperor to the right, the bust in armour and draped.

℞. S.P.Q.R . OPTIMO . PRINCIPI. In the field S. C. A trophy of arms composed of Dacian shields, spears, a standard like a Roman *vexillum*, and other arms; the front shield has a peculiar decoration.

The display of the arms of the vanquished on these different trophies are interesting, for they make known to us the variety of arms and armour used by the Dacians and their allies, all of whom the Romans were accustomed to call barbarians.

A good black Second Brass coin.

513.

IMP . CAES . NERVAE . TRAIANO . AVG . GER . DAC . P.M . TR . P . COS . V . P.P. The laureate head of the emperor to the right.

℞. S.P.Q.R . OPTIMO . PRINCIPI. In the exergum DA . CAP. A pile of arms of different sorts, on which a person entirely naked is kneeling to the right with his hands bound behind him as a captive; on his head is a round cap.

This and the next coin also refer to the capture of Dacia.

Another good black Second Brass coin from the collection of M. Rollin, of Paris.

514.

IMP . TRAIANO . AVG . GER . DAC . P.M . TR. P. The laureate head of the emperor to the right.

℞. COS . V . P . P . S . P . Q . R ; OPTIMO . PRINCIPI. In the exergum DAC . CAP. A Dacian captive, with his hands bound behind him, seated to the left on a pile of arms. In front of the pile are several ornamented shields, behind which are several spears and two falchions. The man is in Dacian dress, long trousers fastened at the ankle, and a loose sort of shirt, and a peaked cap on his head.

Arms of the vanquished were usually burned on the battle-field as an offering to Mars; but I find no record of any captive soldier having been offered upon the pile as a victim in sacrifice to the god of blood and slaughter. It can, therefore, only be viewed as representing the very complete destruction made by the emperor, and not the sacrifice of any human being.

A fine denarius from the cabinet of Mr. Gwilt.

515.

IMP . CAES . NERVAE . TRAIANO . AVG . GER . DAC . P.M . TR . P . COS . V . P.P. The radiate head of the emperor to the right.

℞. S . P . Q . R . OPTIMO . PRINCIPI. In the exergum S. C. Peace standing to the left with a full cornucopiæ on her left arm; in her right hand she holds a torch, with which she is setting fire to a pile of arms on the ground before her.

This type refers to the conclusion of the Dacian campaign, and the cessation of the war upon the death of Decebalus; thus aptly illustrating the motto on the coins of Cromwell, "Pax queritur bello."

A good unpatinated Second Brass coin. Weight 208½ grains.

516.

IMP . CAES . NERVAE . TRAIANO . AVG . GER . DAC . P.M . TR . P . COS . V . P.P. The laureate head of the emperor to the right.

℞. S.P.Q.R. OPTIMO . PRINCIPI. In the exergum S. C. Roma armed, seated to the left on a cuirass, with ornamented shields and various arms around her. Her clothes do not quite reach her knees. Her right hand extended holds a little winged Victory, who presents her with a wreath; her left hand holds her spear erect; her right foot is resting on a helmet lying on the ground, and her left foot is placed on a human head wearing a round cap.

This device representing Roma treading on a human head is intended to signify the complete subjugation and conquest of Dacia. Decebalus, the king, being slain in the last battle, his head was taken off and sent to Rome as a trophy and token of the victory and conquest. It is an appropriate device, therefore, that the engraver should represent Roma treading on the head of her vanquished foe.

It is very rare to find this type in so perfect a state as to show the bearded head with a cap, for generally the head here so clearly shown is so rubbed down as to render it impossible to distinguish whether it be a globe, a head, or a helmet. The only specimen I ever saw in similar perfection was in the cabinet of M. Herpin, Paris.

A remarkably fine light brown coin, weight 424½ grains, from the Devonshire cabinet.

517.

IMP . CAES . NERVAE . TRAIANO . AVG . GER . DAC . P.M . TR . P . COS . V . P.P. The laureate head of the emperor to the right.

℞. S . P . Q . R . OPTIMO . PRINCIPI. In the field S. C. A female standing to the left; her right hand extended holding an olive-branch; on her left arm she bears a cornucopiæ filled with fruits; at her feet is a human head and bust in profile, and wearing a cap; her right foot is pressing on its shoulders.

This type is considered by some as Peace pressing her foot on the head of

Tellus, as if to signify that Peace caused the earth to give out its abundance. That is true one way; but for that purpose the head was not necessary. I consider it a type of peace being gained by the defeat and death of Decebalus, and the resumption of agricultural employments, producing abundance as their natural results.

A fine water-gold-coloured coin, from the Ramsay Cabinet.

518.

IMP . CAES . NERVAE . TRAIANO . AVG . GER . DAC . P . M . TR . P . COS . V . P.P.   The laureate head of the emperor to the right.

℞. S . P . Q . R . OPTIMO . PRINCIPI.   In the exergum S. C.   The emperor standing in a chariot decorated with Victories and trophies, and drawn by four horses at a gentle pace to the left; in his right hand he holds out an olive branch; in the left hand he bears a sceptre surmounted by an eagle; the reins of the horses are fixed in front of the chariot.

A coin commemorating the second triumph, which was decreed to Trajan for his victorious campaign and conquest of Dacia. This triumph was celebrated in A.D. 107.

A very fine dark green coin, from the Devonshire Cabinet.   Weight 408½ grains.

519.

IMP . CAES . NERVAE . TRAIANO . AVG . GER . DAC . P . M . TR . P . COS . V . P.P.   The laureate head of Trajan to the right.

℞. S . P . Q . R . OPTIMO . PRINCIPI.   In the exergum S. C.   The emperor bareheaded and in military costume standing to the left, his right hand holding a fulmen; in the left a spear, rather behind; at his left side is a winged Victory, bearing a palm-branch in her left hand; with her right hand she is placing a wreath on the head of the emperor.

Another type referring to the Dacian victories.

A very fine brown coin.   Weight 371¼ grains.

520.

IMP . CAES . NERVAE . TRAIANO . AVG . GER . DAC . P . M . TR . P . COS . V . P.P.   The laureate head of the emperor to the right.

℞. S . P . Q . R . OPTIMO . PRINCIPI.   In the exergum S. C.   The emperor standing to the left, bareheaded and in military costume, his cloak pendent from his shoulders; in his left hand he holds a spear; the right hand is placed on his right knee, and his right foot rests on a human head which is upon the ground.

Also a type referring to the conquest of Dacia.

A good sound coin without patina. Weight 362¼ grains.

521.

IMP . CAES . NERVAE . TRAIANO . AVG . GER . DAC . P . M . TR . P . COS . V . P.P. The laureate head of the emperor to the right.

℞. S.P.Q.R . OPTIMO . PRINCIPI. In the field S. C. Roma armed standing to the left, her spear in the left hand; her right hand extended holds a Victoriola bearing a palm-branch in its left hand, and with the right presenting a wreath. At the feet of Roma is a person in Dacian dress, kneeling on the right knee with hands uplifted as if supplicating for mercy.

A very good bronze coin. Weight 402½ grains.

522.

IMP . CAES . NERVAE . TRAIANO . AVG . GER . DAC . P . M . TR . P . COS . V . P.P. The laureate head of the emperor to the right.

℞. S . P . Q . R . OPTIMO . PRINCIPI. In the field S. C. Roma armed, standing to the left, as on the preceding coin, but the suppliant at her feet is a female, whose hair is tied behind the head in a Grecian knot.

A very good light brown coin. Weight 391 grains.

523.

IMP . CAES . NERVAE . TRAIANO . AVG . GER . DAC . P . M . TR . P . COS . V . P.P. The laureate head of the emperor to the right.

℞. S . P . Q . R . OPTIMO . PRINCIPI. In the exergum S. C. A female naked below the waist seated on a throne to the left; her right hand extends an olive-branch towards a Dacian kneeling before her with his hands raised in suppliant attitude.

These coins all refer to Dacia, which was the grand event and subject of record with the mint-masters at this period of the reign of Trajan. These three coins are not very frequent, especially in so fine a state.

A fine bronze coin from the Gwilt Cabinet.

524.

IMP . CAES . NERVAE . TRAIANO . AVG . GERM . DAC . P.M. The laureate head of the emperor to the right.

℞ TR . P . VII . IMP . IIII . COS . V . P.P. In the exergum S. C. Roma armed, seated on a cuirass to the right, her spear in the left hand, her left foot resting on a helmet lying on the ground; her right hand is extended to receive a small Victory presented to her by the emperor who stands before her in senatorial costume.

The TR . POT . VII . gives the date of this coin in A D. 104, to commemorate the return of the emperor to Rome from his successful campaign in Dacia, signified by his presenting Roma with the Victoriola, and being himself clothed in the garments of peace.

Claudian gives the character of Trajan as follows:

———————— Victura feretur
Gloria Trajani; non tam quod Tigride victo,
Nostra triumphati fuerint provincia Parthi,
Alta quod invectus stratis capitolia Dacis:
Quam patriæ quod mitis erat ————

A dark green coin, in fine condition; from the Gwilt Cabinet.

525.

IMP . CAES . NERVAE . TRAIANO . AVG . GER . DAC . P.M . TR . P . . . . The laureate head of the emperor to the right.

℞. S . P . Q . R . OPTIMO . PRINCIPI. In the exergum S. C. A narrow-looking temple with eight columns in front; a statue is standing between the two centre columns. The pediment triangular, and decorated with several statues, also statuary in the tympanum, and the friezes are ornamented likewise.

A nice pale green coin. Weight 312¼ grains.

526.

IMP . CAES . NERVAE . TRAIANO . AVG . GER . DAC . P.M . T . TR . P . V . P.P. The head of Trajan to the right, with radiate crown.

℞. S . P . Q . R . OPTIMO . PRINCIPI. In the exergum S. C. A temple of eight columns, very beautifully delineated.

A remarkably fine pale green coin in Second Brass.

527.

IMP . CAES . NERVAE . TRAIANO . AVG . GER . DAC . P.M. TR . P . COS . V . P.P. The laureate head of the emperor to the right.

℞. S . P . Q . R . OPTIMO . PRINCIPI . S . C . inscribed in four lines within a broad wreath of oak-leaves and acorns.

A coin incident upon the Dacian victories.

A very fine coin in red Cyprian copper. Weight $400\tfrac{1}{4}$ grains.

528.

IMP . CAES . NERVA . TRAIAN . AVG . GERM . DACICVS . P.M. The laureate head of the emperor to the right.

℞. . . . . . . CONGIAR . . . SECVND . In the exergum S. C. The emperor, or his legate, robed, seated on a curule chair to the left, placed on a high *suggestum*; at his right hand is a tripod brasier as if to burn perfume. In front of the legate is another *suggestum*, rather lower than that on which he is seated. On this is a small square seat, with a person seated employed writing at a small table before him. A person is standing at the right side of the legate, holding up a frumentarian tablet. A citizen is ascending the steps, in front of the person who is writing, with his robe extended, as to receive the donation. Argelati, Clinton, and Eckhel put the date of this congiary A.D. 104. Vaillant says of this type, " Hic nummus primæ formæ pro raro recensetur."

A black coin, from the Devonshire Cabinet, but not in very good preservation. Weight $402\tfrac{1}{4}$ grains.

529.

IMP . CAES . NERVAE . TRAIANO . AVG . GER . DAC . P.M. TR . P . COS . V . P.P. The laureate head of the emperor to the right, the bust in armour, with a military cloak.

℞. S . P . Q . R . OPTIMO . PRINCIPI . In the exergum S. C. A triumphal arch with outer wings and very much decorated with sculptures; over the arch is a triangular pediment filled with sculptures, and above that a square plinth bearing in front the letters I . O . M . (IOVI . OPTIMO . MAXIMO.), and surmounted by a chariot with six horses; trophies and Victories at the sides, and captives at the foot of the trophies; sculptures are also in different compartments all down the front of the outer wings, the last compartment on each side appearing to have a wolf and twins in it.

This is considered to be a representation of the arch of Trajan, which, in commemoration of his victories, was erected at Rome near to the amphitheatre, and of which there are some remains still existing. Admiral Smyth, No. 128 of his cabinet, looks upon this arch as "probably forming the vestibulum or porch of the Capitol mentioned in the Panegyric," but I do not find any reference of this sort in the Panegyric: chapter ix. of that work refers to a triumph, but not in such terms as to designate any arch.

This coin is not, I believe, mentioned by Eckhel in his work, vol. vi., which is rather singular.

It is in remarkably fine preservation, of a dark or black brown colour, from the cabinet of the Earl of Pembroke. Weight 404¼ grains.

530.

IMP . CAES . NERVA . TRAIANO . AVG . GER . DAC . . . . The laureate head of the emperor to the right.

℞. S . P . Q . R . OPTIMO . PRINCIPI. In the field S. C. A column spirally ornamented with sculptures standing on a square base, at the angles of which eagles are placed; the column is surmounted by a robed statue of the emperor with the right hand extended, in the left a spear or *hasta pura*.

This column was erected by the Senate and people of Rome to the military fame and honour of the emperor on the final overthrow of the Dacians and the reduction of their country to the condition of a Roman province. When completed it was 128 feet high, having within it 185 steps to reach the top, and 45 openings or windows for light. The statue of the emperor on the top was 20 feet in height, making 148 feet in the whole. It was placed in the centre of Forum Trajani, where it stands at the present day, and is one of the most remarkable objects in Rome. The sculptures with which it is adorned form a most valuable and interesting historic record for enabling artists and antiquaries to obtain a knowledge of the arms, accoutrements, ceremonials, military habits and tactics both of the Romans and of the Dacians, amounting in the whole to 2,500 figures, each figure being nearly three feet high, and appearing all to be executed by the same artist.

It was these sculptures that it is said Raffaelle studied, and confessed that whatever was found to be elegant in his paintings he was indebted for to the sculptures on this column. Julio Romano and others have also studied from it.

It was designed and executed under the superintendence of the celebrated Apollodorus of Damascus, who erected the bridge over the Danube.

In the year 1588 Pope Sixtus V. ordered the architect Fontana to repair the column in such places as were dilapidated by time, and he set up the statue of

St. Peter in gilded metal from a model by Tomasa della Porta in lieu of that of Trajan, but I do not find what became of the statue of Trajan.

Dion, *in Hadriano*, says, "Trajani ossa in illius columna condidit;" or as Cassiodorus, "Ossa in urnâ aureâ collocata sub columnâ Fori quæ ejus nomine vocatur recondita sunt."

In the pontificate of Paul III. the base of the column being much hidden by accumulated earth and ruin, it was ordered to be cleared, and the following inscription was discovered on the base:

SENATVS . POPVLVSQVE . ROMANVS
IMP . CAES . DIVI . NERVAE . F . NERVAE . TRAIANO
AVG . GERMANICO . DACICO . PONT . MAX . TRIB .
POT . XVII . IMP . VI . COS . VI . P . P . AD . DECLARANDUM
QVANTAE . ALTITVDINIS . MONS . ET . LOCVS . TANTIS
RVDERIBVS . SIT . EGESTVS.

Various readings of the latter part of this inscription have been given, in consequence of the absence of the letters IS in TANTIS, and RVDERI in RVDERIBVS. This is taken from Salmon. i. 242. See also Donati, Eckhel, Pitiscus. Another inscription describes the victories of the emperor.

The tribunician date xvii. as the time when the column was inaugurated, would place it in the year A.D. 114.

A coin in very good condition, dark brown colour. Weight 443¼ grains.

531.

IMP . CAES . NERVAE . TRAIANO . AVG . GER . DAC . P . M . TR . P . COS . V . P.P. The laureate head of Trajan to the right.

℞. S . P . Q . R . OPTIMO . PRINCIPI. In the exergum S. C. A temple of eight columns: between the two centre columns is a statue standing on a square plinth; the pediment is triangular, and ornamented with statuary at its apices, and there are various sculptures in the tympanum.

A dark brown coin. Weight 380¼ grains.

532.

IMP . CAES . NERVAE . TRAIANO . AVG . GER . DAC . P . M . TR . P . COS . V . P.P. The laureate head of the emperor to the right.

℞. S . P . Q . R . OPTIMO . PRINCIPI. In the field S. C. A large club standing upright, its thickest end resting on the skin of a lion's head and shoulders.

A complimentary coin, comparing the victories of Trajan over the Dacians to the success of Hercules in his combat with the Nemean lion.

A very good black Second Brass coin. Weight 168¾ grains.

533.

IMP . CAES . NERVAE . TRAIANO . AVG . GER . DAC . P . M . TR . P . COS . V . P . P. The head of the emperor to the right, with radiate crown.

℞. S . P . Q . R . OPTIMO . PRINCIPI. In the field S. C. A Roman cuirass or suit of body-armour more adapted for a general officer than a common soldier, but no helmet.

A very good brown Second Brass coin.

534.

IMP . CAES . NERVAE . TRAIANO . AVG . GER . DAC . P . M . TR . P . COS . V . P . P. The laureate head of the emperor to the right.

℞. S . P . Q . R . OPTIMO . PRINCIPI. In the field S. C. Three military standards; the middle one bears an eagle holding a fulmen in its claws; the standard on the right side is surmounted by a wreath, that on the left side bears a hand; there are wreaths and other decorations on the staff of each standard.

I take this device as intended to compliment the army on the successful campaign in Dacia.

A pale green coin, very fine indeed, of Second Brass. Weight 184¼ grains.

535.

IMP . CAES . NERVAE . TRAIANO . AVG . GER . DAC . P . M . TR . P . COS . V . P . P. The laureate head of the emperor to the right.

℞. S . P . Q . R . OPTIMO . PRINCIPI. In the field S. C. A female standing to the left; at her right side is the prow of a galley; in her right hand she holds the tiller of a rudder; on her left arm she bears a cornucopiæ filled with fruits.

A very good light-brown coin. Weight 435¼ grains.

536.

IMP . CAES . NERVAE . TRAIANO . AVG . GER . DAC . P . M . TR . P . COS . V . P . P. The laureate head of the emperor to the right.

℞. S . P . Q . R . OPTIMO . PRINCIPI. In the field S. C. and in the exergum ALIM . ITAL. A female standing full front looking to the left; her right hand holding some wheat-ears, and extended over a small figure at her right side, wrapped in a toga and holding some object in its left hand; on her left arm she bears a full cornucopiæ.

By some writers this coin is represented to have been struck to commemorate the relief afforded by the emperor to many of the provinces of Italy, which had suffered from famine, floods, and earthquakes.

By others it is considered as referring to the institutions founded and endowed with lands by Trajan, for the maintenance of the poor citizens of Rome and their children, as well as affording relief to the poor citizens and their families in the various provinces of Italy, institutions which the local authorities of the different districts were compelled to provide for, on similar principles to the relief created in England for the assistance of the poor by the statute of Queen Elizabeth.

It would appear that this system was first commenced by the Emperor Nerva, as we have seen recorded on his coin. In Gruter, Inscriptions, p. 1084, there is the following tablet:—

IMP . NERVAE . TRAIAN . AVG . GERM .

P . MAX . TRIB . POTEST . COS . IIII . P . P .

NOMINE . PVELLORVM . PVELLARVMQVE .

VLPIANORVM .

EXSC.

A very fine brown coin. Weight 383½ grains.

537.

IMP . CAES . NERVAE . TRAIANO . AVG . GER . DAC . P . M . TR . P . COS . V . P . P . The laureate head of the emperor to the right.

℞. S . P . Q . R . OPTIMO . PRINCIPI . ALIM . ITAL . in the exergum; S. C. in the field. A female with a small togated figure by her right side, as on the preceding coin, but she holds no wheat-ears over him, nor has he anything in his left hand, but holds his dress with his right hand.

This coin was struck on the same occasion as the preceding.

A fine bronze Campana coin, tinged with green. Weight 419½ grains.

538.

[IMP . CAES . NERVAE . TRA]IANO . AVG . GER . [DAC . P.M . TR . P . COS . V . P . P .] The laureate head of the emperor to the right.

℞. S . P . Q . R . OPTIMO . PRINCIPI . In the exergum ALIM . ITAL . In the field S. C. The emperor robed, seated to the left on a curule chair; his left hand holds a *hasta pura*, his right hand extended towards a female who stands before him and presents an infant child to him.

This coin was struck on the occasion related in the two preceding coins; it is the rarest of the series.

The conduct of Trajan in providing for the poor, as already detailed, forms a prominent subject in the Panegyric of Pliny the younger upon the character and conduct of Trajan, ch. xxvi. xxvii. and xxviii.; and, although Pliny was the personal friend of the emperor, and may be supposed to have written with partiality, yet it is supported by other ancient writers.

In the year 1747 there were found at Velcia, an ancient town about eighteen miles from Piacenza, some brazen tablets, recording the fact of large sums of money being given by Trajan, and describing all the lands and farms which had been purchased with these benefactions, both at Velcia and elsewhere. Eckhel, *in Trajano*, vol. vi. p. 424, thus speaks of the circumstance: "Proximum pro temporis serie monumentum quod hanc Trajani beneficentiam comprobet est insignis tabula ænea quantivis pretii anno 1747 in agro Placentino eruta, lata pedes xs. alta pedes vs. pondere librarum DC. in quam commentati sunt Muratorius et Gorius in opere Florentiæ edito in folio, 1749, et quæ describitur a Sebastiano Donato in Supplem. ad Nov. Thes. Muratorii, part ii. page 437, in cujus exordio legitur: OBLIGATIO. PRAEDIORVM. OB . ÆS . DECIES.QVADRAGINTA.QVATVOR. MILLIA . VT . EX . INDVLGENTIA . OPTIMI . MAXIMIQVE . PRINCIPIS .IMP. CAES.NERVAE. TRAIANI . GERMANICI . DACICI . PVERI . PVELLAEQVE . ALIMENTA . ACCIPIANT, &c. Ex titulo DACICI . eruimus tabulam hanc confectam inde ab anno v.c. 856."

A dark green coin, in middling condition, from the Pembroke collection. Weight 436½ grains.

539.

IMP . CAES . NERVAE . TRAIANO . AVG . GER . DAC . P.M . TR . P . COS . V . P.P. The laureate head of the emperor to the right.

℞. S . P . Q . R . OPTIMO . PRINCIPI. In the field S.C. A female standing full front looking to the left, her right hand holding wheat-ears; at her feet is a corn-modius, out of which ears of corn are rising; on her left arm she bears a cornucopiæ filled with fruits; in the back-ground on her left side is the stern of a galley, implying the supply of corn for the city brought by sea from some of the provinces.

A very fine dark green coin. Weight 400⅜ grains.

540.

IMP . CAES . NERVAE . TRAIANO . AVG . GER . DAC . P.M . TR . P. COS . V . P.P. The laureate head of the emperor to the right.

℞. CONGIARIVM . TERTIVM. In the exergum S. C. The emperor or his legate seated to the left on a curule chair, placed on a raised tribunal, in front of whom another person is seated, and is making a donation to a citizen who is ascending the steps to receive it; in the background at the side of the second person another is standing holding up a tablet, and at the right side of the legate is placed a large tripod brasier.

This coin was struck A.D. 107, in which year Trajan had his triumph for the conquest of Dacia, when he made a distribution of his third congiary to the people of Rome. Yet Eckhel seems afraid to decide, and says, "Quo anno Trajanus tertiam hanc liberalitatem erogaverit decidi nequit." Vaillant says, "Hic nummus primæ magnitudinis inter rariores collocatur."

A very fine black brown coin from the Campana Cabinet. Weight 432½ grains.

541.

IMP.CAES.NERVAE.TRAIANO.AVG.GER.DAC.P.M.TR.P.COS.V.P.P. The laureate head of the emperor to the right.

℞. S.P.Q.R.OPTIMO.PRINCIPI. In the field S. C. Roma armed standing looking to the left; her right hand extended holds a Victoriola presenting a wreath. In her left hand Roma holds her spear, the point resting on the ground in token of peace.

A very good black coin. Weight 401¼ grains.

542.

IMP.CAES.NERVAE.TRAIANO.AVG.GER.DAC.P.M.TR.P.COS.V.P.P. The laureate head of the emperor to the right.

℞. S.P.Q.R.OPTIMO.PRINCIPI. In the exergum ARAB. ADQVIS. In the field S. C. A female standing full front looking to the left and holding an olive-branch in her right hand; at her right side is a camel, an emblem of Arabia; her left arm supports her robes and also bears a *sceptrum*; or it may be intended for the *calamus aromaticus*, also an emblem of Arabia.

Arabia is thus spoken of by Ovid:—

"———————————— Sit dives amomo,
Cinnamique, costumque suam, sudataque ligno
Thura ferat, floresque alios Panchaia tellus,
Dum ferat et myrrham."
METAM. lib. x.

Seneca likewise:—

" Cinnami sylvas Arabes beatos
Vidit." ŒDIP. act. i.

A very fine brown coin, exchanged with Mr. Gwilt. Weight 410¼ grains.

543.

IMP.CAES.NERVAE.TRAIANO.AVG.GER.DAC.P.M.TR.P.COS.V.P.P. The laureate head of the emperor to the right.

℞. S.P.Q.R.OPTIMO.PRINCIPI. In the exergum ARAB.ADQ. In the field S. C. A female standing as described on the last coin, only instead of a camel there is an ostrich at her right side; her left arm supports her robes, and also bears a *sceptrum*, or *calamus aromaticus*. The ostrich and camel are both of them natives of Arabia; they are therefore fit emblems of the country.

These two coins are intended to record the subjugation of Arabia. From the time of Augustus until Trajan, neither the emperors or their generals had been able to subdue the Arabs. In A.D. 104, 105, Trajan, by his generals, managed to reduce the greater part of Arabia to the Roman dominion; but, as with the Arabs of the present day, it was only a temporary submission, which was thrown off at the first convenient opportunity.

This event is considered to have been completed, and Arabia rendered part of the empire in the eighth year of Trajan's reign, when A. Cornelius Palma was the governor of Syria, and accomplished this affair.

Occo describes this coin of Arabia with the ostrich as being in the cabinet of Ph. Ed. Fugger, a celebrated and wealthy family in Germany, which possessed a fine collection of coins and other antiquities

A good brown coin. Weight 393¼ grains.

544.

IMP.CAES.NERVAE.TRAIANO.AVG.GER.DAC.P.M.TR.P.COS.V.P.P. The laureate head of the emperor to the right.

℞. S.P.Q.R.OPTIMO.PRINCIPI. In the exergum S. C. The emperor robed standing to the left on a square base placed on a long plinth, decorated in front with festoons; in his left hand he holds a *hasta pura*, and an olive-branch in his right hand; a Victory floating in the air on his left side is placing a wreath on his head; on each side at his feet is a figure with uplifted hands; on the plinth in front on each side of the emperor are four eagles, each holding in its beak a military standard.

Admiral Smyth, No. 133 of his Cabinet, considers this coin to have been struck A.D. 111, to commemorate the peace bestowed by Trajan on Armenia and Parthia, *sed quære*, for Trajan had not subdued Armenia or Parthia at the date of the consulate marked on this coin. May it not have been struck to record the distribution of honours to several of the petty kings of the various countries traversed by Trajan on journeying to Parthia and Armenia?

A good dark brown coin from the Devonshire Cabinet. Weight 354½ grains.

545.

IMP . CAES . NER . TRAIANO . OPTIMO . AVG . GER . DAC . P.M . TR . P. The laureate head of the emperor to the right, shoulders draped.

℞. CONSERVATORI . PATRIS . PATRIAE. In the exergum S. C. Jupiter standing to the left, a large cloak pendent from his shoulders; his right hand extended holds one side of the cloak spread out as a protection to the emperor, who is robed and stands on the right side of Jupiter, and holds up his right hand as if addressing some persons, or in token of thanks for protection afforded.

This is a highly interesting coin. It is mentioned by Argelati only in the silver series of Trajan, and he places it under the date of cos. VI. A.D. 114.

Jupiter is frequently introduced on coins of the emperors, but only on the coins of this emperor in this peculiar character of conservator or preserver of the father of his country, the usual legend being IOVI . CONSERVATORI, and applicable to Jupiter only, meaning Divine Providence.

Domitian had great reverence for Jupiter Conservator, and erected a temple to him.

I do not find this type is mentioned by Eckhel *in Trajano*.

A middling black coin from the Campana Cabinet. Weight 384¼ grains.

546.

IMP . CAES . NERVAE . TRAIANO . AVG . GER . DAC . P . M . TR . P . COS . V . P.P. The laureate head of the emperor to the right.

℞. S . P . Q . R . OPTIMO . PRINCIPI. In the exergum S. C. A temple of eight columns in front, having on each side a columnar arcade or portico, not in width or continuation of the front of the temple, but extending from it in an oblique direction; between the two middle columns of the temple, which are a little apart, an idol is seated; in the tympanum of the pediment another figure is seated with a recumbent figure on each side; on the apex above is a statue holding in its right hand a *hasta pura*, and at each corner is another statue; the tops or gable-like roofs of the side porticoes bristle with ornaments.

This is supposed to represent a temple erected by Domitian to Jupiter Custos; but from its peculiar construction and porticoes, I do not believe that to be a correct opinion. As the emperor Trajan erected many costly temples and public buildings at Rome, he may have repaired the temple of Jupiter Custos and made additions to it. There is no coin of Domitian having on it the representation of a temple like that on the present coin, and had such a temple been built in his time, his vanity would scarcely have allowed it to go unrecorded on a coin.

A very fine black green coin from the Ramsay Cabinet. Weight 413 grains.

547.

IMP . CAES . NERVAE . TRAIANO . AVG . GER . DAC . P . M . TR . P . COS . V . P . P.   The laureate head of the emperor to the right.

℞. S . P . Q . R . OP . . . .   A temple of eight columns in front, having on each side a columnar arcade or portico in the same way as on the preceding coin; in the tympanum and on the apices of the pediment there are statues, as on the last coin.

The outer column on each side of the temple has a square base in front on which a statue is standing; there is also a sedent figure, apparently a Roma, on a base between the two centre columns, which are a little apart to display the idol. There are six steps to approach the temple extending the whole width, but the first or lowest step is made to extend on each side of the porticoes so as to become the first or lowest of the steps; there is also in front of the steps, opposite to the division of the columns where the idol is seated, an altar, square, large size, and decorated in the front and on the top; there are four steps in front of the altar to enable a person to ascend and reach on to the top; on either side of the altar is an S. C.

The type of this coin is much more rare than that of the preceding. I have never yet seen it in a sale. I procured this coin from the cabinet of Mr. Gwilt, F.S.A., the architect, the renovator of the church and ladye chapel of St. Mary Overy in Southwark, at the foot of London Bridge.

A fine aurichalcum.

548.

IMP . CAES . NERVAE . TRAIANO . AVG . GER . DAC . P . M . TR . P   COS . V . P . P.   The laureate head of the emperor to the right.

℞. S . P . Q . R . OPTIMO . PRINCIPI.   In the exergum S. C.   Hygeia seated to the left, feeding a snake which rises from an altar standing at her feet.

A fine coin, mottled orange and red colour. Weight 327½ grains. From Cureton the dealer.

549.

IMP.CAES.NERVAE.TRAIANO.AVG.GER.DAC.P.M.TR.P.COS.V.P.P. The laureate head of the emperor to the right.

℞. S.P.Q.R.OPTIMO.PRINCIPI. No S. C. The laureate head of the emperor to the left, the bust in armour with a military cloak.

A good dark green Second Brass coin. Weight 140¼ grains.

550.

IMP.CAES.NERVAE.TRAIANO.AVG.GER.DAC.P.M.TR.P.COS.V.P.P. The laureate head of the emperor to the right.

℞. S.P.Q.R.OPTIMO.PRINCIPI. In the exergum S. C. The emperor and an attendant standing on a low base to the left; they are both in robes, and the emperor has raised his right hand in the act of addressing four citizens who stand before him with their hands raised in applause; behind the citizens are three obelisks, at the base whereof is a recumbent figure to the right, resting the left arm on a chariot wheel, and embracing the obelisks.

I agree with Oiselius in the attribution of this type, as being the *allocutio* to the citizens, to be "ob Ludos Circenses exhibitos, id enim obeliscus sive potius fragmentum ejus cui fœmina seminuda adjacet indicare videtur."

The consulate of this coin is v. which causes it to be ranked with the coins of the Circus Maximus. It is very rare indeed, especially in anything like a good condition. I obtained this fine black coin by exchange with Mr. Gwilt's, my own not being quite so good. Vaillant says "rarissimus est."

551.

IMP.CAES.NERVAE.TRAIANO.AVG.GER.DAC.P.M.TR.P.COS... The laureate head of the emperor to the right.

℞. S.P.Q.R.OPTI......CIPI. In the exergum S. C. A view of the Circus Maximus, in which appears rising from the centre of the *spina*, that runs the whole length, the Egyptian obelisk brought to Rome by Augustus; at each end of the *spina* are the *metæ*; in the front of the building are the *ostia* or openings, for the admission of the spectators to the interior of the building.

The Circus Maximus is said to have been constructed originally by Tarquinius Priscus (Livy, i. 35; Dion. Hal. p. 200); and, he being of noble Hetruscan family, and one of the early kings of Rome, he sent to Hetruria for race-horses and pugilists to perform in the circus. Valerius Maximus, on the contrary, says that the Circensian Games, or games of the Circus, were first instituted by Romulus, under the name of *consualia*.

The Circus was placed in the valley between the Aventine and Palatine hills. It was first built of wood, but after several reparations it was ultimately constructed of stone. Oiselius, in tab. xcvii. gives from a very rare coin of Augustus a very good view of the Circus as it was in the reign of Augustus: subsequently to that time it was again repaired, and Trajan, on his return from Dacia, enlarged it so as to render it capable of containing, as is said, 200,000 spectators. (Donati, 222.)

In Eckhel, vi. 427, after quoting from Dio, he says, "Etiam Pausanias inter magnifica Trajani opera recenset Hippodromum duorum stadiorum longitudinem equans."

A very good yellow brassy coin, from the Pembroke Cabinet. Weight 379½ grains.

552.

IMP . CAES . NERVAE . TRAIANO . AVG . GER . DAC . P . M . . . . The laureate head of the emperor to the right.

℞. S . P . Q . R . . . . In the exergum S. C. A view of the Circus Maximus, in which an animal is seen running on the right between the obelisk and the *metæ*; in front of the building are the *ostia*.

This coin was struck on the same occasion as the preceding and following coins. After the return of Trajan to Rome, he exhibited a grand display of games for the amusement of the Roman people, extending to a period of 123 days. The Circensian Games on this occasion caused the slaughter of a large number of wild animals which had been collected for the purpose, besides the gladiators.

A good dark green coin. Weight 378½ grains.

553.

IMP . CAES . NERVAE . TRAIANO . AVG . GER . DAC . P . M . TR . P . COS . V.P.P.   The laureate head of the emperor to the right.

℞. S . P . Q . R . OPTIMO . PRINCIPI. In the exergum S. C. A view of the Circus Maximus in which an animal is seen (apparently a horse with his rider) between the obelisk and the *metæ*; in front are the *ostia*; leading into the interior of the building.

This coin is the most perfect of the kind that one could wish to see or possess. It is untouched by acid or engraving tool, remarkably fine, and of black colour; from the Ramsay Cabinet. A coin of this type, but I consider not quite so fine, although very nearly, was sold in the Earl of Gainsborough's sale for 40 guineas, at Messrs. Sotheby and Wilkinson's, in November 1858.

Vaillant says, " Hic nummus primæ formæ rarissimus est."

554.

ALEXANDER. Heroic head covered with or wearing a lion's skin as a cap. In the field in front of the face there is a small leaf or part of a palm-branch.

℞. *No legend*. The interior of the Circus Maximus consisting of the obelisk and two *metæ* standing on the *spina*; no other part of the building appears. On the *spina*, between the obelisk and *metæ*, are *bestiarii*, as they were termed, combatants engaged with wild beasts; while in the upper and lower parts of the field are chariots with drivers, called *essedarii*, who are racing with each other, or engaged in combat, which last was frequently the case.

In having to mention the Circus Maximus represented on the preceding coins, and the games which were there exhibited, I have added the present and next piece (or coin) as continuing the representations of the games or combats which were performed in the Circus. The present is from the Pembroke Collection, and is well known from its having been referred to by various authors, and engraved in numismatic works, where reference has been made to the exhibition of the Circensian Games. It is of the class called *contorniati*, and, although such medals are well authenticated and acknowledged to be of Roman mintage, yet it has been a *vexata questio* with numismatic antiquaries for a very long period of time, whether the *contorniati* were coins, or *missilia* or tickets of admission to particular seats or parts of the theatre appropriated to individuals of a certain rank; they are generally of the size of medallions, and have the appearance usually of having been cast in moulds for the occasion; sometimes they were struck from dies, as the next piece will show.

"Venuti, who wrote in A.D. 1730, is of opinion that the *contorniati* are chiefly of the period of Honorius, A.D. 395—423. We think they were struck somewhat earlier, about the time of Constantinus Maximus, 306—337. Moreover, Honorius having abolished the games of the amphitheatre for ever, it is not probable that he should strike *contorniati*, which pieces are generally supposed to have been given away at public games, the Circus, &c.; there was a '*trouvaille*' of fine *contorniati* at Rome, in 1844."—Curt.

The above is about the usual estimate of the time when the *contorniati* were first minted, but I consider it is quite erroneous; for they occur from the time of Julius Cæsar (*vide* Morell), and frequently have good representations or portraits of the different emperors, besides better workmanship than can be found among the regular coins of Constantine or Honorius. In my opinion, the *contorniati* were struck in the times of the emperors whose portraits they represent, for it is not likely that they would be the offspring of a degraded and debased coinage and very inferior artists, incapable of producing the fine work that is on some of them.

Although they may in great strictness and propriety be considered as relating to the Eternal City, yet they are seldom introduced into cabinets as *historic records*, which is an error in judgment, in my opinion, and I differ in that view of the subject. The obverse of this *contorniate* bears the fictitious head of Alexander the Great, which no doubt was intended as an heroic illustration applicable to the combats of the Circus.

A fine brassy medallion-sized *contorniate*, from the Pembroke Cabinet. Weight 470¼ grains.

555.

DIVO . NERVAE . TRAIANO. A laureate head to the right, being a very rude attempt at a portrait of Trajan.

℞. *No legend.* The *spina* of the Circus Maximus, with the obelisk in the centre, and the *metæ* at either end, and on the right another object likewise, similar to that which on the preceding token is on the left side of the *spina*. Beyond the *spina* is a person on horseback to the right; and to the left is another person, a *bestiarius*, on foot, engaged in combat with an animal resembling a lion. Before the *spina*, in the exergum, a chariot combat of *essedarii* seems to have been concluded by the death of one of the parties; and in the field above are two quadrigæ racing after each other, one on either side of the obelisk.

From the subjects above represented, this token is different from the Pembroke token, and, being in very fine first-rate condition, well struck, and not cast, as usually happens, and as large as a medallion, the whole subject is very distinct, and no doubt the field above and below the *spina* was intended by the artist to represent the arena, with the races and combats of the *essedarii* and other gladiators.

A remarkably fine black *contorniate* with green tinge, from the cabinet of M. Sabatier, St. Petersburg.

556.

IMP . CAES . NERVAE . TRAIANO . OPTIMO . AVG . GER . DAC . P . M . TR . P . COS . VI . P . P. The laureate head of the emperor to the right, shoulders draped.

℞. SENATVS . POPVLVSQVE . ROMANVS. In the exergum FORT . RED.; S. C. underneath. A female seated to the left; her right hand holds the tiller of a rudder, her left arm supports a cornucopiæ filled with fruits.

A brown bronze-green coin, very fine. Weight 431¾ grains.

557.

IMP. CAES. NERVAE. TRAIANO. AVG. GER. DAC. P. M. TR. P. COS. VI. P. P.   The laureate head of the emperor to the right.

℞. FORTVNAE. REDVCI. In the exergum S. C. A female seated to the left with rudder and cornucopiæ, as on the preceding coin, her left foot resting on a stool.

A fine black coin. Weight 395½ grains.

558.

IMP. CAES. NERVAE. TRAIANO. AVG. GER. DAC. P. M. TR. P. COS. VI. P.P.   The laureate head of Trajan to the right, shoulders draped.

℞. DACIA. AVGVSTA. In the exergum PROVINCIA. with S. C. underneath. A female seated on a piece of rockwork to the left; on her head she has a round cap; in her left hand she has a standard bearing an eagle, held transversely over her left shoulder; she has on her knees two young children.

This type betokens the annexation of Dacia and her inhabitants (the children) as a province of the Roman empire, and from respect to the courage of the Dacians, the province was honoured with the title of Augusta.

A black coin in very good condition.

559.

IMP. CAES. NERVAE. TRAIANO. OPTIMO. AVG. GER. DAC. P. M. TR. P. COS. VI. P.P. The laureate head of the emperor to the right, shoulders draped.

℞. IMPERATOR. VII. in the exergum, with S. C. underneath. The emperor in military costume seated on a curule chair placed on a tribunal to the right; two attendants, also in military attire, are standing there on his left hand, one rather behind the other. The emperor extends his right hand towards a number of soldiers who stand before him fully armed, and with several eagles and standards; a horse is mixed with them, and apparently carries a soldier with a *vexillum*, the cavalry banner. In front of the tribunal, with his back to the emperor, a soldier is standing bare-headed, seeming to repeat and enforce the words of the emperor, who is much applauded by the assembled military, as indicated by the number of hands held up by the soldiers.

This coin, with the subsequent coins of IMPERATOR VIII. and IMPERATOR VIIII. are supposed to relate to the successes of Trajan over the Parthians, for which he was saluted with the title of Imperator by the soldiers.

A very good black coin from the cabinet of Baron Koller. Weight 396 grains.

560.

IMP . CAES . NERVAE . TRAIANO . AVG . GER . DAC . P . M . TR . P . COS . VI . P. P. The laureate head of the emperor to the right, shoulders draped.

℞. S . P . Q . R . OPTIMO . PRINCIPI. In the exergum VIA TRAIANA. S. C. underneath. A female naked to the waist reclining to the left against a bank, her face turned to the right; she holds a branch in her left hand, and on her right knee supports a chariot wheel, an emblem of travelling.

This type records the repairs executed by order of Trajan in the ninth year of his reign on the Via Appia, a road which passed through the Pontine Marshes; it was originally made by the censor Appius Claudius Cæcus (whence its name), a celebrated orator in the time of the Republic, but he carried it only from Rome to Capua, a distance of 130 miles. Augustus continued it to Brundusium. Trajan, at a very great expense, put it in repair the whole distance from Rome to Brundusium, from which circumstance it was named Via Trajana. Some portions of it are still remaining in the vicinity of Naples. In vol. ii. of Hillard's "Six Months in Italy," published in 1853, there is a short and pleasing account of the Appian Way, written from the author's own personal view of the road, its numerous objects, and the surrounding country.* The whole length was 350 miles, and was well paved throughout the whole line, for Trajan spared no expense to render it complete in every respect. Road-making was a prominent characteristic of Roman government. In Gruter, pp. 151, 152, we have the following inscription:

IMP . CAESAR . DIVI . NERVAE . F .
NERVA . TRAIANVS . AVG .
GERM . DACIC . PONT . MAX . TR . P .
XIII . IMP . VI . COS . V . P. P . VIAM . A .
BENEVENTVM . BRVNDVSIVM . PECV
NIA . SVA . FECIT .

On which Eckhel, vol. vi. p. 421, says: "Exstat hoc marmor hodieque in oppido dicto Biscigallia. In marmore Gruteri habemus CURATORUM VIAE . NOVAE . TRAIANAE . et apud eundem, CURATORES TRIUM TRAJANORUM." The subject represented on this reverse formed part of a basso-relievo in the arch of Trajan, from which it was taken down and worked into the arch of Constantine, erected

---

* A more scientific account of the Via Appia may be seen in Lumisden's Remarks on the Antiquities of Rome, 4to.

to record the victories gained by Constantine over Maxentius, and it is still to be seen at Rome.

A very nice green and mottled red coin in fine condition. Bought of the late Matthew Young. Weight 418¾ grains.

561.

IMP.CAES.NERVAE.TRAIANO.AVG.GER.DAC.P.M.TR.P.COS.VI.P.P. The laureate head of the emperor to the right.

℞. S.P.Q.R.OPTIMO.PRINCIPI. In the exergum S.AQVA.TRAIANA.C. A river-god reclining to the left under (or I should say in front of) an arched grotto; in his right hand he has a sedge or reed, which he rests on his right knee; beneath him in the stonework is a small opening from which water is flowing, instead of from an urn, the usual attribute of a river-god.

This type commemorates the construction of the conduit by which Trajan caused the stream called Aqua Marcia to be conveyed to that part of the city lying about the Aventine Hill; it was called the Aqua Marcia from the early king Ancus Marcius, who originally conveyed the water from the lake Fucinus, situate about thirty miles from Rome, and now called Celano

It appears by an inscription quoted by Donati, p. 263, that the conduit of Trajan was repaired by order of the emperor Caracalla. The water was the sweetest and most wholesome that was brought to Rome.

A very good brown coin.

562.

IMP.CAES.NERVAE.TRAIANO.AVG.GER.DAC.P.M.......... The laureate head of the emperor to the right.

℞. S.P.Q.R.OPTIMO.PRINCIPI. In the exergum FORVM.TRAIANI. with S.C. underneath. A grand edifice, adorned with sculptures, columns, and trophies, which was erected by order of Trajan by the architect Apollodorus, after the Dacian war had terminated. On the portico was a representation of Trajan in a chariot drawn by six horses, attended by Victories, with trophies at each side. In the niches at the sides of the building were placed the statues of the different generals and chief officers and others who had distinguished themselves in the Dacian war. In the area of the portico attached to the forum there was placed an equestrian statue of Trajan, and in the middle of the forum stood the famous column surmounted by his statue.

This was the most splendid of all the various edifices erected by Trajan, and it remained in great perfection to the time of Constantius, who is described by

Ammianus Marcellinus to have been astonished when he beheld it—"hærebat attonitus"—an expression well borne out by Cassiodorus and others in their remarks upon this magnificent building, which seems to have surpassed every other building of the kind that had ever before been erected in Rome.

In the life of Pope St. Gregory, it is said that when he saw the *vestigia* of this forum, he was so astonished—"tantæ substructionis admiratus consilium auderet supremum Numen implorare ut ab æternis inferni pœnis eximeretur Trajani architectus"—superstition of another class—Eckhel, vi. 432, *in Forum Trajani*.

A good dark green coin. Weight 409½ grains.

563.

IMP . CAES . NERVAE . TRAIANO . AVG . GER . DAC . P . M . TR . P . . . . The laureate head of the emperor to the right, shoulders draped.

℞. S . P . Q . R . OPTIMO . PRINCIPI. In the exergum BASILICA . VLPIA. with S. C. underneath. A grand edifice very much resembling the Forum in its external appearance, being adorned with statuary figures above, but no statues in the niches at the sides.

This building was erected by Trajan at the same period as the Forum. The *basilicæ*, of which there were several at Rome, were public buildings covered over at the top, and thus differing from the Forum, which was open to the air. In these buildings, all the causes and law-suits were tried before the judges of the courts. The *basilica* of Trajan was much frequented, and was decorated with many statues.

These two buildings, the Forum and Basilica, are supposed to have been erected in A.D. 114, after the reduction of Armenia and Mesopotamia.

I have observed on various coins of these types of the Forum and Basilica, that the buildings are very indistinctly made out by the die-engraver; the present coins are a fair criterion of their workmanship.

A pale green coin in good condition, from the Campana Cabinet. Weight 328¼ grains.

564.

IMP . CAES . NERVAE . TRAIANO . AVG . GER . DAC . P . M . TR . P . COS . VI . P.P. The laureate head of the emperor to the right, shoulders draped.

℞. S . P . Q . R . OPTIMO . PRINCIPI. In the exergum S. C. An equestrian figure of Trajan to the left, the horse in the attitude of stepping forward. The emperor in civil attire and bareheaded, holding a spear in his right hand, the point resting on the ground.

This type I consider represents the equestrian statue of the emperor which stood in the area of the portico of the Forum. A coin of similar type in the cabinet of the Duke of Croye and Arschot is marked in its legend ADVENTVS. AVGVSTI; but the catalogue does not distinguish its metal or size, and attributes its coinage to the return of the emperor to Rome mentioned in the Panegyric of Pliny; but this, I think, is incorrect, for although the word *adventus* is used, yet the figure is more in the character of the equestrian statues of other Roman emperors, and the die-engraver may have borrowed the figure from the statue in the Forum to save himself the trouble of making a new design for an *Adventus*.

A good dark brown coin. Weight 344½ grains.

565.

IMP . CAES . NERVAE . TRAIANO . OPTIMO . AVG . GER . DAC . P . M . TR . P . COS . VI . P.P.
The laureate head of Trajan to the right, shoulders draped.

℞. IMPERATOR . VIII . in the exergum, with S. C. underneath. The emperor in military costume seated to the right on an X-shaped stool placed on a high tribunal; behind him, at his left side, are two persons in military attire; on the ground a person is standing with his back to the emperor, and facing the soldiers, who are in front of the tribunal; some of the soldiers bear standards, of which one is an eagle; amongst them also is a horse, but without a rider.

This coin and device is usually considered to relate to the victories obtained by Trajan and the Roman armies over the Parthians; but it is, I think, doubtful whether it applies to the first or the second of his campaigns against them. My opinion is, that the coin applies to the first of the campaigns in the sixth consulate. For Trajan subsequently in the eighteenth year of his reign, A.U.C. 868, had a rupture with Cosrhoes, the then Parthian king, and marched his armies into Parthia and seized Ctesiphon the capital city of Cosrhoes, who fled and thus saved his life, and Trajan received the title of Parthicus, which is not in the obverse legend of this coin.

It is very probable that the salutation of Trajan as Imperator for the ninth time, which we shall see on a subsequent coin, was given on this latter occasion, for, although there does not appear any change in the date of the consulate, yet we have some little guide in the words of the legend.

A fine black coin. Weight 373¼ grains.

566.

IMP . CAES . NERVAE . TRAIANO . OPTIMO . AVG . GER . DAC . P . M . TR . P . COS . V . P . P.
℞. PORTVM . TRAIANI. In the exergum S. C. The representation of an hexagonal port or basin for shipping, the entrance being placed on the lower part of the coin, with the S. C. in front at the exergum; it is surrounded with buildings of different descriptions; the entrance is narrow, having buildings on each side of it; three vessels appear lying at anchor, or moored to the wharves, which we should say were before the buildings fronting the basin.

Argelati, *in Trajano*, A.U.C. 858, A.D. 105, notices the coin PORTUM . TRAIANI. as "Portus variis ædificiis ornatus in cujus medio triremis Imperatoria ornata et aliæ triremes," which he describes as referring "ad Portum a Trajano prope Centum Cellas ædificato cujus meminit Plinius, epist. 31, lib. vi. referendus nummus." And the next following coin he describes " PORT . OST . portus Ostiensis qualis in Neronis nummis cum tribus navibus;" and he refers to the coin he so quotes as being in the Arschot Cabinet, tab. xxxiii. No. 23, adding, " Portum Ostiensem aliquâ insigni refectione a Trajano auctum nummo hoc intelligere licet silentibus historicis."

Occo describes the coin PORTUM TRAIANI as " Portus Ostiensis formâ octangulâ variis ædificiis ornatus, ut tabernis mercium, armentariis, catenâ ferreâ præclusus, in cujus medio navis Imperatoria et aliæ triremes;" and mentions the coin as being " inter picturas Alb. Pr. nummus est apud Jul. Rom."

Eckhel also speaks of it in an uncertain manner in his vol. vi. 426, " Portus variis ædificiis ornatus in cujus medio triremes;" he then says, "Tres sunt Italiæ portus qui hunc Portus Trajani titulum vindicari sibi posse videntur: I. Centum Cellæ, hodie Civita Vecchia, de quibus sic coævus (Plinius), Villa pulcherrima apud hanc urbem cingitur viridissimis agris, imminet littori cujus in sinu fit cùm maximò portus [et cùm prolixè enarrasset rationem novi operis, addit] habebit hic portus etiam nomen auctoris. II. Ostia ex vetere scholiaste Juvenalis qui ad hujus versus 76 et 77, satyra xii. :

> Tandem intrat positas inclusa per æquora moles,
> Tyrrhenamque Pharon porrectaque brachia sursum.

Sic commentatur—inclusa per æquora—portum Augusti dicit sive Trajani—porrectaque—quia Trajanus portum Augusti restauravit in melius et interius tutiorem sui nominis fecit. III. Ancona—nam in Arcu Trajani qui integer adhuc adstat in portu Anconæ, hoc legitur—epigramma premissis ejus titulis et TR. POT. XVIII. (Oiselius says TR. P. XVIIII.) Inscrip. Gruteri, pp. 246, 247.

> PROVIDENTISSIMO . PRINCIPI . SENATVS . P. Q. R.
> QVOD . ACCESSVM . ITALIAE .
> HOC . ETIAM . ADDITO .
> EX . PECVNIA . SVA .
> PORTV . TVTIOREM . NAVIGANTIBVS . REDDIDERIT .

Omnibus rite expensis verisimillimum videtur hunc PORTVM . TRAIANI . esse Portum Centum Cellarum qui totus Trajani opus fuit, quemque discrtè Plinius *habiturum nomen auctoris* testatur—atque etsi Ostiensis etiam portus dicatur Trajani lævius tamen præ Pliniano est scholiastis testimonium qui in veris nominibus poterit hallucinari; et ut illud demus quoque verisimile non est voluisse Senatum in monetâ prædicare portum a Trajano tantum restauratum auctumque, et negligere alterum Centum Cellarum ab eo immensis sumptibus e fundamento excitatum; multo minus intelligi poterit Portus Anconitanus, quem amplificatum quidem a Trajano et tutiorem redditum constat, at non ab eo appellationem traxisse."

Thus Eckhel inclines to attribute the type on this coin to the port at Centum Cellæ. Seeing how inaccurately the coin and its intent is described by these writers, it makes me think they never saw the coin or the port of Civita Vecchia itself; for the port is not octangular, nor is there any mark of or for a chain or boom across the entrance. They could not surely have had the coin before them, for the port of Trajan in all the coins (very few indeed) and engravings I have seen is six-sided, or hexagonal.

This coin of the portus Trajani has (like the coin of Trajan with the arch of a bridge on it) been a *vexata questio* with numismatic antiquaries; but now, with the assistance of Monsieur Texier's discoveries and drawings of the remains of the Port of Ostia, which we have already noticed on the coin of Nero, looking at the *vestigia* he has excavated, traced, and designed, the question seems to be put at rest, for there appears to be no doubt now that the *portus Trajani* depicted on this coin is the *Trajanello* indicated on his plan, which we have given *in Nerone*, and here repeat; the Trajanello, or port of Trajan, being the inner basin to the port of Claudius (or Ostia); and if the two coins be put together and compared with the drawings of M. Texier they will be seen to form the outer port of Ostia and the inner basin of Trajanello.

In confirmation of my view of the question, I find, on referring to the Arschot Cabinet, the port there depicted, as the coin that is quoted is an exact representation of the Portus Trajani on the present coin. And it is thus described by Gevartius: " Portus Ostiensis a Trajano ornatus aut firmatus," Scholiast Juvenalis ad Sat. xii. "Trajanus Portum Augusti restauravit et interius tutiorem sui nominis fecit. Vide Cluverium *in Italia*." Likewise, Oiselius in the cixth plate of his Thesaurus, gives the type of a coin precisely like the *Portus Trajani* on the present coin, and it is called on the reverse PORT. OST., and the preceding coin which he depicts is the reverse—AVGVSTI. PORT. OST. of Nero, the latter being a circular haven, as we see on the coins of Nero, the other being a six-sided or hexagonal basin, as we see on the present coin. Oiselius describes it as a coin of Trajan "cum inscriptione PORT. OST. quia et ipse Trajanus Portum Ostiensem ornavit et firmavit—ut habet Scholiastes vetus ad Juvenal, sat xii.—Trajanus portum Augusti restauravit in melius, et interius tutiorem sui nominis fecit: ita ut jam geminus esset portus; alter *exterior* Augusti Portus dictus, *interior* alter Trajani Portus appellatus. Vid. Ph. Cluverius, Italiæ Antiquæ lib. iii. cap. iii." Oiselius describes the port as *geminus*; thus being like unto Mons. Texier's plan, the inner and the outer ports being conjoined. So that I consider, whether the legend around the hexagonal port of Trajan on his coins be PORT. OST. or PORTUM TRAIANI, it refers to the construction of the port Trajanello added to the Claudian port Ostia, and forming the interior harbour or basin of that port—the words PORT. OST. being an indication on the coin of Trajan of the share taken by Trajan in enlarging the port of Ostia, and rendering it more commodious for shipping; so that, whether the words are PORT. OST. or PORTUM TRAIANI, the port intended and represented is precisely the same in each coin, and the port now called Trajanello is the only port intended. Eckhel is wrong in supposing this coin can in any way apply to Centum Cellæ or Civita Vecchia as it is now called, for Civita Vecchia, although originally constructed by direction and order of Trajan, yet is a circular port, like the port of Ostia; so that, after all research and inquiry, this coin, showing an hexagonal port, refers to the increased accommodation and extension given by Trajan's orders to the port of Ostia, forming the inner basin termed in Mons. Texier's plan Trajanello.

This coin is very rare; it is a black coin, in good condition, from the Herpin Cabinet. Vaillant calls it "rarissimus."

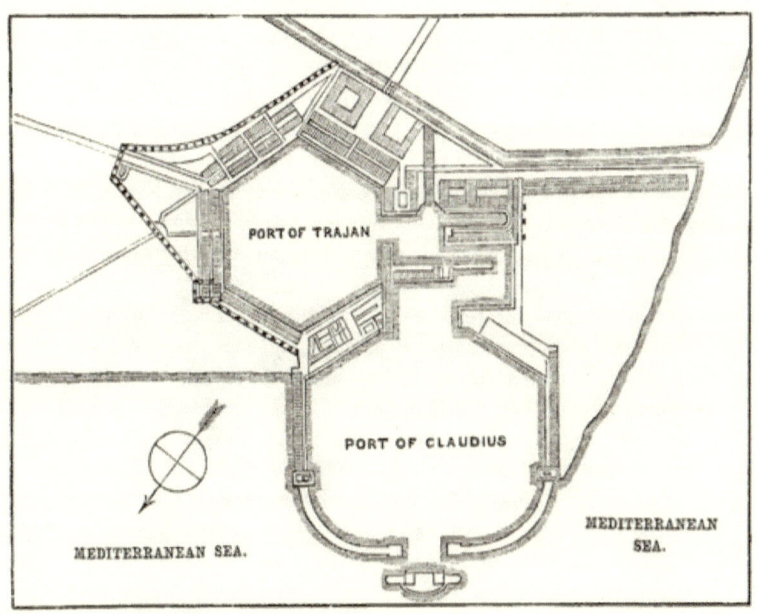

567.

IMP . CAES . NER . TRAIANO . OPTIMO . AVG . GER . DAC . PARTHICO . P. M . TR. P . COS . VI . P.P. The laureate head of the emperor to the right, shoulders draped.

℞. ARMENIA . ET . MESOPOTAMIA . IN . POTESTATEM . P. R . REDACTAE. In the field S. C. The emperor in military costume standing full front holding a spear in his right hand, with a *sceptrum* on his left arm; at his feet, on his left side, a female is seated, wearing a short tunic and trousers as an Oriental, with a mitre or pointed cap on her head; behind her is a recumbent river-god holding a sedge or reed in his right hand, his left arm resting on an urn, from which a stream of water is flowing. On the ground, at the right foot of the emperor, is another river-god, in the same posture, with a sedge or reed in his left hand, his right arm resting on an urn, from which also water is flowing.

A very good brown coin, more particularly the reverse. Weight 331½ grains.

568.

IMP . CAES . NER . TRAIANO . OPTIMO . AVG . GER . DAC . PARTHICO . P . M . TR . P . COS . VI . P . P. The laureate head of the emperor to the right, shoulders draped.

℞. ARMENIA . ET . MESOPOTAMIA . IN . POTESTATEM . P . R . REDACTAE . In the field S. C. The emperor in military costume standing full-front, holding a spear in his right hand, and on his left arm bearing a *sceptrum;* his left foot is placed on the body of a female who is prostrate at his feet, her face turned away from the emperor; she wears a pointed cap, short tunic, and trowsers, as an Oriental. Behind her is a river-god in recumbent position, resting his left arm on an urn, from which water is flowing. On the other side of the emperor, at his right foot, is another river-god with his right arm resting on an urn from which water is flowing.

The rivers personified on these coins are the Tigris and Euphrates, between which Armenia and Mesopotamia are situated. The successes obtained by Trajan in his last expedition against the Parthians are the subjects recorded. The conquered provinces were under the dominion of the Parthian kings, and were the first territories of any importance in the East that Trajan reduced to the sway of the Romans, after which he marched against Cosrhoes, and ultimately reduced his country also to the Roman yoke, for all which successes the Senate bestowed upon Trajan the title of *Parthicus,* as appears by the obverse legend on these and subsequent coins. Argelati, *in Trajano,* places these coins in the date A.D. 115.

A fine Campana coin of pure aurichalcum. Weight 432 grains.

569.

IMP . CAES . NER . TRAIANO . OPTIMO . AVG . GER . DAC . P . M . TR . P . COS . VI . P . P . The laureate head of the emperor to the right, shoulders draped.

℞. IMPERATOR . VIIII . in the exergum, with S. C. underneath. The emperor in military attire, seated on an X stool to the right, addressing several armed soldiers who stand before him bearing eagles and other standards; amongst them is a horse, to signify the cavalry being partakers in the assemblage; their hands are raised towards the emperor as applauding his address to them.

Argelati, *in Trajano,* places this coin in A.D. 116, and cites it as "ex Col. Trajan. 6," thereby implying that this type is represented on the Column of Trajan. Morell in his plates of the sculptures on the Trajan Column, at No. 6, gives a representation of an *allocutio* to the troops, but there is no number VIIII, or any number to it to signify what *allocutio* is intended. The *allocutio* on the column cannot refer to any other than an address made to the troops at some period of the

Dacian war; for, as the whole of the figures and groups on the Trajan Column are representative of the Dacian campaigns, the *allocutio* on the column depicted in Morell cannot refer to any other than one made in that war. The *allocutio* recorded on the present coin, having been made some years after, must therefore refer to a transaction some years subsequent to the Dacian campaigns, and there is no subject so appropriate as the campaigns in Parthia, and the reduction of Armenia and Mesopotamia, being the last of Trajan's campaigns, and IMPERATOR VIIII. being the last salutation of Imperator that is recorded of Trajan.

A fine dark brown coin from the cabinet of Colonel Stewart. Weight 367½ grains.

570.

IMP . CAES . NER . TRAIANO . OPTIMO . AVG . GER . DAC . PARTHICO . P . M . TR . P . COS . VI . P.P. The laureate head of the emperor to the right, his shoulders draped.

℞. SENATVS . POPVLVSQVE . ROMANVS. In the exergum S. C. Two elegant trophies of arms side by side.

Havercamp, in describing this and the following coin as they appear in the Christina Cabinet, refers them both to the conquest of Dacia, and he calls them Dacian trophies. In this I differ with him. The Dacian victories occurred in the early part of Trajan's reign, and the coins on which they are recorded are of the fifth consulate.

In the fourth consulate the titles of Trajan end with that of Germanicus, as referring to his victories in Germany. In the fifth consulate the title Dacicus was added, and continued into the sixth consulate. In the sixth consulate the title Parthicus is added. These two trophies being on a coin of the sixth consulate, and the title Parthicus being introduced, evidently authorizes this coin to be applied to the successes gained over Dacia as the first trophy, and to Parthia as the second trophy. If it were confined to Dacia only, one trophy would suffice, although it may be said the two trophies refer to the two Dacian campaigns, which I do not consider likely, for, if it were so, the word PARTHICO would not be added to the titles on the obverse of this coin.

A very fine earthy or grey-tinted black Second Brass coin from the Campana cabinet. Weight 158⅛ grains.

571.

IMP . CAES . NER . TRAIANO . OPTIMO . AVG . GER . DAC . PARTHICO . P . M . TR . COS . V . P . P. The head of the emperor to the right with radiate crown, his shoulders draped.

℞. SENATUS . POPVLVSQVE . ROMANVS. In the exergum S. C. The emperor in military costume, full front to the right, is in the act of rushing out from between two trophies; on the one to the right he has placed his right hand, in his left hand he holds a spear and is touching the trophy at his left side.

Referring to the note on the subject of the type on the preceding coin, it may be further said that the present type may not only be considered as recording all that is commemorated on the other coin, but it likewise shows the emperor in the act of hastening from his successes over the Dacians in search of further victories, which ended in his campaigns in Parthia, and the complete overthrow of the Parthian king, and the taking of Ctesiphon and Babylon, the chief cities possessed by the Parthians, the former being the metropolis of their empire and the chief residence of their kings. It was at Ctesiphon that Trajan found the massive golden throne of the Parthian kings which he sent to Rome, where it remained in the time of Hadrian, who promised the Parthians he would return it to them, but he forgot to do so.

The capture of Ctesiphon extended the Roman empire beyond the river Tigris. The senate, in their joy at Trajan's constant success, and having bestowed so many titles on him, at last, as embracing all their praise, passed a decree that he should be at liberty to enter the city of Rome in triumph as a conqueror whenever he pleased.

At the sale of the collection of the coins of M. Herpin of Paris at Messrs. Sothebys' in 1857, there was a coin of Trajan in First Brass I should have liked to have purchased. No explanation was given of its type; it was beautifully perfect, and the reverse was, I think, described as a countryman or colonist ploughing; but it represented Trajan in civilian costume ploughing with two oxen, signifying his enlargement or extension of the empire, virtually of the boundaries of Rome. We see a similar type on the coins of Commodus; with him it was the affected vanity of a crack-brained fellow, who had never been out of Rome whilst emperor; but in Trajan it was the energetic progress of a warrior extending the boundaries and conquests of the empire.

A fine brown Second Brass coin. Weight 227½ grains.

572.

IMP . CAES . NER . TRAIANO . OPTIMO . AVG . GER . DAC . PARTHICO . P.M . TR . P. COS . VI . P . P. The laureate head of the emperor to the right, his shoulders draped.

℞. REX . PARTHIS . DATVS. In the exergum S. C. The emperor bare-headed, in military costume, seated to the left on an **X** shaped seat placed on a raised tribunal; a military officer is standing at his left hand, and appears to have his sword in his right hand, which he holds across his breast, having the point in his left hand in the same style as the military salute of an officer of a battalion infantry company at the present day. In front of the tribunal, with his back to the emperor, a person is standing, on whose head the emperor is placing a crown or diadem as king; before this person, and kneeling on her right knee, is a female personifying Parthia with hands extended to receive the king.

This type represents the crowning of Parthamaspates, a prince of Parthia, who was selected by Trajan to be their king, and whom he crowned himself when at Ctesiphon, with much pomp and ceremonial. This prince continued a faithful ally to the Romans until the death of Trajan, upon which event the Parthians drove their new king from his throne, and, with other Eastern nations, revolted from the dominion of the Romans, who for many years after were unable to reduce any portion of those countries again to their power.

The ceremony represented on this coin is thus described by Dio., lib. lxviii. s. 30—" Itaque ut Ctesiphontem venit, Romanis omnibus Parthisque qui tum aderant in magnam planitiem congregatis, consecnsoque alto tribunali Parthamaspatem imposito diademate Parthis regem præfecit."

This coin was struck A.D. 116. The sixth consulate is the last that is mentioned on the coins of Trajan; and it is to be observed, from the number of coins bearing the fifth and sixth consulates, whereon events are recorded which have occurred through a series of many succeeding years, that, as regards the emperor, the consulates were evidently not successively annual.

It is a fine coin of yellowish green tint, from the Devonshire Cabinet. Weight 421½ grains.

573.

IMP . CAES . NER . TRAIANO . OPTIMO . AVG . GER . DAC . PARTHICO . P . M. The laureate head of the emperor to the right, shoulders draped.

℞. REGNA . ADSIGNATA. In the exergum S. C. The emperor in military costume seated to the left on a **X** shaped chair placed on a tribunal; a person stands on each side of him. Three persons are standing in front; the first holds out his right hand to receive something which is presented to him by the emperor; the person on the emperor's left also extends his hand to the second person in front.

This type relates to the assignment of dominions to the kings of Armenia, Mesopotamia, and Parthia, which was done by Trajan in the nineteenth year of his reign, for in the year following he made a second expedition against Arabia, from which country he was, however, obliged to retire after several severe engagements. He afterwards died at Selinus, where his body was burned with the usual honours, and his ashes conveyed to Rome by his widow the empress Plotina, who had accompanied him to the East. Selinus was afterwards called Trajanopolis; it is a town in Cilicia, and is now called Salinti. Admiral Beaufort describes many remains of antiquity there; among them the most remarkable is a low massive edifice composed of well-cut large blocks of stone containing a single vault; there is every reason to suppose this was the basement of some splendid superstructure, nothing of which now remains.

"I cannot find (says Admiral Sir Francis Beaufort) what honours were paid to his (the emperor Trajan's) memory by the Cilicians, but it seems highly probable that a mausoleum should have been erected in the city where the decease of so accomplished and so popular an emperor took place; and, if so, it is equally probable that this building was designed for that purpose." (Lares et Penates, p. 34.)

We have no funereal coins of Trajan.

A brown coin in middling condition, from the Devonshire Cabinet. Weight $412\frac{1}{2}$ grains. It is a rare coin, and very seldom in good condition. Vaillant says "rarissimus est."

574.

IMP . CAES . NER . TRAIANO . AVG . GER . DAC . P . M . TR . P . COS . VI . P . P. The laureate head of the emperor to the right, shoulders draped.

℞. SENATVS . POPVLVSQVE . ROMANVS. In the field S. C. A female standing full front, looking to the left; in her right hand she holds a caduceus : on her left arm she bears a cornucopiæ filled with fruits.

A water-gold coin from the Thames, from my friend C. R. Smith. Weight $385\frac{5}{8}$ grains.

575.

[IMP . CAES . NERVAE] . TRAIANO . AVG . GER . DAC . P . M. The unlaureate head of the emperor to the left, the bust full front and in armour.

℞. S . P . Q . R . OPTIMO . PRINCIPI. In the field S. C. A female standing to the left holding a *hasta pura* in her left hand; in her right hand she has some ears of corn; at her right foot is a corn-modius.

A dark green coin. Weight $413\frac{1}{4}$ grains.

576.

IMP . CAES . NER . TRAIANO . OPTIMO . AVG . GER . DAC . PARTHICO . P . M . TR . P . COS . VI . P . P. The laureate head of the emperor to the right, shoulders draped.

℞. PROVIDENTIA . AVGVSTI . S . P . Q . R. In the field S. C. A stately female standing full front, looking to the left; her right hand holds a short staff pointed downwards towards a globe on the ground at her feet to the right, and, being circular, it represents the world, or Roman world, *orbis Romanus*; her left hand holds a *hasta pura*, and her left elbow rests on a short column that is placed at her left side.

A fine bronze coin. Weight 364½ grains.

577.

IMP . CAES . NER . TRAIANO . OPTIMO . AVG . GERM. The head of the emperor to the right, with radiate crown.

℞. DAC . PARTHICO . P . M . TR . POT . XX . COS . VI . P . P. A large thick wreath of laurel; S. C. within it.

This reverse records the honour of the triumphal wreath which was bestowed on Trajan upon the accomplishment of his successes in the East, and which, by the tribunician date, would be in A.D. 117.

The Senate had already struck a coin with the civic wreath of oak-leaves and acorns in honour of the emperor's victories over the Dacians, and the reduction of their country to the condition of a Roman province, as we have already noticed; but the legend on the present coin has the titles OPTIMO and PARTHICO. By the latter word it is evident that the honours now accorded were for the success of the emperor and his armies in Parthia. This coin, therefore, of the mintage A.D. 117, in the twentieth and last year of Trajan's reign, refers to the complete overthrow of the Parthian kingdom in the preceding year: and with this coin we end our series of the Latin coins of Trajan.

A fine black Second Brass coin. Weight 123½ grains.

The following coins are Alexandrian coins in Large Brass, and are retained for the excellence of their preservation, as well as for their historic interest. Several of them are unique and unpublished. They were obtained some years back from Mr. Borrell, of Smyrna, a gentleman well known in the numismatic world for his skill and abilities.

Mr. Samuel Sharpe, in his work of "Ægypt under the Romans," ed. 1842, p. 57, says, "The Ægyptian coinage of the eleventh year of Trajan is very remarkable for its beauty:" also, "on this series of the coins of Trajan we find a rich variety of fables, taken both from Ægyptian and Greek mythology."

Mr. Sharpe might, with great propriety, have taken the whole range of the Alexandrian coins of Trajan, for in the few specimens now following it will be seen that up to the twentieth year of Trajan the Ægyptian mint produced many very beautiful specimens of great historic interest.

The Ægyptian year was different in its arrangement to the year of the Romans. The Roman year commenced on the first day of January, and ended on the thirty-first day of December, and consisted of 365 days, according to the plan of Julius Cæsar, and which mode of reckoning is now almost universally adopted throughout Europe. The Ægyptian agriculturists commenced their year on the day of the heliacal rising of the Dogstar, that is, about the 18th day of July; while for the dates of king's reigns and civil purposes a year was used of 365 days, which would consequently have a moveable new year's day. By a decree of Augustus, the year of Julius Cæsar or the Julian year of 365 days and a quarter was used.

We must, therefore, consider that in the following coins, the years to which they refer are calculated by the Julian periods, as established by the decree of Augustus.

We have made these few remarks on the Ægyptian and Roman modes of reckoning the term of a year, because on the imperial Alexandrian series of coins, as applicable to the Romans, the Julian mode of reckoning was taken and used at the mint, and the date of its coinage was impressed on each coin, and reckoned by letters of the Greek alphabet answering to numbers, thus rendering certain what is uncertainty in the Roman coinage, which we are obliged to reckon by consulate or tribunician power, the former of which is by no means accurate for fixing the date of an event, as we have had occasion to remark in the coins of cos . v . ranging through several years, and cos . vi . the same.

The tribunician date is the most certain means of fixing the period of an event on a Roman coin; but on the coins of some of the emperors the TR . POT. is marked without the addition of the number or date of the tribunician year.

578.

. . . . ΓΕΡΜ . ΔΑΚ . . . . . . The laureate head of the emperor to the right.

℞. *No legend.* The emperor in a quadriga passing gently to the right; his right hand is raised, and in his left he holds a sceptre ornamented at the top with an eagle. In the field above the horses are the letters LIA, or Leucubantos II., being the date of the eleventh year of the reign of Trajan, when it was struck at the mint.

TRAJAN. 291

It is most probable from the legend on the obverse bearing the word ΔΑΚΙΚ, or DACICVS, that this type has reference to the successful campaigns of Trajan in Dacia, and the emperor is in his triumphal chariot for these successes; but by the Roman coin the triumph for Dacian victories took place A.D. 107, in the tenth year of Trajan's reign. Still, allowing Alexandria to be a distant province of the empire, the triumphal record might without any impropriety appear on a coin minted in a province some time after the event had occurred, and yet have reference to such event. I consider there can be no doubt this type refers to the triumph for Dacian victories.

A fine brown coin. Weight 319¼ grains.

579.

ΑVΤ.ΤΡΑΙΑΝ.ϹΕΒ.ΓΕΡΜ.ΔΑΚΙΚ. The laureate head of the emperor to the right.

℞. A square temple with a large triangular pediment; in the tympanum is a round object; each of the lower angles of the pediment is supported by two massive columns, and apparently intercolumniated; in the centre between the columns is the large figure of an idol holding a *hasta pura* in its left hand, its right hand extended towards an altar which is at the right side; in the field at the sides are the letters LIA.

A very good brown coin. Weight 342½ grains.

580.

ΑVΤ.ΚΑΙ.ΝΕΡ.ΤΡΑΙΑ.ϹΕΒ.ΓΕΡ . . . . The laureate head of the emperor to the right.

℞. *No legend.* The emperor in a car drawn by two centaurs to the right, his right hand raised, the left holding a sceptre. The centaur to the right has turned his head to the emperor, and with its right hand presents him a Victoriola; the centaur to the left hand of the emperor is looking forward, and extends its left hand with a Victoriola which is presenting a wreath; above them in the field is the date LIB or 12.

A brown coin with fine reverse. Weight 315¾ grains.

581.

Legend defaced. The laureate head of the emperor to the right.

℞. *No legend.* A small figure in a car drawn to the right by two large winged serpents, in an undulatory posture and motion, each of them having a sort of feathered plume on its head. In the exergum LIB.

The car drawn by winged serpents is the attribute of Ceres. See the Dialogues of Agostini, the Archbishop of Tarragona. See also Ceres described, in a car drawn by serpents, in a painting discovered in an ancient Hetruscan tomb at Tarquinii. (Dennis, Hetruria, vol. i. p. 348, *in notis*.) The winged serpents also belong to the Ægyptian mythology.

A brown coin, with fine reverse. Weight 425¼ grains.

582.

ΑΥΤ.ΤΡΑΙΑΝ.CΕΒ.ΓΕΡΜ..... The laureate head of the emperor to the right, shoulders draped.

℞. *No legend.* A Victory in a car drawn by two horses to the right, having the reins in her left hand, whilst with her right she holds up a wreath. LIB. in the field above the horses.

A very good brown coin. The device beautifully designed. Weight 342 grains.

583.

............ΓΕΡΜ.ΔΑΚΙΚ. The laureate head of the emperor to the right.

℞. *No legend.* A trophy of arms to the right, before which is a Victory with a palm-branch in her left hand; in her right hand she holds some ornament she is about to affix to the trophy. In the field LIB.

A good-conditioned brown coin. Weight 405¼ grains.

584.

... ΤΡΑΙΑΝ.CΕΒ.ΓΕΡΜ.ΔΑΚΙΚ. The laureate head of the emperor to the right.

℞. *No legend.* Isis seated on a throne to the right; she is crowned with a lotus-flower, and in her lap she has a small figure of Horus; a hawk is perched at each corner of the back of her throne. In the field LIB.

A fine brown coin. Weight 363½ grains.

585.

ΑΥΤ.ΤΡΑΙΑΝ.CΕΒ.ΓΕΡΜ.ΔΑΚΙΚ. The laureate head of the emperor to the right.

℞. *No legend.* A triumphal arch of three entrances, the centre arch being large and high, those at the side being smaller; broad friezes go across the whole front over the arches; on the summit above the centre arch are six horses abreast, as if drawing a chariot; at each side at the ends are sculptured figures. In the field LIΓ, or the year 13.

Another fine brown coin. Weight 371½ grains.

586.

AVT. KAI. TPAIAN. CEB. ΓEP. ΔAKIK. The laureate head of the emperor to the right.

℞. *No legend.* A large figure of Osiris, full front, having a modius on his head; on each side, in the upper part of the field, are two ornamented German or Dacian shields, crossed; his left hand is extended towards an eagle which is perched on a short column at the left side, and his right hand holds a patera over a peculiarly-formed altar at his right side. In the field LIΓ.

This figure is not that of an Osiris proper, but of Osiris Apis or Serapis.

A good brown coin. Weight 456¼ grains.

587.

AVT. TPAIAN. CEB. ΓEPM........ The laureate head of the emperor to the right, the bust in armour.

℞. *No legend.* The front of a temple supported by a single column at each end of the pediment, which is narrow, and has in the tympanum apparently a *scarabæus* or a globe with extended wings. In front is a figure which appears to be crowned with wheat-ears, bearing a cornucopiæ on the left arm. In the right hand she holds up a *sistrum;* at her feet, on the right, an animal is seated, which, by the arching of the back, seems to be a cat; on the left side a dog is seated; both of these animals being objects of Ægyptian veneration. In the field LIΓ.

A very good brown coin. Weight 314½ grains.

588.

AVT. TPAIAN. CEB. ΓEPM. ΔAKIK. The laureate head of the emperor to the right, shoulders draped.

℞. *No legend.* The emperor in a car drawn to the right by four elephants without their riders; his right hand extended holds an olive branch, in his left hand he has a sceptre surmounted by an eagle. Over the elephants, in the field, is the date LIΔ, or year 14.

This coin is unpublished; it is a very fine brown coin. Weight 308⅞ grains.

589.

ΑΥΤ. ΤΡΑΙΑΝ. ϹΕΒ. ΓΕΡΜ. ΔΑΚΙΚ. The laureate head of the emperor to the left.

℞. *No legend.* The twin brothers Castor and Pollux with stars over their heads, each having his horse by his side, and holding his spear, the one in his right hand, the other in his left hand, so that their points cross at the top. The date of this coin is ʟɪє, or year 15.

This is also an unpublished coin; it is in very fine condition, brown in colour. Weight 280⅞ grains.

590.

ΑΥΤ. ΤΡΑΙΑΝ. ϹΕΒ. ΓΕΡΜ. ΔΑΚΙΚ. The laureate head of the emperor to the right.

℞. *No legend.* Nilus recumbent to the left; in his right hand he holds a reed or sedge, in the left a cornucopiæ filled with fruits; underneath him is a crocodile moving to the right; above in the field ʟɪє.

A very good brown coin. Weight 349¼ grains.

591.

ΑΥΤ. ΤΡΑΙΑΝ. ϹΕΒ. ΓΕΡΜ. ΔΑΚΙΚ. The laureate head of the emperor to the right; the bust in armour, the front of the breast-plate decorated with victories.

℞. *No legend.* Jupiter seated to the left, with the *hasta pura* in his right hand; in his left he has what appears to be a reed or sedge; on the ground, at his right side, is a large eagle with its head turned looking at Jupiter. In the field ʟɪs, or year 16.

Another very good brown coin. Weight 349¼ grains.

592.

ΑΥΤ . ΤΡΑΙΑΝ . ϹΕΒ . ΓΕΡΜ . ΔΑΚΙΚ . The laureate head of Trajan to the right; the bust in armour.

℞. *No legend.* A female standing to the right, holding with both hands a ship's sail, which has swollen outward; at her left side is a short round column, on the upper part of which are two tritons, one on each side, and above, on a short projection from the first part of the column, a small figure is standing; above in the field are the letters LIS, year 16.

This coin was struck on the occasion of the emperor leaving Ægypt. He took his departure from the port of Alexandria, as represented by the sail in the hands of the female being swollen outward, a type of his leaving with a fair wind. The type on this coin, which is not particularly rare, except for state of preservation, is usually called Isis Pharia; the female figure signifying Isis as Preserver, and the short column intending a pharos, watch-tower, or lighthouse.

A very fine coin, black colour, from the Brice Cabinet. Weight 427½ grains.

593.

ΑΥΤ . ΤΡΑΙΑ . ϹΕΒ . ΓΕΡΜ . ΔΑΚΙΚ . The laureate head of the emperor to the right.

℞. *No legend.* Two females, one seated to the left holding a *hasta pura* in the left hand; in her right hand she has some ears of corn; on her head there appears a lotus-flower. The other female is standing before her as if she were speaking to her, and holds in her right hand a long jointed torch with fire burning on the top; with her left hand she places a small globe on the lap of the seated female; there appears to be a veil at the back part of the head falling on to her shoulders. The date is LIS, or year 16.

A brown coin; very fine reverse. Weight 420⅔ grains.

594.

ΑΥΤ.ΤΡΑΙΑΝ.ϹΕΒ.ΓΕΡΜ.ΔΑΚΙΚ. The laureate head of the emperor to the right.

ΕΙΡΗΝΗ.ΚΑΙ.ΟΜΟΝΟΙΑ. Peace and Concord. Two females standing opposite each other, their right hands joined; the one to the right holds up in her left hand some ears of corn; the one to the left has on her left arm a cornucopiæ filled with fruits; the date in the field LIS, or year 16.

A very fine brown coin. Weight 313½ grains.

595.

ΑΥΤ.ΤΡΑΙΑΝ.ϹΕΒ.ΓΕΡΜ.ΔΑΚΙΚ. The laureate head of the emperor to the right, shoulders draped.

℞. *No legend.* The emperor in military costume is standing full front and looking to the left, holding a spear erect in his right hand, his cloak folded round his left arm, and a sceptre or *parazonium* in his left hand; at his feet to the right is a person in Oriental costume kneeling down, his face raised towards the emperor as if speaking to him, his hands extended forward in token of supplication. In the field LIII.

This coin is inedited; its type signifies the same event as on the Latin coin *ante* relating to Dacia.

A fine brown coin. Weight 230 grains.

596.

ΑΥΤ.ΤΡΑΙΑΝ.ϹΕΒ.ΓΕΡΜ.ΔΑΚΙΚ. The laureate head of the emperor to the right, shoulders draped.

℞. *No legend.* A graceful female figure reclining on a couch to the left, supported at the shoulders by cushions; at her left side is a rudder; her right hand crossed over holds the tiller; on her head is a lotus-flower. In the field above her is the date LIΘ, or year 19.

A very fine brown coin. Weight 295 grains.

597.

ΑΥΤ . ΤΡΑΙΑΝ . ϹΕΒ . ΓΕΡΜ . ΔΑΚΙΚ.   The laureate head of the emperor to the right.

℞. *No legend.* The emperor laureate, and in full military costume, is seated on a curule chair to the left, holding a spear in his left hand; his right hand is extended towards a female who stands before him wearing a turreted crown, representing Alexandria; her left hand holds a *hasta pura*, with her right hand she presents a wreath to the emperor. In the field LIΘ.

Another very fine brown coin. Weight 250¾ grains.

598.

ΑΥΤ . ΤΡΑΙΑΝ . ϹΕΒ . ΓΕΡΜ . ΔΑΚΙΚ.   The laureate head of the emperor to the right, shoulders draped, and in armour.

℞. *No legend.* Jupiter laureate, seated on a throne to the left; on his left arm he supports rather a clumsy representation of a fulmen, in the right hand he holds a *hasta pura;* at the right side of his seat is a large eagle with its head turned looking towards him. In the field are the letters LIΘ, or year 19.

Another very fine brown coin. Weight 300½ grains.

PLOTINA.

POMPEIA PLOTINA, the wife of the emperor Trajan, was one of the most estimable of the Roman empresses. Her family, and the place and time of her birth, are unknown. She had been married to Trajan for a considerable period before his adoption by Nerva, and died childless in A.D. 129, having survived her husband twelve years. She was a woman of amiable manners, and lived in the greatest harmony with Marciana and Matidia, the former being the sister of Trajan and the mother of Matidia, whose daughter Sabina was married to Hadrianus, who, by the influence of Plotina, was adopted by Trajan (although the old emperor did not much like him), and afterwards succeeded him in the sovereignty.

The coins of Plotina, Marciana, and Matidia are very rare, but not equally rare with Domitia and two or three other empresses whose coins are almost unattainable.

599.

PLOTINA . AVG . IMP . TRAIANI. The head of the empress to the right wearing a frontal coronet, the hair dressed in plaits and hung in a long plaited loop behind; her shoulders slightly draped.

℞. FIDES . AVGVST. In the field S. C. A female standing to the right; her left hand extended holds a patera or small punnet containing fruits; in her right hand she has some ears of corn.

A good aurichalcum coin. Weight 347 grains.

600.

PLOTINAE . AVG . TRAIANI . AVG. The head of the empress to the right, her hair dressed as on the preceding coin.

℞. VENERI . GENETRICI. In the field S. C. Venus standing to the right; her right hand raises her veil; the left presents an apple.

This type is again represented on the coins of Sabina, and also of Faustina Senior. At Rome a temple was erected to Venus Genetrix by Scipio Africanus the younger.

The precise counterpart of this coin was sold in the Earl of Pembroke's collection. The Pembroke coin is mentioned in Eckhel, vi. p. 466; it is so similar to the present coin as to make me believe they both came from the same dies.

A black coin in good condition.

601.

PLOTINA . AVG . IMP . TRAIANI. The head of the empress to the right; hair dressed as before.

℞. AETERNITAS. In the field S. C. A veiled female standing full front looking to the right with the *hasta pura* in her left hand, her right hand raised as if speaking.

There is no doubt this coin is genuine, but, it being unknown in any collection, and the coins of Plotina being very rare, any coin with a new reverse is generally doubted; in the present case it is a most appropriate type. It is a struck coin of Roman aurichalcum, and in fine condition. It was formerly in the cabinet of Mr. Benwell. Weight 463½ grains.

A similar reverse is to be seen on the coins of Faustina Junior.

MARCIANA.

MARCIANA was the sister of the emperor Trajan; the period of her birth is unknown; she was married, but to whom and when is also unknown. It is considered she had become a widow before the adoption of Trajan by the emperor Nerva. She continued on terms of great friendship with her brother and the empress Plotina up to the time of her death, which occurred in about A.D. 114.

Marciana was the mother of Matidia and the grandmother of Sabina the empress, wife of Hadrian.

602.

DIVA . AVGVSTA . MARCIANA. The head of Marciana to the right, with ornamented frontal coronet, her hair braided with great taste at the back of her head; the shoulders draped.

℞. CONSECRATIO. On the exergum S. C. An eagle standing full front with expanded wings, its head turned to the right.

A fine large well-spread First Brass coin of yellowish green earthy look. Weight 405¼ grains.

603.

DIVI . AVGVSTA . MARCIANA. The head of Marciana to the right, as on the last coin; shoulders draped.

℞. EX . SENATVS . CONSVLTO. In the exergum S. C. A decorated car drawn to the left by two elephants, each having its rider; on the car is placed a throne, on which is a seated figure with veiled head to represent Marciana, holding a patera in the right hand, in the left a *hasta pura*.

A black brown coin, fine condition. Weight 346 grains.

MATIDIA.

MATIDIA was the daughter of Marciana and niece of the Emperor Trajan, and mother of Sabina, who was married to Hadrian. The time and place of her birth are not known, nor have we as yet any record of the person to whom she was married or when, or the date of her decease. History supplies very scanty materials of information regarding her, and coins still less.

604.

MATIDIA . AVG . DIVAE . MARCIANAE . F. The head of Matidia to the right, with frontal coronet; the hair is carefully dressed, and drawn up behind and braided with strings of pearl; shoulders draped.

℞. PIETAS . AVGVST. In the exergum S. C. A female standing to the left; her hands are placed on the heads of two children, who stand one on each side looking up to her.

This type represents the princess and her two daughters Sabina and Matidia, the latter of whom died in early life, although it is not known when. Sabina, the other daughter, became the wife of Hadrian.

Pietas, as a virtue, is on the Roman coins mostly represented veiled, but when that is the case, it is usually accompanying some act of religious ceremony, not so when merely of a moral character.

A good dark green coin from the Thomas Cabinet. Weight 445¾ grains.

HADRIAN.

The tribunician dates of Hadrian's reign are as follows. The Emperor Trajan died August A.D. 117; thus —

A.D.				Trib. Pot.			
117.	August to 31st December,		117	Trib. Pot.	1	— cos. 1.	
118.	January 1 to December 31,		118	,,	2	— ,,	2. et Ti. Cl. Fuscus Salinator.
119.	,,	,,	119	,,	3	— ,,	3. et Q. Junius Rusticus.
120.	,,	,,	120	,,	4		
121.	,,	,,	121	,,	5		
122.	,,	,,	122	,,	6		
123.	,,	,,	123	,,	7		
124.	,,	,,	124	,,	8		
125.	,,	,,	125	,,	9		
126.	,,	,,	126	,,	10		
127.	,,	,,	127	,,	11		
128.	,,	,,	128	,,	12		
129.	,,	,,	129	,,	13		
130.	,,	,,	130	,,	14		
131.	,,	,,	131	,,	15		
132.	,,	,,	132	,,	16		
133.	,,	,,	133	,,	17		
134.	,,	,,	134	,,	18		
135.	,,	,,	135	,,	19		
136.	,,	,,	136	,,	20		
137.	,,	,,	137	,,	21		
138.	,,	to June	138	Hadrian died 22			

PUBLIUS ÆLIUS HADRIANUS was the son of Ælius Hadrianus Afer, (a cousin of the Emperor Trajan,) and Domitia Paulina, descendants of an ancient Hetruscan family in Umbria. He was born at Rome A.D. 76. At the age of fifteen he joined the army, and in A.D. 101 he was made quæstor; afterwards, in A.D. 105, he was elected tribune of the people.

Before he became quæstor he married Sabina, the daughter of Matidia, and thus became nearly allied to the imperial family. Nevertheless, he was no favourite with the old emperor Trajan, who never conferred any particular honours upon him.

The empress Plotina not having any children of her own to succeed to the imperial purple, she used her friendly offices and influence with Trajan, and procured him to adopt Hadrian as his successor. Hadrian succeeded in A.D. 117; and after reigning prosperously for nearly twenty-two years, he expired at Baiæ A.D. 138, leaving no child. He had, however, adopted Ælius Cæsar as his successor; but he dying in A.D. 135, he selected Marcus Antoninus, afterwards called Antoninus Pius, to be the future emperor.

The coins of Hadrian are very numerous, and with some exceptions are easily to be obtained at sales; and in Large Brass they are generally of a good-sized module, and rounded flan; but as a general rule, the ordinary coins of Hadrian are difficult to be obtained in fine preservation, which renders it by no means easy to have a series of coins in good regular size and condition. Some devices are very rare indeed, especially when in fine condition.

The coins in this series are all of fine module, the earlier coins especially.

605.

IMP . CAES . DIVI . TRA . PARTH . F . DIVI . NER . NEP . TRAIANO . HADRIANO . AVG. The laureate head of Hadrian to the right, the bust in armour.

℞. PONT . MAX . TR . POT . COS. In the exergum FORT . RED. In the field S. C. Fortune seated to the left on a throne; her right hand extended holds the tiller of a rudder; on her left arm she bears a full cornucopiæ.

At the time of the emperor Trajan's death, Hadrian, who commanded the army in Syria, was at Antioch, to which place the news was conveyed to him; and he then returned to Syria, and from thence to Rome.

By the *tribunicia potestas* not having any number, this coin was struck A D. 117, to record the return of Hadrian to Rome from Syria. Although according to Eckhel, vol. vi. p. 477, Hadrian returned to Rome through Illyria A.D. 118; and he refers to Spartianus in proof, and the type ADVENTVS is quoted. If that be so, and the ADVENTVS type is to mean the actual arrival of Hadrian in Rome, then the present type is anticipatory and supplicatory for the safe arrival of Hadrian.

The coins of Hadrian, with the designations of the emperor Trajan, are those which were struck at the commencement of the reign. Soon after then the titles of Trajan are omitted, and ultimately it is merely the legend HADRIANVS. AVGVSTVS.

A good brown coin. Weight 364¼ grains.

606.

IMP . CAES . DIVI . TRAIAN . AVG . F . TRAIANO . HADRIAN . OPT . AVG . GER . The laureate head of the emperor to the right, the bust in armour.

℞. DAC . PARTHICO . P . M . TR . P . COS . P . P . In the field S. C. and in the exergum CONCORDIA. A female seated on a square seat to the left; her right hand extended holds a patera, her left elbow rests on the back of her chair, on the ground by her left side is a cornucopiæ.

By the CONCORDIA I apprehend is implied the good understanding which had been produced between the emperor Trajan and Hadrian by the good offices of the empress Plotina which occasioned the adoption of Hadrian. It would not have been proper to have made the legend CONCORDIA . AVGVSTORVM as we find on the coins of Aurelius and of Verus, for, although it was understood that Hadrian would become the successor of Trajan, yet the latter had not nominated Hadrian either CAESAR or AVGVSTVS. The mint-master could therefore only use the word CONCORDIA to signify the event, and then only *ex post facto*, and to compliment Hadrian when he became emperor.

The present coin is of the first consulate, and the first tribunician period, A.D. 117.

A yellowish black coin very fine. Weight 504½ grains.

607.

IMP . CAES . DIVI . TRAIAN . AVG . F . TRAIANO . HADRIANO . OPT . AVG . GER . The laureate head of Hadrian to the right, the bust in armour.

℞. DAC . PARTHICO . P . M . TR . P . COS . P . P . In the field S. C., and in the exergum CONCORDIA. A female seated to the left; her right hand extended holds a patera, her left elbow rests on the head of a small figure placed on a square base at the side of the chair, on the ground by her left side is a full cornucopiæ.

In noticing the preceding coin, we have already stated the cause which we apprehend occasioned this type. It is evident, from the inscriptions and titles on this and the preceding coin, the word COS . being used singly without any numeral, that they were struck on the accession of Hadrian, and in his first consulate, thus shewing by the termination P. P. or PATER. PATRIAE that the title was conferred on Hadrian immediately on his accession to the sovereignty in A.D. 117.

Argelati, *in Hadriano*, describes two denarii of Hadrian with the respective types ADOPTIO and PIETAS having COS. P. P., and two other denarii, PIETAS and IVSTITIA, having COS. P. P., placing all four coins under the date A.D. 117, and the same with two brass coins inscribed CONCORDIA with COS. P. P.

Occo likewise, in describing a denarius of Hadrian of the type PIETAS, and also one of the type IVSTITIA, with the legends very nearly alike, and also a brass coin with legends similar to those on the present coin, including the P. P. on each, places them all under the date A.D. 118.

That the word COS. singly without numeral is applied to the first consulate or year of his accession is evident from another coin noticed by Occo, a denarius, the reverse CONCORDIA, with the reverse legend TR. POT. COS. DES. II., shewing the COS. to be for the first consulate, the TR. POT. to be for the first tribunician year, and that the DES. was a notification that he was nominated (*designatus*) to be elected consul for the second time, having already been Consul I. This coin is also placed under the date A D. 118; beside the COS. singly, there is the TR. POT. singly; had it been in the second or third year, it would probably have been TR.P. II. or TR.P.III.; but the COS. and TR. P. being without any number clearly show this and the other coins whereon they are found to be of the first year of the reign.

Eckhel, in vol. vi., p. 515, enters into a very long dissertation on the time when the title P.P. or PATER. PATRIAE was conferred on Hadrian, and which, from marbles and ancient histories, he seems to consider as commencing in the eleventh year of his reign; but coins struck in his first and second consulates, that is in A.D. 117 and 118, clearly establish the fact that the title was borne by him at that period. Historians who do not consult coins may easily fall into mistakes; but coins struck at the very time cannot err, and it is by them that the conjectures of historians are to be rectified. Eckhel, judging from marbles, may have been misled by an inscription terminating with the numerals II. to signify two or second consulate, or second year, and he may thus have been led to call it eleven.

I will add further this remark as to the P.P.—that no master of the mint would have allowed his coin dies to have been thus engraved, unless the title had been authorised by the Senate; for had he ventured so to do, he would have stood in danger of great disgrace, if not of his life; besides the S. C. or *senatus consulto*, is evidence of the coin having been struck by a decree of the Senate; therefore, with all due respect for those excellent writers, I see no reason at present for denying the ascription of the P.P. to Hadrian on becoming emperor, or why he should have waited eleven years for it.

I will just add a remark by Eckhel regarding the P.P., that it may be borne in mind in collecting coins of Hadrian of cos. II. After observing upon a coin said to have the reverse legend cos. II. P. P. only—" Satis est enim advertere nullum nummum Consulatus II. hactenus cognitum offerre memoratam hanc capitis epigraphen, aut etiam caput quale pictura exhibet loco protomes, quam hoc anno fuisse in usu in prolegominis ad nummos Consulatus III. affatim probavi."

The coin Eckhel alludes to he thus describes:

HADRIANVS . AVGVSTVS. Caput laureatum.

℞. COS . II . P.P. Cybele quadrigis leonum invecta.

The head he speaks of is the large-sized head to the right, without any drapery on the shoulders; and I have never yet seen it on the coins of Hadrian until the third consulate, although Eckhel quotes it as of cos . II.

A fine green coin. Weight 381¼ grains.

608.

IMP . CAES . DIVI . TRAIAN . AVG . F . TRAIAN . HADRIAN . OPT . AVG . GER. The laureate head of Hadrian to the right, bust in armour.

℞. DAC . PARTHICO . P . M . TR . P . COS . II . P.P. In the exergum S. C. Two persons robed standing opposite each other, the one on the right delivering a *mundus* or globe to him who stands on the left; this type is emblematic of the adoption of Hadrian by Trajan. In Occo, p. 223, there is a denarius quoted with nearly the same legends as the present coin, struck in the first consulate of Hadrian, and on which the word ADOPTIO appears, the type being described thus: " duæ figuræ togatæ jungentes dextras; " and in p. 224 he quotes a brass coin having similar legends to the present, with the addition of CONCORDIA, with the type, " duæ figuræ dextris tenentes globum."

The present type is the first noticed by Admiral Smyth in the series of Hadrian's coins in his cabinet. It is a fine dark green coin. Weight 359 grains.

609.

IMP . CAES . TRAIANVS . HADRIANVS . AVG. The laureate head of the emperor to the right.

℞. PONT . MAX . TR . POT . COS . II. In the exergum ADVENTVS . AVG and S. C.

underneath. Roma seated to the right on a cuirass, behind which is a shield; her left hand holds a spear upright; her right hand extended joins the emperor's right hand, who is before her in his robes.

This type records the arrival of Hadrian in Rome, on his accession to the sovereignty; from its consulate, it appears to have been struck soon after his arrival, which would place the mintage early in the year 118.

A very fine dark green coin. Weight 400¼ grains.

610.

IMP . CAESAR . TRAIANVS . HADRIANVS . AVG. The laureate head of the emperor to the right.

℞. PONT . MAX . TR . POT . COS . II. In the exergum FORT . RED . and S. C. underneath. A female with her head veiled, seated to the left, her left foot resting on a stool; in her right hand she holds the tiller of a rudder; her left arm bears a cornucopiæ filled with fruits.

This type refers to the return of Hadrian to Rome from Syria, and may, with propriety, be taken in conjunction with the preceding coin ADVENTVS.

A fine dark green coin.

611.

IMP . CAES . DIVI . TRA . PARTH . F . DIVI . NER . NEP . TRAIANO . HADRIANO . AVG. The laureate head of the emperor to the right, bust in armour.

℞. PONT . MAX . TR . POT . COS . II. In the exergum S. C. Three military standards. The centre one bears an eagle, type of the legionary forces. That on the right has the *manipulus*, and that on the left bears a wreath, both of them applying to cohorts.

The type records the fidelity of the army to the new emperor. The full legend on the obverse shows this coin to have been struck in the first years of the emperor's reign.

A very fine light green coin in Second Brass. Weight 184¼ grains.

612.

IMP . CAES . DIVI . TRA . PARTH . F . DIVI . NER . NEP . TRAIANO . HADRIANO . AVG. The laureate head of the emperor to the right.

℞. IMP . CAES . DIVI . TRA . PARTH . F . DIVI . NER . NEP . TRAIANO . HADRIANO . AVG. The laureate head of the emperor to the right.

Both these heads are in the same style, and it is very evident they are not the produce of accident in mis-placing the dies, but that the coin was struck from dies engraved for the occasion. There are two or three sorts of these bicipitous coins of Hadrian, and there is also one of Trajan; but I do not remember ever to have seen similar coins of other emperors, and all I have seen have, like this, been in Second Brass.

A very good brown coin from the cabinet of Sir George Musgrave.

613.

IMP . CAESAR . TRAIANVS . HADRIANVS . AVG. The laureate head of the emperor to the right.

℞. PONT . MAX . TR . POT . COS . II. In the field S. C. and in the exergum ANNONA . AVG. A female standing in profile to the right, a cornucopiæ by her left arm; at her left foot on the ground is a corn-modius; in the background, on the left, is part of a galley, intimating that the supply of corn had come by sea.

A very good brown coin.

614.

IMP . CAESAR . TRAIANVS . HADRIANVS . AVG. The laureate head of the emperor to the right, with full bust.

℞. PONT . MAX . TR . POT . COS . II. In the field S. C. and in the exergum LIBERALITAS . AVG. The emperor or his deputy seated to the left on a curule chair, placed on a high square *suggestum*, his right hand extended. In front of him is another person seated on a stool placed on a square base, but a little lower down; he is in the act of putting something into the lap of a citizen who stands before him with his robe extended to receive the donation. At the right hand of the second sedent figure a female is standing with her right hand raised holding a tablet.

This type records the first of the liberalities or donations made by Hadrian to the citizens of Rome, and being the first it was made on his accession. Eckhel, *in Hadriano*, vol. vi. 476, cites a coin in the Vienna Cabinet representing a liberality bestowed by the emperor Hadrian by proxy before he arrived at Rome, and bearing the date of cos. only, thus denoting that it was made in the first consulate; but the liberalities of Hadrian are all numbered, and, the present having LIBERALITAS . AVG. only, we may fairly conclude it is the type of the first donation. Eckhel accounts for the distribution of two liberalities being so quickly made, by quoting Spartianus, cap. vii.—" Hadrianus ad refellendum tristissimam de se opinionem quod occidi passus esset uno tempore quatuor consulares Romam venit, et, ad comprimendam de se famam, congiarium duplex præsens populo dedit, ternis jam per singulos aureis se absente divisis."

This is a remarkably fine light green coin, from the Devonshire Cabinet; rarely met with in so good a condition. Weight 393¼ grains.

615.

IMP . CAESAR . TRAIANUS . HADRIANUS . AVG. The laureate head of the emperor to the right, with full bust.

℞. PONT . MAX . TR . POT . COS . II. In the exergum LIBERALITAS . AVG . II. with S. C. underneath. The emperor or his deputy, with other persons seated and standing in the manner represented on the preceding coin.

From this coin being struck in the same consulate as the preceding *liberalitas*, it may be considered to be the liberality mentioned by Spartianus under the words "congiarium duplex," as quoted above, thus making two liberalities in one year, which Spartianus says were bestowed that the attention of the citizens might be withdrawn from the circumstance of four men of consular dignity having been put to death by Hadrian.

A good brown coin. Weight 366¼ grains.

616.

IMP . CAESAR . TRAIANUS . HADRIANVS . AVG. The laureate head of the emperor to the right.

℞. PONT . MAX . TR . POT . COS . DES . III. In the field S. C., and in the exergum ANNONA . AVG. A female standing to the left, a corn-modius at her right side, with ears of corn rising out of it; ears of corn are also in her hand; on her left arm is a full cornucopiæ; behind her, in the background to the left, is the stern of a galley, intimating it was an importation of corn from a province beyond sea.

A remarkably fine greenish-black coin. Weight 411¼ grains.

617.

IMP . CAESAR . TRAIANUS . HADRIANUS . AVG . P . M . TR . P . COS . III. The laureate head of the emperor to the right.

℞. RELIQUA . VETERA . HS . NOVIES . MILL . ABOLITA. In the field S. C. A lictor bearing his axe and fasces on his left arm standing to the left; in his right hand he holds a torch, with which he is setting fire to a bundle of papers piled up before him.

This coin and the two that follow record the munificent act of Hadrian soon after his arrival in Rome, in ordering all the bonds and registers of public debts which had been accumulating for many years, and were owing to the treasury by a great number of the patricians and citizens of Rome, and the provinces and *municipia*, amounting to between seven and eight millions of pounds sterling, to be burned, which was done accordingly in the Forum Trajani.

A good brown coin. Weight 377¼ grains.

618.

IMP . CAESAR . TRAIANVS . HADRIANVS . AVG . P . M . TR . P . COS . III. The laureate head of the emperor to the right.

℞. RELIQVA . VETERA . HS . NOVIES . MILL . ABOLITA. In the exergum S. C. A lictor with his axe and fasces on his left arm standing to the left, holding a torch in his right hand and setting fire to a pile of papers on the ground; in front of him are two citizens with hands raised in applause.

A good brown coin also. Weight 368½ grains.

619.

IMP . CAESAR . TRAIANVS . HADRIANVS . AVG . P . M . TR . P . COS . III. The laureate head of the emperor to the right.

℞. RELIQVA . VETERA . HS . NOVIES . MILL . ABOLITA. In the exergum S. C. A lictor with his axe and fasces on his left arm standing to the left, and with a torch in his right hand; he is setting fire to a pile of papers on the ground before him; in front are three citizens, who raise their hands in applause.

We have just stated the cause for these types being struck. It seems, although this munificent act of Hadrian took place on his first arrival in Rome, there is no doubt, from the type being repeated in the third consulate, the Senate considered it a matter most worthy to be kept in remembrance on the coinage. Spartianus, *in Hadriano*, c. vii. says—"Ad colligendum autem gratiam nihil prætermittens, infinitam pecuniam quæ fisco debebatur privatis debitoribus in urbe atque Italia in provinciis vero etiam ex reliquis ingentes summas remisit, syngraphis in foro Divi Trajani quo magis securitas omnibus roboraretur incensis;" and Dio also, lib. lxix. s. 8, says, "Ut Romam venit quidquid aut fisco aut publico Romanorum ærario debebatur remisit, sexdecem annorum definiens tempus ex quo et usque ad quod tempus beneficium istud observandum esset."

Eckhel, vol. vi. p. 478, calculates the value of these debts at about sixty millions of Austrian florins, or thirty millions of Roman scudi—"scutorum Romanorum."

A very good brown coin from the Devonshire Cabinet. Weight 360¼ grains.

620.

IMP . CAESAR . TRAIANVS . HADRIANVS . AVG . P . M . TR . P . COS . III. The laureate head of the emperor to the right.

℞. LIBERTAS . PUBLICA. In the exergum S. C. A female seated to the left on a throne; her right hand holds an olive-branch, the left bears a *hasta pura*, her left foot resting on a stool.

This type was probably occasioned by the satisfaction the Senate and people of Rome felt on finding themselves enjoying a state of public peace and liberty brought about by the emperors Nerva and Trajan, and which it was evidently the intention of Hadrian to keep undisturbed.

A fine brown coin. Weight $382\frac{1}{4}$ grains.

621.

IMP . CAESAR . TRAIANVS . HADRIANVS . AVG. The laureate head of the emperor, with full bust.

℞. PONT . MAX . TR . POT . COS . III. In the field S. C.; and in the exergum LIBERTAS . RESTITVTA. The emperor seated to the left on a curule chair placed on a square base, his right hand extended towards a female who stands before him as speaking to him, and presenting an infant with her left hand; the child's hands are stretched out towards the emperor; by her right hand the female leads another child who is at her right side.

A fine greenish brown coin. Weight $407\frac{1}{2}$ grains.

622.

IMP . CAESAR . TRAIANVS . HADRIANVS . AVG. The laureate head of the emperor to the right.

℞. PONT . MAX . TR . POT . COS . III. In the field S. C. In the exergum LIBERTAS . RESTITVTA. The emperor and the female and children, as on the other coin, save that the female has placed her left foot on a high stool to enable her to lean nearer towards the emperor.

On the coins of Trajan, *ante*, we have the type ALIMENTVM . ITALIAE on three coins recording the bounty given and provided by the late emperor Trajan for the maintenance of the children of poor citizens throughout Italy and the provinces, the third coin we have so described being in its representation very like the two present coins.

The emperor Hadrian carried his benevolence in these matters far beyond what had been done by the emperor Trajan; hence arose the significant type of the present coins, although the legends on the reverses do not impute any such benevolences as the words on the coins of Trajan imply.

A fine coin in aurichalcum. Weight 438¾ grains.

623.

IMP . CAES . TRAIANVS . HADRIANVS AVG . The laureate head of the emperor to the right, bust in armour, with his military cloak on the shoulders.

℞. P . M . TR . P . COS. III. In the field S. C. Spes gradient to the left in her usual manner.

A fine earthy green coin. Weight 334¼ grains.

624.

IMP . CAESAR . TRAIANVS . HADRIANVS . AVG. The laureate head of the emperor to the right, bust in armour, with his military cloak fastened on the shoulder.

℞. P . M . TR . P . COS . III. In the field S. C. Minerva standing to the left with her spear in the left hand, her shield at her left side; at her right side a fire is burning on a brazier altar supported on a single stem resting on three extended feet; she is in the act of strewing something on the fire.

A rich coffee-coloured brown coin, remarkably fine, from the Thomas Cabinet. Weight 392¾ grains.

625.

HADRIANVS . AVGVSTVS . P . P. The laureate head of the emperor to the right.

℞. COS . III . in the exergum, and S. C. in the field. The emperor standing to the left, his right hand extended towards the empress Sabina, who stands on the right, her right hand extended towards the emperor; between them Roma is standing armed, with her spear in her left hand, while with her right hand she is joining the hands of the emperor and empress.

Argelati, *in Hadriano*, quotes an aureus of the first year of Hadrian, with the reverse CONIVGIVM . AVG .; and he describes it "Imp. jungit dextram Imperatrici, inter medio sacrificio cupidines tres supervolant," a coin which refers to the marriage of Hadrian with Sabina, the grandniece of the emperor Trajan. This took place in the year of Rome 853, A.D. 100, at the commencement of the reign of Trajan. The present coin refers to the same subject, and by the presence of Roma it is clear the marriage was agreeable to the citizens.

The aureus in Argelati was struck Y.R. 870, A.D. 117. Occo says it was in

A.D. 118, and that the legend on the obverse, combining all the titles of Trajan with Hadrian, shows it was struck at the commencement of the reign of Hadrian; whereas the legend on the present coin shows it was struck several years after, for the legend HADRIANVS. AVGVSTVS first began to be used about the year 872, and was continued for the remainder of his reign.

The type is appropriately of the early part of the reign; I have, therefore, introduced it after Spes and Minerva, as the hope of the people that wisdom would guide the emperor during his reign; but the legend on the obverse denotes it as having been struck many years after the event had taken place. Sabina is supposed to have been poisoned A.D. 137.

A good black coin from the Campana Cabinet. Weight 484½ grains.

626.

IMP . CAESAR . TRAIANVS . HADRIANVS . AVG . P . M . TR . P . COS . III. The laureate head of the emperor to the right.

℞. AETERNITAS . AVGVSTI. In the field S. C. A female standing to the left, having in each hand a bust; that in the right hand has a radiate crown, and the bust in the left hand has a crescent.

These types of the sun and moon are representations of the emperor and empress, and are intended to signify or express the wishes of the people, that as the sun and moon were eternal, so they hoped for a long reign of the emperor, and that he might have posterity to succeed him to all eternity.

We have noticed a similar coin of Domitian, *ante*, and it occurs again in Antoninus Pius, *post*. We have also noticed *in Augusto* the signification of the radiate crown and crescent, as applicable to Augusta and Livia.

A Second Brass dark brown coin. Weight 209½ grains.

627.

IMP . CAESAR . TRAIANVS . HADRIANVS . AVG . P . M . TR . P . COS . III. The laureate head of the emperor to the right.

℞. CONCORDIA EXERCITVVM. In the exergum S. C. A female standing full front, her head turned to the left, supporting a military standard in each hand; that to the right has an eagle, the one in her left hand has a wreath.

The type of this coin is to signify the fidelity to, and satisfaction of, the armies with the government of Hadrian, although he was not a man of military enterprize and adventure.

A fine black coin. Weight 395¼ grains.

628.

IMP . CAESAR . TRAIANVS . HADRIANVS . AVG.   The laureate head of the emperor to the right.

℞. PONT . MAX . TR . POT . COS . III.   In the exergum S. C.   Roma armed seated on arms to the left; her right hand extended holds a Victoriola, in her left hand she has her spear, her right foot supported by a helmet lying on the ground.

A dark green coin in very fine condition.   By Mr. Cureton; from the Trattle and Neve Cabinets.   Weight 370½ grains.

629.

IMP . CAESAR . TRAIANVS . HADRIANVS . AVG.   The laureate head of the emperor to the right.

℞. PONT . MAX . TR . POT . COS . III.   In the exergum SECVR . AVG; in the field S. C.   A female seated on a throne to the left; her right hand holds a *hasta pura*, her left arm rests on the back of the throne supporting her head with her hand, her left foot resting on a stool.

A very fine dark green coin.   Weight 464⅜ grains.

630.

IMP CAESAR . TRAIANVS . HADRIANVS . AVG . P . M . TR . P . COS . III.   The laureate head of the emperor to the right.

℞. LIBERALITAS . AVG . III.   In the exergum S. C.   The emperor or his deputy wearing a cap, seated to the left on a curule chair placed on a low *suggestum*; behind his left shoulder a person is standing as if prompting him; a female stands at his right hand holding up a tablet; in front of the *suggestum* a citizen is standing holding up his robe to receive a donation.

Argelati, *in Hadriano*, places this type under the date A.D. 118.   Occo places it in A.D. 119.

A very fine dark green coin.   Weight 385 grains.

631.

IMP . CAESAR . TRAIAN . HADRIANVS . AVG . P . M . TR . P . COS . III.   The laureate head of Hadrian to the right; bust in armour, with military cloak.

℞. PIETAS . AVGVSTI.   In the field S. C.   A female veiled and robed standing to the right, her head rather thrown back, both her hands raised in supplication; at her feet is an altar, on which a fire is burning.

A very fine brown coin with green tinge.   Weight 428¼ grains.

632.

HADRIANVS . AVG . COS . III . P . P.   The laureate head of the emperor to the right, shoulders draped.

℞. PIETAS . AVG.   In the field S. C.   A female standing full front, both her hands extended as if in prayer; at her right side is a decorated altar, on which a fire is burning; at her left side is a stork—a bird that with the ancients was an emblem of piety.

A very fine green coin from the Ramsay Cabinet.   Weight 400 grains.

633.

IMP . CAESAR . TRAIANVS . HADRIANVS . AVG . P . M . TR . P . COS . III.   The laureate head of the emperor to the right.

℞. PROVIDENTIA . DEORVM.   In the field S. C.   The emperor gradient to the left, his right hand raised towards a sceptre held in the talons of an eagle, which appears before him with expanded wings, as if floating down to him with the sceptre from the sky.

By some persons the eagle may be supposed to be bearing a *fulmen*, as the bird of Jove; but the legend would rather make me consider that by the Divine Providence, "Providentia Deorum," the sceptre of power had been conferred on Hadrian, that through him the gods might be disposed to bestow blessings on the Romans.

A black coin; middling good.   Weight $358\frac{1}{4}$ grains.

634.

IMP . CAESAR . TRAIANVS . HADRIANVS . AVG.   The laureate head of the emperor to the right.

℞. PONT . MAX . TR . POT . COS . III.   In the field S. C.   A female standing full front, looking to the left, holding a caduceus in her right hand, on her left arm she bears a cornucopiæ filled with fruits.

A fine pale yellow green coin.

635.

IMP . CAESAR . TRAIANVS . HADRIANVS . AVG . P . M . TR . P . COS . III.   The laureate head of Hadrian to the right.

℞. LOCVPLETATORI . ORBIS . TERRARVM.   In the exergum S. C.   The emperor seated to the left on a curule chair placed on a *suggestum*.   By his right side a female is standing, who is pouring the contents of a cornucopiæ into the lap of two citizens, who stand in front holding up their robes to receive the donation.

Hadrian is the only emperor on whom the Senate conferred this complimentary title, expressive of his liberality and munificence to the citizens of Rome as well as to the Provinces—the words ORBIS . TERRARVM having a wide-spread signification, but in reality meaning the Roman World. By this conduct Hadrian justified the assumption of the type and legend of the preceding coin, PROVIDENTIA DEORVM, intimating that he was deputed by Divine Providence to be a blessing to mankind.

The conquests of Sylla, Lucullus, and Pompeius, and latterly of Trajanus, opened a new world to the Romans, and extended their dominion beyond the rivers Tigris and Euphrates.

Horace says—

Possis nihil urbe Româ visere majus.

Ovid says—

Jupiter arce suâ totum cum spectat in orbem,
Nil nisi Romanum quod tueatur habet.

These were the praises bestowed in the time of Augustus, but Hadrian was 100 years later. The legend on the coin is highly adulatory; at the same time, in conjunction with the lines of Horace and Ovid (who, be it remembered, were courtiers as well as poets), it exhibits the inflated style of boasting which the Romans were in the habit of assuming within their own city, to be afterwards circulated to the world and posterity. But with how much greater truth can these compliments be bestowed on Britain of the present day—the despised Britannia, the *sævos Britannos* of the boastful Roman.

Vaillant describes this coin, "inter præstantissimos et rarissimos recensetur."

A sort of pale green mottled red Campana coin. Weight 396 grains.

636.

IMP . CAESAR . TRAIANVS . HADRIANVS . AUG. The laureate head of the emperor to the right, bust in armour.

℞. P . M . TR . P . COS . III. In the field S. C. Ceres standing full front looking to the left, holding wheat-ears in her right hand; in her left hand she bears a long torch, the end of it resting on the ground, and a fire burning on the top.

A dark brown coin; very fine. Weight 402½ grains.

637.

IMP . CAESAR . TRAIANVS . HADRIANVS . AVG. The laureate head of the emperor to the right.

℞. PONT . MAX . TR . POT . COS . III. In the field S. C. A female standing full front looking to the left; in her right hand she holds a caduceus, on the left arm she supports a cornucopiæ filled with fruits.

A very fine green coin. Weight 377½ grains.

638.

IMP . CAESAR . TRAIANVS . HADRIANVS . AVG . P . M . TR . P . COS . III. The laureate head of the emperor to the right.

℞. ANNONA . AVGVSTI. In the exergum S. C. A female seated on a throne to the right, supporting with both hands a full cornucopiæ; at her feet is a cornmodius, with ears of corn from the top, her right foot resting on a small footstool.

A dark green coin. Weight 405⅜ grains.

639.

IMP . CAESAR . TRAIAN . HADRIANUS . AVG. The laureate head of the emperor to the right, bust in armour, with cloak.

℞. P . M . TR . P . COS. III. In the exergum EXPED . AVG. and in the field S. C. The emperor, bareheaded and on horseback, prancing to the left; his right hand raised, his left hand holding a spear upright, his cloak flying from his shoulders behind.

This coin appears to have been struck on the declaration of war with the Roxolani and Sarmatii, whom Hadrian defeated, and returned to Rome after he had made a peace with those countries. This is the only military campaign made by Hadrian during the whole of his reign; his visit to Britain was just in time to prevent the necessity of a campaign. Argelati places this event in A.D. 120, the fourth year of the reign of Hadrian.

A good brown coin. Weight 372½ grains.

640.

IMP . CAESAR . TRAIANVS . HADRIANVS . AVG . P . M . TR . P . COS . III. The laureate head of the emperor to the right.

℞. VICTORIA AVGVSTI. No S. C. A Victory volant to the right, bearing in her hands a trophy carried transversely in an attitude of offence.

A light green coin, in very good condition. Weight 411₈ grains.

641.

IMP . CAESAR . TRAIAN . HADRIANVS . AVG. The laureate head of the emperor to the right, bust in armour.

℞. P . M . TR . P . COS . III. V . RT.—AVG. across the field on either side of Roma, with S C under the words so separated. Roma armed standing to the right, holding her spear in her right hand, a *parazonium* in her left hand; her left foot rests on a helmet placed on the ground.

A very good brown coin. Weight 380½ grains.

642.

IMP . CAESAR . TRAIAN . HADRIANVS . AVG. The laureate head of Hadrian to the right, bust in armour.

℞. P . M . TR . P . COS . III. Across the field VIRT.—AVG. with S. C. under the words. Roma as on the preceding coin, only standing to the left; her spear in her left hand, in her right a *parazonium*; her right foot rests on a helmet lying on the ground.

This coin and the two which precede refer to the victories gained over the Roxolani and Sarmatii.

It is a fine dark green coin. Weight 422⅛ grains.

643.

IMP . CAESAR . TRAIANVS . HADRIANVS . AVG . P . M . TR . P . COS . III. The laureate head of the emperor to the right.

℞. SALVS . PVBLICA. In the field S. C. A female standing to the left, holding in her left hand a rudder against her left shoulder, the blade of it being above the shoulder; her right hand extended holds a globe, and her right foot rests on a globe. This is a very uncommon type of Salus.

A good green Second Brass coin. Weight 197¼ grains.

644.

IMP . CAESAR . TRAIANVS . HADRIANVS . AVG . P . M . TR . P . COS . III. The laureate head of Hadrian to the right, shoulders draped.

℞. MONETA . AVGVSTI. In the field S. C. A female standing full front, looking to the left; in her right hand she has a pair of scales, on her left arm she bears a full cornucopiæ.

This is a very rare type. I never saw it at a sale until it appeared amongst General Ramsay's coins, from whence I obtained it.

A very fine pale green coin.

645.

IMP . CAES . HADRIANVS . AVG . COS . III. The laureate head of the emperor to the right, bust in armour, with military cloak.

℞. ANN . DCCCLXXIIII . NAT . VRB . P . CIR . CON. A male figure unclothed to the waist, having a cap on his head, is reclining at full length to the left; the face bearded and turned to the right towards three obelisks standing on a base, and which are embraced by the left arm of the figure; the right hand supports a chariot-wheel on his lap.

This is an aureus, in excellent preservation, from the Pembroke Collection. Weight 110¾ grains.

It is a most interesting type and legend, and differs from all others of the same or any other metal, inasmuch as numismatic writers invariably describe the recumbent figure as being a female. This error I apprehend is occasioned by the present device on the reverse being taken from that of the VIA . TRAIANA, *ante* No. 560. On that coin there can be no doubt of it being a female figure, and thus has arisen the opinion of it being a female on the present device. But the figure on the present coin is evidently a male figure; the cap on the head, the beard, and the anatomical delineation of the bust and abdomen are large and muscular, resembling the bust of the *Jupiter Victor* on the coins of Domitian, and the recumbent figure of *Tiberis* on the coins of Antoninus Pius; all which appearances are inconsistent with the idea and figure of a female.

Admiral Smyth in his Cabinet, No. 152, describing the Large Brass coin of this type, places it as the first of the coins of the third consulate; but there is a great difficulty in saying in which of the early years of the third consulate it was struck. It is evidently in one of the early years on account of the date of the legend, which according to some calculations would be in A.D. 121, and according to others in A D. 123. Again, it is by the legend on the obverse evidently an early struck coin of the third consulate, for we shall see in subsequent coins that, in about three years after the commencement of the third consulate, or even earlier, the obverse legend was much shortened by having it only HADRIANVS . AVGVSTVS.

The difficulty the coin presents by its peculiar device is not the date only, but also the particular occasion for which it was struck.

It is described by Oiselius in his work, p. 483, ed. 1677, "ANN . DCCCLXXIIII . NAT . VRB . CIR . CON. Figura feminea fere nuda humi sedens, dextrâ rotam genu alteri impositam sustinens, et sinistro brachio complectens tres metas circi. Inscriptio indicat circum quendam ab Hadriano conditum, quamvis nemo veterum meminerit, nec ejus rei ulla mentio uspiam præterquam in hoc nummo fiat, tempusque unà adsignet istud nempe factum anno octingentissimo septuagesimo quarto *natae vrbis;* per rotam autem et metam cursus certamen bigis aut quadrigis circum metas in circo fieri soliti denotatur."

When the learned Oiselius wrote this description he must have had before him a coin with an imperfect legend, or he would not have omitted the P. with the CIR . CON. Argelati, *in Hadriano,* is of a similar opinion that the coin commemorates the building of a circus by the emperor, of which no vestige is now remaining. The coin he quotes has the P. in the legend. Occo also quotes an aureus with the legend similar to the present, having the P. and the figure with the wheel and the three obelisks. He likewise cites an aureus of the same year with the reverse defined simply by the words " cum circo ; " thus stating that an engraving of a circus was to be found on an aureus of Hadrian, but there is no legend of the reverse given by Occo, if it had one.

Vaillant reads the inscription as " Anno 874 natali urbis populo circenses concessit." Hardouin considers it should be read " Anno 874 natali urbis primum circenses constitutæ." Others again dispute whether the P. means " populus," " plebeii, " publici," or " primus."

It is something singular that on the coins mentioned in the Christina Cabinet, and the Florentine Cabinet, and in Oiselius, the P. is omitted.

After all the conjectures of numismatic writers respecting this device the more reasonable supposition appears to be that, on the birthday of Roma, in the year of the city 874, the emperor, to increase the festivities of the anniversary, or for some other cause now unknown, in addition to the games then usually celebrated, ordered the exhibition of the Circensian Games, and thus gave, as Vaillant writes, " populo circenses concessit," a greater entertainment to the people on the occasion.

This I consider to be the more proper and reasonable solution of all the difficulty, for had Hadrian erected a circus on the occasion to be a lasting record of the event, the aureus " cum circo " cited by Occo would have had a legend similar to the present legend, or of similar import, and accompanied by a representation of the circus so erected; and there is every reason to suppose we should have had, in addition to the aureus, a denarius, and also a representation of the building on some Large Brass coins, like as we have the Circus Maximus on the Large Brass coins of Trajan and the Coliseum of Titus; but there are no such coins known.

One thing however is clear, the three *metæ* or obelisks and the wheel of the chariot evidently refer to the chariot-races which formed part of the Circensian Games. Eckhel, in vol. vi. p. 501, describes a similar coin in gold in Mus. Cæs. reverse "mulier humi sedens d. rotam. s. tres obeliscos seu conos complexa;" but he does not give any solution of the question why this was struck.

Vaillant, describing an aureus of this type says, "Cùm nulla sit circi ab Hadriano conditi mentio apud Historiæ Scriptores, mulier per rotam cursus bigarum et quadrigarum certamen, per metas illud in circo peractum denotat." Adding, "Hic nummus aureus rarissimus est."

The conclusion I arrive at, therefore, is this—that the legend is fairly to be rendered thus:—

ANNO DCCCLXXIIII . NATALI . VRBIS . POPVLO . CIRCENSES . CONCESSIT. The date 874 also is equal to the year A.D. 121, as indisputably shown by calculation from Tacitus, who places the submission of Caractacus before Claudius to A . U . C . 803 or A.D. 50; then add the number of years passed between the time of Claudius to the early part of Hadrian, being 71, which, added either to the 803 or the 50, the two dates will be produced thus:—

$$
\begin{array}{cc}
\text{A . U . C . 803} & \text{A.D. 50} \\
71 & 71 \\
\hline
874 & \text{equal to A.D. 121}
\end{array}
$$

and it will be proved that the present coin was struck in 874, as its legend implies.

The foundation-day of Rome was accustomed to be celebrated on the 21st day of April, being the festival day of *Pales*, the goddess of sheepfolds and pastures; her festivals were called *Palilia*, when the country people, who were the earliest inhabitants of Rome, besought the goddess of shepherds to protect and increase their flocks, and to pardon their involuntary violation of consecrated spots; purifying themselves by passing through a fire of straw, like those which were kindled on May-day in the Middle Ages. (Niebuhr, i. 226.)

From this period, that is to say, the third consulate, the legend on the obverse of the coins of Hadrian is altered; the titles CAESAR and TRAIANVS cease, for which omission Hadrian has by some writers been accused of ingratitude in so soon forgetting the memory of Trajan, and the benefits he had received from his adopted father and patron. This change took place in the early part of the third consulate, or third year of his reign. Soon after then he began his travels, and the coins record the third consulate only, throughout the remainder of his reign.

For the purpose of rendering the following series of Hadrian's coins more interesting, and with an endeavour to fix the probable periods of his reign which the events recorded on them illustrate, I shall now introduce a short narrative of the succession of events by way of index or reference to the coins which follow.

Numismatists, for want of proper attention, generally class them all together, and place them in order alphabetically; thus their historic reference and chronology are confounded and lost. I shall therefore place them historically, according to the following short narrative of the journeys taken by Hadrian:—

Upon the death of the Emperor Trajan, Hadrian, being declared his successor, arrived at Rome from Antioch and Syria in the first year, and in the same year he remitted the debts due to the imperial treasury.

In the second year there was a war with the Roxolani and Sarmatii, who were defeated, as we have already noticed.

In the third year Hadrian began his travels, and visited Gaul and Germany; he thence returned to Gaul and crossed over to Britain; while in Britain he traversed all those parts subject to the Roman arms, and gave directions for building the wall across the northern part of the island, to repress the incursions of the Picts. He afterwards returned to Gaul, and proceeded towards the southern parts, and at Nismes, amongst other public works, he built the Amphitheatre, remains of which are still in existence.

From Gaul he went into Spain, and at Tarraco he rebuilt the Temple of Augustus. There also he narrowly escaped assassination by an insane man. He afterwards returned to Rome.

In the fourth and fifth years he proceeded to Athens, and returning he passed through Cilicia, Lycia, Pamphylia, Cappadocia, Moesia, Bithynia, Phrygia, giving directions for rebuilding temples and other edifices in different cities and places.

In the fifth year also he visited Achaia, and from thence he proceeded to Athens, where he was initiated into the Eleusinian mysteries.

In the sixth and seventh years he appears to have visited Egypt for a short time, and then returned to Rome.

In the eighth year he visited Nicomedia and Bithynia, where he rebuilt temples and other public buildings which had been recently destroyed by earthquakes, whence the coin was struck, RESTITVTORI . BITHYNIÆ. Also the coin with the temple KOINON.

In the ninth year Hadrian passed over into Africa, from whence he afterwards returned to Rome.

In the tenth year he remained in Rome, and built a temple to Roma, and one to Venus.

In the eleventh year Hadrian returned to Asia and visited Cappadocia; from thence he went to Syria, Palestine, and Arabia.

In the twelfth and thirteenth years he was travelling in Egypt.

In the fourteenth and fifteenth years he completed his visit to Egypt, and went into Syria.

In the sixteenth year he went to Thracia, Macedonia, and Athens. In this year also the Jews revolted, but were finally overthrown and ejected from Jerusalem, and completely dispersed.

In the seventeenth year he quitted Athens, and returned to Rome, where he continued.

In his twenty-second year, being ill, he retired to Baiæ, where he died A.D. 138.

The years of reign and the years of travel vary two to three years or so, occasioned by the chronologies as reckoned by different writers having a variation, a point we have already noticed. Excepting this, we believe the preceding notes of Hadrian's travels to be nearly correct, and they show that the coins of the provinces visited by him cannot be arranged in an alphabetical order to be historic. If so, Arabia, visited by him in his eleventh year, would precede Gaul and Britain, which were visited by Hadrian eight or nine years before.

As some guide, also, we have the coin just noticed with the age of the city upon it, which can thus be brought in conjunction with the reckonings of the years of the Christian æra.

I have compared the foregoing arrangement with that proposed by Eckhel, vol. vi. p. 480, and on fully considering it with the events occurring at each period, and the before-mentioned allowance of variations of two or three years, and which even Eckhel himself admits occur with some writers, I see no reason to be dissatisfied. By the arrangement I have made, to which I have been guided entirely by the coins themselves, the visits of the emperor to the different provinces of the empire, and the military reviews of the different legions and auxiliary troops quartered in the provinces, fall into their proper places; although it is not presumed that the dates are entirely perfect, the absence of any notice of the tribunician dates as they arose precluding all possibility of making a complete arrangement.

646.

HADRIANVS . AVGVSTVS. The laureate head of the emperor to the right.

℞. COS . III. In the exergum S. C. Roma armed, seated on a cuirass to the left, a shield behind her; her right hand extended holds a Victoriola presenting a wreath and bearing a palm-branch; on her left arm she supports a cornucopiæ filled with fruits; her right foot rests on a helmet lying on the ground.

The obverse of the coins now begins to bear a large head of Hadrian, with name and title only, like as the present; occasionally the consulate is added, as on the next coin.

The present is a fine black coin.

647.

HADRIANUS . AVG . COS . III . P . P. The laureate head of the emperor to the right, shoulders draped.

℞. ADVENTVI . AVG . ITALIAE. In the field S. C. The emperor standing to the right, his right hand raised in the attitude of addressing a female who stands before him to the left, having a cornucopiæ on her left arm; in her right hand she holds a patera, and is in the act of pouring on to a fire burning on an altar, standing between her and the emperor.

The types of these two coins seem to represent the emperor being in Rome, after his expedition against the Roxolani, and previous to his starting upon his travels to Gaul and other places.

A roughish green coin.

648.

HADRIANVS . AVGVSTVS. The laureate head of the emperor to the right.

℞. COS. III. In the exergum EXPED . AVG. S. C. in the field. The emperor, bare-headed and in military costume, on a prancing horse, to the left, his right hand raised as if addressing some persons.

Hadrian commenced his visits to the different provinces of the empire in about the third year of his reign. We therefore place an expedition coin to denote his starting off on a tour. When it is intended as a military departure to the army for a campaign, the legend is PROFECTIO . AVG. and the emperor is accompanied by armed soldiers (see the coin of Trajan, *ante*); not so when it is a tour of inspection. And, as Hadrian was not a warrior seeking conquests over adjoining nations, there is no coin of PROFECTIO representing him starting with his soldiers on a military expedition.

The present is a fine brown coin. Weight 373¾ grains.

649.

HADRIANVS . AVG . COS . III . P . P. The laureate head of the emperor to the right, shoulders draped.

℞. ADVENTVI . AVG . GALLIAE. In the exergum S. C.. The emperor robed standing to the right; opposite to him on the left a female is standing to personify Gallia; she is in the act of pouring from a patera on to fire burning on a decorated altar which stands between her and the emperor; a beast is lying on the ground at the back of the altar, as if intended for sacrifice; the emperor holds his robes with his left hand; his right hand is raised as addressing a speech to Gallia.

The arrival of Hadrian in Gaul is here recorded, upon which occasion much public rejoicing took place. It was usual with Hadrian to review the Roman troops in garrison in the provinces at the different cities he passed through on his tour of inspection. Many of these reviews are recorded on the coins, and present very interesting devices. We shall see them noticed on different occasions; but I have not seen a coin with a review of the troops, or any of them, which were stationed in Gaul, although there were several Roman garrisons in that country.

This is a beautifully coloured orange-red coin.

650.

HADRIANVS . AVG . COS . III . P . P. The laureate head of Hadrian to the right; shoulders draped.

℞. RESTITVTORI . GALLIAE. In the exergum S. C. The emperor robed standing to the right; with his right hand he is raising a female (representing Gallia) who is kneeling on the ground before him.

This is a remarkably fine black coin from the Ramsay Cabinet.

651.

HADRIANVS . AVG . COS . III . P . P. The laureate head of the emperor to the left; shoulders draped.

℞. RESTITVTORI . GALLIAE. In the exergum S. C. The emperor robed standing to the right; with his right hand he is raising a female (Gallia) who is kneeling on the ground before him.

These coins not only record the fact of Hadrian's visit to Gaul, but also the benefits he bestowed on the different cities and towns he visited, and the restoration of their fallen condition.

After passing a considerable time in Gaul, engaged in redressing complaints and grievances, and setting the various municipal institutions to rights, he departed for Germany.

A very good brown coin from the Devonshire Cabinet. Weight $433\frac{1}{4}$ grains.

652.

HADRIANVS . AVG . . . . . The laureate head of the emperor to the right; shoulders draped.

℞. EXERC. in the upper verge, GERMANICVS. in the exergum, S. C. underneath. The emperor on his horse to the right, his right hand raised, addressing three soldiers who stand before him; the first bears an eagle, the other two have standards.

By these ensigns it was intended to represent the Roman legions and other troops which were reviewed by the emperor when he visited a province. In the present instance it is a representation of the troops in Germany which Hadrian reviewed during the time he was there.

After a tour in Germany, and visiting different places, he returned to Gaul, and passing over the sea went to Britain.

A black coin, the reverse being very good. Vaillant calls it "rarissimus."

653.

HADRIANVS . AVG . COS . III . P . P. The laureate head of the emperor to the right; shoulders draped.

℞. EXERCITVS at the right side; RAETICVS in the exergum, with S. C. underneath. The emperor on his horse standing to the right, addressing three soldiers who stand before him with standards of various sorts.

Rætia, the modern Tyrol and Grisons, was a Roman province. The inhabitants rendered themselves formidable to the Romans by their frequent incursions into the Roman territories. They were at last vanquished and their country reduced to the condition of a Roman province by Drusus.

A good brown coin, scraped a little. Said by Vaillant to be "rarissimus."

654.

HADRIANVS . AVG . COS . III. The laureate head of the emperor to the right; shoulders draped.

℞. . . . . BAETIC . . . in the exergum. The emperor standing on a low dais to the right, an attendant behind; in front of him, on the ground at his left side, is a lictor. Three soldiers are standing before the emperor, each bearing a standard.

These two coins record the review of the troops stationed in Rætia by Hadrian in the early part of his reign, when, passing through Germany and Gaul, he visited the northern provinces of the empire, including Rætia, in his tour.

A brown coin, but middling for condition.

655.

HADRIANVS . AVGVSTVS. The unlaureate head of the emperor to the left; shoulders draped.

℞. FELICITATI . AVG. in the upper verge, and COS. III. P . P. in the exergum; S. C. on either side the field. A large galley rowed to the left, having a small sail on a sort of bowsprit at the head. In the stern two standards erect, one bearing an eagle, showing that some person of rank is on board.

A very good black coin from the cabinet of Sir Robert Abdy. Weight $437\frac{1}{4}$ grains.

656.

HADRIANVS . AVGVSTVS. The laureate head of the emperor to the right.

℞. COS . III. In the field S. C. Neptune standing to the left, his right foot resting on the prow of a galley with the rostrum outward. Some drapery is thrown in easy carelessness across the right thigh. In his right hand he holds an acrostolion, or the ornament from the stern of a galley. In his left hand he has a trident, the prongs upward. On his head he wears a round-shaped cap, with a spike at the top.

This device appears to have been taken from the Greek tetradrachm of Demetrius I. surnamed Poliorcetes, who lived and reigned B.C. 294 to 287.

A very good dark-green coin.

657.

HADRIANVS . AVG . COS . III . P . P. The laureate head of the emperor to the right; shoulders draped.

℞. ADVENTVI . AVG . [BRI]TAN[NI]AE. In the exergum S. C. The emperor robed, standing to the right; his right hand raised, addressing a female who stands opposite to him, wearing a short dress, with apparently a helmet on her head, and holding a spear in her left hand, thus denoting the character of the Britons. In her right hand she has a patera, from which she is pouring on to a fire burning on an altar standing on the ground between her and the emperor. At the foot of the altar an animal is lying as if for sacrifice.

This type records the arrival of Hadrian in Britain, which occurred in A.D. 120 or 121, and according to some other writers in A.D. 122 or 123. It would seem by the narrative of Camden, in his Britannia, that Hadrian came to Britain just in time to prevent the Britons from throwing off the Roman yoke. Speed, in his Chronicle (chap. xvii.), describes Hadrian as coming to Britain accompanied by three legions (a force of about 13,000 men, infantry and cavalry), to enable him more effectually to put down the insurrection which had arisen, and which he ultimately suppressed. Speed places the arrival of Hadrian in Britain in A.D. 124.

Whilst he was in Britain the emperor made many very useful regulations for the government of the province, and visited several parts of the island. He also caused a wall to be built, extending from the river Eden in Cumberland to the Tyne in Northumberland, for the purpose of repressing the incursions of the northern tribes of Picts and Caledonians. This wall was afterwards repaired and increased in strength by Antoninus Pius, and afterwards by Septimius Severus. It is very commonly called the Roman Wall, Hadrian's Wall, and the like, at the present day. The most recent account of it, containing all the valuable materials of his predecessors, is contained in the work of the Rev. J. C. Bruce, LL.D. of Newcastle-upon-Tyne.

The present coin is brown, but in middling condition. It is an extremely rare device. Weight 361¼ grains.

Vaillant says this type "primi moduli eximiæ raritatis est."

658.

The legend obliterated. The laureate head of the emperor to the right.

℞. *Legend obliterated.* Britannia seated two-thirds front to the left; her left elbow rests on the upper edge of a large oval shield at her left side; the lower edge of it is on the ground. In her left hand she holds a spear transversely, her right elbow resting on her right knee. Her right foot is placed on a mound of earth, or piece of rock-work.

We have a type representing Britannia precisely in this attitude in Hadrian's Second Brass coins. The Large Brass Britannia coins of Hadrian are not known, the present is the only one I ever saw. They are met with frequently in Second Brass, and generally in very middling condition.

Vaillant describes a First Brass coin of Hadrian Britannia in these terms: "*Britannia.* Figura muliebris sedens—pede dextro rupibus imposito, sinistrâ caput sustentans, dextrâ hastam gerit, innixa cubito ingenti clypeo;" adding, "Hic nummus primæ magnitudinis rarissimus, secundæ inter rariores computatur." This description is also fully borne out by the next coin.

The present coin is in very poor condition, it being much rubbed by ancient wear; but sufficient of the type, &c. is remaining to have enabled Mr. Fairholt to make the drawing of Britannia from it. It is a Large Brass coin from the Thomas Cabinet, and if perfect would be remarkably rare, and of very great price. Weight 322⅜ grains.

659.

.... RAIANVS.HADRIA .... VG. The laureate head of the emperor to the right.

℞. PONT . MAX . TR . POT . COS . III. In the exergum BRITANNIA. In the field S. C. A female seated two-thirds front to the left, her right foot resting on a mound of earth, or piece of rock-work; her right elbow resting on her right knee, her head leaning upon her right hand; at her left side is a large oval shield with a spike in the middle; her left elbow rests on the upper verge of the shield, and she holds a long spear in her left hand transversely, the point resting on the ground near her left foot.

The present coin was found in digging in a garden in Whitechapel Mount. It was given me by the late Mr. Spencer (frequent aeronaut with Mr. Green), who had it from the person who found it. The metal is red copper, and the coin is much corroded on the obverse; the reverse is good.

A Second Brass coin, and answering on the reverse to the description we have given from Vaillant of a Britannia in Large Brass. Weight 135½ grains.

660.

IMP.CAESAR.TRAIANVS.HADRI...... The laureate head of Hadrian to the right.

℞. PONT . MAX .... In the exergum BRITANNIA. In the field S. C. A female seated in the manner represented on the preceding coins, but leaning more forward, and her shield more slanting.

This coin, also a Second Brass, was obtained by young Edwards * from a London excavation. It is in good condition considering. Weight 121⅜ grains.

661.

IMP . CAESAR . TRAIANVS . HADRIANVS . AVG. The laureate head of the emperor to the right.

℞. .... OT . COS . III. In the exergum BRITANNIA. In the field S. C. A female with spear and shield seated, as represented on the preceding coins.

* August, 1859. This month young Edwards died at his house in Aldersgate Street, London. He was a kind, intelligent, painstaking young man, and a good antiquary. I had known him many years.

Hadrian remained in Britain nearly a year, after which he passed over to Gaul, and from thence he went to Spain before he returned to Rome.

Mr. Noel Humphreys in his work on Roman Coins, p. 196, contradicting what is said by Vaillant in his Numismata Selectiora, says, "The so-called Britannia on Roman coins beneath the inscription BRITANNIA is not Britannia, but the goddess Roma seated on a rock, symbolising the subjugated province. A similar figure appears on coins recording other conquests."

It is evident from this remark that Mr. Humphreys knows very little of Roman coins. He cannot be a collector, nor has he taken the trouble to inquire and examine any good cabinets, public or private, wherein are found any of the coins of emperors on which provinces of Rome or subjugated countries are symbolised. I should like to know what coins "recording other conquests" have such a figure? Besides, what business has Roma to be sitting on a rock? Rome is not an island, or built on an island. Had he compared *Roma*, as represented on the coins of Nero *only*, with the representations of provinces on any of the coins of the emperors, he would never have written the above comment.

The coins on which Roma is represented, whether of Nero or any other emperor, almost invariably have the word ROMA on the reverse, either in the exergum or on the side of the field, thus indicating who and what is intended by the figure. The attributes of Roma are always of a warlike and aggressive character; she always wears her helmet, and has her sword, spear, and shield; she is almost always seated on a cuirass with arms of various sorts around her to signify the spoils of the vanquished; in her right hand generally a Victoriola, or small image of Victory, and her right foot placed on a helmet or an orb, signifying by the latter her subjugation of the world—so great was the vanity of the Romans.

But a conquered province is almost invariably represented bearing a Roman standard; sometimes it is a legionary eagle, but no sword, with the exception of Dacia; not wearing any helmet on the head; often a cap or some covering, according to the custom of the country; sometimes trousers, as may be seen on a coin of Antoninus, and also in the coin of Britannia of Antoninus, where she is represented sitting on a rock to signify the insulation of the country; a cap on her head, a standard in her right hand, a spear in her left hand, and shield at her left side, all signifying the warlike character of the people. So also Dacia is represented; but, instead of a spear in her left hand, she has a curved sword or falchion, something similar to what the Dacians are represented with on the Trajan column: this sword some writers have erroneously designated a sickle.

How does Mr. Humphreys interpret the representation of a Britannia on a coin of Antoninus, where, without any helmet, but having a standard in her right hand, with her spear and shield, she is sitting on a globe placed on water?

I feel, therefore, bound to say, that Mr. Humphreys, as a popular author, ought to be more cautious?

A good brown Second Brass coin.

662.

HADRIANVS . AVG . COS . III . P . P. The unlaureate head of the emperor to the right.

℞. EXERC . BRITANNI . in the exergum; S. C. at the sides of the field. The emperor is standing to the right on a dais raised a little from the ground; he is in military costume, and bareheaded; his right hand is raised addressing three soldiers, who stand before him carrying military standards.

This coin possesses much interest. It is an ancient forgery, and is retained in the cabinet for the following reasons:—It was purchased more than twenty years ago; and on comparing it with Speed's Chronicle (chap. xvii.) there is a wood-cut of an *allocutio* of Hadrian—*a very correct resemblance of this coin*—so that it might be said this very coin was before the artist when he made the engraving.

The *allocutio* of Hadrian to the forces in Britain is also recorded on a coin bought out of the Campana Collection for the British Museum; it is but in middling condition, as may be seen by the cast of it which follows this coin, and the emperor is there represented on horseback addressing the soldiers. That coin is said to be unique, but that is an error, for the present is a very good cast from an original coin; and if Speed's wood-cut were taken from a genuine coin instead of the present one, that would prove that the British Museum coin is not unique; besides, Argelati, *in Hadriano*, A.D. 126, refers to two coins; he states the first, "Imp. in suggestu stans alloquitur milites," and quotes Vaillant, tom. 1, fol. 61; the next he states short, "Imp. alloquitur milites."

Vaillant describes the EXERCITUS BRITANNICUS thus: "Imperator paludatus stans in suggestu adloquitur cohortes—in aliis Imperator eques," and he puts it "inter rariores."

Occo, in *Hadriano*, A.D. 121, cites a coin, "ADLOCVTIO BRITANNICA. Imp. alloquitur cohortes pedestres, M. Fug."; and in A.D. 125 he cites another, "EXER. BRITANNICVS, S. C. Imp. cum tribus militibus:" thus some of the coins so quoted entirely resemble the type of the present coin, and they prove that the British Museum coin is not unique, either as to it being a single coin or a coin of peculiar type.

The same coins are likewise referred to by Eckhel, in *Hadriano*, vol. vi. p. 403.

The wood-cuts of coins introduced in Speed's Chronicle were made from the collection of Sir Robert Cotton, to which Speed was allowed access, A.D. 1610. Many coins which were so borrowed were never returned to Sir Robert Cotton, and thus were dispersed to other collections; the coins that remained are in the British Museum, and went there with the Cottonian MSS. They are now so commingled with others that they cannot be distinguished; but there was no EXERCITUS. BRITANNICVS in the British Museum until the Campana coin was bought, so that Sir Robert Cotton never had his—it may be this—coin returned to him.

The present is a good brown coin. Weight 342½ grains.

663.

HADRIANVS . AVG . COS . III . P . P. The unlaureate head of the emperor to the right.

℞. DISCIPLINA in the exergum, with AVG underneath. The emperor bareheaded, with military cloak, marching to the right, followed by three soldiers in single file also bareheaded. Instead of bearing standards, they carry their personal baggage on their spears, packed in parts, in the same way as is represented on the Trajan column, where Roman soldiers are represented in marching order with their personal baggage, and bareheaded. The emperor is holding a scroll or short staff in his left hand; the soldiers have their swords on their right side.

This excellent coin, an aureus, was obtained some years back from the bed of the Thames at Chelsea by young Edwards, who, with his brother long since dead, and Mr. Eastwood, were the principal parties engaged in collecting antiquities from the Thames, and from excavations made in London, for Mr. Charles Roach Smith, whose collection, called Roman London, was bought by the British Museum, where it is now to be seen.

The type of DISCIPLINA, representing the emperor on a march at the head of some soldiers, is frequent on the coins of Hadrian; but I have never met with it on the coins of any other emperor, although there is such a type in Antoninus. So also the number of galley coins, and coins of EXPEDITIO and FORTUNA . REDUX, which I consider were struck as representative of Hadrian moving about from place to place during the whole of his reign; also the frequent representation of Neptune, signifying the freedom from tempest when the emperor went anywhere by sea, thus giving him a safe passage; for some of these types are not found on the coins of any other emperor so as to contradict the interpretation I say that they have under Hadrian.

There are types of ALLOCUTIO to the army of almost every province Hadrian visited, and there is no doubt that, coupled with the DISCIPLINA, they allude to the evolutions and manœuvres at his different reviews of the armies in the provinces when he visited them, and inspected the several legions quartered there. In allusion to Hadrian's military drills, and the hardships he was accustomed to endure at times as an example and to encourage his troops, the poet Florus wrote—

> Ego nolo Cæsar esse,
> Ambulare per Britannos,
> Scythicas pati pruinas;

alluding also to the scanty fare Hadrian at such times subsisted upon; for it is related of Hadrian that he inured his legions to military discipline by his own example, partaking also of the usual coarse food of the Roman soldiers. It is to this conduct Spartianus, in his Life of Hadrian, attributes his death from disease, brought on by his continual exposure to the weather; but by his perseverance, and the reforms he introduced, Hadrian had the satisfaction, without being a prince of warlike disposition, of restoring the Roman armies throughout the whole empire to a most efficient state of discipline.

Admiral Smyth, in noticing his coin of this type, No. 159 in his Cabinet, says, "Hadrian established pioneers and a staff corps;" but Antonius and Augustus had, in a great measure, done this before in the *Cohors Speculatoria*, of which a coin is to be found among the legionary coins of Antonius we have already noticed. The *Cohors Speculatoria* was a detachment as guides or field engineers;

they are not mentioned by Vegetius, De Re Militari; but Varro, a military commander in Spain in the time of Julius Cæsar, and an earlier writer, defines the word *speculator* " quem mittimus ante ut respiciat quæ volumus." (Varr. lib. v. 8.) The *speculatores* were really spies or scouts, their duty being "ad omnia exploranda" (Adam, p. 377); thus strictly to examine or explore the nature of the country the army was to pass through or occupy, and its adaptation and fitness for military manœuvres. The same course was observed in their naval expeditions; the *speculator* was to observe from the masthead of the galley the nature of the shore the vessel was approaching, and where about would be the best landing-place, or the nature and disposition of an enemy's fleet in time of war.

We now add a coin as an invocation to Neptune for the emperor's safe journey across the sea on his return to Gaul on his way back to Rome. It is rather strange, but it does not appear from their index that the Vienna Cabinet have this type.

664.

. . . . IANVS . AVGVSTVS. The laureate head of Hadrian to the right.

℞. COS . III. In the field S. C. Neptune standing to the right holding his trident erect in his right hand, his left foot resting on the prow of a galley, the *rostra* outward; some drapery loosely spread across his left knee, and his left elbow resting on his knee; in his left hand he has a dolphin—type of the tranquillity of the waters of which Neptune was ruler, to let the emperor have a safe and pleasant passage.

A fine black coin from the Gwilt Cabinet.

665.

HADRIANVS . AVGVSTVS. The unlaureate head of the emperor to the right, shoulders draped.

℞. FELICITATI . AVG. in the upper part of the field, and COS . III . P.P. in the exergum, with S. C. on either side of the field.

A fine galley rowing to the left; the *gubernator* in the stern is with his right hand giving some directions, it would seem, to a person who stands at the head of the vessel looking towards him, and extending his hand also to the *gubernator*.

The figure-head or sign of the galley is a Mars, or warrior, armed and in a fighting attitude; there are three standards fixed upright in the stern, one of them being an eagle.

After Hadrian had completed his inspections in Britain he crossed the sea to

Gaul. Rutupiæ, on the south coast of Britain, now known as Richborough, was the port to which and from which the Romans were in the habit of sailing when passing to and from Gaul. Its importance at that period is testified by the immense remains of a fortified castellum which have been discovered there, of which a relation is made by my respected friend C. Roach Smith in his work on Richborough, Lymne, and Reculver. From Rutupiæ the Romans crossed to Boulogne, and so entered or quitted Gaul. We therefore regard this galley as placed at the emperor's command, and that a person of high rank is on board is signified by the eagle in its stern.

I do not recollect to have seen anywhere a galley with an armed warrior at the bow, either as a figure-head or a warrior combating with a supposed foe; the present figure has a shield on the left arm, the right hand raised in the act of throwing a spear.

A very fine brown coin from the cabinet of Mr. Durmer.

666.

HADRIANVS . AVG . COS . III . P . P. The laureate head of the emperor to the right, shoulders draped.

℞. ADVENTVI . AVG . HISPANIAE. In the exergum S. C. The emperor robed standing to the right; his right hand raised as addressing a female who stands facing him to the left, pouring from a patera on to a fire burning on an altar standing between them; at the foot of the altar, is an animal for sacrifice; the female holds an olive-branch on her left arm.

The type records the arrival of Hadrian in Spain, which was about the latter part of the year A. D. 122; and then he wintered at Tarraco (Tarragona). After he had inspected the legions and visited several places, Hadrian returned to Rome.

During the time he was at Tarraco he was attacked by a slave and nearly lost his life, but he contented himself with treating the man as a maniac and consigning him to the care of medical men to be taken charge of, instead of putting him to death.

I cannot learn what particular coins relating to Spain are in the royal cabinets at Madrid. I have had the inquiry made, and been informed there is no printed index; but, considering that Spain, including Lusitania, now known as Portugal, was for a very long period in the power of the Romans, and held in much estimation, there should be considerable collections of Roman coins in the public libraries of Spain, as well as in the hands of private individuals.

A fine water-gold coloured Campana coin. Weight $404\frac{1}{2}$ grains.

667.

HADRIANVS . AVG . COS . III . P . P.   The unlaureate head of Hadrian to the right, shoulders draped.

℞. RESTITVTORI . HISPANIAE.   In the exergum S. C.   The emperor standing to the right in his robes; before him a female is kneeling who he raises from the ground by her right hand; she bears an olive-branch over her left shoulder.

A very good red-brown coin.   Weight 389¼ grains.

668.

HADRIANVS . AVG . COS . III . P . P.   The unlaureate head of the emperor to the right, shoulders draped.

℞. RESTITVTORI . HISPANIAE.   In the exergum S. C.   The emperor robed standing to the left; he is raising a female from the ground by her right hand; on her left shoulder she bears an olive-branch.

A black-green coin, in very good condition.   Weight 364¼ grains.

669.

HADRIANVS . AVG . COS . III . P . P.   The laureate head of the emperor to the right, shoulders draped.

℞. HISPANIA in the upper verge of the field; S. C. in the exergum.   A female reclining in easy posture to the left; her left arm rests on a mound of earth or piece of rock, her right hand extended holds an olive-branch, at her feet is a rabbit.

A dark green coin.   Weight 396½ grains.

670.

HADRIANVS . AVG . COS . III . P . P.   The laureate head of the emperor to the right, shoulders draped.

℞. HISPANIA . in the upper part of the field; in the exergum S. C.   A female reclining to the left as on the preceding coin, but no rabbit at her feet.

By the testimony of several of the ancient writers, Spain in many parts abounded in rabbits, whence the little animal was used as a type of the country.   It is thus alluded to by Catullus—

Cuniculosæ Celtiberiæ fili.

It was likewise renowned for its abundance of olive-trees, which it retains at the present day, and their fruit still continues to be an article of considerable commercial benefit to the country.   This is alluded to by the olive-branch which

HISPANIA bears on the coins. The two Roman poets, Martial and Claudian, speak of the olives of Spain as an attribute of the country—

> Bœtis olivifera crinem redimite coronâ,
>   Aurea qui nitidis vellera tingis aquis,
> Quem Bromius, quem Pallas amat.
>
> MART. lib. xii. ep. 99.

> ———glaucis tum prima Minervæ
> Nexa comam foliis, fulvâque intexta micantem
> Veste Tagum, tales profert Hispania voces.
>
> CLAUD. DE LAUD. STIL. l. 2.

A yellow-brown coin, very good condition. Weight 438 grains.

671.

HADRIANVS . AVG . COS . III . P . P. The laureate head of the emperor to the right, bust in armour.

℞. EXERC . HISPAN. in the exergum; S. C. underneath. The emperor bareheaded and apparently in military costume, with a cloak on his shoulders and left arm, and a short spear in his left hand, is standing to the left on a low dais raised from the ground; his right hand is extended as addressing the soldiers who stand before him; before the emperor and facing the soldiers a lictor is standing, with his axe and fasces on his left shoulder; the soldiers bear military standards, one of them being an eagle; the head and forelegs of a horse appear amongst them, to represent the cavalry of the legions, as on the ALLOCUTIO coins of Galba and Trajan already noticed.

This coin is unique in this country; it is large in size, black in colour, and in very fine preservation, and particularly interesting as recording the review of the Spanish legions by Hadrian whilst he was in Spain. Having concluded his tour of inspection of the Roman towns and garrisons, Hadrian returned to Rome, when he had been absent more than a year.

It is from the cabinet of Captain Faber. Weight 368½ grains.

672.

HADRIANVS . AVG . COS . III . P . P.   The unlaureate head of the emperor to the right, shoulders draped.

℞. DISCIPLINA . AVG. in the exergum; S. C. on either side of the field. The emperor bare-headed, with military cloak, and a short staff in his left hand, marching to the right, followed by an officer and four *signiferi* bearing different standards; their swords on their right sides. All are marching in single file.

This is a fine large spread black coin.

673.

HADRIANVS . AVGVSTVS.   The laureate head of the emperor to the left.

℞. COS . III . P . P.   The emperor or some cavalry officer on a horse to the right, having a spear in his right hand, brought to the charge, as on the DECVRSIO coins of Nero, *ante*.

This is a device of cavalry review; the officer is in armour with his military cloak flying from his shoulders, and the attitude of the horse is as if it were stopped in its career by the word of command to *halt*. It is an uncommon device of Hadrian, but is well applicable to a review of troops, therefore I introduce it with the Spanish army.

It is a very good black Second Brass coin. Weight 164½ grains.

674.

HADRIANVS . AVG . COS . III . P . P.   The laureate head of the emperor to the right, shoulders draped.

℞. FORTVNA . REDVCI.   In the exergum S. C.   The emperor, robed and bare-headed, standing to the right; his right hand joined with the right hand of a female who stands opposite to him, having a cornucopiæ on her left arm.

This type expresses the satisfaction of the Roman people on the return of

Hadrian to the city, and the two following coins are of like import, in acknowledgment of his safe arrival.

A very fine red-green Campana coin. Weight 357¼ grains.

675.

HADRIANVS . AVG . COS . III . P . P. The laureate head of the emperor to the right, shoulders draped.

℞. ADVENTVS . AVG. In the exergum S. C. Roma armed standing to the right, with her spear in her left hand; her right hand clasps the right hand of the emperor, who is robed and standing before her.

A fine green Campana coin. Weight 395⅞ grains.

676.

HADRIANUS . AVGVSTVS . The laureate head of the emperor to the left.

℞. COS . III. In the exergum S. C. Roma, armed, seated on arms to the left, holding a Victoriola in her right hand presenting a wreath; on her left arm she bears a full cornucopiæ; the arms, being a cuirass, helmet, shield, quivers, and a bow, are all well displayed.

A dark brown coin in fine condition.

677.

HADRIANVS . AVG . COS . III . P . P. The laureate head of the emperor to the right.

℞. SALVS . AVG. In the exergum S. C. A female standing full front looking to the left; her left elbow rests on a short column placed at her side; a snake is winding round her left arm, and, crossing her bosom, raises its head over her right shoulder towards a bowl, which she holds up in her right hand for the snake to feed out of.

A supplicatory coin or type for the health of the emperor on his return to Rome.

A dark green coin in fine condition. Weight 362 grains.

678.

HADRIANVS . AVGVSTVS . P . P. The laureate head of the emperor to the right.

℞. HILARITAS . P . R. In the field S. C., and in the exergum COS . III. A female standing to the left, holding in her right hand a palm-branch, the stem of it resting on the ground; on her left arm she bears a full cornucopiæ; at her right side is a small male figure holding up his hands; and on her left side is a small female figure also holding up her hands.

This and the two following coins seem to have been struck to express the joy of the people of Rome (P. R.) under the government of Hadrian. It is useless to attempt to refer such coins to any particular year or event in the reign of Hadrian, for, being all marked COS. III., they may range through the whole period; but I consider them as appropriate to a return of Hadrian to Rome, especially in the early part of his career. I have therefore introduced them at this period, which would be about the years A.D. 122, 123.

A very fine black coin. Weight 374 grains.

679.

HADRIANVS.AVG.COS.III.P.P. The laureate head of the emperor to the right, shoulders draped.

℞. FELICITAS.AVG. In the exergum S. C. The emperor standing to the right, holding a scroll in his left hand; his right hand joined with the right hand of a female standing to the left, holding a caduceus on her left arm.

A very fine bronze Campana coin. Weight 437½ grains.

680.

HADRIANVS.AVG.COS.III.P.P. The laureate head of the emperor to the right, shoulders draped.

℞. FELICITAS.AVG. In the field S. C. A female standing to the left; her right hand extended holds an olive-branch; in her left hand she holds a long caduceus staff, resting the end on the ground.

A water-gold Campana coin. Weight 401¾ grains.

681.

HADRIANVS.AVGVSTVS. The laureate head of the emperor to the right.

℞. COS.III. in the exergum, but no S. C. An eagle standing on a *fulmen*, its head turned to the right; at its right side is an owl standing on an ornamented shield, and at its left side there is a peacock with its tail fully expanded.

Admiral Smyth, No. 26, Addenda in his Cabinet, commenting on a coin of this type, calls it *pantheistic*, but it is not explained; however, I look on the type as a very adulatory compliment to the emperor, for, being interpreted, it signifies love, wisdom, and power, the three attributes of divinity.

In the Christina Cabinet there is a Greek coin with a type of the same import; it represents Jupiter seated on a throne, with Minerva on his right hand, Juno on the left, the signification being the same as on the present coin, the three birds being those assigned in the mythology of the ancients to those three deities, the eagle to Jupiter, the owl to Minerva, and the peacock to Juno. Minerva, or Wisdom, is said to have sprung armed from the brain of Jupiter, and Love, or Juno his sister, was united to Jupiter, or Power, as his wife,—thus Power, ruled by Love and Wisdom.

In Vaillant's work "Numismata Selectiora," being a description of the medallions in the cabinet of the Abbé de Camps, there is a medallion of Trajan, with a reverse of Jupiter, standing in the middle with an eagle at his right foot, and holding a *fulmen* in his right hand, the *hasta pura* in his left. At his right side is Minerva wearing her helmet, and with spear in her right hand, a shield at her left side, and an owl at her right side; on the left of Jupiter is Juno with her peacock beside her on the right, holding the *hasta pura* in her left hand.

A remarkably fine large black coin from the cabinet of Capt. Faber. Weight 446¼ grains.

682.

HADRIANVS . AVG . COS . III . P . P.   The laureate head of the emperor to the right, shoulders draped.

℞. CAPPADOCIA. In the field S. C. A female in warlike attire, standing full front, her head turned to the left, wearing a turreted crown; her right hand extended holds what is generally termed a representation of Mount Argæus; in her left hand she holds a banner, or vexillum, the staff resting on the ground; the skin of some wild animal is pendent behind from her shoulders; the paws are seen on each side of her dress, which reaches just above her knees, with buskins half-way up on her legs.

After Hadrian's return from Spain he remained at Rome for a time, attending to the affairs of the state. In the following year he went to Athens; from thence he returned by way of Cilicia, Lycia, Pamphylia, Cappadocia, Phrygia, and Bithynia.

The present type is a personification of Cappadocia in Asia Minor, between the rivers Halys and Euphrates and the Euxine Sea. The inhabitants were reckoned, in the time of the republic, of a dull and submissive disposition, and addicted to vicious courses; they refused freedom and independence when offered them by the Romans, but begged for a king; and a man of rank, named Ariobarzanes, was appointed. Subsequently, in the civil wars of Pompey and Julius Cæsar, Ariobarzanes joined with Pompey; after whose defeat and death, and also the subsequent death of Julius Cæsar, Ariobarzanes was continued in his government by the powerful interest of Cicero. Cappadocia is also a type on the coins of Antoninus Pius, *post*.

A good water-gold Campana coin. Weight 392½ grains.

683.

HADRIANVS . AVG . COS . III . P . P. The laureate head of the emperor to the right, shoulders draped.

℞. EXER . CAPPAD[OCIVS] in the exergum, and S. C. at the sides of the field. The emperor, bare-headed and on horseback, standing to the right; his right hand raised, addressing soldiers who stand before him, each of them bearing a standard, the one who is first in front having his sword on the left side.

A very rare coin, recording the review of the Roman forces in Cappadocia by the emperor, on his visit to that province in his way back to Rome.

A fine water-gold coin. Vaillant says this type, in First Brass, "eximiæ raritatis et elegantiæ est."

684.

HADRIANVS . AVG . COS . III . P . P. The laureate head of the emperor to the right, shoulders draped.

℞. EXER . MOESICVS . in the exergum, and S. C. on either side of the field. The emperor standing to the right, a little raised from the ground by a turf, or dais, addressing four armed soldiers; the first is in front, with his back to the emperor, and bearing a legionary eagle, and there are three other standards with the rest of the soldiers.

This is also a very rare coin, recording a review of the Roman forces in Moesia by Hadrian, after he had left Cappadocia on his way, returning to Rome. Moesia is the Bulgaria of the present day.

Another fine water-gold coin.

685.

HADRIANVS . AVG . COS . III . P.P.   The laureate head of the emperor to the right, shoulders draped.

℞. ADVENTVI . AVG . PHRYGIAE . . . .   The emperor, robed and bareheaded, standing to the right; his right hand raised, addressing a person who stands on the left wearing a short tunic to the knees; on his head he has a cap, rather high, and ornamented at the top with a crescent; in his left hand he holds a shepherd's crook; between the two there is an altar with a fire burning, over which the person holds a *patera* as if pouring on it a libation; at the back of the altar some animal is lying as for sacrifice.

Phrygia was divided by the ancients into Major and Minor. It appears to have been situate between Bithynia, Lydia, Cappadocia, and Caria; its inhabitants were reckoned an effeminate race of people.

A fine mottled green red coin from the cabinet of Sir George Musgrave. Vaillant says, "inter raros numeratur."

686.

HADRIANVS . AVG . COS . III . P.P.   The unlaureate head of the emperor to the right, shoulders draped.

℞. RESTITVTORI . PHRYGIAE.   In the exergum S. C. The emperor, robed, standing to the left, extends his hand to a female kneeling before him on her right knee; a robe or mantle is pendent from her shoulders, and an ornamented vest or tunic reaches to her knees; it resembles the lappets of a cuirass: in her left hand she has a shepherd's crook; on her head she wears the cap, or Phrygian bonnet, as it is often termed, which was peculiar to the country, and singular in its form at the top, being curved as if intended to represent the crest or ornament of a helmet.

The visit of Hadrian to Phrygia here recorded took place on his way back to Rome in the same year that he visited Cappadocia. The benefits bestowed by him on the Phrygian province are implied in the term or title *Restitutor*.

A fine black coin from the Gwilt Cabinet, which Vaillant terms *rarus* only.

687.

HADRIANVS . AVG . COS . III . P . P.   The laureate head of the emperor to the right; shoulders draped.

℞. RESTITVTORI . ACHAIAE.   In the exergum S. C.   The emperor, robed, standing to the left; his right hand extended, raising a female who is kneeling before him; between them is a vase with a flower rising out of it.

Hadrian appears to have visited Achaia when on his way to Athens; after finishing his inquiries and bestowing his benefactions he went on to Athens, and afterwards returned to Rome.

Oiselius, p. 101, quoting from Spartianus, says, in reference to this type, "Post hoc per Asiam et insulas ad Achaiam navigavit, &c. et in Achaiâ quidem illud observatum ferunt quod cùm in sacris multi cultros haberent, cum Hadriano nullus armatus ingressus est."

A very fine black Campana coin. Weight $466\frac{3}{5}$ grains.

688.

HADRIANVS . AVGVSTVS. The radiate head of the emperor to the right.

℞. COS. in the upper verge of the field over a winged horse that is galloping to the right at full speed; under the horse S. C. and $\overline{\text{III}}$.

The Pegasus or winged horse was a Greek emblem; we therefore place it to represent Athens, which was visited by Hadrian after he left Achaia. Pegasus in the ancient mythology is said to have sprung from the blood of Medusa when killed by Perseus, and as soon as born, according to Ovid, he flew to Mount Helicon and there fixed his residence; on which spot he raised a fountain, called Hippocrene, by striking his foot on the earth.

Whilst Hadrian was at Athens he was initiated in the Eleusinian mysteries. The mythology of the ancient Greeks was in its origin not a mere mass of wild and idle fables, but rather a series of beautiful allegories embodying elevated lessons of wisdom. The story of Pegasus the winged horse is an interesting instance of this. The horse is a symbol of the intellect by whose energies we advance on the path of truth—a winged horse is an intellect gifted with sublime ideas, thus having the power to soar. Bellerophon could not destroy the triple monster Chimæra until he obtained the assistance of Pegasus; and in like manner Chimæra, representing the monstrous fallacies which waste the minds of the superstitious and ignorant, can only be overcome by a vigorous and heaven-taught understanding.

Pegasus also struck the side of Mount Helicon, the abode of the Muses (by whom the ancients represented Science), and opened the fountain Hippocrene, out of which the sacred waters flowed which give to genius of every kind its inspiration. By this the wise among the ancients sought to intimate, in their own graceful imagery, that, when the heaven-taught and vigorous intellect penetrated beneath the surface of things, the waters of truth furnish the votaries of the Muses (the Sciences) with all the gushing streams of poetry, music, and grace, and other sciences. Now, from this explanation, and from the circumstance of Hadrian having visited Egypt, the metropolis of hieroglyphics,—from his having dwelt at Athens, the capital of ancient mythology,—from his reputed love of learning,—to say nothing of his capabilities as a writer, or of his genius as a poet, —I am inclined to think that the Pegasus was employed by the mint-master in its primary use and meaning among the ancient Greeks, and consequently it was intended as a compliment, symbolically to express Hadrian's admiration for high and recondite learning—the Pegasus representing Athens as the seat of learning.

A fine pale yellow-green Second Brass coin.

689.

HADRIANVS . AVGVSTVS. The unlaureate head of the emperor to the right, shoulders draped.

℞. FELICITATI . AVG. In the exergum COS . III . P . P. at the sides of the field S. C. A fine galley rowed to the left; two standards are at the stern, signifying that some person of rank is on board; a small bowsprit and sail at the head; the *gubernator* sits in a hutch or covered place at the stern.

We place a galley now to signify the emperor embarked on his return to Rome, after visiting Athens and other places.

A good black coin.

690.

HADRIANVS . AVG . COS . III . P . P. The unlaureate head of the emperor to the right, shoulders draped.

℞. FORTVNAE . REDVCI. In the exergum S. C. The emperor standing to the right, his right hand joined with that of a female, who stands on the left opposite to him, bearing on her left arm a cornucopiæ filled with fruits.

A type of Hadrian having arrived at Rome after his tour.

A fine red bronze Campana green coin. Weight 378¼ grains.

691.

HADRIANVS . AVGVSTVS. The laureate head of the emperor to the right.

℞. COS . III. In the exergum S. C. Roma armed sitting on a cuirass to the left; her clothes reach to her knees only; her right hand extended holds a Victoriola; on her left arm she bears a full cornucopiæ, her right foot placed on a helmet lying on the ground; her buskins reach half up her legs, and show their lacing and ornaments very plainly.

A mottled red coin from the Ramsay Cabinet, very fine.

692.

HADRIANVS . AVGVSTVS. The laureate head of Hadrian to the right, shoulders draped.

℞. IOVI . OPTIMO . MAXIMO . S . P . Q . R . inscribed in four lines within an oak-wreath.

A compliment to Hadrian. After Hadrian had returned to Rome from Athens, he remained at home for two or three years before he started again on his travels, and during this time it would seem many coins were struck, of which the reverses all represent subjects of a peaceful character.

A very good bronze coin.

693.

HADRIANVS . AVGVSTVS . The laureate head of the emperor to the right.

℞. COS . III . and in the exergum LIBERALITAS . AVG . IIII . S. C. at the sides of the field. The emperor, or his deputy, seated to the left on a curule chair placed on a raised tribunal; at his right hand is a female, pouring corn, or some other article, from a cornucopiæ into the lap of a citizen, who stands in front, holding his robe with both hands to receive the donation.

This type is quoted by Argelati *in Hadriano*, A.D. 125, as being ex Angel. f. 148, No. 36. He describes it thus, "Imp. sedens cui assistit alia figura in sinum fundens ex cornucopiæ pecunias tertiæ adstanti;" and adds, "Liberalitas hæc quarta, videtur esse illa de qua Spartianus scribit, 'Absente Hadriano congiarium P. R. datum ternis Aureis in singulos divisis;' qui verò sedet in substructione vel consul, vel alius imperatoris vicem gerens."

It is a very scarce coin, and, when found, it is seldom in a condition fit to put in a cabinet, and the legends rarely readable. The present is a good black coin; and Vaillant says, "Hic nummus primi moduli eximiæ raritatis est."

694.

HADRIANVS . AVGVSTVS. The laureate head of the emperor to the right; shoulders draped.

℞. CLEMENTIA . AVG . COS . III . P . P. In the field S. C. A robed female standing to the left, with a *hasta pura* in her left hand; her right hand extended holds a *patera*.

A good brown coin, *e* Cureton. Weight 456¼ grains.

695.

HADRIANVS . AVGVSTVS. The laureate head of Hadrian to the right, shoulders draped.

℞. INDVLGENTIA . AVG . COS . III . P . P. In the exergum S. C. A female seated to the left on a throne, with a *hasta pura* in her left hand; her right hand extended and open.

A beautiful wax-like coin, from the Brice Cabinet. Weight 377 grains.

696.

HADRIANVS . AVGVSTVS. The unlaureate head of Hadrian to the right.

℞. INDVLGENTIA . AVG . P . P. In the exergum COS . III. and in the field S. C. A female seated to the left, as on the preceding coin, her right hand extended and open.

A fine black Campana coin. Weight 428 grains.

697.

HADRIANVS . AVG . COS . III . P . P. The laureate head of Hadrian to the right.

℞. FIDES . PVBLICA. In the field S. C. A female standing to the right, holding wheat-ears in her right hand; with her left hand raised she presents a small basket or punnet of fruits.

A fine green bronze coin, from the Thomas Cabinet. Weight $411\frac{1}{2}$ grains.

698.

HADRIANVS . AVG . COS . III . P.P. The laureate head of the emperor to the right.

℞. AEQVITAS . AVG. In the field S. C. A female standing to the left holding a pair of scales in her right hand; in the left hand she has the *hasta pura*.

A good brown coin from the cabinet of H. Robson. Weight $438\frac{2}{3}$ grains.

699.

HADRIANVS . AVG . COS . III . P . P. The laureate head of the emperor to the right.

℞. IVSTITIA . AVG. In the exergum S. C. A female seated to the left; her right hand extended holds a patera; in her left she bears the *hasta pura* upright.

These two coins seem to record an acknowledgment by the Senate of the integrity of Hadrian's conduct in the administration of justice. The emperor was so desirous of having one uniform system of law throughout the empire and provinces that he caused the whole of the laws to be revised and digested under the superintendence of Salvius Julianus, an eminent lawyer of that period, and ultimately they were compressed into one body or code, which was called "The Perpetual Edict;" thereby intending that from thenceforth this code of laws should be in use throughout the empire, and serve as the standard for any amendments which might be required at a future period.

A black green middling coin. Weight 320¼ grains.

700.

HADRIANVS . AVGVSTVS. The laureate head of the emperor to the right.

℞. COS . III., and in the exergum S. C. The emperor, robed, standing in front of a temple or other public building; his right hand raised in the act of addressing some citizens, who stand before him with their hands raised in token of applause.

A brown coin in good condition. Weight 369½ grains.

701.

HADRIANVS . AVG . COS . III . P.P. The laureate head of Hadrian to the right.

℞. FELICITAS . AVG. In the field S. C. A female standing to the left; in her right hand she holds a caduceus, at her right foot is a wheel, on her left arm she bears a full cornucopiæ.

The wheel is more usually attributed to Fortune, but it is equally appropriate here, as showing by the revolving of a wheel how uncertain is human happiness—ever changing and revolving in its daily course with the life of man.

A middling good brassy coin. Weight 372¼ grains.

702.

HADRIANVS . AVG . COS . III . P.P. The laureate head of the emperor to the right.

℞. FORTVNA . AVG. In the field S. C. A female standing to the left; her right hand rests on the tiller of a rudder, on her left arm she bears a full cornucopiæ.

A brown bronze coin. Weight 392 grains.

703.

HADRIANVS . AVGVSTVS. The laureate head of the emperor to the right.

℞. [COS . III], and in the exergum [LI]BERALITAS . . . . . The emperor or his deputy seated to the right on a curule chair placed on a *suggestum*; at his left side a person is standing, and in the act of pouring some articles from a cornucopiæ into the lap of a person who stands in front holding up his robe to receive the donation, whilst another person who has received his gift is folding his robe and walking away.

This donation, although it is not marked as the fifth, yet seeing all the others except the first are numbered, but none of them representing the persons engaged to be standing and sitting in the same positions in which the figures on this reverse are placed, we may fairly consider it to be the fifth liberality, and mark it accordingly, until the fifth does appear with its number defined; but if any coin be so marked it must be remarkably scarce, for I have never yet seen it in any cabinet, public or private, nor at sale, neither do I find it in Occo or in Argelati; but Vaillant, describing the different liberalities, notes them as to rarity in the following manner:—"Diversi sunt Liberalitatis typi cum plurimis figuris. Primus obvius, secundus rarus, tertius et quartus triti, quintus rarissimus, sextus inter rariores, septimus rarus; omnes sunt primæ magnitudinis;" and, in regard to the type of a single figure, he says, "Omnes Liberalitates cum solâ figurâ inter rariores collocandi exceptis primâ et sextâ."

A brown coin in middling condition. Weight 391^2 grains.

704.

HADRIANVS . AVGVSTVS. The laureate head of the emperor to the right.

℞. COS . III. In the field S. C. A female robed to the feet standing to the right; in her left hand she holds a bow, in her right hand an arrow.

A drab-coloured coin, very fine. Weight 386 grains.

705.

HADRIANVS . AVG . COS . III . P . P. The laureate head of Hadrian to the right.

℞. *No legend.* S. C. either side of the field. A female robed to the feet standing to the left; her right hand extended holds an arrow; in her left hand she has a bow.

A very good dark green coin. Weight 399 grains.

706.

HADRIANVS . AVGVSTVS. The laureate head of the emperor to the right.

℞. COS . III. In the field S. C. A female with arrow and bow in her hands standing to the right, as on the first preceding coin.

There is no doubt from the bow and arrow held by the female represented on these three coins that it is intended as a personifiation of Diana, the bow and arrow being peculiar to her; but her clothing, as here represented, is rather an impediment to her for the chace. Generally, Diana is represented with her legs bare, wearing buskins, her clothes only to the knees, and a quiver of arrows over her shoulders. See her *in Antonino, post.*

A very fine black coin from the Gwilt Cabinet.

707.

HADRIANVS . AVG . COS . III . P . P . The laureate head of Hadrian to the right.

℞. PROVIDENTIA . AVG. In the field S. C. A female standing looking to the left; at her right foot is placed a globe, to which she points with her right hand; in her left hand she has the *hasta pura.*

A type signifying the watchfulness of Hadrian for the welfare of the Roman world, denoted by the globe to which the hand of the female is pointing.

A good brown coin. Weight 376¼ grains.

708.

HADRIANVS . AVG . COS . III . P . P. The laureate head of Hadrian to the right.

℞. *No legend.* S. C. in the field. Victory standing to the right, her right hand raised towards her face; in her left hand she has an olive branch, which she holds in a drooping position towards the ground.

A fine bright green coin. Weight 318⅞ grains.

709.

HADRIANVS . AVGVSTVS . The laureate head of Hadrian to the right.

℞. COS . III. In the field S. C. A female warrior standing to the left; her right hand extended presents a sword with the belt; her right foot rests on a helmet lying on the ground; in her left hand she holds a spear, the point on the ground.

We have already noticed two coins like the present on the reverse, excepting they have the word VIRTVS, or VIRT. short, on each of them. The figure on this reverse has the same import, although the word VIRTVS is not introduced. We therefore rank it as a compliment to the valour of the emperor, for by VIRTVS the Romans meant valour or courage, and not virtue in the modern designation of the word, and it is thus used in describing a warrior—

" Haud ulli veterum in VIRTVTE secundus."

A light brown coin, in fine preservation. Weight 463¼ grains.

710.

HADRIANVS . AVGVSTVS. The laureate head of Hadrian to the right.

℞. COS . III. In the exergum EXPED . AVG. S. C. It is not noticed in history at what precise period Hadrian visited Dacia; but, as he started off in about his eighth year to visit Nicomedia and Bithynia, we put his visit to Dacia as forming part of the tour he then made.

The emperor is represented on this coin on horseback galloping to the left; he is in armour, with his military cloak floating from his shoulders; he looks forward, his right hand is raised, and he seems to wear a helmet or a pointed cap.

A dark brown coin.

711.

HADRIANVS . AVG . COS . III . P . P. The laureate head of the emperor to the right, shoulders draped.

℞. DACIA in the exergum; S. C. in the field. A warlike figure seated to the left on a rock; the right hand holds a Roman military ensign, the left a curved sword.

A rich light brown. Weight 409½ grains.

Dacia was conquered by the emperor Trajan, as we have already seen recorded on his coins. Trajan built a bridge over the river Danube, thus connecting the Dacian territory to the Roman, and Dacia became a Roman province, with Roman garrisons. Although history is silent as to the date of Hadrian's visit to Dacia, yet that he did go there is proved by this coin and the others which refer to Dacia; besides, after his view of Trajan's magnificent bridge, he gave orders for it to be demolished, observing that by the same means that the Roman armies passed the Danube the Dacians and other barbarians could likewise pass over.

Dacia, as we have said, *in Trajano, ante*, is now known as the principalities of Moldavia, Transylvania, and Wallachia, forming parts of the Austrian and Turkish empires. It comprises the whole of the immense district lying between the river Dneister, which takes its rise in the Carpathian Mountains in Gallicia, and falls into the Black Sea or Euxine at Akerman, and the Lower Danube. Hungary and Transylvania were originally called the kingdom of Dacia.

712.

HADRIANVS . AVG . COS . III . P . P. The laureate head of the emperor to the right, shoulders draped.

℞. DACIA in the exergum; in the field S. C. A warlike figure personifying Dacia sitting to the left on a rock, wearing a cap, a cloak passing across the bosom and falling over the left shoulder, a short tunic to the knees, and trousers reaching to the ancles; the right hand holds a Roman military standard surmounted by an eagle; in the left hand a curved sword.

A very fine light brown coin, from the cabinet of Sir George Musgrave.

713.

HADRIANVS . AVG . COS . III . P . P.   The unlaureate head of the emperor to the right.

℞. . . . . DACIC . . . in the exergum.   The emperor on a horse to the right, his right hand raised addressing three soldiers who are before him bearing military standards, the first of them being an eagle. The emperor wears a cap or helmet without crest, which is uncommon, for amongst all the representations of Hadrian on the reverses of coins the head is rarely to be seen covered.

714.

HADRIANVS . AVG . COS . III . P . P.   The laureate head of the emperor to the right, shoulders draped.

℞. EXERC . DACICVS. S. C. underneath; all in the exergum.   The emperor on his horse to the right, his right hand raised addressing three soldiers who stand before him, each of them bearing a military standard, the one in the middle being an eagle.

A good black-green coin from the cabinet of General Ramsay.

715.

HADRIANVS . AVG . COS . III . P . P.   The laureate head of the emperor to the right, shoulders draped.

℞. DISCIPLINA . AVG.   In the exergum, with S. C.   The emperor, bareheaded, holding a short staff in his left hand, is marching gently to the right, followed by an officer whose head is also uncovered, and he is followed by three *signiferi*, who wear their usual and peculiar costume of an animal's skin with its head over their heads; the first of them carries an eagle.

A very good brown coin.

These three coins record the reviews of the Roman legions quartered in Dacia at the time of Hadrian's visit there. After these expeditions the emperor returned to Rome; but we will pass over that interval, and proceed with the tour to Nicomedia and Bithynia.

716.

HADRIANVS . AVG . COS . III . P . P.   The laureate head of the emperor to the right, shoulders draped.

℞. RESTITVTORI . NICOMEDIAE.   In the exergum S. C.   The emperor standing to the left, raising with his right hand a kneeling female, who wears a turreted crown, and carries a rudder in her left hand, the blade of it appearing over her left shoulder.

A brown coin in good condition. Weight 376 grains.

Nicomedia was the capital of Bithynia; it was founded by Nicomedes, the first king of Bithynia, about 278 years before the Christian æra. The kings of Bithynia were maintained on their throne by the Romans, who treated the country rather as a province of the empire than as an independent state. Nicomedes IV. dying B.C. 75 without issue, left his kingdom and all his possessions to the Roman people, and it thus became a complete Roman province, and Hadrian visited it as a province of the empire, as he did the other provinces.

Admiral Smyth, referring to the coin of Nicomedia in his cabinet, reckons it one of the rarest of the Hadrian series. I never had another opportunity of obtaining this coin, although waiting for years to do so, and I have only seen it once since then. Vaillant says, "Hic nummus primæ formæ rarissimus et elegantissimus est."

717.

HADRIANVS . AVG . COS . III . P . P. The unlaureate head of the emperor to the right, shoulders draped.

℞. ADVENTVI . AVG . BITHYNIAE. In the exergum S. C. The emperor in his robes standing to the right, his right hand raised, addressing a female who stands before him to the left; between them is a decorated altar on which a fire is burning, and the female is pouring on to the fire from a patera she holds in her right hand. In her left hand she holds a rudder to her shoulder, on her head is a turret crown; at the side of the altar, on the ground, there is an animal lying, as for sacrifice.

A good brown coin, from the Devonshire Cabinet. Weight 341 grains.

These two coins, and the four which follow, commemorate the visits of Hadrian to the province of Bithynia, where he bestowed many benefits on the cities, and especially Nicæa and Nicomedia, which had suffered severely from earthquakes.

The most known of these two cities is Nicæa, now called Isnic, and belonging to Turkey; at Nicæa the first general council of Christian bishops was held, in A.D. 325. There is now nothing to be seen of its ancient splendour but an aqueduct. The greater part of the inhabitants used to be Jews. The country around is famous for corn and wine. The rudder borne by the female representing the province, is occasioned by the northern part of the country bordering on the Euxine Sea, the inhabitants of those parts being a maritime people.

718.

HADRIANVS . AVG . COS . III . P. P.   The laureate head of the emperor to the right, shoulders draped.

℞. RESTITVTORI . BITHYNIAE. In the exergum S. C. The emperor standing to the right, his right hand extended towards a female in plain head-dress kneeling before him on her left knee; on her left arm she bears a rudder.

A dark green coin, from the Campana Cabinet.

719.

HADRIANVS . AVG . COS . III . P. P.   The unlaureate head of the emperor to the right, shoulders draped.

℞. RESTITVTORI . BITH . . . . In the exergum S. C. The emperor standing to the right, his right hand extended towards a female kneeling before him on her left knee, wearing a turreted crown and bearing a rudder on her left arm.

A dark green coin. Weight 378¼ grains.

720.

HADRIANVS . AVG . COS . III . . .   The unlaureate head of the emperor to the right, shoulders draped.

℞. RESTITVTORI . BITHYNIAE. In the exergum S. C. The emperor standing to the left; his right hand extended, raising a kneeling female, who wears a turreted crown, and has the rudder of a galley in her left hand.

A good brown coin. Weight 409¼ grains.

721.

ΑΥΤ . ΚΑΙC . ΤΡΑΙ . ΑΔΡΙΑΝΟC . CΕΒ. The laureate head of the emperor to the right.

℞. A temple of eight columns. In the tympanum is a sculpture of the wolf and twins. The word ΚΟΙ—ΝΟΝ divided, and half placed on each side of the field by the side of the columns. In the exergum is the word ΒΕΙΘΥΝΙΑC.

The temple on this coin is supposed to represent the magnificent temple built by Hadrian on his visit to Bithynia, and dedicated to all the gods, in imitation of the Pantheon at Rome. The word ΚΟΙΝΟΝ signifying common to all [the gods]; *pantheon* meaning the same thing.

Montfaucon quotes this coin; he says that the words signify that it was struck by the community of Bithynians.

After Hadrian had completed his tour in Bithynia and adjacent parts he crossed the sea to Africa; this was in the ninth year of his reign. We therefore place a sailing galley at his disposal, and invoke the kindness of Neptune to let him have a safe passage.

HADRIANVS . AVGVSTVS. The unlaureate head of Hadrian to the right; bust in armour, and draped.

℞. FELICITATI . AVG. on the sail of a galley; COS . III . P . P . in the exergum. A large galley with mast and square sail steering away to the right; military standards are erect in the stern, and a figure is standing at the head; but whether it is a person belonging to the vessel or the sign or figure-head of the vessel is rather doubtful.

A splendid coin, in the very finest preservation, from the Devonshire Cabinet, displaying every part of the vessel very perfectly, its apparel and tackle all clearly defined. This coin is very rare indeed in so perfect a state. It is frequently found as a forgery, of which the next coin is a good specimen, and I retain it in the cabinet because it was sold to a gentleman by a workman employed in the removal of Old London Bridge, who said he had just dug it up in clearing among the foundations, and the gentleman, not understanding coins, believed the man's story and bought the coin. It was then covered with dirt, easily washed off, and was given by the gentleman to my friend, C. Roach Smith, as a great curiosity, and he gave it to me.

Weight 463¾ grains.

723.

HADRIANVS . AVGVSTVS. The unlaureate head of Hadrian to the right; bust in armour, and draped.

℞. FELICITATI . AVG. on the sail of a large galley steering away to the right, as on the preceding coin.

A yellow-brown coin.

This is the forgery above-mentioned.

724.

HADRIAN . AVGVSTVS. The laureate head of the emperor to the right; the Modena silver eagle in the field, at the back of the head.

℞. COS . III. In the field S. C. Neptune standing to the left holding his trident in the left hand; his right foot rests on the prow of a galley, the beaks outward; in his right hand he holds an *acrostolion*, and some drapery is thrown over his right knee.

We place these coins to represent the passage of Hadrian across the Mediterranean Sea to Africa after he had completed his visitation of Bithynia and the adjacent countries.

Neptune being so frequent a type on the coins of Hadrian, I am led to believe it was used to signify the safe passage of Hadrian to different places by water, so likewise with the great number of coins having galleys on the reverse; I have therefore introduced them whenever a journey by water required the use of a galley.

The types of the galley, of Neptune, and the *Expeditio*, are almost exclusively confined to Hadrian, which I consider was occasioned by his being continually visiting some one or other of the provinces.

A fine coin, bronze; formerly in the cabinet of the Duke of Modena, as proved by the small silver eagle at the back of the head.

725.

HADRIANVS . AVG . COS . III . P . P. The laureate head of the emperor to the right, shoulders draped.

℞. AFRICA in the upper part of the field. S. C. in the exergum. A female reclining to the left, wearing as a head-dress the skin of an elephant's head with its trunk raised in front; her right hand extended holds a scorpion; on her left arm she bears a cornucopiæ filled with fruits, and leans on a mound of earth or piece of rock; at her feet is a basket with ears of corn coming out of the top. The scorpion held by Africa is thus spoken of by Lucan—

    ——— quis fata putaret
    Scorpion, aut vires maturæ mortis habere?
    Ille minax nodis et recto verbere sævus
    Teste tulit cælo victi decus Orionis. Lib. ii.

A good brown coin. Weight 372⅜ grains.

726.

HADRIANVS. AVG. COS. III. P. P. The laureate head of the emperor to the right, shoulders draped.

℞. ADVENTVI. AVG. AFRICAE. In the exergum S. C. The emperor standing to the right, his right hand raised, as addressing a female who stands before him wearing the elephant head-dress; her right hand extended holds a patera, from which she is pouring on to the fire burning on an altar placed between them; at the foot of the altar an animal is lying for sacrifice.

Hadrian passed into Africa about the year A.D. 128, and returned to Rome the same year. The present coin came from some excavation about Boxmoor in forming the London and Birmingham Railway. There were several Roman urns and other Roman remains found about Boxmoor.

The coin is of yellow colour, as from water, in perfect condition; it is a scarce reverse. Weight $335\frac{1}{2}$ grains.

727.

HADRIANVS. AVG. COS. III. P. P. The laureate head of the emperor to the right, shoulders draped.

℞. RESTITVTORI. AFRICAE. In the exergum S. C. A female wearing the elephant head-dress kneeling on her right knee before the emperor, who stands to the left, with his right hand raising her from the ground; in her left hand she has some ears of corn, and three plants of corn spring from the ground between her and the emperor.

Africa was the great granary of Rome; hence the introduction of the ears of corn. Horace also alludes to it thus—

Frumenti quantum metit Africa.—Sat. iii. lib. 2.

728.

HADRIANVS. AVG. COS. III. P. P. The unlaureate head of Hadrian to the right.

℞. RESTITVTORI. AFRICAE. In the exergum S. C. A female wearing the elephant head-dress kneeling to the right before the emperor, who stands to the left, and with his right hand raises her from the ground (as depicted on the preceding coin), with ears of corn in her hand, and ears of corn on the ground before the emperor.

Hadrian did not stay for a long period in Africa before he returned to Rome;

we will therefore accompany him in a visit to Mauretania, and afterwards take shipping for Rome.

These two coins are black in colour, and in fine preservation; the latter of them is from the cabinet of General Ramsay.

729.

HADRIANVS . AVG . COS . III . P . P.   The unlaureate head of the emperor to the right, shoulders draped.

℞. ADVENTVI . AVG . MAVRETANIAE.   In the exergum S. C.   The emperor robed standing to the right; before him is a female wearing a short dress to the knees with a round cap on her head, and bearing on her left shoulder a standard; her right hand extended holds a patera over a fire burning on an altar standing between her and the emperor; the altar is a narrow circular altar, apparently of stone, and by its side is a lamb.

A good brown coin of greenish tint.

730.

HADRIANVS . AVG . COS . III . P . P.   The laureate head of the emperor to the right, shoulders draped.

℞. ADVENTVI . AVG . MAVRETANIAE.   In the exergum S. C.   The emperor robed standing to the right, his right hand raised as addressing a female who stands before him wearing an elephant head-dress; in her left hand she holds upright a *vexillum* or cavalry banner, the staff resting on the ground, her dress reaching only to her knees; her right hand, holding a patera, is extended to a fire burning on a tripod altar, at the foot of which is seemingly the head and trunk of an elephant.

A good coin, the reverse yellow-brown, very distinct.

These coins record the arrival of Hadrian in the province of Mauretania, now Morocco; the difference of the reverses renders them very interesting.

731.

HADRIANVS . AVG . COS . III . P . P.   The laureate head of the emperor to the right, shoulders draped.

℞. MAVRETANIA.   No S. C.   The province personified by a female standing to the right, by the side of a spirited horse, which she holds with her left hand, as if by a bridle, or by its mane; in her right hand she has two spears; her dress, very scanty, reaches to her knees.

Mauretania, the present kingdom of Fez and Morocco, became a province of the Roman Empire in the time of the Emperor Claudius. Horace, in allusion to the use of the spear by the Moors, says,

Integer vitæ scelerisque purus
Non eget Mauri jaculis.

The native inhabitants were black, or of very dark complexion, whence their name, Mauri. It would seem, by the female (or province) being represented with a horse, that they were then as celebrated for their breed of horses as they are at the present time. Their skill in horsemanship resembled that of their neighbours, the Numidians, thus described by Silius Italicus:

Hic passim exultant Numidæ, gens inscia fræni :	On his hot steed, unused to curb or rein,
Queis inter geminas per ludum mobilis aures	The black Numidian prances o'er the plain ;
Quadrupedum flectit non cedens virga lupatis :	A wand betwixt his ears directs his course,
Altrix bellorum bellatorumque virorum	And, as a bridle, turns th' obedient horse.
Tellus.	

A black coin, in good condition.

732.

HADRIANVS . AVG . COS . III . P. P. The laureate head of the emperor to the right, shoulders draped.

℞. MAVRETANIA. In the exergum S. C. The province personified by a female standing to the left by the side of a fiery horse, which she holds with her right hand; in her left hand she has two spears; her dress reaching to her knees, and a cap on her head.

A good black-coloured coin.

The Mauri were also inhabitants of Mauretania in that part now called Algiers; it was the eastern part of Mauretania. They are sometimes classed as distinct provinces; but each was equally noted for its breed of horses, and skill in horsemanship.

The horse on these coins of Mauretania may also be considered an emblem of the warlike genius of the people, thus alluded to by Virgil, Æneid, lib. 3 :

Bello armantur equi, bella hæc armenta minantur.

733.

HADRIANVS . AVG . COS . III . P. P. The laureate head of the emperor to the right, shoulders draped.

℞. MAVRETANIA. In the exergum S. C. A female, representing the province, walking to the right, and leading a horse with her right hand; her dress reaches to the knees; on her left shoulder she carries two spears. Claudian, speaking of the Numidian cavalry, asks the question:

——— An Mauri fremitum raucosque repulsus	Can Moors sustain the press in close-fought fields
Umbonum et vestros passuri cominus enses?	Of shortened falchions and repelling shields?
Non contra clypeis tectos galeisque micantes	Against a host of quiv'ring spears ye go,
Ibitis; in solis longè fiducia telis.	Nor helm nor buckler guard the naked foe;
Exarmatus erit, cùm missile torserit, hostis,	The naked foe, who vainly trusts his art,
Dextra movet jaculum, prætentat pallia lævâ,	And flings away his armour in his dart:
Cetera nudus eques, sonipes ignarus habenæ,	His dart the right hand shakes, the left uprears
Virga regit, non ulla fides, non agminis ordo,	His robe, beneath his tender skin appears.
Arma oneri, fuga præsidio—	Their steeds, unrein'd, obey the horseman's wand,
	Nor know their legions when to march or stand:
	In the war's dreadful laws untaught and rude;
	A mob of men, a martial multitude.

A fine light green coin, from the cabinet of General Ramsay.

734.

HADRIANVS . AVG . COS . III . P.P.   The unlaureate head of the emperor to the right, shoulders draped.

℞. MAVRETANIA. In the exergum S. C. A man walking to the left in front of a horse, which he is leading with his right hand, and carrying two spears in his left hand.

These four coins, representing Mauretania, delineate the province in various positions. There are no other representations of the province than as on these coins, which are not easily procured as a complete series.

The present is a brown coin, rather worn. Weight 402¼ grains.

735.

HADRIANVS . AVG . COS . III . P.P.   The laureate head of the emperor to the right, shoulders draped.

℞. EXERCITVS in the upper verge of the field. In the exergum MAVRETANICVS, with S. C. under it. The emperor on a horse to the right; his right hand raised addressing three soldiers who stand before him, each of them carrying a standard, the foremost of them being an eagle.

A fine green coin from the cabinet of General Ramsay.

Vaillant calls the coin "rarissimus."

736.

HADRIANVS . AVG . COS . III . P.P. The unlaureate head of the emperor to the right, shoulders draped.

℞. DISCIPLINA . AVG. in the exergum; S. C. at the sides of the field. The emperor, bareheaded, with military cloak, is marching to the right followed by four soldiers, three of them bearing military standards; the emperor holds a scroll or short staff in his left hand.

The types on these two coins commemorate the review and manœuvres of the Roman legions and forces stationed in Mauretania when Hadrian visited the province during his tour in Africa.

A brown coin in good condition.

737.

HADRIANVS . AVGVSTVS. The laureate head of the emperor to the right.

℞. COS . III., and across the field NEP.—RED., with S. C. under the words, which are divided by the figure of Neptune, who stands to the right, wearing a large round cap. In his right hand he holds a trident, the prongs upward; his left foot rests on the prow of a galley, the *rostra* outward; his left arm resting on his left knee; in his left hand he holds a bunch of coral or sea-weed, or perhaps an *acrostolion;* some drapery is hanging in a careless manner over his left knee.

The inscription of NEP.—RED. across the field of this coin records a return by sea from a distant country. Oiselius, in Pl. xxxvi. No. 12, speaking of a coin of Titus with the legend NEP.—RED. says, "NEP*tuno* RED*uci* dicatus hic nummus ob reditum Titi Romam per mare." Neptune had great honours paid to him at Rome. During the *Ludi Consuales* horses and mules were exempt from labour, and were led through the streets decked with garlands.

Admiral Smyth, describing a Neptune reverse of Hadrian, No. 155, says that he holds a *hasta pura*. I think his coin must be a little imperfect, for the trident is Neptune's peculiar weapon, and the *hasta pura* belongs to Jupiter and peaceful deities, or personifications of moral virtues—the *hasta pura*, or pointless spear, being the wand or staff of Divinity. The wand, or *hasta pura*, is used by certain officers of state attendant on royal personages on state occasions at the present day—by the Lord Chamberlain and other like officers—called Gold Stick, or Silver Stick, or Black Rod, according to its ornamentation; also, the office of Lord High Steward for the trial of a peer is created by the delivery of a wand, the *hasta pura*, and on the termination of the trial the Lord High Steward breaks the wand, and declares the court dissolved.

I should prefer considering Neptune as holding a bunch of coral or sea-weed instead of the *acrostolion*, which was the ornamental part of the stern of a galley, and was a token of a naval victory, it being customary to break away the *acrostolion* from the stern of any hostile ship that might have been taken in battle, and there is no record of any naval engagement having occurred during the reign of Hadrian. The coral or sea-weed would therefore be an appropriate emblem to the peaceful reign of Hadrian.

A very fine pale green coin.

738.

HADRIANVS . AVGVSTVS . The unlaureate head of the emperor to the left; shoulders draped.

℞. FELICITATI . AVG. In the exergum COS . III. S. C. at each side of the field. A large galley, very high in the stern, in which are placed a *vexillum* and another standard; at the head is a sort of bowsprit with a small sail, a round or fiddle-head scroll, below which are the *rostra*. It is full of men, who are rowing away to the left. The *gubernator* at the stern is giving some directions to a person who stands at the head of the vessel. The standards indicate some person of rank being on board.

Hadrian's journeys by sea were fit subjects for the die-engravers to commemorate. It is to be observed that a galley was made by the ancients to signify a government, as the vessel of the state under the guidance of the emperor and senate, as the pilots and *gubernatores*; yet, as there are more galley coins of Hadrian than of all the other emperors, we may fairly consider that, although some were emblems of his good pilotage of the state vessel, yet others were intended to express the satisfaction of the people at finding the emperor return in safety from a sea-voyage after visiting distant provinces of the empire, for they invariably have the legend FELICITATI . AVG. on the reverse with the galley, and on the sail at times, when the galley carries sail.

A fine black-green coin. Weight 388½ grains.

739.

HADRIANVS . AVGVSTVS . P . P. The laureate head of the emperor to the right, shoulders draped.

℞. COS . III. In the exergum FORT . RED. and S. C. in the field. Fortune seated to the left holding a rudder in her right hand; on her left arm she bears a full cornucopiæ.

The *Fortuna redux* seated with a rudder I consider refers to the emperor's return to Rome by sea, indicated by the rudder, as part of the tackle of a galley. The type of *Fortuna redux*, a female standing, her hand joined with the emperor's, seems a greeting of the emperor when he has returned from a journey by land. There is, doubtless, a distinction in the coins of the emperor Hadrian, implied by *Fortuna redux* being in different attitudes; which I can only account for by considering one class as referring to a voyage by sea, and the other to a journey by land.

A brown coin, from the cabinet of Mr. Robson. Weight 419¼ grains.

740.

HADRIANVS . AVG . COS . III . P . P . The laureate head of the emperor to the right.

℞. IOVI . CVSTOD. In the exergum S. C. Jupiter seated to the left, holding a *fulmen* in the right hand, which he rests on the right knee; in the left hand he holds a *hasta pura*.

The type of this coin seems to be a recommendation of the emperor to the protection of Jupiter.

A black coin. Weight 433¼ grains.

741.

HADRIANVS . AVGVSTVS. The laureate head of the emperor to the right.

℞. HILARITAS . P . R. In the exergum COS . III . and S. C. in the field. A female standing to the left, holding a palm-branch in her right hand; on her left arm she bears a full cornucopiæ, a child on each side of her with its hands raised.

This type has been already noticed *ante;* but I introduce it again here to signify the joy or satisfaction expressed by the people of Rome on Hadrian's return to the city after his tour in the distant provinces of the empire; for it is a type that was frequently minted in the reign of Hadrian, and may be termed a common reverse of his time, excepting as to its state of preservation.

A good brown coin.

742.

HADRIANVS . AVGVSTVS. The laureate head of the emperor to the right.

℞. CO . . I . . . In the exergum ANNONA . AVG . and in the field S. C. A female seated to the right making a donation to a person who stands in front to receive it; in the background is the stern of a galley, thus indicating that the supply of corn came to Rome by sea.

A Second Brass black coin, very good. Weight 214¼ grains.

3 A

743.

HADRIANVS . AVGVSTVS. The laureate head of the emperor to the right, shoulders draped.

℞. TRANQVILLITAS . AVG . P . P. In the exergum COS . III; in the field S. C. A female standing full front, her head turned to the left; in her right hand she has a *hasta pura;* her left arm rests carelessly on the top of a short column at her left side.

This type is rare; the coin is of gold colour, from lying in water. Weight, $414\frac{1}{2}$ grains.

744.

HADRIANVS . AVG . COS . III . P . P. The laureate head of the emperor to the right.

℞. SALVS . AVG. In the field S. C. A female standing to the right feeding a snake, which rises from an altar before her.

A good brown coin. Weight $428\frac{3}{4}$ grains.

745.

HADRIANVS . AVGVSTVS. The laureate head of the emperor to the right.

℞. COS . III. In the field S. C. A female standing full front looking to the left; in her left hand she bears a *hasta pura;* in her right hand she holds a pair of scales, the emblem of justice.

This type is most likely in allusion to the emperor's righteous conduct as judge and chief officer of the state.

It is a fine black coin. Weight $398\frac{1}{8}$ grains.

746.

HADRIANVS . AVG . COS . III . P . P. The laureate head of the emperor to the right, shoulders draped.

℞. TELLVS . STABIL. In the exergum S. C. A female reclining to the left, her left arm resting on a basket of fruits, her right hand placed on a globe, which is at her right side.

A good coin, yellow brassy. Weight $392\frac{5}{8}$ grains.

747.

HADRIANVS . AVG . COS . II .... The laureate head of the emperor to the right.

℞. PAX . AVG. In the exergum S. C. A female seated on the throne to the left; her right hand, extended, holds an olive branch; in her left hand she has the *hasta pura*.

Argelati, *in Hadriano*, places this type in A.D. 131, but there is no historic record of a war followed by a peace in that year; the only affair of the kind was the revolt of the Jews, but that was in A.D. 134-5; so I place the coin in the present period, about A.D. 128-9, as signifying the peaceful state of Rome and the provinces at that period of Hadrian's reign. The only type of Pax mentioned by Occo is described "Pax typus, dextrâ ramum, sinistrâ cornucopiæ;" and it is placed in A.D. 119, in the second consulate of Hadrian. In that case the type would apply to the repression of the insurrection of the Roxolani. The legend on this coin on the obverse is a little corroded; but I consider, from its general appearance and similitude to the others, that it is a coin of cos. III.

A good brown coin. Weight 395⅜ grains.

748.

HADRIANVS . AVG . COS . III . P . P. The laureate head of the emperor to the right, shoulders draped.

℞. LIBERALITAS . AVG . VI. In the exergum S. C. A female standing full front, looking to the left, holding up a tablet in the right hand; on her left arm she bears a cornucopiæ filled with fruit.

It is not easy to give any specific dates to these coins of liberalities bestowed on the citizens. By Occo this liberality is placed in A.D. 126; but that date cannot be correct, for he places LIBERAL . VII. in the same year, and also in A.D. 121, which are quite inconsistent with each other.

This is a fine black coin, from the cabinet of the Duke of Devonshire. Weight 417 grains.

749.

HADRIANVS . AVGVSTVS. The laureate head of the emperor to the right, shoulders draped.

℞. ROMVLO . CONDITORI. No S. C. The emperor, bare-headed, in military costume, walking at a quick pace to the right, bearing on his left shoulder a trophy of arms; in his right hand he carries a spear, the point forwards.

Hadrian remained at Rome for a long period after his return from Africa, and built some temples and other edifices, whence the compliment of this legend.

The coin is of a dark mottled green colour, in very fine condition, from the cabinet of General Ramsay.

750.

HADRIANVS . AVG . COS . III . P . P.   The unlaureate head of the emperor to the right.

℞. VOTA . PUBLICA.   The emperor in pontifical vestments and veiled head, standing to the left; in his right hand he holds a *patera*, with which he is making a libation on a fire burning upon a tripod altar placed before him on the right.

We have already noticed, *in Augusto*, the custom established by Augustus for the reigning emperor, in every tenth year of his reign, to make his offering of the decennalian vows on resuming the Tribunicia Potestas. I therefore introduce this fine denarius as belonging to the tenth year, or at furthest the eleventh, of Hadrian; for the legend being VOTA PVBLICA, in my opinion this type has reference to his performing the ceremony of the decennalian vows, although I have not found any other record of the fact. Vaillant mentions a First Brass coin with the reverse legend VOT . PVB. and thus describes the type: "Imperator velatus sacrificans supra tripodem, victimario, popa et tibicine assistentibus;" adding, "Hic nummus primi moduli præstantissimus et rarissimus est." On the present coin the emperor is performing sacrifice alone; but the description of Vaillant and the present coin prove, I should say beyond a doubt, that the ceremonial usual on renewal of the decennial vows was all duly performed, and at the proper period, although history is silent on the question.

751.

HADRIANVS . AVGVSTVS.   The laureate head of the emperor to the right, shoulders draped.

℞. FELICITATI . AVG. above a galley rowing to the left; COS . III . P . P. in the exergum, and S. C. at the sides. The galley has two ensigns set up in the stern, to denote a person of rank is on board.

Hadrian, after being some time quiet at Rome, started off to visit the provinces in the eastern part of the empire. We thus see and consider him on board the galley sailing to Asia. The figure-head of the galley appears to be a triton blowing a large open-mouthed trumpet or sea-shell.

A very good brown coin.

752.

HADRIANVS . AVGVSTVS.   The laureate head of the emperor to the right.

℞. COS . III.   In the field S. C.   Neptune standing to the left resting his right foot on the prow of a galley, the beaks outward; some drapery is thrown across his right thigh, and his right elbow rests on it; his right hand holds an *acrostolion*, in his left he holds his trident upright.

This type we may consider as praying the aid of Neptune to give the emperor a safe passage in his journey over the seas.

It is a brown coin in good condition.

753.

HADRIANUS . AVG . COS . III . P. P. The unlaureate head of Hadrian to the right, bust in armour.

℞. ADVENTVI . AVG . ASIAE. In the exergum S. C. The emperor robed standing to the right, his right hand raised addressing a female who stands before him to the left, and with her right hand is pouring from a patera upon a fire burning on an altar between them; on the ground, by the side of the altar, an animal is lying for sacrifice.

After his arrival in Asia and inspection of the towns, Hadrian went into Syria, Judea, Arabia, and Ægypt, passing the latter part of his journey mostly in Ægypt.

A green coin, from General Ramsey's cabinet.

754.

HADRIANVS . AVG . COS . P. P. The laureate head of the emperor to the right, shoulders draped.

℞. EXERC . SYRIAC. S. C. underneath; all in the exergum. The emperor bareheaded, on his horse, to the right; his sword at his right side, his right hand raised, addressing five soldiers who are before him, bearing four standards, the first a *vexillum*, the second a wreath, the third an eagle, the fourth a hand; the fifth has no standard, thus showing that the figures on the standards represent all the divisions of the troops quartered in Syria

It is a good brown coin, from the Duke of Devonshire's Cabinet. Weight 386¾ grains. Vaillant says this coin "inter rariores scribendus est."

755.

HADRIANVS . AVG . COS . III . P. P. The unlaureate head of the emperor to the right, shoulders draped.

℞. EXERC . SYRIACVS, in the exergum; S. C. underneath. The emperor on horseback, to the right, is addressing four soldiers who stand before him, each bearing a standard.

A good brown coin. Weight 368¼ grains.

756.

HADRIANVS . AVG . COS . III . P. P.   The unlaureate head of the emperor to the right, shoulders draped.

 S. C. in the field. The word DISCIPLINA, usually in the exergum, is corroded. The emperor, with his head uncovered, and wearing his military cloak, is marching to the right, holding in his left hand a scroll, or short staff. He is followed by an officer in military attire; and behind them are three soldiers, each bearing a standard.

We place this coin as commemorative, with the two preceding coins, of the reviews, and marches, and manœuvres of the troops in garrison in Asia, at the time Hadrian visited the province.

The present is a good green coin.

757.

HADRIANVS . AVG . COS . III . P. P.   The unlaureate head of Hadrian to the right, shoulders draped.

℞. IVDAEA in the exergum; no S. C. The emperor robed, seated on a curule chair to the left; an official person is standing at his right hand, holding up a wand of office, as if to command silence among the spectators, or audience. The emperor extends his right hand to a female wearing a turret crown, who falls on her right knee before him. Two naked children are in front, between her and the emperor, one of whom approaches the emperor's feet; the other raises its right hand to its mother, and the third is at her left side, in the background.

This beautiful and interesting coin, from the cabinet of the Vicomte Jessaint at Paris, is unique; I do not find it noted anywhere; the nearest approach to it, if it may be so considered, is in Oiselius, pl. xvii. p. 86, also, Occo's description of a coin, in Eriz. Ant. Aug. Tab. 71, which may represent the coin given in Oiselius; but the engraving of that coin in Oiselius shows it to be a different device to the present, though the nearest I have found. The description given by

Occo is but meagre, yet one must conclude it embraces all the device would admit of: he says, *in Hadriano*, p. 230, "IVDAEA. figura muliebris cum puerulis cui Imp. dextram porrigit."

The present coin is in pure aurichalcum, without patina. When I first had it there was much dirt upon it. I cleaned it all away, and found it a pure brass, and untouched by graving tool, or any trick played with it; which satisfied me of its being a genuine coin, as perfect as it came from the Roman mint.

758.

HADRIANVS . AVG . COS . III . P . P. The laureate head of the emperor to the right, shoulders draped.

℞. ADVENTVI . AVG . IVDAEAE. In the exergum S. C. The emperor robed, standing to the right, his right hand raised, addressing a female who stands before him, with her right hand presenting him a globe; between them is an altar, on which a fire is burning, and some animal on the ground by the altar for sacrifice. A little child is standing on each side of the female.

A good brown coin, from the Devonshire Cabinet. Weight 320¼ grains.

759.

HADRIANVS . AVG . COS . III . P . P. The laureate head of the emperor to the right, shoulders draped.

℞. ADVENTVI . AVG . IVDAEAE. In the exergum S. C. The emperor robed, standing to the right, his right hand raised, addressing a female who stands before him; she appears to have an *acerra*, or incense box, on her left arm, and, with her hand held over a fire, to be burning incense before the emperor on an altar which stands on the ground between them. On each side of the female stands a child; the one on her left side appears to have in its hands what is usually termed a palm-branch, from which circumstance it is considered a rarer type than the preceding; but they are both difficult to obtain, even in a poor condition.

Admiral Smyth, No. 176 in his Cabinet, under the title of this reverse, mentions the expulsion of the Jews from Jerusalem. That event, however, did not take place until the nineteenth year of the reign of Hadrian, whereas these coins were struck to commemorate the visit of Hadrian to Judæa in the eleventh year of his reign.

In the sixteenth year of his reign Hadrian was compelled by the rebellious conduct of the Jews to chastise them, and they were quieted for a time; but on their resuming their turbulent conduct he subsequently took possession of Jerusalem and entirely expelled and dispersed them, and from that hour they have ever ceased to exist as a nation. The walls of the city, which had escaped destruction in the siege of Titus, were broken down and razed to the ground; and the name of the city was changed, it being called AELIA . CAPITOLINA; and Hadrian decreed death to any Jew who should set his foot in the city.

We have already, *in Vespasiano*, noticed the denunciations against the Israelites, mentioned in Deuteronomy, ch. xviii. v. 64-68; we need not therefore repeat them on the present coin; but the Jews are, and will be for several ages, a living testimony of the truth of the Holy Scriptures, of which they have been the *custodes*, and of our Lord's prophecies, recorded in the Holy Gospels, until they are gradually absorbed among other peoples and nations of this earth.

The present is a good green coin, from the Campana Cabinet.

760.

HADRIANVS . AVG . COS . III . P . P. The laureate head of the emperor to the right, shoulders draped.

℞. ADVENTVI . AVG . ARABIAE. In the exergum S. C. The emperor standing to the right, addressing a female who stands to the left, having in her right hand a patera from which she is pouring on to a fire burning on an altar before her; on her left arm she bears a *sceptrum*, or as some say the *calamus odorata*, which we should now call a stick of cinnamon, a produce of Arabia.

A good coin of green tint. Weight 380 grains.

761.

HADRIANVS . AVG . COS . III . P . P. The laureate head of the emperor to the right, shoulders draped.

℞. RESTITVTORI . ARABIAE. In the exergum S. C. The emperor standing to the right, with his right hand raising a female who is kneeling before him on the ground on her left knee; at her right side is a camel, and in her left hand she bears the *calamus odorata*.

After Hadrian had visited Syria he went to Palestine and Judæa; from thence to Arabia, and then to Ægypt. His visit to Arabia is thus recorded on these coins.

A brown coin, procured from Mr. Hoffman of Paris. Weight 380¼ grains.

These two coins are seldom to be met with.

762.

HADRIANVS . AVG . COS . III . P . P. The laureate head of the emperor to the right, shoulders draped.

℞. AEGYPTOS in the upper verge of the field ; S. C. in the exergum. A female reclining to the left, her left arm resting on a basket of fruit; in her right hand she holds up a *sistrum,* at her feet is an ibis perched on a short column.

After Hadrian had visited Palestine and Judæa, passing by Arabia, he travelled into Ægypt, and remained there about two years. Lucan thus describes Ægypt :

> Syrtibus hinc Libycis tuta est Ægyptus : at inde
> Gurgite septeno rapidus mare summovet amnis :
> Terra suis contenta bonis, non indiga mercis,
> Aut Jovis ; in solo tanta est fiducia Nilo. Lib. viii.

A dark green coin in fine condition, from the Devonshire Cabinet. Weight 416½ grains.

763.

HADRIANVS . AVG . COS . III . P . P. The laureate head of the emperor to the right, shoulders draped.

℞. AEGYPTOS, in the upper verge of the field ; S. C. in the exergum. A female reclining to the left, her left arm resting on a basket filled with fruits; in her right hand she holds up a *sistrum;* at her feet is an ibis perched on a short column with wings nearly expanded, as if about to fly, or just returned from a flight.

In Vaillant, ed. 1743, vol. i. p. 57, there is a coin cited of this type, but of a prior date, thus : " IMP . CAES . TRAIAN . HADRIANVS . AVG . P . M . TR . P . COS . II. Caput Hadriani laureatum. rev. AEGYPTOS. Figura muliebris humi sedens, dextrâ sistrum, cubiti lævo innixo canistro frugum. Ibis ante pedes."

Vaillant adds this comment : " Hic nummus primæ formæ rarus est." It would seem that a coin of Ægypt of the date COS . III. was unknown to him ; but the date COS . II. puts the quære, when did Hadrian visit Ægypt? or did he visit Ægypt twice, and thus account for COS . II. ? On referring to Mr. Sharpe's book, I find Hadrian visited Ægypt in the sixth year of his reign, A.D. 122, and again in his fifteenth year, A.D. 131, when he was accompanied by the Empress Sabina; and Mr. Sharpe refers to triumphal coins (Alexandrian) bearing the date of that year. Argelati, *in Hadriano,* also quotes the coin mentioned by Vaillant, but no other is noticed by him. Eckhel does not mention any AEGYPTOS . S . C . COS . III.

A very fine dark coin, from the Gwilt Cabinet.

764.

HADRIANVS . AVG . COS . III . P . P.   The unlaureate head of the emperor to the right, shoulders draped.

℞. AEGYPTOS in the upper verge ; S. C. in the exergum. A female reclining to the left, her left arm resting on a basket of fruits ; in her right hand is the *sistrum*, and at her feet the ibis stands perched on its column.

The ibis was held as a sacred bird among the ancient Ægyptians; it was viewed in the light of a beneficent deity, from its living upon and destroying the serpents and other noxious reptiles with which the country abounded.

The *sistrum* is also an emblem of Ægypt, it being an instrument like an elongated horseshoe, made of brass, fixed on a handle, with loose bars across from side to side (as shown on the coin), which made a jingling noise when it was shaken, and I should consider that some specimens were made with the horseshoe-like part hollow, to increase the sound. It was carried by the priests of Isis, and used by them in their religious ceremonies.

Juvenal, ridiculing the Ægyptian deities, speaks of the ibis also:

> Quis nescit, Volusi Bithynice, qualia demens
> Ægyptus portenta colat ? Crocodilon adorat
> Pars hæc, illa pavet saturam serpentibus Ibim ;
> Effigies sacri nitet aurea Cercopitheci.   Sat. xv.

The *sistrum* is also noticed by Claudian as—

> ———————— Nilotica sistris
> Ripa sonat ————

Lucan also, alluding to the introduction of Ægyptian gods, says—

> Nos in templa tuam Romana accepimus Isin
> Semideasque canes, et sistra jubentia luctus.

A very good dark green coin.   Weight 415½ grains.

765.

HADRIANVS . AVG . COS . III . P.P.   The laureate head of the emperor to the right, shoulders draped.

℞. AEGYPTOS in the upper verge of the field ; S. C. in the exergum. A female reclining to the left, her left arm resting on a basket of fruits, with the *sistrum* and ibis, as represented on the preceding coins.

This coin is singular, being of lead; it was formerly in the Dimsdale Collection, lot 531 in the sale catalogue, and was bought by M. Young, the dealer, for thirty-one shillings. It is unique. It is not mentioned in Ficorini's work Di Antichi Piombi.

766.

HADRIANUS . AVG . COS . III . P. P. The laureate head of the emperor to the right, shoulders draped.

℞. NILVS in the upper verge of the field; S. C. in the exergum. A river-god, representing Nilus, reclining to the right; in his left hand he holds a cornucopiæ filled with fruits, and a child stands on each side supporting it. A hippopotamus is coming out from some sedges at the feet of Nilus.

It will be seen there is no urn with water flowing from it introduced in the coins of Ægypt which represent the Nile, thus signifying that the source of that celebrated river was at that time unknown; it is not yet discovered, but in the course of time there is little doubt its source will be traced in the mountains of Abyssinia, or a far interior country bearing some other name.

We need not enter into long remarks about this celebrated river. Antiquarian curiosity may be fully satisfied in reading the works of Bruce, and other persons who have at different times made excursions to explore the less frequented parts of Ægypt, Abyssinia, and Æthiopia.

A fine green mottled red coin. Weight 350 grains.

767.

HADRIANVS . AVG . COS . III . P . P . The laureate head of the emperor to the right, shoulders draped.

℞. *Legend corroded.* In the exergum S. C. The river-god Nilus, reclining to the right, his right arm resting on the head of a sphinx, by the side whereof a figure is standing; in the right hand Nilus bears a reed or sedge; on the left are three children playing, one of them sitting astride on a great hippopotamus; the floating water of a river appears under Nilus, and beneath the water is a crocodile at full length moving to the left.

A good dark green coin. Weight 341 grains.

768.

HADRIANVS . AVG . COS . III . P . P . The unlaureate head of the emperor to the left, shoulders draped.

℞. NILVS. In the exergum S. C. The river-god reclining to the left, his left arm resting on the head of two small figures; his right hand supports a cornucopiæ filled with fruits, by the side of which is a child; a child's head also appears peeping over his left shoulder; at his feet is a hippopotamus coming towards him with a little child on its back; under him are the undulations of water bearing a crocodile swimming to the right.

A good dark green coin. Weight 446¼ grains.

769.

ΑΥΤ . ΚΑΙ . ΤΡΑΙΑΝ . . . .   The laureate head of the emperor to the right, shoulders in armour and draped.

℞. ΛΔѠΔΕΝ in the exergum. Nilus reclining to the left, his head crowned with reeds; in his left hand he holds a reed or sedge, and under him is a large crocodile moving to the right; in his right hand he supports a full cornucopiæ; above in the field are the Greek letters ιγ . signifying the thirteenth year of the reign of Hadrian, A.D. 129, as the year of its being struck at the mint at Alexandria, for it is an Ægyptian coin of Alexandria.

There is a celebrated colossal figure of Nilus, with all the attributes of children, crocodile, sphinx, &c. as on the coin, in the Vatican Collection at Rome. It is sculptured in black basalt, or Æthiopian marble, and was brought by Vespasian to Rome and placed in the Temple of Peace. A representation of it may be seen in Oiselius, p. 566.

The sixteen children attendant on Nilus have been supposed to signify the sixteen months of the river. Mr. Sharpe designates the sixteen children, or cupids, to mean sixteen cubits, the desired overflow of the Nile.

The coin is dark brown in colour and in fine condition; the weight 406¼ grains.

770.

HADRIANVS . AVG . COS . III . P . P.   The unlaureate head of the emperor to the right, shoulders draped.

℞. NILVS . in the upper part of the field; S. C. in the exergum. The river-god reclining to the right, holding a full cornucopiæ in his left hand; at his feet is a crocodile looking towards him, and under him is another crocodile swimming to the left; there are no children about him.

A fine Second Brass yellow coin; no patina. Weight 174¼ grains.

771.

HADRIANVS . AVG . COS . III . P . P.   The laureate head of the emperor to the right, shoulders draped.

℞. NILVS in the upper part of the field; in the exergum S. C. The old river-god reclining to the left, holding a sedge in his left hand, his left arm resting on the head of a small figure like a sphinx; his right hand holds a full cornucopiæ; at his feet is a hippopotamus coming towards him; underneath him is a crocodile. There are no children introduced.

Both of these creatures, the crocodile and the hippopotamus, are emblems of Ægypt, they being indigenous to that part of the world.

A fine black green Second Brass coin.

772.

HADRIANVS . AVG . COS . III . P . P. The laureate head of the emperor to the right.

℞. *No legend.* S C. in the field. The emperor, bareheaded, in military costume, standing to the right; in his right hand he holds a spear upright, in his left hand a *parazonium;* his left foot is placed on a crocodile that is on the ground, its head much raised.

By the attitude of the emperor, and the position of the crocodile, it would seem to represent a conquest; but that event was accomplished in the time of Julius Cæsar, recorded on the gold and silver coins of Augustus; the present is therefore to be considered as signifying the continued subjection of Ægypt to the dominion of the Romans.

773.

HADRIANVS . AVG . COS . III . P . P. The laureate head of the emperor to the right, shoulders draped.

℞. ALEXANDRIA. In the exergum S. C. A female reclining to the left, a reed or stem of wheat in her left hand; her left arm rests on a basket filled with fruits; in her right hand she has some ears of corn, and at her feet some stems of wheat are represented growing.

Alexandria, the city of Ægypt so celebrated in history for its schools of philosophy, was built originally by Alexander the Great B.C. 332, on the western side of the Delta. He intended to have made it the capital city of Ægypt, its situation giving it great commercial advantages. The commodities of India were brought there by the caravans, and from thence dispersed throughout the coasts of the Mediterranean. Amongst other things, Alexandria was renowned throughout the then known world for its extensive and valuable library, as well as its schools for mathematics and philosophy. In the early Christian times it also acquired a name for its abounding in theological disputants, and its controversies upon different religious

374   RECORDS OF ROMAN HISTORY.

opinions. During the first centuries, the names of Origen, Herodian, Eusebius, Arius, Athanasius, and many others, as well pagan as christian, are well known to theological antiquaries, and were all connected at different periods with Alexandria. Murders and massacres of all sorts, both christian and pagan, were perpetrated at different periods in a long succession of years. One remarkable in history is the murder of Hypatia, a young female of most excellent beauty and character, and one of the most eminent teachers of mathematics and philosophy. She was deemed a pagan, and was barbarously murdered by the Christians, as they were called.

The city, however, continued to flourish as a commercial city until the seventh century, when, on the invasion of Ægypt by the Saracens, Alexandria was taken by Amrou, the general of the Caliph Omar; and on the first day of the month Mohana, the Mahometan new year's day, being the 22nd December, 640, Ægypt ceased to be a Roman province. The then existing magnificent library was burned by order of the caliph, who used the maxim of ignorance, saying, whatever books that were good in the library their goodness would be found in the Koran, and whatever were of an opposite character it was right should be destroyed; and with this direction all were burned, and it is said its numerous volumes supplied during six months fuel for the 4,000 public baths which were in the city. A very interesting account of Alexandria, as the chief city of Ægypt under the Romans, is to be found throughout Mr. Sharpe's book. It is still a place of considerable commercial importance in relation with Europe, although chiefly inhabited by the followers of Mahomet.

The present is a fine black coin. Weight 410¼ grains.

774.

HADRIANVS . AVG . COS . III . P . P .   The unlaureate head of the emperor to the right.

℞. ADVENTVI . AVG . ALEXANDRIAE. In the exergum S. C. The emperor in the foreground robed and standing to the left; with his right hand he clasps the right hand of a person before him, also robed, and holding in his left hand transversely a *hasta pura;* on his head he has the *modius,* the emblem of Jupiter Serapis, or Osiris. Between them on the ground is an altar with fire burning on it. By the side of the emperor another person is standing in profile, whose hand is raised as addressing a fourth person, who in like manner stands in profile by the side of Jupiter Serapis with hand raised holding a *sistrum,* and having on the head an ornament—we should say a minute lotus flower, the emblem of Isis.

Argelati classes this coin under A.D. 123, which would be in the seventh year of the reign of Hadrian, but I think he is in error; for, although Hadrian visited Ægypt in the sixth year of his reign, yet it nowhere appears that the Empress Sabina was then with him, so that the four figures would not be all applicable to the visit in the sixth year, when he was alone. But it was in the fifteenth year of his reign when he again visited Ægypt accompanied by the Empress Sabina, of which fact Mr. Sharpe says there is the record by an inscription to that effect cut on the colossal statue of Amunothph, at Thebes. Eckhel, also, descanting upon the visit of Hadrian to Alexandria in his fifteenth year, refers to other authors, saying, " Illud Pocockius ipse cruri sinistro celebratæ in superiore Ægypto Memnonis statuæ insculptum excepit," and gives the date coinciding with the date cut on the statue " ut videre est apud Dorvillium (in Charitonem, p. 524).

> Audivi loquentis ego Publius Balbinus
> Voces divinas Memnonis qui et Phamenoph,
> Veni vero una cum amabili regina Sabina,
> Horæ vero primæ Sol habuit cursum,
> Domini Hadriani quinto decimo anno,
> Dies vero habuit Athyr viginti et quatuor."

Thus we learn from this inscription, transcribed from the left leg of the statue, that the Empress Sabina, being in Ægypt, visited the statue in the fifteenth year of the reign of Hadrian, and on the 24th day of the (Ægyptian) month Athyr, which, by Julian computation, would be on the 20th day of November. (Eckhel, vi. p. 490-1.)

This is a very fine black coin, from the cabinet of Mr. Gwilt, formerly in the cabinet of Colonel Bainbridge. It is very rarely to be seen.

775.

AVT . KAIC . TPAIAN . AΔPIANOC . CEB. The laureate head of the emperor to the right, shoulders draped.

℞. *No legend.* Isis and Osiris, or Jupiter Serapis, in profile, side by side, to the right. It is an elegant portrait of the goddess, having the lotus-flower on her head.

Osiris in fine profile, in the style of Jupiter Olympius, has the *modius* on his head; L on the right of the field.

From the beauty of Isis and the majestic features of Osiris, the die of this coin's reverse was evidently cut by some skilful Greek artist. It is a coin of the Alexandrian mint; the date is obliterated. From the cabinet of the Cavalier Campana. It is of a pale drab colour. Weight 304¼ grains.

776.

ΑΥΤ . ΚΑΙC . ΤΡΑΙΑΝ . ΑΔΡΙΑΝΟC . CΕΒ. The laureate head of Hadrian to the right, shoulders draped.

℞. *No legend.* Isis to the left, and Osiris to the right, in profile; between them Horus. Isis has the lotus-flower on her head, Osiris has the *modius*. Horus standing opposite to Osiris places his right hand to his mouth; in his left hand he carries a cornucopiæ; on his head he has a flower; underneath is a royal eagle with expanded wings; by its side is the date LIH, or 17, A.D. 133.

A very fine black coin. Weight 332¼ grains.

777.

ΑΥΤ . ΚΑΙC . ΑΔΡΙΑΝΟC. The laureate head of the emperor to the right, shoulders draped.

℞. *No legend.* Two serpents standing opposite each other, upright, on their tails; the one on the left is so thick in the throat and body that if it had feet it would represent a crocodile; each has a flower on its head, and their tails are so coiled as to give them good support in the erect posture; a large ear of corn seems to protrude from the coil of the tail of the serpent on the right, and a flower from the tail of that on the left; underneath in the exergum are the letters of date LIH, or year 17, A.D. 133.

With the ancients the serpent was an emblem of immortality; for this reason, it served as a general sign of consecration. The serpent was sometimes represented with a radiated head, and sometimes with the crest or comb of a cock. It was made an emblem of immortality, because of its renewing itself annually by casting off its skin.

This type is mentioned and figured in Spanheim, p. 265; the only differences are, the serpent on the left delineated in his work is *mammifera*, or with the breasts of a female, and neither of them has any flower at the tail. Spanheim states them as intended to represent Isis and Osiris, the one on the left being intended for Isis.

778.

...... PAIAN .. ΔRIAN ..... The laureate head of the emperor to the right.

℞. *No legend.* A sphynx couchant to the left; in front of her forefeet is a wheel.

A brown coin, rather worn, from the cabinet of Mr. Sabatier of St. Petersburg.

These four Ægyptian coins record the visit of Hadrian to Ægypt; and, as he had been residing there for two or three years, visiting most of the cities and towns, and causing public buildings to be erected, there was a considerable mintage of coins to him struck at different times at the Alexandrian Mint, and all the reverses of these coins are eminently types appropriate to Egypt.

When Hadrian visited Alexandria he caused the decayed parts of the city to be repaired, and bestowed many benefits on its citizens, who, after he had quitted their country, amused themselves in writing satires upon him.

The signification of a sphynx is given by Clemens of Alexandria in his Stromata, lib. v. where he says, "That the Ægyptians were accustomed to place sphynxes at the doors of the temples, animals which are a symbol of obscurities and enigmas; signifying by this that things divine were not to be noised abroad everywhere and to all, but ought to be kept secret, in order that, carrying with them as they did so great a majesty, they might be held in the greater reverence." Clissold, p. 393.

The sphynx of the heathen mythology is represented with the head and breasts of a woman, the body of a dog, the tail of a serpent, the wings of a bird, the paws of a lion, and a human voice. It is supposed that this figure was emblematic of a warrior-daughter of Cadmus, who laid waste the country about Thebes by her incursions, and was thus interpreted: the lion's paw expressed her ferocity, the body of the dog her lasciviousness, her enigmas the snares she laid for strangers and travellers, and her wings the dispatch she used in her expeditions—being a sort of feudal or baronial robber of very ancient times.

The enigma of the sphynx, which was solved by Œdipus, is well known.

779.

HADRIANVS . AVGVSTVS. The laureate head of the emperor to the right.

℞. COS . III. and across the field on either side of Neptune the words NEP .... RED. with S. C. under them respectively.

Neptune, unclothed, standing to the right, his left foot resting on the prow of a galley, the beaks outward, his left elbow on his left knee; in his left hand he holds an *acrostolion*, some drapery is lying in careless manner across his left thigh; in his right hand he holds a trident, the teeth of which rest on the ground.

A very fine brown coin, from the cabinet of Mr. Vint of Colchester, the ancient *Camulodunum*.

780.

HADRIANVS . AVGVSTVS. The laureate head of the emperor to the right, shoulders draped.

℞. FELICITATI . AVG.; in the exergum COS . III . P . P .; and on either side S. C. A galley in full sail to the left with bending mast, the wind apparently blowing strong; there are several persons also at the oars; in the stern a *vexillum* and another standard are set up.

These two coins are placed here to represent the emperor crossing the sea to Italy on his return from Syria, whither he had gone after visiting Egypt.

Hadrian, after quitting Egypt and Syria, crossed over to Thracia and Macedonia, and thence returned to Rome, taking Athens in his route. The devices on the two coins imply a safe and prosperous passage.

The present coin is a fine black Second Brass coin. Weight 204¼ grains.

Coins representing a galley with mast and sail as well as rowers, are very rare.

781.

HADRIANVS . AVG . COS . III . P . P. The unlaureate head of the emperor to the right, shoulders draped.

℞. FORTVNAE . REDVCI.; in the exergum S. C. The emperor robed standing to the right, Fortune to the left, their right hands joined; Fortune is supporting on her left arm a cornucopiæ filled with fruits.

A very fine pale-green coin from the Campana Cabinet. Weight 368¼ grains.

782.

HADRIANVS . AVG . COS . III . P . P. The unlaureate head of the emperor to the right, shoulders draped.

℞. ADVENTVI . AVG . ITALIAE. In the exergum S. C. Hadrian standing to the right with his right hand raised, addressing a female who stands before him, and bears a full cornucopiæ on her left arm; her right hand, holding a patera, is extended towards the emperor; between them is a small circular altar, at the foot of which an animal is lying for sacrifice.

A good brown coin. Weight 393¼ grains.

783.

HADRIANVS . AVG . COS . III . P . P. The laureate head of the emperor to the right, shoulders draped.

 RESTITVTORI . ITALIAE. In the exergum S. C. The emperor standing to the right, raising from the ground a female who is kneeling before him, bearing on her left arm a full cornucopiæ.

These three coins record the return of Hadrian to Rome after his excursion to the provinces; the coins of these types have no tribunician dates by which to know the particular periods of journey they refer to, they therefore admit of being placed to each return of Hadrian after visiting distant countries; they appear to be a welcome to him on his return to Rome, but the next coin is the most interesting of them all, upon the subject of his travels.

Weight of this coin 353½ grains.

784.

HADRIANVS . AVG . COS . III . P . P. The laureate head of the emperor to the right, bust in armour, with military cloak.

℞. *No Legend.* Roma armed standing to the right, with her spear in the left hand, the point resting on the ground. The emperor stands before her robed, their right hands joined; in his left hand the emperor has a small baton scroll, or *chartam involutam;* behind him a female is standing naked, with her hands tied behind her back. At the feet of Roma is a reclining female figure, bearing on the left arm a cornucopiæ filled with fruits, whilst at the feet of the emperor and the captive is a sea deity having a dolphin on his left arm, a type of Oceanus. There is no S. C.

From the peculiarity of the figures on this reverse, and in the absence of a legend, it is not easy to decide positively and with a certainty the intent and meaning of this device. It seems to me to be a commemoration of the return of the emperor to Rome after his visiting the different provinces of the empire, when

Roma gives him a welcome on the occasion. The various provinces, both those to be reached by a sea voyage as well as those overland, are represented by the two figures at the feet of Roma and the emperor respectively. The object, which of the whole at first appears the least capable of explanation, is the captive female standing behind the emperor; unless we suppose that the female in a state of bondage is to represent all the provinces he visited, and that he found them all settled and quiet (or still content to bound) under the Roman dominion.

I think I may say this coin is unique and unknown; the nearest approach, after much research, that I have been able to find, is in Vaillant, who in his work "Numismata Imperatorum" (ed. 1692, p. 194), describes a medallion of Hadrian in these terms: "Sine epigraphe Imperator togatus stans dextram porrigit mulieri galeatæ—pone Hadrianum genius stat seminudus—hinc figura insidet monticulis quibus nititur, illinc mulier decumbens humi, lævâ innixâ urnæ aquas vomenti cui impositus est delphinus."

It does not appear from Vaillant what is the condition of the above-quoted medallion; if it were imperfect from the corrosion of time, it is possible it may have been like the present medallion, and Vaillant, misled by the corrosion, may have imagined those parts of the medallion which he describes that are not on the present coin; but the known attributes or adjuncts of the different figures warranted him in supplying those deficiencies; for instance, the figure with the dolphin may have had some oxydation near to it, disfiguring or obliterating the dolphin, and he mistook it as intended for an urn, but the urn is not the attribute of a *mulier*, but of a river deity, the urn being an emblem of the mountain, and the water flowing out of the urn an emblem of the stream descending from the mountain, which ultimately becomes the river.

The figure with the dolphin on the present coin is a male figure, and with a beard, and, by his not having any urn, the dolphin, as a sea fish, becomes an attribute or emblem of the sea, or Oceanus; the urn being the attribute of an inland river, as on the coin of Antoninus Pius, the reverse TIBERIS, or the river Tiber, personified, with an urn at his left side, from which a stream of water is flowing.

The other reclining figure on the right is a female, and, being represented with a cornucopiæ filled with fruits, personifies abundance. The captive female may be considered as representing collectively all the provinces visited by Hadrian, by whom she is standing, and which still continued bound or at peace under the Roman dominion.

We may thus conclude that the device signifies the abundance and tranquillity that Rome and the provinces enjoyed from the prudent government, care, and foresight of the emperor, as well as being the result of his constant watchfulness and inspection of the various provinces of the empire, causing them to be content to remain subject to the government of the Romans; for all which Rome congratulates the emperor on his return to the Eternal City.

The present medallion has been very carefully cleaned from dirt, without adding to or in any way taking from or altering the figures, the whole of which remain entire, and their distinctive characters are uninjured in the smallest degree.

It is a beautiful brown coin from the Devonshire Cabinet, but passed unnoticed at the sale. Weight 425¾ grains.

785.

HADRIANVS . AVG . COS . III . P . P. The laureate head of the emperor to the right.

℞. LIBERALITAS . AVG . VII. In the exergum S. C. The emperor or his legate seated to the left on a curule chair raised on a square *suggestum*; at his right side a female is standing, and is in the act of pouring from a cornucopiæ some of its contents into the lap of a citizen, who stands in front with his robe extended to receive the donation.

This is the last donation recorded by coins to have been made by Hadrian. It is not easy or scarcely possible to arrange the dates when his donations were made; but as they happen to be marked so as to show their number, one can place them in fair proportion to the different periods of his reign, being assisted a little by the titles given him on the obverse legend. Had the tribunician number been put in the legend, the date could have been immediately and correctly ascertained.

A very fine black coin from the Devonshire Cabinet. Weight 382¾ grains.

786.

HADRIANVS . AVG . COS . III . P . P. The unlaureate head of the emperor to the left, shoulders draped.

℞. ADVENTVI . AVG . THRACIAE. In the exergum S. C. The emperor standing to the right, his right hand raised addressing a female, who stands to the left with a patera in her right hand pouring a libation on a fire burning on an altar, at the side whereof is an animal for sacrifice.

After his visit to Ægypt, Hadrian returned by Syria, and crossing the sea went into Thrace and Macedonia, and other parts adjacent; he then returned to Athens, where he remained some time, for it was a favourite place with him, and then went back to Rome.

A good black coin from the Cabinet of Mr. Benson. Weight 363¼ grains.

787.

HADRIANVS . AVG . COS . III . P . P. The laureate head of the emperor to the right, shoulders draped.

℞. RESTITVTORI . MACEDONIAE. In the exergum S. C. The emperor robed standing to the left, with his right hand raising a female, who is kneeling on the ground before him.

Macedonia, the kingdom of Alexander the Great and his father Philip, was adjoining Thracia. It continued to be an independent monarchy until the time of Perses, or Perseus, the last king of Macedonia. He had reigned about seven years when he got into war with the Romans, and after four years' contest with them he was defeated by L. Æmilius Paulus at the battle of Pydna, B.C. 168. Perseus being taken prisoner was brought to Rome, when, after walking in the triumphal procession, he was allowed to retire into private life, and died at Alba, and his kingdom became annexed to the Roman empire as a province.

A very good brown coin. Weight 346½ grains.

788.

HADRIANVS . AVG . COS . III . P . P. The laureate head of the emperor to the right, shoulders draped.

℞. ADVENTVS . AVGVSTI . In the exergum S. C. Roma armed standing to the right, her spear in her left hand, the point resting on the ground; she joins right hand with the emperor, who is robed, standing before her to the left, with his head uncovered, thus bidding him welcome back to Rome.

A good dark green coin.

789.

HADRIANVS . AVG . COS . III . P . P. The laureate head of the emperor to the right, shoulders draped.

℞. FORTVNAE . REDVCI . In the exergum S. C. The emperor robed standing to the right; his right hand clasps the hand of Fortuna, who stands before him to the left, bearing on her left arm a full cornucopiæ.

A good brown coin.

790.

HADRIANVS . AVGVSTVS. The laureate head of the emperor to the right.

℞. COS . III. In the exergum S. C. Roma armed, seated to the left on a cuirass; behind her is an ornamented shield, the edge resting on what appears to be a helmet; her right hand extended holds a Victoriola having a wreath and palm branch in its hands; on her left arm she bears a cornucopiæ filled with fruits.

A very good black coin.

791.

HADRIANVS . AVG . COS . III . P . P. The laureate head of the emperor to the right.

℞. HADRIANVS . AVG . COS . III . P . P. The unlaureate head of the emperor to the right.

We have before noticed a similar instance of bicipitous coin in the Trajan series. Such coins are rarely met with, and are very singular and curious; they are not the result of accident, but are intentional; but I have been unable as yet to learn the reason why they were so struck. I have never met with them in Large Brass.

A poor conditioned Second Brass coin from the Cabinet of Sir George Musgrave.

792.

HADRIANVS . AVG . COS . III . P . P. The laureate head of the emperor to the right.

℞. S. C. within a laurel-wreath. This seems to be a coin of compliment or congratulation to the emperor, being as if a laurel-wreath were presented to him in full senate to express their opinion and satisfaction with his conduct.

A fine brown coin. Weight 186¼ grains.

793.

HADRIANVS . AVG . COS . III . P . P. The laureate head of the emperor to the right, shoulders draped.

℞. ANNONA . AVG. In the field S. C. A corn *modius* with two poppies rising from the centre, and four ears of corn, two on each side.

A memorial of the annual supply of corn for the city.

A fine brown coin. Weight 211½ grains.

794.

HADRIANVS . AVG . COS . III . P . P.   The laureate head of the emperor to the right, shoulders draped.

℞. FELICITAS . AVG .; in the field S. C. A female standing to the left bearing a full cornucopiæ on her left arm; in her right hand she holds a caduceus.

A fine dark green coin.

795.

IMP . CAESAR . TRAIANVS . HADRIANVS . AVG . P . M . TR . P . COS . III . P . P.   The laureate head of the emperor to the right.

℞. RESTITVTORI . ORBIS . TERRARVM.   In the exergum S. C. The emperor robed with head uncovered standing to the left, raising with his right hand a female who is kneeling before him to the right wearing a turret crown, and bearing on her left knee a globe.

This coin records the advantages gained by the provinces from the visits of the emperor. By the legend on the obverse it would seem to have been struck before the time when Hadrian had made his tours of the various provinces of the empire; but by the words of the reverse legend it is more applicable to the period when the emperor had completed all his visits; certainly the latter period would be the most fitting and appropriate for bestowing upon him the title of "Restorer of the world," *i.e.* of the Roman world, or provinces under their dominion, of which he had been so liberal a benefactor. The coin of LOCVPLETATORI . ORBIS . TERRARVM bears a similar signification. Spartianus, *in Hadriano*, says, "Nullus fere principum tantum terrarum tam celeriter peragravit;" and soon after, "in omnibus pene urbibus et aliquid edificavit et ludos edidit."

Although the obverse title is in full as on the earlier coins, yet it bears the COS . III. This last consulate, and the subject of the device and title on the reverse, mark it as a coin belonging to the time when all the visits of Hadrian had ended: for that reason I have placed it the last in the series except the galleys.

It is a fine black coin from the Cabinet of General Ramsay. Weight 356¼ grains.

796.

HADRIANVS . AVGVSTVS.   The unlaureate head of the emperor to the right, shoulders draped.

℞. FELICITATI . AVG . on the upper verge of the field; COS . III . P . P . in the exergum; S. C. at the sides. A large galley rowed to the left by six men; the pilot appears in the hutch at the stern giving his directions; an *acrostolion* rises above the hutch, and beside it are two military standards; a small sail, or some object of singular form, appears on the head of the vessel.

In this and the subsequent galley coins there are varieties in their construction and fittings; I have therefore retained them as proper subjects of reference when required. Galley coins of Hadrian are very frequent, and, being usually treated unceremoniously, their peculiarities pass unobserved. The galley is seldom represented as rowed to the right, or under sail.

The figure at the head of a galley was sometimes viewed as the deity under whose tutelage the vessel was placed; at other times it signified its name. Virgil, Æneis, lib. x. and Silius Italicus, lib. xiv. allude to the figure-head of a Triton:—

> Hunc velut immanis Triton et cærulea concha
> Exterrens freta, &c.—VIRGIL.

> Ducitur et Libya puppis signata figuram
> Et Triton captivus.—SIL. ITAL.

> Est mihi sitque precor flavæ tutela Minervæ
> Navis.—OVID. TRIST. l. i. El. x.

These galley coins are in excellent condition, mostly brown and dark green in colour, and were selected nearly all from the cabinets of Sir Robert Abdy, Sir George Musgrave, the Duke of Devonshire, &c.

797.

HADRIANVS . AVGVSTVS. The laureate head of the emperor to the right.

℞. FELICITATI . AVG. In the exergum COS . III . P . P. S. C. at the sides. A galley with five men rowed to the left; the pilot is seated in the hutch at the stern, over which is an *acrostolion*, but no standards; a small sail on a bowsprit at the head, which has a fiddle scroll, and the rostrum underneath; the vessel sits low in the water, as if it were heavily laden.

798.

HADRIANVS . AVGVSTVS. The laureate head of the emperor to the left, shoulders draped.

℞. FELICITATI . AVG. In the exergum COS . III . P . P . and S. C. at the sides. A galley rowed to the left by six men; in the stern are two standards; the stern is raised high; the pilot appears under the hutch, and an *acrostolion* rises above; at the head there is a figure like a Triton.

The Triton being a sea-deity is a very frequent sign on galleys. In the Acts of the Apostles (chap. xxviii.) the departure of St. Paul, and the crew and soldiers who were all wrecked at the island of Melita, is narrated; and in verse 11, the vessel they embarked in is thus described: "And after three months we departed in a ship of Alexandria which had wintered in the isle, whose sign was Castor and Pollux," the sign being what is now called the figure-head, and intimating the name of the vessel.

799.

HADRIANVS . AVGVSTVS. The unlaureate head of the emperor to the right.

℞. FELICITATI . AVG . on the upper verge of the field, COS . III . P . P . in the exergum, S. C. at the sides; a fine galley rowed by six men to the left; a pilot sits in the hutch in the stern, over which is an *acrostolion*; two standards erect in the stern; instead of a figure at the head there is a short bowsprit with a sail on it.

800.

HADRIANVS . AVGVSTVS. The laureate head of the emperor to the right, shoulders draped.

℞. FELICITATI . AVG . on the upper verge. In the exergum COS . III . P . P . and S. C. at the sides. A galley rowed to the left by six men; the pilot sits in the hutch in the stern, over which there is an *acrostolion*; two standards are erected in the stern; at the head there is no sail or figure.

801.

HADRIANVS . AVGVSTVS. The unlaureate head of the emperor to the right, shoulders draped.

℞. FELICITATI . AVG. on the upper verge; COS . III . P . P . in the exergum, and S. C. at the sides. A large galley rowed by six men to the right; the pilot sits in the stern, where two standards are hoisted; at the head is the figure of a Triton, but no small sail or bowsprit.

802.

HADRIANVS . AVGVSTVS. The laureate head of the emperor to the left, shoulders in armour, and draped.

℞. FELICITATI . AVG . on the upper verge; COS . III . P . P . in the exergum, and S. C. at the sides. A long galley rowed by five men to the left; the stern rather high, with the hutch and the pilot much aft; over the hutch an *acrostolion*; two standards erect in the stern; at the head is some figure, but no sail or bowsprit.

803.

HADRIANVS . AVGVSTVS. The laureate head of the emperor to the right.

℞. FELICITATI . AVG . on the upper verge of the field; COS . III . P . P . in the exergum, and S. C. at the sides. A large galley rowed by six men to the left; the pilot sitting in the hutch at the stern; two military standards erect in the stern also.

804.

HADRIANVS . AVGVSTVS. The laureate head of the emperor to the right, bust in armour.

℞. FELICITATI . AVG . on the upper verge of the field; COS . III . P . P . in the exergum; S. C. at the sides. A galley rowed to the left by five men; the pilot is in his hutch at the stern, with *acrostolion* over it; two standards erect at the sides; a small bowsprit with a sail on it at the head.

805.

HADRIANVS . AVGVSTVS. The laureate head of the emperor to the right, bust in armour, with military cloak.

℞. FELICITATI . AVG . on the upper verge; COS . III . P . P . on the exergum; S. C. at the sides. A smartly-built galley rowed by five men to the left; a small bowsprit with sail at the head. In the stern the pilot is sitting in his hutch, with *acrostolion* above and two military standards, one a *vexillum*.

806.

HADRIANVS . AVGVSTVS. The laureate head of the emperor to the right.

℞. COS . III . on the upper verge; S. C. in the exergum. A small straight-built galley moving to the right; the stern has no raised work or poop, but is a straight run from the bulwark at the side, upon which is the pilot's hutch, with a sort of pillar behind surmounted by a large *acrostolion*; at the head is a small bowsprit with a sail furled in two folds; a very long upright scroll-head with beaks under, one of them being level with the water; the run of the stern from the bulwarks gives the stern a long overhanging counter. There are no standards in the stern.

807.

HADRIANVS AVGVSTVS. The laureate head of the emperor to the right.

℞. COS . III . above and S. C. under a small galley rowed by five men to the right, having a straight bulwark at the side, running out to a long counter at the stern, as on the preceding coin; the pilot's hutch at the stern with *acrostolion* above; no standards set up; a long bowsprit and small sail at the head; a fiddle-head scroll in front and three *rostra* beneath.

808.

HADRIANVS . AVGVSTVS. The laureate head of the emperor to the right.

℞. COS . III . above; S. C. in the exergum. A small galley rowing to the right, three men engaged, and the pilot is standing in front of his hutch, behind which is an upright curved work formed of the termination of the counter at the taffrail, which does not rake away from the body of the vessel, as on the last two coins. A small bowsprit without sail; a scroll-head, with three beaks or *rostra* under.

809.

HADRIANVS . AVGVSTVS. The unlaureate head of the emperor to the right, shoulders in armour, and draped.

℞. FELICITATI . AVG . above, in the field; COS . III . P . P . in the exergum; S. C. at the sides. A handsome well-formed galley rowed by five men to the left; the pilot sits in a large hutch at the stern, where there are also two standards, but no *acrostolion*; at the head is a bowsprit, with a small sail on it.

810.

HADRIANVS . AVGVSTVS. The laureate head of the emperor to the right, shoulders draped.

℞. FELICITATI . AVG . above, in the field; COS . III . P . P . in the exergum; S. C. at the sides. A galley rowed by six men to the left, having at the head a bowsprit and small sail, and two standards set up in the stern; the pilot is standing in front of his hutch, giving directions.

811.

HADRIANVS . AVGVSTVS. The laureate head of the emperor to the right, shoulders draped.

℞. FELICITATI . AVG . in the field above; COS . III . P . P . in the exergum; S. C. at the sides. A galley rowed by six men to the left, having a bowsprit and small sail at the head; two standards erect in the stern; the pilot sitting in front of his hutch.

812.

Legend obliterated. The laureate head of Hadrian to the right.

℞. CONSECRATIO. S. C. on either side of a globe, on which an eagle is standing with expanded wings looking to the right.

I do not find this type in brass, either in Occo, Argelati, or Eckhel; but Occo and Argelati have it in silver. Eckhel has it in gold likewise; it is thus described:

HADRIANVS AVGVSTVS. Aquila insistens globo.

I do not doubt but a consecratio coin was struck in brass as well as in gold and silver. The present coin came from the cabinet of the Cavalier Campana. It is a Large Brass coin; but, although a real Roman minted coin, I doubt its having been struck with this particular reverse on it.

The Emperor Hadrian, to prepare for the reception of his body after death, caused a large and magnificent building to be erected on the banks of the Tiber; it was called *Mausoleum Hadriani*. The mausoleum which was erected by Augustus as his burial-place and that of his successors had given the first idea to Hadrian, and as the mausoleum of Augustus was nearly full, Hadrian by this building intended to provide a resting-place for the mortal remains of himself and his successors.

The mausoleum Hadriani was constructed at great cost and was much ornamented with statuary and sculpture, all which have during successive ages been destroyed, but the main body of the building remains. It was occupied in A.D. 985 by Crescentius Nomentanus, whence it was called the fortress or Tower of Crescentius. He being expelled by Otho the Third, it was reduced by Boniface the Ninth to the form of a citadel, and Alexander the Sixth surrounded it with fortifications. Pope Urban the Eighth furnished it with cannon and mortars made from metal which he had plundered from the Pantheon of Agrippa, and he placed a governor and garrison in the building and called it the Castle of St. Angelo, by which designation it is known at this day.

SABINA.

JULIA SABINA was the daughter of Matidia, the granddaughter of Marciana, and the grandniece of the emperor Trajan; by the aid of the empress Plotina she was married to Hadrian in A.D. 100, and died in A.D. 137-8, either by her own hand or, as is supposed, poisoned by the orders of Hadrian, who treated her very ill, although it was in consequence of his marrying her that he was, at the instigation of Plotina, adopted by the emperor Trajan as his successor to the empire.

The coins of Sabina are not particularly common; the devices generally allude to moral virtues.

813.

SABINA . AVGVSTA . HADRIANI . AVG . P.P. The head of the empress to the right, her hair braided in many plaits, and decorated with a coronet, which in some respects resembles the coronets of Marciana and her mother Matidia; shoulders draped.

℞. *No legend.* S. C. in the exergum. Ceres seated to the left on a basket shaped like a barrel; with her right hand she presents three ears of corn, in her left hand she holds a long torch with a fire burning on the top.

The coronet worn by the empress on this coin is of three parts; the first band is narrow and joined to the second, which is broad, and both are ornamented with indentations joining into each other; added to these is a third band, narrow at the side, and progressively rising to a sort of pointed crown or coronet, which seems in the original crown worn by Sabina to have been ornamented with jewels; the narrow band is flattened out at the end, as if to fix it by its elasticity on the side of the head by the temples, reminding one of the flat gold bands worn over the forehead and sides of the head by the women in Friesland, in Holland, at the present day.

I do not find the peculiar construction and ornamental work of the Sabina coronet mentioned in its particulars by any numismatic writer, and I may be catechised for pedantry in noticing it with such minuteness, but I consider every thing that presents itself to notice on a coin should be specified, for it is by such particulars that we become more acquainted with the personal customs, habits, and appearance of individuals of rank, whose influence in society generally had an important weight in the course of human affairs.

This is a fine dark green coin. Weight $371\frac{1}{4}$ grains.

814.

SABINA . AVGVSTA . HADRIANI . AVG . P.P. The head of Sabina to the right, her hair braided close to the head, and a short tail-knot behind, a very small coronet in front, and behind that a broad wreath of wheat-ears; the shoulders draped.

℞. *No legend.* S. C. in the exergum. Ceres seated to the left on a basket, as on the preceding coin.

The wreath of wheat-ears I do not find to occur on the coins of any of the empresses but Sabina. Livia Augusti has a wreath of myrtle. Domitia the same, or laurel, but the wheat-ears are for the empress Sabina, and, excepting on the present coin, they are only to be seen on the Second Brass coins of Sabina.

The present is a black coin, from the Campana Cabinet; the obverse fine, but the reverse not so good. Weight 346 grains. It is a very rare coin.

815.

SABINA . AVGVSTA . HADRIANI . AVG . P. P. The head of the empress to the right, her hair braided and decorated with a coronet as on the first coin, shoulders draped.

℞. *No legend.* In the exergum S. C. Vesta seated to the left, having the *hasta pura* in her left hand; her right hand, extended, holds a little idol palladium.

A fine bright green coin. Weight 480¼ grains.

816.

SABINA . AVGVSTA . HADRIANI . AVG . P. P. The head of the empress to the right, her hair braided and decorated with a coronet as on the preceding coin, the shoulders draped.

℞. *No legend.* In the exergum S. C. Vesta seated to the left, as just before described.

A fine black coin. These types of Ceres and Vesta are represented so like each cach other that they may be easily mistaken if a little worn. To distinguish the types it must be observed whether the seated figure holds in the right-hand ears of corn or a palladium, and the coin should not have a permanent place in the cabinet unless the distinction be clearly made out. There is also another distinction to be observed, and more likely to be seen, even though a little worn. Ceres is almost, I may say, invariably seated on a basket, which at times has a neatly-worked pattern. Vesta is constantly found seated on a throne or decorated chair.

The coins of Sabina, on which she is represented with a head-dress like that of Marciana Matidia, are much less frequent than the coins representing her with her hair dressed as we shall see on the next coins.

817.

SABINA . AVGVSTA . HADRIANI . AVG . P. P. The head of the empress to the right, her hair dressed in a broad rolled band raised in the front of the head like a coronet, and fastened with a narrow fillet passing round the head and just over the forehead; the back hair falling behind ends in a knot or broad loop, shoulders draped.

℞. VESTA. In the exergum S. C. Vesta seated on a throne to the left holding a *hasta pura* in the left hand; her right-hand, extended, bears a little idol palladium; her left foot rests on a stool.

The head-dress here given to the empress is the one most frequently found delineated on her coins; it may therefore be fairly considered as representing that style in which she was most usually accustomed to appear.

The style of head-dress on other coins, such as on the first in this series, may have been adopted out of compliment to her mother and aunt, or may have been such as the empress may herself have used on some particular occasions of state ceremony.

The present is a fine brown coin from the Campana collection. Weight 483½ grains.

818.

SABINA . AVGVSTA HADRIANI . AVG . P . P. The head of the empress to the right; her hair dressed with rolled band and long loop knot, as on the last preceding coin, shoulders draped.

℞. CONCORDIA . AVG . in the field S. C. A female standing to the left; her right-hand extended holds a patera, on her left arm she bears a double cornucopiæ.

This type is generally found on the coins of empresses to signify the amity existing between the emperor and his wife; the cornucopiæ being double, also denotes that plenty and happiness in a twofold quantity are the result of the good understanding between the parties.

Considering the barbarous manner in which the wives of some of the Roman emperors were treated by their husbands, the type of *Concordia* is a fulsome adulatory falsehood executed by a servile mintmaster to endeavour to cover or palliate the iniquity of his emperor, and infer blame to the empress, should she be disgraced by him at some future time.

Seneca, in his tragedy of Medea, Act i., wishes Concordia to be propitious to the marriage with Jason, and, although he does not mention Concordia by name, yet by the qualities described she is well delineated.

——————— Asperi
Martis sanguineas quæ cohibet manus,
Quæ dat belligeris fœdera gentibus,
Et cornu retinet divite copiam.

A good brown coin   Weight 419¼ grains.

819.

SABINA AVGVSTA . HADRIANI . AVG . P . P. The head of the empress to the right, her hair dressed in the ordinary way, shoulders draped.

℞. CONCORDIA . AVG. In the exergum S. C. A female seated to the left on a throne; in her right-hand she holds a patera, her left elbow rests on the head of a small statue placed on a pedestal at the left side of her throne.

820.

SABINA AVGVSTA HADRIANI . AVG . P . P. The head of the empress to the right, with a laurel-wreath and a small coronet over the front hair at the forehead, the hair in large folds (not a roll band), and tied in a small thick knot at the back of the neck, shoulders draped.

℞. CONCORDIA . AVG . in the exergum S. C. A female seated on a throne to the left; her right-hand holds a patera, her left elbow rests on the head of a small statue standing on a pediment by the side of the throne.

Although the wreath on the head of Sabina appears formed of small laurel-leaves, it might be termed a myrtle wreath, but that the leaves appear very thick, and thus more like to laurel.

A fine Second Brass black coin from the cabinet of Monsieur Rollin at Paris, 1847.

821.

SABINA . AVGVSTA . HADRIANI . AVG . P . P. The head of the empress to the left, her hair dressed plain with the back hair in a long loop-knot over her shoulder; a broad wreath of ears of corn encompasses the head, the shoulders draped.

℞. CONCORDIA . AVG. In the exergum S. C. A female seated on a throne to the left, her right-hand extended holding a patera; at the side of the throne within the bars of the lower part is a full cornucopiæ; her left elbow rests on the head of a small statue at the side of the throne, as on the preceding coins.

The cornucopiæ seems to be an emblem of the benefits arising from a good understanding, or concord, existing between the emperor and his wife; but I take it the type applies only in strictness to the early period of the marriage, for not only were there no children, but in a few years after their marriage disagreements arose, Hadrian treated his wife very ill, and he discreditably allowed her to be as badly or even worse treated by others.

The head of Sabina being bound with a wreath of wheat-ears is complimentary, as representing her in the character of Ceres. The sacred rights of Ceres, or the Bona Dea, were celebrated by females only, and the empress on such occasions would be likely to be the chief actor in the ceremonial, and be distinguished by a wreath of wheat-ears. At Rome there were five different temples erected to *Concordia*.

3 E

The coins of Sabina which give portraits to the left are not very usual, and the wreaths render them more uncommon.

822.

SABINA . AVGVSTA . HADRIANI . AVG . P. P. The head of the empress to the right, her hair dressed with rolled bands as on the former coins, shoulders draped.

℞. PIETAS. In the field S. C. A female standing full front looking to the right; a child is standing on each side of her, on each of whose heads she places one of her hands.

This is one of the rare devices of Sabina; it is a beautiful bright green coin, from the cabinet of General Ramsay. Weight 425½ grains.

823.

SABINA . AVGVSTA . HADRIANI . AVG . P. P. The head of the empress to the right, her hair dressed as on the preceding coin.

℞. PIETAS. In the exergum S. C. A female seated to the left, her right hand extended, holding a patera; in her left hand she holds a *hasta pura* transversely.

This is a nice yellow bronze coin. Weight 404¾ grains.

824.

SABINA . AVGVSTA . HADRIANI . AVG . P . P . The head of the empress to the right, her hair dressed in rolled band confined by a ribbon, as on the preceding coins.

℞. IVNONI . REGINAE. In the field S. C. A female robed and standing to the left, bearing a *hasta pura* in the left hand; the right hand, extended, holds a patera.

There were two or three temples at Rome dedicated to Juno Regina, who was so called—" Quod et conjux Jovis deorum atque hominum Regis esset." She was represented in sculpture, according to the description of Albricius, " Erat fœmina in throno sedens sceptrum regium tenens in dextrâ—ejus caput nubes tenebant opertum super diadema quod capiti gestabat."

Juno had several other offices or duties attributed to her, for which correspondent temples were erected, wherein she was worshipped—as Juno Pronuba; Juno Lucina; Juno Moneta (as such she was guardian of the treasury), and the Roman mint for the coining of the money was in her temple on the Capitoline Hill; and as Juno Sispita, or Sospita, a temple was erected to her at Lanuvium, the birthplace of Antoninus Pius.

This is a scarce type of Sabina; the coin is but in poor condition; and, though of Large Brass size, is of very light weight, being only 166½ grains.

825.

SABINA . AVGVSTA . HADRIANI . AVG . P . P . The head of the empress to the right, her hair dressed with rolled bands, as on the other coins, shoulders draped.

℞. VENERI . GENETRICI . in the field S. C. Venus draped, standing full front looking to the right, her left hand raised holding an apple, her right hand lifted to her head supports a veil.

Venus as the goddess received great veneration from Julius Cæsar, who affected to be descended from her through Æneas the Trojan hero. At the battle of Pharsalia, Cæsar gave as his watchword or signal "Venus Victrix," and made a vow that if he obtained a victory he would erect a temple to Venus; having gained the battle, Cæsar soon after caused a temple to be built to Venus Genetrix, "eique spolia de hostibus dedicavit." He also placed on the statue of Venus which was in the temple the celebrated gorget or breast ornament of pearls, which he had brought from Britain, "thoracem de margaritis Britannicis."

After the death of Cæsar, Augustus placed in the temple a statue of Cæsar, having a star represented above his head, in token of the flaming star or comet which was seen at Rome after the death of Cæsar, as we have already noticed *in Cæsare*.

The festival of Venus Genetrix was held at Rome on the kalends of October. This type is also introduced on the coins of Faustina senior, *post*.

A good yellow coin, presented me by Professor Donaldson.

826.

SABINA . AVGVSTA . HADRIANI . AVG. P. P. The head of the empress to the right, her hair dressed in rolled bands with long looped knot as before noted, shoulders draped.

℞. PVDICITIA. In the exergum S. C. A female seated on a throne to the left; her right-hand raised to her head appears slightly to lift a veil from her face; her left foot rests on a stool.

At Rome Pudicitia was worshipped as a goddess, and had her temples, the one to Pudicitia Patricia, the other to Pudicitia Plebeia. The origin of the latter temple is said to have been occasioned by the following incident. The temple of the goddess Pudicitia Patricia could only be entered by Roman ladies who were of patrician families by birth, and this rule was kept so strictly, and with so much jealousy, that when Virginia, the wife of Volumnius, a Roman of consular dignity, determined to enter, she was forcibly put out because she was herself of plebeian birth. However, in revenge for the affront so put upon her, she exhorted the plebeian women to venerate the goddess Pudicitia, and erected a temple in part of her house that equalled the temple of Pudicitia Patricia.

I believe the temple of Pudicitia Plebeia is now embodied with the church of St. Mary Cosmedin.

The Athenians were content to dedicate only an altar to Pudicitia, without distinction of Patricia or Plebeia.

Pudicitia is thus described by one of the Roman poets:—

>Ergo sedens velat vultus, obnubit ocellos,
>Ista verecundi signa pudoris erant.
>
>She sits, her visage veiled, her eyes concealed;
>By marks like these was chastity revealed.

These lines most aptly designate the figure on the reverse of this coin, or of any other coin of an empress on which Pudicitia is represented sitting.

827.

SABINA . AVGVSTA . HADRIANI . AVG. The head of Sabina to the right, with the Marciana coronet head-dress, shoulders draped.

℞. HADRIANVS . AVGVSTVS. The unlaureate head of Hadrian to the right.

This is a brown Second Brass coin in good condition; it is a very rare coin; for Eckhel *in Sabina,* vol. vi. p. 521, quotes one in Mus. Cæs. in Second Brass, with the following legend on the obverse:

SABINA . AVGVSTA . IMP . HADRIANI . AVG . epigraphe rarissima; the reverse being "S. C Ceres sedens d. spicas s. facem;" and he says, "Hanc capitis epigraphen in nullo hactenus Sabinæ nummo videre mihi contigit, intelligo, omissum juxta HADRIANI . nomen PATRIS . PATRIAE titulo."

ÆLIUS CÆSAR.

LUCIUS AURELIUS CEJONIUS COMMODUS VERUS, known by coins as Ælius Cæsar, descended from an illustrious Hetruscan family, was adopted by the emperor Hadrian, A.D. 135, as his successor, by the names of Lucius Ælius Verus. He thus became Cæsar, and was elected consul A.D. 136; afterwards he was created prætor, and sent to govern in Pannonia. He subsequently returned to Rome, and died in January A.D. 138, Y.R. 891. Upon which event Hadrian, in the month of March following, adopted Marcus Antoninus, surnamed Pius, who succeeded him in the sovereignty in the month of June, 138.

The coins of Ælius are not numerous and are of very few types; they are not very generally met with, and the brass coins are almost generally in very poor condition.

828.

AELIVS . CAESAR. The unlaureate head of Ælius to the right.

℞. TR . POT . COS . II.; in the field S. C. Spes gradient to the left; in her right-hand she holds up a lotus flower, with her left hand she supports her clothes.

A fine dark green coin from the Cabinet of the Duke of Devonshire. Weight 370½ grains.

829.

L . AELIVS . CAESAR. The unlaureate head of Ælius to the right, shoulders draped.

℞. TR . POT . COS . II.; in the exergum CONCORD., and S. C. in the field. A female seated to the left; her right hand extended holds a patera, her left elbow rests on the top of a cornucopiæ, which is at the side of her chair.

Concordia on this coin may be considered as signifying the good understanding which existed between Hadrian and Ælius.

A good brown coin. Weight 474¼ grains.

830.

L . AELIVS . CAESAR. The unlaureate head of Ælius to the right, shoulders draped; very fine; head struck up high; showing fine bold workmanship.

℞. TR . POT . COS . II.; in the field S. C. Fortune standing full front, looking to the right, supporting a cornucopiæ on her left arm; in her right hand she holds the tiller of a rudder. Spes approaches close to her on her left, as if about to address her, holding up a lotus flower in her right hand; with her left hand she supports her robe.

A very good black coin from the Cabinet of Mr. Gwilt, by exchange.

831.

L . AELIVS . CAESAR. The unlaureate head of Ælius to the right.

℞. TR . POT . COS . II.; and across the field the divided word PAN-NONIA, with S. C. underneath; between the divisions of the word a female is standing to the left, full front, holding her robe with her left hand; in her right hand she holds a *vexillum*.

Ælius was, after his adoption by Hadrian, appointed governor of Pannonia, which I conclude was the occasion of this type being struck to him.

This is an unpatinated coin from the Cabinet of Sir G. Musgrave; it is very unusual to find this scarce type in such good condition, although not first rate.

832.

L . AELIUS . CAESAR. The unlaureate head of Ælius to the right, shoulders draped.

℞. TR . POT . COS . II. In the field S. C. A female standing to the left, her right hand extended holds up a lotus-flower; on her left arm she bears a full cornucopiæ, and her left hand rests on the top of a rudder.

833.

L . AELIVS . CAESAR. The unlaureate head of Ælius to the right.

℞. TR . PO .... II. S. C. in the field. In the exergum SALUS. Hygeia seated to the left, feeding a snake that rises from an altar before her.

A good mottled brown coin, from the cabinet of M. St. Croix.

834.

L . AELIVS . CAESAR. The unlaureate head of Ælius to the right.

℞. TR . P .... II. across the field PIETAS, with S. C. underneath. A female standing full front, looking to the left; her hands are raised in the attitude of prayer; at her right side is an altar, with fire burning on it.

A good brown coin.

www.ingramcontent.com/pod-product-compliance
Lightning Source LLC
Chambersburg PA
CBHW050845300426
44111CB00010B/1138